WORLD EVENTS	MUSIC AND MUSICIANS	FIGURES IN THE ARTS AND HUMANITIES
1528: Baldassare Castiglione, *Il cortegiano*	late 1520s–1591: Vincenzo Galilei	
	1528–1600: Claude LeJeune	
1534: English Reformation	ca. 1532–1594: Roland de Lassus	1532–1589: Jean-Antoine Baïf
1536: Calvinist Reformation	1539: First Calvinist psalter	1538–1612: Battista Guarini
	1543–1623: William Byrd	1541–1614: El Greco
1545–1563: Council of Trent	1545–1607: Luzzasco Luzzaschi	1542–1591: St. John of the Cross
	ca. 1549–1611: Tomas Luis da Victoria	1544–1595: Torquato Tasso
	ca. 1550–1602: Emilio de' Cavalieri	
	ca. 1550–1618: Giulio Caccini	
	1553–1599: Luca Marenzio	
	1553–1612: Giovanni Gabrieli	
1558–1603: Reign of Elizabeth I in England	1558: Gioseffe Zarlino, *Le istitutioni harmoniche*	
	1558–1602: Thomas Morley	
	ca. 1560–1613: Carlo Gesualdo	
	ca. 1560–1627: Lodovico Grossi da Viadana	1561–1626: Francis Bacon
	1561–1633: Jacopo Peri	1564–1616: William Shakespeare
	1567–1643: Claudio Monteverdi	1564–1642: Galileo Galilei
	1571–1621: Michael Praetorius	1573–1631: John Donne
	1585–1672: Heinrich Schütz	1577–1640: Peter Paul Rubens
	1586–1630: Johann Hermann Schein	
	1587–1654: Samuel Scheidt	
	1588: Nicolas Yonge, *Musica transalpina*	1588–1679: Thomas Hobbes
	1597: Thomas Morley, *A Plaine and Easie Introduction to Practicall Musicke*	1596–1650: René Descartes
	1598: Peri, *Dafne*	1598–1680: Gianlorenzo Bernini
1600: Wedding of Henry IV of France and Marie de' Medici	1600: Peri, *Euridice*; Cavalieri, *Rappresentatione di Anima e di Corpo*	
	1601: *The Triumphs of Oriana*	
	1602: Caccini, *Le nuove musiche*; Viadana, *Cento concerti ecclesiastici*	
	1605–1674: Giacomo Carissimi	1606–1669: Rembrandt van Rijn
	1607: Monteverdi, *Orfeo*	1606–1684: Pierre Corneille
1610–1643: Reign of Louis XIII in France, Richelieu as prime minister		1608–1674: John Milton
1611: King James translation of Bible	1616–1667: Johann Jacob Froberger	1622–1673: Molière
1618–1648: Thirty Years' War		1623–1662: Blaise Pascal
	1632–1687: Jean-Baptiste Lully	1632–1675: Jan Vermeer
	ca. 1637–1707: Dieterich Buxtehude	1632–1677: Baruch Spinoza
	1637: First public opera house, Venice	
1643–1715: Reign of Louis XIV in France	1640: *Bay Psalm Book* published in Massachusetts	1639–1699: Jean Racine
1649–1660: English Commonwealth under Cromwell	1653–1706: Johann Pachelbel	1642–1727: Isaac Newton
	1653–1713: Arcangelo Corelli	
	1658–1709: Giuseppe Torelli	
	1659–1695: Henry Purcell	
1660: Restoration of monarchy in England		1667–1745: Jonathan Swift
	Philipp Telemann	
	1683–1764: Jean-Philippe Rameau	1684–1721: Antoine Watteau
	1685–1750: Johann Sebastian Bach	
	1685–1757: Domenico Scarlatti	
	1685–1759: George Frederic Handel	
	1686–1768: Nicola Porpora	
	1689: Purcell, *Dido and Aeneas*	1694–1778: Voltaire
	1699–1783: Johann Adolf Hasse	1698–1792: Pietro Metastasio
	ca. 1700: Invention of fortepiano	1703–1770: François Boucher
	1701–1775: Giovanni Battista Sammartini	1706–1790: Benjamin Franklin
	1710–1736: Giovanni Battista Pergolesi	1707–1793: Carlo Goldoni
	1714–1787: Christoph Willibald Gluck	1712–1770: Jean-Jacques Rousseau
1712–1786: Reign of Frederick the Great in Prussia	1714–1788: Carl Philipp Emanuel Bach	1714–1795: Raniero Calzabigi
	1717: Couperin, *L'Art de toucher le clavecin*	
	1717–1757: Johann Stamitz	
	1722: J.S. Bach, *Well-Tempered Clavier*, 1; Rameau, *Traité de l'harmonie*	1724–1804: Immanuel Kant

IDEAS AND STYLES IN THE WESTERN MUSICAL TRADITION

IDEAS AND STYLES IN THE WESTERN MUSICAL TRADITION

Douglass Seaton

Florida State University

 Mayfield Publishing Company
Mountain View, California
London • Toronto

Copyright © 1991 by Mayfield Publishing Company

Library of Congress Cataloging-in-Publication Data

Seaton, Douglass.
    Ideas and styles in the western musical tradition / by Douglass
Seaton.
        p.   cm.
    Includes bibliographical references and index.
    ISBN 0-87484-956-X (cloth)
    1. Music—History and criticism.   I. Title.
ML160.S407   1991
780′.9—dc20   90-6669
                                                                                        CIP
                                                                                        MN

Manufactured in the United States of America

10 9 8 7 6 5 4 3 2 1

Mayfield Publishing Company
1240 Villa Street
Mountain View, California 94041

Sponsoring editor, Janet M. Beatty; managing editor, Linda Toy; production editor, Carol Zafiropoulos; copy editor, Loralee Windsor; text and cover designer, Cynthia Bogue. The text was set in 10 1/2/12 1/2 Berkeley Book by Thompson Type, and printed on 50# Finch Opaque by Arcata Graphics.

Cover photo credits Detail, St. Cecilia's Marriage Feast. Used by permission of Walters Art Gallery, Baltimore. Bach selection from musical manuscript autograph, Bach P25. Used by permission of Deutsche Staatsbibliothek Berlin Musikabteilung. John Cage selection © 1960 by Henmar Press Inc. Used by permission of C.F. Peters Corporation.

Text credits appear on a continuation of the copyright page, p. 409.

TO THE INSTRUCTOR

At the heart of *Ideas and Styles in the Western Musical Tradition* is the premise that we study music history in order to become better musicians—whether performers who wish to play or sing more sensitively, composers looking for inspiration in the musical experience of earlier composers, or listeners hoping to hear more.

We become better musicians by confronting and exploring the musical thinking of other musicians. Our performances are better when we understand what and how musicians in the past have intended to communicate with their audiences. Our compositions can be more interesting and better crafted when we know how other composers have set themselves artistic problems and solved them. Our listening can be more perceptive and fulfilling when we know all these things and are aware of the cultural contexts in which music has been conceived and performed.

Approach

One can, of course, write a book that is primarily a cultural history of music in Western civilization; alternatively one might adopt a more technical viewpoint and compose a history of musical style. The history of music presented here takes a balanced approach between consideration of external influences on music and internal changes within the art itself. The text emphasizes that musicians inevitably operate in particular historical contexts and that those contexts just as inevitably affect their music and musical experience. It draws connections between political and social world events and contemporaneous musical events and developments, and it particularly stresses the parallels in music, the other arts, and philosophy. But equally, it discusses how musicians through history have reacted to the music of their predecessors, at times building upon and at times challenging the assumptions of their own pasts.

Ideas and Styles also offers a new approach that makes it not just a compilation of information but a coherent view of the history of Western music. This approach draws on ideas that have been established in recent scholarly studies but as yet have not been assimilated into any general survey of the cultural and historical changes in musical thinking and style. In my view, the history of the Western musical tradition is best regarded not as one of changing traits of style *per se* but as one of changing models for musical expression. These models in turn justify the articulation of music history into periods, for they constitute the foundations on which the style characteristics of music in those periods have been based. They also account for historical divisions and connections at different levels. The change of music's aesthetic assumptions from mathematical/symbolic to literary ones is crucial to explaining the great separation of music-historical periods in the fifteenth century. From the fifteenth through the nineteenth centuries the continuous reliance on literature for expressive models and the successive exploration of the approaches of different literary genres accounts for both unifying and dividing factors: Poetry served as the expressive model for music in the Renaissance, rhetoric in the Baroque period, and finally drama in the Classic-Romantic period. In the last of these cases, the understanding that the dramatic model was being developed from the middle of the eighteenth century through the end of the nineteenth justifies the view of that period as one, divided into two phases, a division less deep than those preceding and following the Baroque period.

Learning theory has clearly shown that information is only absorbed and retained when it is incorporated into some coherent pattern. The approach to music history here does not, therefore, intend to turn the reader into a data-storage-and-retrieval system, but instead hopes to encourage critical and creative musical thinking. The facts of history can by no means be discounted, of course, for ideas without information are as useless as they are insubstantial; facts—names, dates, places, and so on—make thoughts concrete and give color and detail to our image of the past. The approach in *Ideas and Styles* is to encourage students to learn as much as possible—as long as they are thinking about what they learn. Mere memorization of names and dates constitutes an exercise in futility; ultimately it defeats the primary object of reading, which should be to stimulate thinking.

Most important, the experience of music itself is crucial to the comprehension of anything we read about it; indeed, the reading is pointless without the music. Since the goal is to learn about music by studying it in the context of the social situations and the philosophical ideas among which it developed, it would be backwards to regard music as a supplement to the textbook. The musician/reader should hear, sing or play, analyze, and discuss as much music as time permits. For this reason, the book has been made as short as possible. Moreover, because this is a book about ideas and styles, and because the goal is to encourage students to apply the principles learned from their reading in their own experience of music, it avoids detailed, bar-by-bar instructions on what the students should examine in a score.

Features

A special feature of *Ideas and Styles* is the use of writings of thinkers, artists, and musicians to identify the ideas that underlie styles of music. The writers quoted range widely from social and political thinkers, to philosophers, to painters, to novelists and poets, and of course to musicians themselves. Rather than provide incidental "enrichment" of the text, the quotations seek to establish what has been thought about the place of music in culture, to illustrate values and patterns of thought, and to demonstrate how critical thinking by musicians provides foundations for music itself. Where possible, foreign-language quotations have been newly translated for this book.

Illustrations have been carefully chosen for *Ideas and Styles* in order to support the content of the text. Pictures show (1) general principles of artistic expression in different periods, (2) music notation when it embodies musical conceptions, (3) places that served as contexts for the playing and singing of music, and (4) ways in which instruments were built and music was performed.

Diagrams and music examples elucidate important concepts in *Ideas and Styles*. These include diagrams of scale formations used by theorists in early periods of music history, the liturgical calendar and the structure of the Mass, and numerous musical forms. The music examples clarify changes in the formation of polyphonic cadences, illustrate Baroque melodic ornamentations, and show the bass lines for important ground-bass forms.

The supplementary material at the ends of the chapters encourages readers to pursue new lines of thought and research. For each chapter there are several Questions for Reflection, intended to stimulate thinking in new directions and synthesis of ideas. Some can be answered from the chapter; some invite readers to think critically and form their own opinions; some may call for further research. In addition, each chapter provides a list of Suggestions for Further Reading.

Ideas and Styles in the Western Musical Tradition includes two appendixes. One is a brief Guide to the Pronunciation of Church Latin. The other is an essay on writing about music, which discusses types of writing, different approaches to particular aspects of music and its history, some sources for research, and suggestions to help students improve their writing in general.

Teaching Aids

Supplementing *Ideas and Styles in the Western Musical Tradition* is a substantial Instructor's Manual. The manual's introductory chapter discusses pedagogical philosophy, outlines sample course syllabuses, and offers ideas for teaching strategies. Each following chapter corresponds to a chapter of the text itself and begins with a chapter overview; several possible teaching objectives; and a list of terms, names, and concepts. There follows a section on classroom approaches, assignments, and topics for discussion; this includes discussion topics to stimulate the exchange of ideas in the classroom, as well as assignments, including some simple composing projects. Next some music for study is recommended, with a discussion of the important style features of each piece and a list of sources for each in historical anthologies of recordings and scores. Finally the manual provides sample test questions in fill-in or multiple choice, true-false/justification, and short essay formats, as well as answer keys.

To help students in their study of music the supplementary materials for *Ideas and Styles* include a worksheet for score study and listening, which guides students to a focused and systematic approach to musical pieces. A set of transparency masters is also available to instructors. These help to amplify the discussion in the text and offer visual representations of abstract ideas.

Acknowledgments

This book has profited immensely from the contributions of many people other than its author. Several classes of students worked with it in its draft stages, patiently noting typographical and factual errors and making suggestions. My colleagues Elias Dann and Jeffery Kite-Powell at The Florida State University provided useful comments. Thanks go especially to my former teaching assistant Marian Wilson for her willingness to teach from the book and to offer her ideas.

The reviewers who read *Ideas and Styles* during its preparation for publication offered both tremendous support and rigorous, always constructive criticism. Their contributions cannot be adequately rewarded, but I acknowledge them here with deep appreciation: Thomas Bauman, Stanford University; John Brobeck, University of Arizona; Gregory Butler, University of British Columbia; Camilla Cai, Kenyon College; Richard S. James, Bowling Green State University; Douglas Lee, Vanderbilt University; Christopher Reynolds, University of California, Davis; and Stan Stanford, Portland State University.

The efforts of Mayfield Publishing Company and its entire staff—especially the firm, tactful, and creative contributions of Janet M. Beatty as sponsoring editor and the painstaking work of Carol Zafiropoulos as production editor—merit the gratitude of the author and readers of this book. The excellent copyediting of Loralee Windsor and design work by Cynthia Bassett Bogue are also gratefully acknowledged.

Finally, there are many who have made the immensely important, intangible contribution of moral support. It would be impossible to list all the friends and colleagues who have alternately prodded and provided encouragement. Most of all I wish to thank my wife, Gayle, without whose humor, patience, intellect, and love none of it would have happened.

TO THE STUDENT

I recently asked my class why they were studying the history of music. One student suggested that music history was a special torture designed as part of the curriculum to punish them for having too much fun with music. Another, more seriously, proposed that it was inherently valuable to memorize the names and dates of important figures and events in the history of music. Yet another thought that studying music history was a way to make music students learn about other fields of cultural history, disguising that intention behind the mask of a music course. Finally, we agreed that the main reason to study the history of music was to make ourselves better musicians. And this is so whether we are primarily players or singers, composers, or listeners.

The real reason to study music history is to encounter musical thinking. Like any other area of human experience and endeavor, music has been approached from many points of view. Performers will present music more effectively if they know what purposes and values inform their music. Composers will enrich their imaginations by understanding other composers' ways of musical thinking and how they have created solutions to musical problems. Listeners will hear more sensitively and alertly when they enrich their understanding with a knowledge of the social contexts and philosophical ideas from which the music sprang. Music in the Western tradition—and, of course, in other traditions as well—is a form of expression and communication. Like any form of communication, it becomes more meaningful when we become more aware of its motives and the foundations of its thought processes.

There are two reasons for approaching the study of musical thinking from a historical perspective, and correspondingly there are two types of music history. First, music is inextricably woven into the fabric of all human activity; that is, history affects music and music affects history. The purposes for music—whether to worship, to glorify political powers, or to entertain the common citizen; the sources of support for music—what countries had the necessary peace and leisure to enjoy it, who had the money to buy it; the philosophical foundations for music—the emphasis on intellect or emotion, the models by which it was expected to achieve expressiveness; the art and literature surrounding music—the architectural spaces in which it was performed, the poetry that was sung; the technological achievements that facilitate music—the means of reproducing scores, the invention of new instruments: all these and many more factors enhance and indeed are inseparable from the understanding of the music itself. Such factors come and go, reinforce or conflict with each other at different times. This book will identify some of these forces that have shaped musical styles.

The second type of music history has to do with the history of music in and of itself. In Western culture musicians, like thinkers in any field, have responded to their past. Such responses may be positive or negative; they may build on what has gone before or may reject it in favor of new directions. Because ideas take time to achieve their full development and because there is no one ideal style, it is common to view the history of music (or cultural history in general) as a series of contrasting though typically overlapping periods, with phases of conception, development, and maturity. We must acknowledge that this way of thinking is peculiarly Western and that it is not necessary to music; other cultures do not view human thought as requiring such forward motion or history as requiring divisions into successive periods characterized by emergence, attainment of full stature, and decline. Moreover, we must not allow our generalizations regarding period styles to obscure the complexity and diversity of a period; individuals differ, the characteristics of one century's music survive into the following centuries, and ideas that have been underground reemerge. Neither should we think that the value of any music depends on its belonging to any particular period or phase within a period. Different types of music incorporate their own value systems, and music of one type cannot be judged by the criteria of another. Further, the conception of a new way of thinking, the exploration and building up of its possibilities, and its full mastery all have values of particular kinds.

Although we may read about the ideas and styles of music in books or discuss them in the classroom, we must *experience* them in music. We may understand the ideas in a book about music, but we will only truly comprehend them through hearing and studying the music. When I first began to study music history, a wise teacher told me, "The history of music is the music itself." I made myself a bookmark with that statement and put it in my music history textbook so that I would be reminded of that truth every day. It is still there.

After all, what we all want to learn is what creative musicians have thought, felt, and expressed in their music. The best thing that a book can do is to lead you deeper into the music itself. So you should spend much more time listening to and analyzing representative works than you do reading. Some works to study will be suggested along the way, and collections of well-chosen pieces are available for analysis. You will be well on your way if you regard this book as a supplement to the music, rather than vice versa!

One last word about what this book is and is not intended to do. It provides, as the title suggests, a look at some important contributions to Western musical thinking. It intends to encourage you to respond with some thoughts of your own about the music you make and hear. But this book is not a comprehensive history of music; there are certainly many interesting events, fine composers, and important musical works that cannot be mentioned here. It is also not a compendium of information that a musically cultured person should know. I hope you will find areas in which you wish to know more, and that you will pursue them in more detailed studies as far as your interest takes you. You may wish to begin with dictionaries and encyclopedias of music, or larger and more detailed histories, or studies of musical philosophy and theory; or you may prefer to go directly to specific books and articles on composers, instruments, genres, and so on. Read widely, enjoy conflicting ideas, and form and refine your own. Most of all, always remember to keep the music foremost!

CONTENTS

4 MEDIEVAL SECULAR SONG AND INSTRUMENTAL MUSIC 45

5 THE DEVELOPMENT OF POLYPHONY 59

6 ## MUSIC IN THE LATE MIDDLE AGES 79

7 ## THE RISE OF THE RENAISSANCE 93

8 THE HIGH RENAISSANCE 107

9 INSTRUMENTAL MUSIC IN THE RENAISSANCE 123

10 THE REFORMATION 133

11 THE WANING OF THE RENAISSANCE 143

12 THE ARRIVAL OF THE BAROQUE 151

13 THE EARLY BAROQUE 167

14 THE HIGH BAROQUE 183

18 THE HIGH CLASSIC PERIOD 257

19 THE RISE OF THE ROMANTIC MOVEMENT 275

20 THE MATURE ROMANTIC PERIOD 299

21 THE TWILIGHT OF ROMANTICISM 321

24 IN THE SECOND HALF OF THE TWENTIETH CENTURY 383

To my students

IDEAS AND STYLES
IN THE WESTERN
MUSICAL TRADITION

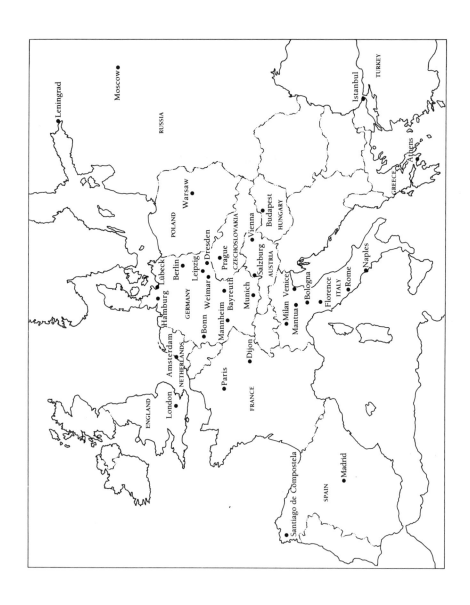

1 MUSIC IN CLASSICAL ANTIQUITY

Music in the Life and Philosophy of Ancient Greece

The culture of ancient Greece has provided the philosophical and intellectual roots for much of later Western culture. Time and again thinkers have returned to the ideas of the great early philosophers to revitalize and redirect contemporary imagination. This once led the philosopher Alfred North Whitehead to speak of all later Western philosophy as a series of footnotes to Plato. In the sense that it provides a model or standard, we refer to the culture of ancient Greece as "classic."

The Greek writers had a great deal to say about music, and we will find that their ideas have influenced Western music at several important stages in its history. But unlike Greek thought, ancient Greek music has not survived in any significant quantity to the present. The total repertoire from which we can study the music itself consists of only a few dozen examples, most of them fragmentary and dating from comparatively late. It is ironic that the Greek philosophers had almost nothing to say about their sculpture and architecture, which still exist, while they devoted a great deal of discussion to their music, which has nearly vanished.

From the writings of the time we know that the Greeks had an active, vibrant musical life. Music played an important role in a variety of social contexts. For example, musical art was intimately connected to literary art. Plato defined music as consisting of words, harmony, and rhythm, while Aristotle listed words, melody, and rhythm as the components of poetry. The epics of Homer were sung, as were the plays of Sophocles and Aeschylus. As in all cultures, music accompanied religious ritual. In addition, there were musical competitions for players and

1

singers, as important as the Olympic athletic contests. And these categories account for only what we would call "art" music; there was surely much folk music as well. The scarcity of surviving ancient Greek music leaves the scholar especially frustrated because what we can learn from the philosophical and theoretical documents is so fascinating.

The organized study of musical phenomena was a lively concern in Greece. The Greeks understood the acoustic properties of musical tones early, and the identification of the simple mathematical relationships underlying the harmonic series were attributed to the mathematician Pythagoras in the late sixth century B.C.

Plato and Aristotle, the two major philosophers of the fourth century B.C., had different views of music—views that have reemerged at various times in the history of musical thought. Plato's roots were in mathematics and abstract thinking, his philosophical affinity was for the ideal, and he viewed the sensible world as merely the shadow of a pure and abstract Reality. For him music derived its value from its reflection of ideal forms, and its purpose was to inculcate excellence rather than to provide pleasure. Aristotle's background in biological studies led him to take a more inductive and empirical approach, and he adopted a more pragmatic view of music. To Aristotle music did not reflect abstractions but imitated human action (*mimesis*); he also allowed for music to be pursued for pleasurable or practical ends.

Music and the Doctrine of Ethos

One of the major contributions of Greek philosophy, shared by both Plato and Aristotle, is the doctrine of *ethos*. Applied to music, this doctrine is the belief that music can powerfully affect human character and behavior. Such beliefs may be found in many musical cultures, of course, most clearly those in which music is related to shamanism. We shall see that it continued to be reflected in much later historical periods, although it is rarely taken literally in Western music today.

The doctrine of ethos was applied to music by the Greek thinkers in a variety of ways. First, music could be related to the spiritual life in the context of religion. The gods of Olympus represented a variety of characters, and the worship of each was necessarily suited to the specific deity. A major distinction was made between the worship of Apollo, which was characterized by discipline and restraint, and that of Dionysus, which was typically emotional, even orgiastic, and in consequence, as one might well imagine, extremely popular. The terms *Apollonian* for music that is abstract and appeals to the intellect and *Dionysian* for music that arouses strong emotions have been employed more recently, and the two inclinations have operated in uneasy tension throughout our music history. The music employed in worship clearly reflected such distinctions. In secular life, as well, music was considered a major component of education. Some Greeks believed that ennobling music could produce a noble and virtuous character, while exposure to lascivious music would lead to a debauched life. Characteristically, when Plato discussed the political organization of the ideal state in his *Republic,* he prescribed certain types of music and forbade others. To Plato the true value of music was its power to educate one to virtue. Equally characteristically, Aristotle believed that even impassioned and Dionysian music had value in inducing emotional release or *catharsis.* He recognized different social circumstances and was less concerned with restricting music to certain types, but rather concentrated on applying to each situation music with the appropriate ethos.

Ethos was understood to be rooted in specific aspects of musical style. One of the aspects of style that contributed to musical ethos was instrumentation. The *lyre* or *kithara,* a stringed instrument, was associated with the cult of Apollo and therefore, naturally, with more noble types of ethos; the *aulos,* a double-barreled reed pipe employed in the Dionysian rites, obviously evoked a sensual and less-disciplined ethos. (Fig. 1.1) In similar fashion, rhythms, that is, poetic meters, had their own ethical force. Finally, pitch patterns, generally referred to as *harmonia* (pl. *harmoniai,* often translated as "mode"), also produced specific ethos. Aristotle (*Politics*) regarded the Dorian harmonia as "steadfast and most manly in character," the Phrygian as leading to ecstasy and emotion, and the Lydian as suitable for children because it had the "capacity to contain both elegance and educativeness." Plato (*Republic*) accepted Dorian and Phrygian music but rejected the Mixolydian and Syntonolydian harmoniai as too mournful, while he considered certain Ionian and Lydian harmoniai "slack" and likely to induce softness and sloth.

Characteristics of Music

Despite the paucity of musical documentation, we can determine some characteristic aspects of Greek music itself. Of primary importance is the connection of music with words. We have already noted the similarity of Plato's and Aristotle's definitions of music and poetry, respectively, and it is clear from the surviving music that the Greek musical archetype was a sung text. One effect of this conception was that musical rhythm corresponded to the rhythm of poetic verse. Since we know that the Greeks employed instruments—the kithara, the aulos, and a wide variety of other instruments, including percussion—vocal performances may well have been accompanied by instruments. There is no evidence, however, that complex textures were used; rather the instruments may have doubled the vocal melodies in monophonic texture or varied from the vocal lines in their ornamentation of basic patterns to produce *heterophony.* There is also evidence of the use of instruments without voices, but such music was apparently improvised. This would have been the case for the competitions of virtuoso instrumentalists and perhaps for dancing.

Figure 1.1
Music contest between Apollo and Marsyas, relief sculpture (320 B.C.).
According to myth, the aulos player Marsyas challenged the god Apollo to a
musical competition. Apollo, playing the lyre, defeated Marsyas and had him
flayed for his insolence. The myth illustrates the relative virtue of the two
most important Greek instruments. (*National Archaeological Museum, Athens*)

Greek Music Theory

Another major contribution made by the Greeks to Western music was a
sophisticated theory of musical pitch organization constructed according to
acoustical principles. The Greeks actually developed the concept of discrete
pitches ordered by frequency into what they called either harmonia or *tonos*
(pl. *tonoi*), a theoretical construct roughly comparable to our idea of a scale.
(Fig. 1.2)

The Greek music theorists viewed their total pitch spectrum according to
a plan known as the Greater Perfect System. This was a series of four intervals
of the fourth or *tetrachords* ("four strings"), placed consecutively so that they
formed two pairs of conjunct fourths (that is, the tetrachords share one common pitch) separated by a whole tone. The addition of one more whole tone
at one end of the spectrum created a span of two octaves. The following
diagram will help clarify this plan; the upper level shows the spectrum divided

Figure 1.2
One form of Greek musical notation is preserved in the first Delphic hymn to Apollo, inscribed on the marble wall of the Treasury of the Athenians at the shrine of Apollo at Delphi. The letters that indicate notes can be seen between the lines of text. (*Archaeological Museum, Delphi*)

into fourths in the Greek fashion, while the lower level indicates the relation to the octave-based scale system (diagonal slashes mark disjunctions; dashes indicate the number of semitone spaces within the tetrachords or octaves; the points of conjunction are indicated by equal signs):

```
    +  tetrachord    tetrachord    tetrachord    tetrachord
    X / 4 - - - - 1 = 4 - - - - 1 / 4 - - - - 1 = 4 - - - - 1

             octave                      octave
    1 - - - - - - - - - - 8 = 1 - - - - - - - - - - 8
```

The theorists also recognized a Lesser Perfect System, composed of three conjunct tetrachords and the added note.

```
    +  tetrachord    tetrachord    tetrachord
    X / 4 - - - - 1 = 4 - - - - 1 = 4 - - - - 1
```

(The Greeks thought of the higher-frequency pitches as being at the "lower" end of the system and vice versa—a consequence of the fact that the kithara was held like the modern guitar with the lowest-pitched strings farthest from the ground—so modern readers have to invert as well as translate their writings. This makes it difficult for modern musicians to keep the patterns clear. In these diagrams, the pitch at the left is the one the Greeks would have thought of as highest but that we would now call lowest, while the pitch at the right is the one they would have called lowest and we would call highest.)

Between the fixed pitches at the ends of each tetrachord came two intermediate pitches; these were not always placed in the same positions, however. There were actually three different ways to fit them in, each of which produced a different *genus* (pl. *genera*) of tetrachord. The *diatonic* genus divided the tetrachord into two whole tones plus a semitone. The *chromatic* genus divided it into two semitones and an augmented whole tone. The *enharmonic* genus reduced the distances separating the three pitches at one end of the tetrachord still further to quarter tones, resulting in a ditone (two-whole-tone) gap to the remaining pitch. The three genera can be depicted as follows:

Diatonic genus -	tetrachord
	4 3 - 2 - 1
Chromatic genus -	tetrachord
	4 3 2 - - 1
Enharmonic genus -	tetrachord
	432 - - - 1

Another aspect of the Greek theoretical concept of pitch organization was the elimination of redundancy by focusing attention on a single or characteristic octave, just as we do today. The Greeks had seven different ways to take an octave from the Greater Perfect System, thus producing divisions of the octave into the various groupings of tonoi (or harmoniai) just as, for example, the diatonic white-key octave scale on a modern keyboard produces a major scale beginning on C or a natural minor scale beginning on A. In the following chart the symbol X has been used for the note of conjunction (i.e., 4=1) between conjunct tetrachords:

Hypodorian tonos	1 / 4 3 - 2 - X 3 - 2 - 1
Hypophrygian tonos	2 - 1 / 4 3 - 2 - X 3 - 2
Hypolydian tonos	3 - 2 - 1 / 4 3 - 2 - X 3
Dorian tonos	X 3 - 2 - 1 / 4 3 - 2 - X
Phrygian tonos	2 - X 3 - 2 - 1 / 4 3 - 2
Lydian tonos	3 - 2 - X 3 - 2 - 1 / 4 3
Mixolydian tonos	4 3 - 2 - X 3 - 2 - 1 / 4
(compare - major	c - d - e f - g - a - b c′
natural minor	A - B c - d - e f - g - a)

The relation of these theoretical constructs to actual Greek music and specifically to the ethical effects attributed to musical modes (harmoniai) by the philosophers is obscure. It is likely that the use of a particular array of tones within the range of the characteristic octave produced certain melodic patterns or formulas that would be common to all pieces employing the same tonos. This would account for the dual usage of the word *harmonia*—in a technical sense by the theorists and in a more empirical sense by the philosophers.

Although the pitch system was quite different from what has been used in Western music for the last few centuries, the attempt to explain music on the basis of a systematic grouping of articulated pitches organized according to acoustical relationships was a major contribution of the Greeks to the history of Western musical thought. As we shall see, a later age found it possible to maintain a great musical culture without such an abstract theoretical foundation. It is significant, however, that the eventual rediscovery of the Greek theoretical heritage encouraged construction of a new system.

Music in Ancient Rome

Music in the culture of Rome was built on the heritage received from Greece. The Romans apparently adapted the music of the Greeks to their own manner of life. Instead of the philosophical and theoretical pursuits that occupied the Greek thinkers, the Romans were more inclined to indulge in music for pleasure.

As a result, musical works became more grandiose and elaborate. The instruments were developed to provide more volume and were played in huge ensembles. At the same time, increased complexity in the melodies gave rise to a new emphasis on virtuosity. This was supported by the influence of Oriental styles that entered Roman culture as a result of military conquest in the East. Wealthy Romans employed professional musicians, including slaves, to entertain at all kinds of social events and adopted the Greek practice of musical competitions. The stars of that time were idolized, fawned over, and lusted after as much as rock stars of the twentieth century. Patricians also aspired to virtuosity. For example, the Emperor Nero's concern for his skill as a kithara player and relative indifference to the crisis in his capital led to the familiar statement "Nero fiddled while Rome burned."

As one would expect, the military conquests of the Roman armies provided one special field for musical development, the field of battle. It is not surprising that this period produced notable developments in brass instruments.

The Romans did not contribute significantly to the philosophy or theory of music as did the Greeks, although they developed and transmitted some of the older Greek ideas and ideals through the early centuries of the Christian era. At the close of that period, however, the Romans made some attempts to consider music from a philosophic viewpoint, in connection with the way music fit into the educational system.

In the fifth century Martianus Capella outlined a program for education based on seven "liberal arts." These were arranged into two divisions: (1) the *trivium,* consisting of the three language arts, *grammatica* (grammar), *rhetorica* (rhetoric or style), and *dialectica* (logic); and (2) the *quadrivium,* comprising the four mathematical disciplines, *arithmetica* (basic mathematics), *geometria* (plane geometry), *musica* (music), and *astronomia* (astronomy). The grouping seems a bit peculiar compared to modern curricula, in which music is placed closer to literature than to mathematics and natural science. Capella assumed, however, that the study of music would deal exclusively with harmonic proportions. Thought of in that way rather than as an expressive art form, music takes a natural place between the study of spatial relationships in geometry and the observation of the regular motions of the stars and planets.

More influential in the history of music than Martianus Capella was the scholar Anicius Manlius Severinus Boethius (ca. 480–524). Boethius followed Capella's lead by writing treatises on each of the seven liberal arts. In his *De institutione musica* (On the organization of music) he codified many of the ancient ideas about music. Like Capella, Boethius was concerned only with what he called *musica speculativa* ("speculative" or "reflective" music, from the Latin *speculum,* meaning "mirror") because by its harmonic proportions music reflects mathematical principles. He addressed the *musicus* (the true musician), who understood the principles of music. Boethius saw no place in the liberal education for *musica practica,* the domain of the mere *cantor* (literally "singer," but including all performing musicians), who had the talent to make beautiful sounds but no understanding of the principles of the art.

Boethius's greatest contribution to musical thought was a classification of music in three divisions. The most important of these was *musica mundana* (the music of the spheres), which was the product of the regular rhythmic motions of the sun, moon, stars, and planets. Such harmonious relationships, Boethius proposed, must produce musical tones, even though these tones could not actually be heard by human ears. (Christian thinkers later reasoned that our inability to hear this heavenly music was caused by the corruption of our senses through Adam's sin.) The second type of music was *musica humana* (human music), the music that gave harmony to human existence. Human harmony would govern life by keeping everything in proportion, both individually and in society; a personality or relationship that was out of proportion would be appropriately described as disharmonious and consequently unmusical. The lowest form of music, *musica instrumentalis,* incorporated all sounding music, including singing. Thus actual music sung or played would present a concrete image of the order of the universe, a reflection—following in the tradition of Plato—of a great principle or higher Reality.

When Roman culture collapsed after the transfer of the imperial capital to Constantinople and the sacking of Rome in the fifth century by northern invaders, there was little time or concern for the finer aspects of life. Survival in a dangerously unstable world became a primary concern. Many of the great documents of Greek culture disappeared from view. As Christianity spread, the relics of pagan art were crowded out and later deliberately suppressed. Therefore we must next turn to the Christian culture.

Questions for Reflection

✥   What is the proper place of music in education? How has this changed since the periods of Plato and Aristotle, Martianus Capella, and Boethius?

✥   How has the understanding of the therapeutic value of music developed since the Greeks?

✥   Study the discussions of music in Plato's *Republic* and Aristotle's *Politics* and compare their ideas.

✥   What did the Greeks know about the acoustical properties of musical tones and the relationships between tones, and how was that reflected in the system of tonoi or harmoniai?

Suggestions for Further Reading

For translations of some of the important discussions of music by the writers cited in this chapter, see Oliver Strunk, *Source Readings in Music History* (New York: Norton, 1950); Andrew Barker, ed., *Greek Musical Writings*, (Cambridge: Cambridge University Press, 1984), vol. 1, *The Musician and His Art.*

Two studies of Greek musical thought are Warren D. Anderson, *Ethos and Education in Greek Music* (Cambridge: Harvard University Press, 1966); Edward Lippmann, *Musical Thought in Ancient Greece* (New York: Columbia University Press, 1964).

2

THE EARLY CHRISTIAN PERIOD

The Growth of the Christian Church and Its Music

Christianity rose just as the power of Rome was passing its peak. It began in a small corner of the Mediterranean where a tiny band of Jews embraced the rabbi Jesus's message that love of God and for one's neighbor was the principle that would redeem humankind, a principle stronger than the law of Moses or the power of Caesar. Of course the ruling powers in both Jerusalem and Rome considered this faith highly subversive. Jesus was executed for treason, and for three hundred years Christians suffered persecution and martyrdom throughout the Roman Empire. In A.D. 313 the Emperor Constantine, who himself became a Christian, issued the Edict of Milan, allowing religious freedom to Christians. The church was free to grow, and it became the dominant power in Western culture. Because of this, it should not be surprising that the history of Western music for a long period becomes the history of the music of the Christian religion.

Our understanding of music from the fourth to the ninth century is also influenced by the fact that the historical evidence preserved from those centuries comes substantially through the church. As the church's power grew, it rooted out paganism and its cultural relics with the same vigor that had been exercised against the church in the three preceding centuries. Meanwhile, with Europe in political turmoil and general learning on the wane, the church's reliance on scripture gave it a special reason to preserve literacy, which pagan religion did not have. Moreover, together with architecture and the visual arts music was an essential medium of worship. And finally, Christian worship was really the only cultural activity whose custodians had the wherewithal to maintain it.

11

It was not to be taken for granted that music would thrive in the young religion, however. There was a certain suspicion of the power music could hold over the minds and hearts of the faithful. Music had been important to the Greek and Roman religious cults and therefore had dangerous associations with paganism. The belief in musical ethos remained strong. It manifested itself in the musical philosophy of the church fathers. The dilemma contemplated by St. Augustine (354–430) in his *Confessions* sums up the problem. On the one hand, the sensuous pleasure derived from music threatened to distract him from the words being sung and turn his attention away from the contemplation of God. Nevertheless Augustine recognized the power of music to fire devotion, especially that of the newer and weaker minds among the faithful, and he recalled "the tears that I shed on hearing the songs of the church in the early days, soon after I had recovered my faith." Indeed, Augustine bears an honorable place in the history of Christian music; according to legend, at the moment of Augustine's baptism by St. Ambrose of Milan the two men extemporized one of the great hymns of the church, "Te Deum laudamus" (We praise thee, O God). Thus he wavered "between the danger that lies in gratifying the senses and the benefits which . . . can accrue from singing."[1] Ultimately, of course, music secured a place in Christian life. Throughout the church's history, however, music has developed within a state of constant tension in which the imaginative and progressive contributions of musicians are held in check to some degree by the severer concerns of churchmen.

The Jewish Heritage

The earliest Christian worship and music naturally came from the Jewish tradition of the apostolic church of the first centuries rather than from pagan Hellenism. Although Judaism did not have a theoretical and philosophical literature to match that of the Greeks, it had as rich a musical tradition as any religion. The exhortations in the Psalms to praise God with songs and musical instruments provide ample evidence of this.

> O sing to the Lord a new song,
>   for he has done marvelous things! . . .
> Make a joyful noise to the Lord, all the earth;
>   break forth into joyous song and sing praises!
> Sing praises to the Lord with the lyre,
>   with the lyre and the sound of melody!
> With trumpets and the sound of the horn
>   make a joyful noise before the King, the Lord!
>
> (Ps. 98: 1, 4–6)

Praise him with trumpet sound;
   praise him with lute and harp!
Praise him with timbrel and dance;
   praise him with strings and pipe!
Praise him with sounding cymbals;
   praise him with loud clashing cymbals!

(Ps. 150: 3–5)

The power of music over the human mind was also part of Jewish experience. The first book of Samuel reports the therapeutic effect of David's harp playing on the troubled King Saul (1 Sam. 16:23). (Fig. 2.1)

Jewish synagogue worship contained several types of worship activities, mostly based on scripture. These included prayer, readings and teaching, and the giving of alms. All these features were carried over into Christian practice.

The Jewish religious musical repertory comprised both scriptural and nonscriptural songs. The scriptural songs included the *psalms* (from the Book of Psalms) and other poetic passages from the religious writings, known as *canticles*. Since the Christian Old Testament retained the Jewish scriptures, the psalms and canticles were naturally retained as well. (Fig. 2.2) The nonscriptural songs were *hymns*, a simpler and more popular genre than the psalms and canticles. Vestiges of the Jewish hymns and their music certainly survived into Christian repertoire, but since they did not have biblical authority they rapidly gave way to newly composed hymns embodying the Christian faith.

The musical style of early Christian music was derived from that of Judaism. The texture of the music was monophonic, although actual performance presumably involved doublings and heterophonic ornamentations. Rhythm was not metered but controlled in general by word rhythms. There were three different means of performing. The simplest was *direct* performance, which consisted of solo or unison performance of the music throughout. Also common was *responsorial* singing, in which a solo singer or leader performed verses of the text, and the entire congregation answered each verse with the following verse or with a response or refrain. Common responses were the simple Hebrew words *amen* (an expression of affirmation) and *halleluja* (praise Jahweh); but these might be more extensive:

O give thanks to the Lord for he is good;
   his steadfast love endures for ever!
Let Israel say,
   "His steadfast love endures for ever!"
Let the house of Aaron say,
   "His steadfast love endures for ever!"
Let those who fear the Lord say,
   "His steadfast love endures for ever!"

(Ps. 118: 1–4)

Figure 2.1
Lorenzo Monaco, "King David" (ca. 1410). King David, to whom many of the psalms are attributed, was depicted not only with the harp but with a variety of other musical instruments by medieval artists. Here he holds a psaltery. (*Metropolitan Museum of Art, Gwynne Andrews and Marquand Funds, and Gift of Mrs. Ralph J. Hines, by exchange, 1965. (65.14.4)*)

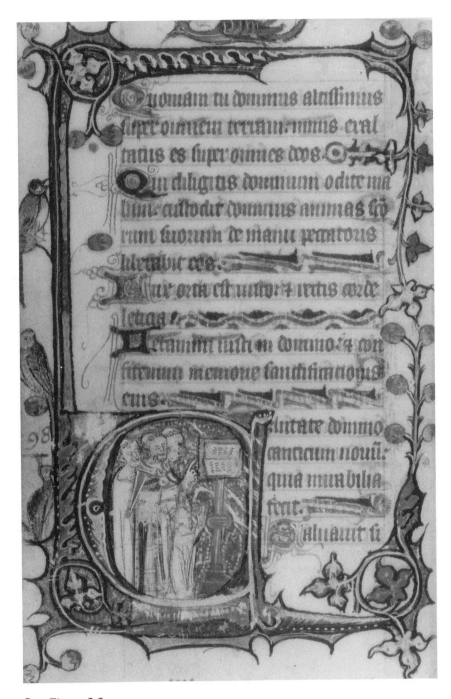

Figure 2.2
Medieval manuscript illumination showing church singers at a lectern, decorating the first letter of Psalm 98, "Cantate Domino canticum novum" (O sing to the Lord a new song). (*Bodleian Library, Oxford, MS. Lyell empt. 4, fol. 133v*)

Given the structure of psalms in paired verses, it was possible to divide the singers into two groups and have them sing in alternation. Such performance is termed *antiphonal*. Direct, responsorial, and antiphonal singing continued in Christian musical practice.

The pitch organization of Jewish music was quite different from that of the Greeks and from our familiar scales. It relied on the principle of *modes* or melodic formulas. The basic units were not individual notes considered as abstract points in tonal space but melodic outlines or prototypes serving as patterns for actual sung phrases. In some cases it appears that the early Christians adopted the melodies themselves. More importantly, however, the principle of melodic construction based on modes became the basis for the music of the church for at least the first ten centuries of its existence.

The Diversification of Practice

In the centuries following the Edict of Milan, Europe gradually became Christianized; but as the religious faith spread, its worship and musical practices diversified. Decentralization of political power led to the formation of smaller, loosely organized nations. Because the means of communication were slow and unreliable, it was difficult to disperse any uniform repertoire or style throughout the continent. Growing pains within the church itself led to a variety of theological opinions associated with different spiritual leaders. Some positions were absorbed into the dogma of the church, while others were rejected as heretical. In this context it is not surprising that the musical tradition was extremely fragmented.

The Eastern Influence

The strongest political, cultural, and musical center was the eastern portion of Christendom, centered in the new capital of the Roman Empire at Constantinople, or Byzantium, to use its traditional name (now Istanbul). The Emperor Constantine had made the city his imperial capital in 330, so that while the Catholic Church remained centered around the pope, the bishop of Rome, an eastern branch of the church grew up in Byzantium. This branch produced the modern Orthodox Church.

The relative stability of the Byzantine empire, which for a thousand years staved off one attack after another from the outside, permitted the development of a highly sophisticated culture. In politics this manifested itself in a system of court intrigue that led to the modern connotation of the epithet *Byzantine*. In Byzantium the Emperor Justinian (483–565) achieved a monumental and intricate codification of the Roman imperial law. He also ordered the building of the great church of Hagia Sophia. (Fig. 2.3) Religious thinkers reveled in the pursuit of arcane details of theology.

Figure 2.3
Hagia Sophia in Istanbul (earlier Constantinople and Byzantium), the greatest
church of the Byzantine era. It was built in the reign of the great emperor
Justinian (r. 527–565), a time when Constantinople exerted ecclesiastical,
political, and artistic domination over Europe. Following the Turkish
conquest of the city in 1453, Hagia Sophia was converted to a mosque.
(*Marburg/Art Resource*)

It should not be surprising that in this context the Byzantine church
developed a repertoire of elaborate, extended musical compositions. Particularly impressive was the huge repertoire of perhaps a hundred thousand or
more hymns. There were a number of special types of musical pieces to ornament worship. Characteristic of the spirit of Byzantine music, the *kontakion*
(pl. *kontakia*) resembled a long, poetic sermon on a biblical text. Each kontakion contains a prologue (*prooimion*) and twenty or more long stanzas, linked
by a shared refrain. Equally grandiose is the *kanon* (pl. *kanones*), a complicated, multisectional piece based on a series of nine biblical canticles. For each
canticle, a kanon provides a so-called ode consisting of several stanzas.

The style of the music could be as complex as the repertoire was extensive.
The performance of these pieces was, of course, conceived as monophonic,
but they were by no means simple. The kontakia and kanones were originally

syllabic, but they developed an elaborate, florid style called *kalophonic* (beautiful sounding), actually a number of different styles of embellishment associated with individual musicians. This, of course, reflects the general melodic tendencies of much Middle Eastern and oriental music.

By the eighth century, the theoretical tonal structure of Byzantine church music was modal; that is, an actual piece of music was based on a given melodic formula. In this it resembled Jewish and other Eastern musical styles. The melodic formula was known as an *echos* (pl. *echoi*). The complete system incorporated eight different echoi, classified in two series of four. In each series the formulas were oriented respectively around the pitch centers d, e, f, and g. This system strongly influenced the development of the music theory of western Europe in the Middle Ages.

Local European Practices

After the fourth century, the churches and monasteries in the different parts of Europe developed a number of local musical idioms. Before we turn our attention to the great centralized musical repertoire that dominated the Middle Ages, a brief note of the evidence of the diversity of the early church is in order.

The religious and musical tradition of Rome itself is commonly termed *Old Roman*. It continued as an oral tradition well into the Middle Ages, when a suitable notation was developed; consequently, a substantial quantity of Old Roman music is available for modern scholars to study and compare to the related, but significantly different, music of the later Catholic church. By comparison, much less is known about the musical repertoires and styles of the "peripheral" regions of northern and western Europe.

St. Ambrose, the fourth-century Bishop of Milan, was a musical leader in the early church. He is credited with promoting the singing of hymns as a means of strengthening faith and fortifying belief in the true doctrines of the Christian religion. He actually composed the texts of several great hymns, though probably not their music. The music and worship practice that was used in Milan is called *Ambrosian* in his honor. Like the Old Roman, the Ambrosian repertoire was eventually notated.

In Ireland, one of the first areas almost entirely converted to Christianity, there was a *Celtic* musical tradition associated with the monasteries founded by St. Patrick in the fifth century. It did not last past the seventh century, and none of the actual music is known today.

Between the sixth and eighth centuries, the Frankish territory, consisting of what is now western France and the Netherlands, also developed a local musical idiom, called *Gallican*. Of the various "peripheral" styles it was undoubtedly the one with the most influence on the later, unified repertoire of the Middle Ages, but the lack of surviving music makes it impossible to determine the nature and extent of the relationship.

The Christians living in the Iberian region (Portugal and Spain) during the domination of the Moors from the eighth to the eleventh centuries were known as Mozarabs. The surviving musical manuscripts of the *Mozarabic* (or Hispanic) tradition are mostly undecipherable.

Out of this diversity of regional political, social, religious, philosophical, and artistic forces, the Middle Ages emerged. The construction of a relatively unified European civilization from the wreckage of Greek and Roman culture was the achievement of the leaders, thinkers, artists, and musicians from the sixth century on. Music holds a proud position in that civilization.

Questions for Reflection

❖   How did the Judaeo-Christian tradition justify theologically the importance of music in its worship?

❖   How did the texts that were sung in Jewish and early Christian worship reflect the needs of an unnotated musical tradition?

❖   What relationships were there between differences in chant traditions and the articulation of national cultural integrity in the early church? How did the continuously expanding church deal with the differences of musical styles among peoples to whom it spread?

Suggestions for Further Reading

The discussion of music in St. Augustine's *Confessions* and some writings of other church fathers are translated in Oliver Strunk's *Source Readings* (see Suggestions for Further Reading in Chapter 1). For other sources of the early church's thought about music, see James W. McKinnon, ed., *Music in Early Christian Literature* (Cambridge: Cambridge University Press, 1987).

On the Jewish musical tradition, see A. Z. Idelsohn, *Jewish Music in Its Historical Development* (New York: Schocken, 1967). The standard study of Byzantine chant is Egon Wellesz, *A History of Byzantine Music and Hymnody*, 2d ed. (Oxford: Clarendon, 1971).

Notes

1. Saint Augustine, *Confessions*, trans. R.S. Pine-Coffin (Baltimore: Penguin, 1961), 239.

3

THE CHANT OF THE MEDIEVAL CHURCH

The Establishment of a Catholic Tradition

One of the great accomplishments of the early Middle Ages was the establishment of a unified Europe on religious and political grounds. An important product of that unification was the development of the musical repertoire commonly known as "Gregorian" chant. It takes this name from Pope Gregory I, who led the Roman church from 590 to 604. As far as can be determined Gregory did not actually compose any of the music. His reputation derived from his consolidation of ecclesiastical authority in Rome and the assertion of the church's power in worldly affairs.

Pope Gregory came from a political background and was a remarkably capable administrator; he was responsible for sending out missionaries who spread not only the Christian faith but also its musical practice throughout Europe. Within the realm of worship and music, Gregory's contributions included the recodification of the parts of the service, the reorganization of the *schola cantorum* (school of singing, the papal choir), and the cultivation of vocal instruction in Roman institutions to train singers to lead the church's music and thereby free priests for other duties.

It is important to remember that music was transmitted orally. The earliest surviving manuscripts with reasonably precise musical notation for the chant date from the end of the ninth century. Like all oral traditions in music, the chant required concentration on a nucleus of simple, fundamental melodic designs, while at the same time it naturally varied from place to place, generation to generation, and singer to singer.

21

The establishment of a single, universal body of church music actually came later, at the time of Charlemagne (ca. 742–814). It was a natural corollary of the attempt to unify the European continent politically, in a sense a propaganda move. Charlemagne well understood the need to base his secular power on the support of the church, and when Pope Leo II was threatened, Charlemagne came to his rescue. Leo in turn crowned Charlemagne Holy Roman Emperor on Christmas day in 800. Partly because of the importance of centering the Catholic musical practice in Rome and partly because of the musical taste of Charlemagne and his father Pepin, the new worship service and music were grounded in the practice described in books sent north from Rome. The compilation of the entire repertoire was directed by the scholar Alcuin (ca. 732–804), who was in charge of the school at Charlemagne's court in Aachen (Fig. 3.1), and elements of the Gallican practice were also assimilated into the final product. In support of the authenticity of this music over the existing regional styles, the legend grew up that Pope Gregory I himself had composed the music under divine inspiration.

The Roman Liturgy

The prescribed order for the conduct of worship is called the *liturgy*. An understanding of the Roman church's liturgy is essential for any understanding of the chant, because the liturgy provides both the context and the shaping plan for the musical expression of chant.

The Roman liturgy can be regarded as the largest unified artistic experience possible, for it encompasses the entire year and is reenacted as a great symbolic ritual each year in a subtly changing but never-ending cycle. Consequently every piece of the chant has its particular place or places within space and time provided by architectural settings and within a gigantic liturgical form. Each day in the *liturgical year* is unique; the form and content of its music are based on its relationship to the two greatest days in the church year—Christmas, which celebrates the birth of Christ and is fixed on 25 December in the Western church, and Easter, which celebrates Christ's resurrection on a movable date in the spring—and to other feasts. (Fig. 3.2)

The liturgical year actually begins on the fourth Sunday before Christmas, which marks the beginning of the season of Advent, the period when the church anticipates the coming of Christ. Advent is the first of two penitential seasons in the liturgical year, which are traditionally marked by prayer, self-examination, and fasting, as well as by relatively austere music and worship. The celebration of Christmastide begins on Christmas day itself and continues for the next twelve days. Then follows Epiphany, the day when the visit of the Magi to the child Jesus is commemorated, and its season, which signifies the

Figure 3.1
The Palatine Chapel of Charlemagne at Aachen. Aachen was Charlemagne's
capital, and the chapel contained his throne. The architecture represents the
imposing, weighty style of the ninth century. (*Marburg/Art Resource*)

manifestation of Christ to the whole world. Epiphany ends with the beginning
of Lent, the second of the penitential seasons, which consists of the forty days
before Easter. The last week before Easter is known as Holy Week. Easter is the
most important festival of the year, since it marks the resurrection of Christ.
The Easter season lasts seven weeks and ends on the Sunday known as Pentecost (fifty days after Easter) or Whitsunday. On Pentecost the church celebrates the gift of the Holy Spirit to the apostles (Acts 2). Then comes Trinity
Sunday and the long season of Trinity, continuing through the summer and

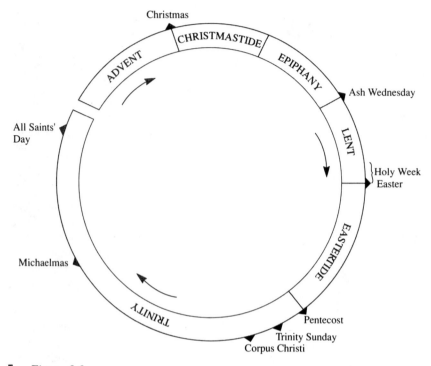

Figure 3.2
The liturgical year, showing the seasons and some of the major festivals of the church.

fall until the arrival of the first Sunday of Advent and the start of a new church year.

There are numerous other festivals in the church, notably St. Stephen's day, the day after Christmas; Corpus Christi, the first Thursday after Trinity Sunday; Michaelmas, 29 September; and All Saints' Day, 1 November. Because the exact date of Easter changes from year to year, it was necessary to establish a complicated hierarchy of celebrations in cases when two liturgical days fell on the same date.

The liturgical calendar may seem strange to modern students, but it need not be thought of as totally foreign. Indeed, some of our familiar secular holidays are based on the liturgical calendar. Mardi Gras (French for "fat Tuesday"), the last day of the season of Epiphany, arose as a "last fling" before the long season of fasting that begins with Ash Wednesday, the first day of Lent. Ash Wednesday is a church holiday (i.e., holy day); Mardi Gras is definitely not. Similarly Halloween (All Hallows Eve) is the night before All Saints'

Day (or All Hallows). All Saints' Day is a church holiday; Halloween probably has its roots in the Celtic pagan observance of the beginning of winter.

Settings for Worship

Within the Roman liturgy for each day there are two different settings for worship: a relatively private one known as the *Divine Office,* which is observed by the cloistered community in a monastery or convent; and a public one, the *Mass.*

Divine Office   The Divine Office has its roots in the Jewish synagogue services and early Christian night vigils from the centuries when the church was still suffering Roman persecution. The standardization of monastic worship, like the governance of monastic life and work in general, was established by the Rule of St. Benedict. Benedict (ca. 480–527) set out detailed regulations to order every aspect of the activities of the monks. The Rule prescribed eight services that articulated the day of study and work, the Divine Office or Canonical Hours. The daily schedule ran approximately as follows:

Matins (morning)—2:00 A.M. (The ever-practical Rule of St. Benedict suggests that "When they arise for the Divine Office, they ought to encourage each other, for the sleepy make many excuses.")
    Private study and prayer

Lauds (praise)—5:00 A.M.

Prime (the first Hour)—6:00 A.M.
    Breakfast (if any)
    Private study
    Possibly Mass
    Work begins

Terce (the third Hour)—9:00 A.M.
    Return to work

Sext (the sixth Hour)—12:00 noon
    Return to work

None (the ninth Hour)—3:00 P.M.
    Dinner. According to the Benedictine Rule, there would normally be only two dishes, and each monk would have a ration of a pound of bread for the entire day. Only the infirm were allotted red meat.
    Private study and prayer

Vespers (evening)—4:00 P.M.

Compline (complete)—5:00 P.M.
    Bed—6:00 P.M.

Obviously worship was an important part of the monastic vocation. The monks dedicated themselves not only to charitable work but also to a career of worship.

The named Offices (Matins, Lauds, Vespers, and Compline) are called the Greater Hours, and their music is more extensive and more complicated and more important to music history than that of the numbered or lesser hours (Prime, Terce, Sext, and None). The book containing the music of the Offices is the *Antiphonary,* that containing only the texts is the *Breviary.* Medieval scribes prepared beautifully decorated breviaries (also known as Books of Hours) for wealthy patrons; among these are some of the most elaborate and famous examples of manuscript illumination.

The musical content of the Offices centers on the singing of psalms; the number of these ranges from three for the Lesser Hours to nine at Matins. The psalms are set off by nonbiblical pieces (the *antiphons* and *responsories*). Except for Matins, each of the Greater Hours climaxes with a canticle. For Vespers the canticle is the *Magnificat* or Song of Mary (Luke 1:46–55, beginning "My soul magnifies the Lord"), and for Compline it is appropriately the Song of Simeon *Nunc dimittis* (Luke 2:29–32, "Lord, now lettest thou thy servant depart in peace"). There is also a hymn in each Office. Besides these elements there are opening and closing formulas, brief passages from the Bible, and prayers. The Offices include neither preaching nor Holy Communion. The entire service does not last long, perhaps fifteen minutes for the Lesser Hours and up to half an hour or a bit more for the Greater Hours on major feast days.

Mass   The Mass is the most solemn service of the liturgy. Like the Divine Office, the Mass originated in the Jewish worship practice, combining the synagogue teaching tradition with the celebration of Holy Communion (also known as the *Eucharist* or the Lord's Supper), derived from the rite of the Jewish Passover. The Mass therefore has two parts. The first part, or teaching service, concludes after the sermon, if there is one, and the statement of the Christian faith in the Nicene Creed (known in music as the *Credo*). The second consists of Holy Communion. In the early days of the church, the teaching service was open to inquirers who were not yet baptized Christians, and they were excused when the faithful prepared for the Eucharist.

The essential structure of the Mass was established in a more-or-less unified pattern much later than that of the Offices, in fact, not until the tenth century. The book that contains the music for the Mass is known as the *Gradual;* the book that contains the text is called the *Missal.* For general use, the most important materials were later collected from the vast total repertoire into the more practical *Liber usualis.*

An important structuring principle in the liturgy is the division of material into those parts of the text that always remain the same and those that change according to the particular day in the liturgical year. The former are called

Ordinary, and the latter are known as *Proper*. In the Offices of Vespers and Compline, for example, the canticles are Ordinary, because these texts are sung every day; the psalms, which change according to the church calendar, are Proper. The same holds true for the Mass. (Figure 3.3) In this case, the parts of the service that were originally intended to be sung by the entire congregation are always the same, or Ordinary; the Proper tended to be reserved for the choir and solo singers. Historically the Mass Proper is older and more closely tied to the texts of the scripture than the Ordinary. In later periods in music history the term *Mass* often refers to a musical setting of the five movements of the Mass Ordinary only, for the practical reason that composers generally wrote only the Ordinary and left the Proper, with its relatively limited usefulness, to the traditional chant.

The complete Mass forms an effective artistic as well as religious experience. Like most large art works, it has a clear shape with well-placed climaxes and distinctly articulated segments. Its structure can be understood in two main divisions: the teaching service and the Eucharist, and these are subdivided into two and three smaller groups of movements, respectively. In the following outline, we shall show this organization, noting which elements belong to the Ordinary and which to the Proper (see also Fig. 3.3).

Within the first half of the Mass, the first subgroup of movements forms a brief opening ceremony. This starts with the singing of the *Introit*, or introductory psalm verse, proper to the day, framed by two statements of a brief independent piece known as an *antiphon*. Then comes the first pair of movements of the Ordinary, the plea for forgiveness *Kyrie eleison* (Lord, have mercy—the only part of the Mass that continued to be sung in Greek after the early days of the church) and the song of praise *Gloria in excelsis* (Glory to God in the highest).

The next portion of the Mass contains the instruction of the congregation through scripture and sometimes a sermon. This part of the service opens with the *Collect* or prayer for the day, which is not sung but read or intoned by the priest, the congregation responding "Amen." The Proper assigns each day two scripture readings. The first reading is an *Epistle* selection taken from the New Testament. It is followed by the singing of a responsorial *Gradual* (from the Latin word *gradus*, meaning "step," because that is where the solo singer stands), and *Alleluia*, which includes a psalm verse. The Gradual and Alleluia, which have the most elaborate music of the Mass, form the service's musical climax. Then the second reading, the *Gospel*, follows. After the Gospel there may be a sermon, but this is optional. The whole first part of the Mass closes with the singing of the *Credo* (I believe in one God), the third musical movement of the Mass Ordinary.

The second half of the Mass begins with the offering of the Eucharistic bread and wine. A musical *Offertory* is sung, followed by the saying of prayers and the Twenty-fifth Psalm. Then the priest says a silent prayer known as the *Secret*.

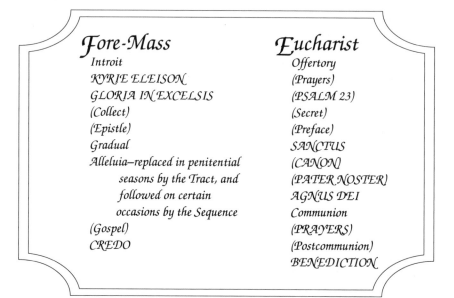

Fore-Mass
Introit
KYRIE ELEISON
GLORIA IN EXCELSIS
(Collect)
(Epistle)
Gradual
Alleluia—replaced in penitential
    seasons by the Tract, and
    followed on certain
    occasions by the Sequence
(Gospel)
CREDO

Eucharist
Offertory
(Prayers)
(PSALM 23)
(Secret)
(Preface)
SANCTUS
(CANON)
(PATER NOSTER)
AGNUS DEI
Communion
(PRAYERS)
(Postcommunion)
BENEDICTION

Figure 3.3
The structure of the Mass. The parts of the Ordinary are shown in capitals, the Proper in lower case. (Sections spoken or intoned rather than sung are indicated by parentheses.)

Next come two prayers: the *Preface,* which belongs to the Proper and is intoned aloud, and the *Canon,* which is Ordinary and is said silently by the priest. After these comes the singing of the fourth musical movement of the Ordinary, the *Sanctus* (Holy, holy, holy).

The actual partaking of Holy Communion forms the liturgical climax and conclusion of the Mass. The *Pater noster* ("Our father"—the Lord's Prayer) is intoned, followed by the singing of the Ordinary *Agnus Dei* ("Lamb of God"). A Proper movement appropriately called *Communion* is then sung. After the Communion come prayers, the *Postcommunion* prayer, and finally the *Benediction,* which is sung. There are only two forms for the Benediction, so it can be regarded as belonging to the music of the Ordinary, but it is so brief that it has rarely been included in compositions of the Mass. Curiously, it is one of these simple formulas, "Ite, missa est," (Go, it is dismissed) that gave the service its name, in Latin *Missa* and, of course, *Mass* in English.

Under special circumstances the form of the Mass may vary somewhat. The Gloria is omitted during penitential seasons, and during Lent the position usually occupied by the celebrative Alleluia is taken by a more somber movement called the Tract. An even more substantial variant is the Mass for the Dead or *Requiem* Mass, so called from the text of its introit, *Requiem aeternam dona eis Domine* (Give them eternal rest, O Lord).

Aesthetic Considerations Regarding the Chant

In order to gain a genuine understanding of any music, it is necessary to imagine it in the context for which it was intended. This is perhaps even more strongly the case for the chant than for other music in our cultural heritage. The chant is distant enough in time from the music that we are accustomed to hearing that it seems foreign. On the one hand, it is simpler than the polyphonic music and stylized forms that govern more familiar styles; on the other hand, its principles and the concepts on which it is based are quite sophisticated, although they are different from those of later music.

That much of this music appears at first somewhat austere should not surprise us, since we know that it belongs in the framework of the liturgy. We must remember that the church fathers, including St. Augustine, were greatly concerned that the music should not distract from the worshipper's meditation on God. To answer this concern, the music eschews virtuosic display that would force the singer to concentrate on the problems of performing and seduce the listener's attention from the music to the singer. Similarly, the spiritual rather than physical focus of the service calls for a style that does not encourage a physical rhythmic response such as clapping or toe tapping.

The early church fathers were also particularly concerned that the music not obscure the words of the chant. However, the style of the chant is not merely adapted to the communication of its texts but also closely dependent on the text for its musical structure. The single-line texture of the music allows the words to come through unimpeded, and, as our analysis will show, the rising and falling inflections of the speaking voice and the grammatical structure of language actually define the music.

The single-line texture of the chant and the suitability of the music for singers of modest technical qualifications bear special significance. The unity of the "community of believers" finds expression in the uniting of voices in a single statement, especially within the religious cloister. Thus the monophonic texture of the chant serves as a symbol of an idea; its simplicity should not by any means be regarded as evidence of primitiveness.

Another aspect of the context in which the chant was sung is the architecture of the churches where it was performed. During the Gregorian and Carolingian periods churches were still somewhat weighty in construction, embodying more solidity than lightness and reflecting firmness of faith rather than soaring ecstasy. The music of the chant has a corresponding sense of gravity and solemnity.

Purely physical aspects of early church architecture offered both problems and opportunities for music. Acoustically, the open space in the nave or central body of the church presented a very "live" environment for music, and hard stone and wood surfaces set up considerable reverberation. This meant that the simple texture of the chant easily filled the space in which it was sung; indeed the sound in a very resonant room could become blurred in detail but produce an audible atmosphere similar in effect to the incense wafted from the thurible in the Mass. The actual design of the space and the placement or movement of singers could also be exploited in the performance of the chant. Processions were, of course, a significant part of the action of worship, and the division of the singers into two groups facing each other in the choir reinforced the effect of antiphonal singing.

The Musical Style of the Chant

The chant was intended to be performed by unaccompanied solo and choral male voices in unison, though undoubtedly in actual practice there were other possibilities. Boys often sang with men, using octave doubling, and in convents of nuns the women could sing the services. The existence of documents by church authorities banning instruments from churches implies that *ad libitum* performance on instruments also took place.

Within the limits of unison singing, variety in sound was achieved by doubling and by contrasting direct, antiphonal, and responsorial performance. Hymns and the chants of the Mass Ordinary were sung in direct fashion. Psalms and the antiphons that framed and articulated them were performed antiphonally. Responsorial chanting increased as more elaborate music developed, and we shall see that the solo portions of responsorial pieces provided a fruitful field for musical experimentation.

We do not have any clear notational evidence of measured rhythm in the style of the chant, but this does not mean that there was no rhythm in the music. The rhythm of the singing derived from that of the spoken language. In Greek and Latin dynamic syllable stress did not contribute to grammar or expression. Syllables fell into the categories long and short, and the linguistic phrase flowed smoothly from beginning to end without the lumpiness that accents give to modern English and German. As a consequence, the musical phrase also flowed smoothly, and the absence of rhythmic meter should be regarded as a natural effect of the language itself.

An important concept in understanding the chant is that the basic musical unit of the chant was originally not the note but the phrase. In the following discussion we must constantly keep in mind that the idea of single pitches as independent, abstract building blocks for the construction of musical pieces arose only after the repertoire was already well established. This will not only help us appreciate the authentic character of the chant but also explain the nature of later musical composition.

The melodic style of the chant was, of course, always guided by the intention of vocal performance. The music proceeds gracefully, without large leaps, and unfolds within a moderate range. The phrase shapes reflect the grammar and inflections of natural speech by rising and falling to parallel the sound and sense of the texts. We can identify three distinct melodic types, used for different types of pieces.

The first and simplest melody type is formed by the *recitation tones*. Used for readings and prayers, these formulas allow the singer to cover long passages clearly and efficiently. They reflect speech patterns in a very simple sense. The pitch contour is almost completely monotone, broken only by the use of a few small upward or downward inflections at punctuations in the text.

Next in simplicity are the *psalm tones*. Employed specifically for singing the verses of the psalms, they can be applied to any psalm text. They are not unlike the recitation tones, but they give a more exaggerated depiction of speech inflection (see Ex. 3.1). The psalm begins with a rising gesture called the *initium* or *intonation*. This brings the voice to a pitch at which the bulk of the verse will be chanted, called the *tenor* (from the Latin *tenere*, to hold). The punctuation in the middle of the verse produces another little melodic gesture, the *mediatio* or *mediant*, which leaves the line suspended on the tenor. (In cases of clear punctuation before the mediant there is an optional dip from the tenor known as the *flex*.) The second half of the verse begins on the tenor, and the verse concludes with a descending figure, the *terminatio*, or *termination*. The second and succeeding verses of the psalm start directly on the tenor, omitting the intonation.

Other chants have more freedom in their melodic construction, with a variety of phrase shapes and greater flexibility in contour. Most of the phrases are arch-shaped or descending curves, so that a grammatical phrase ending is indicated by a downward inflection. Much of the repertoire is constructed from a few archetypal phrases with characteristic beginning, central, and ending functions, each phrase adapted as necessary to the words of that particular moment in the text. This process is known as *centonization*.

We have noted several times the essential connection between the text and music in the chant. It is also important to consider the manner in which the syllables were matched to the music (text underlay). The simplest procedure is to move quickly through the text without changing pitch on any syllable; such a setting is called *syllabic*. Syllabic text setting is naturally used for music intended to be sung by untrained singers or by large groups such as entire congregations. It is also the most efficient way of handling long texts. As a result, a long movement of the Mass Ordinary, for example the Credo, is generally set syllabically. The opposite procedure is *melismatic*, that is, a single syllable stretches through a considerable amount of melodic motion. Pieces with short texts and chants intended for soloists or trained choristers are more likely to be set melismatically.

The musical forms of the chant are quite varied. There are strophic forms in the hymns, for example, where the text comprises a series of identically structured stanzas that are sung to the same music. A related special case is the singing of the psalm tones. A few of the liturgical texts suggest symmetrical musical forms. For example, the complete text of the Kyrie of the Mass reads

Kyrie eleison	Lord, have mercy
Kyrie eleison	Lord, have mercy
Kyrie eleison	Lord, have mercy
Christe eleison	Christ, have mercy
Christe eleison	Christ, have mercy
Christe eleison	Christ, have mercy
Kyrie eleison	Lord, have mercy
Kyrie eleison	Lord, have mercy
Kyrie eleison	Lord, have mercy

The musical settings of this text sometimes, though not always, adopt a ternary or ABA structure. Most chants have rather free forms. These are often motivically unified by the recurrence of variants of a few model phrases in irregular arrangements, the result of the process of centonization mentioned earlier.

The Music Theory of the Chant

In the course of the centuries, liturgical music grew in quantity and complexity. At the same time the church recognized that teaching singers by rote led to alterations of the sacred repertoire through the natural process of oral transmission. Moreover, it was obvious that it would be desirable to have more efficient ways of teaching singers to master their extensive repertoire than simply through painstaking memorization. From these concerns and needs came a system of theory and musical notation.

To gain control over such a vast body of material as the chant repertoire, church musicians needed some method of classification. This meant that they had to examine individual pieces in detail and, consequently, to identify separate pitches and their relationships. The reemergence of some of the treatises of ancient Greek music theory, which relied on the identification of individual pitches, helped facilitate the creation of a new pitch system that ultimately developed into the theory of the church or ecclesiastical *modes*.

An important early accomplishment was the definition of the psalm tones. By carefully considering the melodies and perhaps regularizing some subtle differences between closely related variants, the theorists identified nine basic formulas that were in use. The first eight were numbered and grouped in pairs according to their pitch configurations; that is, psalm tones 1 and 2 share some elements of whole-step and half-step arrangement, as do psalm tones 3 and 4, and so on. Those in each pair differ in the placement of the tenor. The ninth psalm tone was named the *Tonus peregrinus* (pilgrim, or wandering, tone); it differs from all the other psalm tones because it adopts a new tenor after its mediant. The psalm tones can be summarized in modern notation as shown in Example 3.1.

Example 3.1

The psalm tones. The nine tones are shown with their components identified. In some cases a tone has a number of different possible terminations, but only one for each has been included here.

This arrangement of the psalm tones into four pairs was undoubtedly influenced by the eight echoi of Byzantine chant (which, however, were organized into two groups of four). Thus the formulation of the medieval modes combined the theoretical traditions of Greek classical theory with Judaeo-Christian practice.

By experience singers discovered that the melodies of certain antiphons linked naturally with some psalm tones and not with others. Examining the details of the pitch patterns in the various antiphons and comparing them to the eight numbered psalm tones, theorists were able to classify the antiphons in a system parallel to the psalm tones. The melodic patterns came to be known as the modes, which were used to classify any free chants in the repertoire.

The most important characteristics of a chant were (1) its cadential tone or *final*, (2) the tone around which its melodic curves generally oriented themselves (the equivalent of the tenor of a psalm tone, but more heavily decorated by melodic motion) or *dominant*, and (3) the melody's general tessitura or *ambitus* (always an approximation). Like the psalm tones, the modes were numbered and grouped in four pairs. Modes 1 and 2 share the same final, d, but differ in their dominant and their ambitus; similarly, modes 3 and 4 share the final e, modes 5 and 6 both have f as their final, and modes 7 and 8 close on g. The dominants and the ambiti of the odd-numbered modes, the *authentic* modes, are higher than those of their even-numbered partners, which are called *plagal*. The following table summarizes the characteristics of the eight modes:

Mode	*Final*	*Dominant*	*Ambitus*
1 (authentic)	d	a	d–d$'$
2 (plagal)	d	f	A–a
3 (authentic)	e	c$'$	e–e$'$
4 (plagal)	e	a	B–b
5 (authentic)	f	c$'$	f–f$'$
6 (plagal)	f	a	c–c$'$
7 (authentic)	g	d$'$	g–g$'$
8 (plagal)	g	c$'$	d–d$'$

Several features of the system are worth noting:

1.   The dominant of each authentic mode is generally a fifth above the final, except for mode 3. The dominant of each plagal mode is a third below the dominant of its corresponding authentic mode, except for mode 8. This reflects a hesitancy about the pitches b and b-flat in the Middle Ages. The pitch b would produce an awkward tritone from f, while the substitution of b-flat would result in a tritone from e. The pitch was, in fact, adjusted in performance according to its context, but as a result it seems to have been regarded as unsuitable for a dominant. Consequently, in modes 3 and 8, where to be consistent the dominant would be b, c$'$ was substituted.

2.   The ambitus of each mode is given as an octave, but in practice the melodies often extend beyond that ambitus. Usually the extension takes the form of a lower neighbor to the final in the authentic modes and of an upper neighbor above the given top note in the plagals. When there is a very wide range, the mode can be considered a "mixed mode," combining authentic and plagal.

3.   There was no standard of absolute pitch; therefore the note names given here indicate only relative pitch. A melody could be sung at any comfortable level.

The next step in making the singers' task easier was to develop a music notation so that they could read the chant rather than having to memorize the music for the entire liturgical year. The first stage was to make sketchy upward, downward, level, arched, wavelike, or zigzag marks in the spaces between the lines of text to remind the singers, who certainly already knew the melodies well, of the general direction of the melodic line. These notations were called *neumes,* and the term continued to be used generically for the signs that indicated pitches throughout the Middle Ages. (Fig. 3.4) The use of neumes seems to date from about the eighth century, corresponding to the attempt to catholicize the Roman chant.

The church musicians soon made progress in the accuracy of pitch indication by using neumes of different sizes, placed at different heights above the words. Such *heighted neumes* gave the singer not only an idea of the direction of the melodic gesture but also a sense of the scope of the gesture and of how high or low a particular figure lay in the total range. Even so, the indication remained rather vague.

Eventually the musicians scratched two straight horizontal lines in the space where the neumes were to be placed, one indicating the note f and the other the note c', and the details of the melodic contour grew still clearer. Later the f line was drawn in red ink and the c' line in yellow or green, an attractive predecessor of clefs. In the eleventh century the addition of two more lines became common, and the use of letter names at the left edge of the c' or f lines completed the development of the staff and clefs used for chant notation.

To indicate precise locations of pitches on the staff, the neumes evolved from their old, rather cursive style to a form in which small squares with or without tails were placed on the lines and spaces of the staff. These square neumes could be combined with one another or with chains of diamond shapes, forming compound neumes or *ligatures.* They might also have hooklike appendages (*plica*) or other ornamental components (e.g., the *quilisma,* which looks rather like the more familiar zigzag sign for a short trill).

The standardization of the four-line staff appears to have been the accomplishment of a theorist and teacher named Guido of Arezzo, who worked in

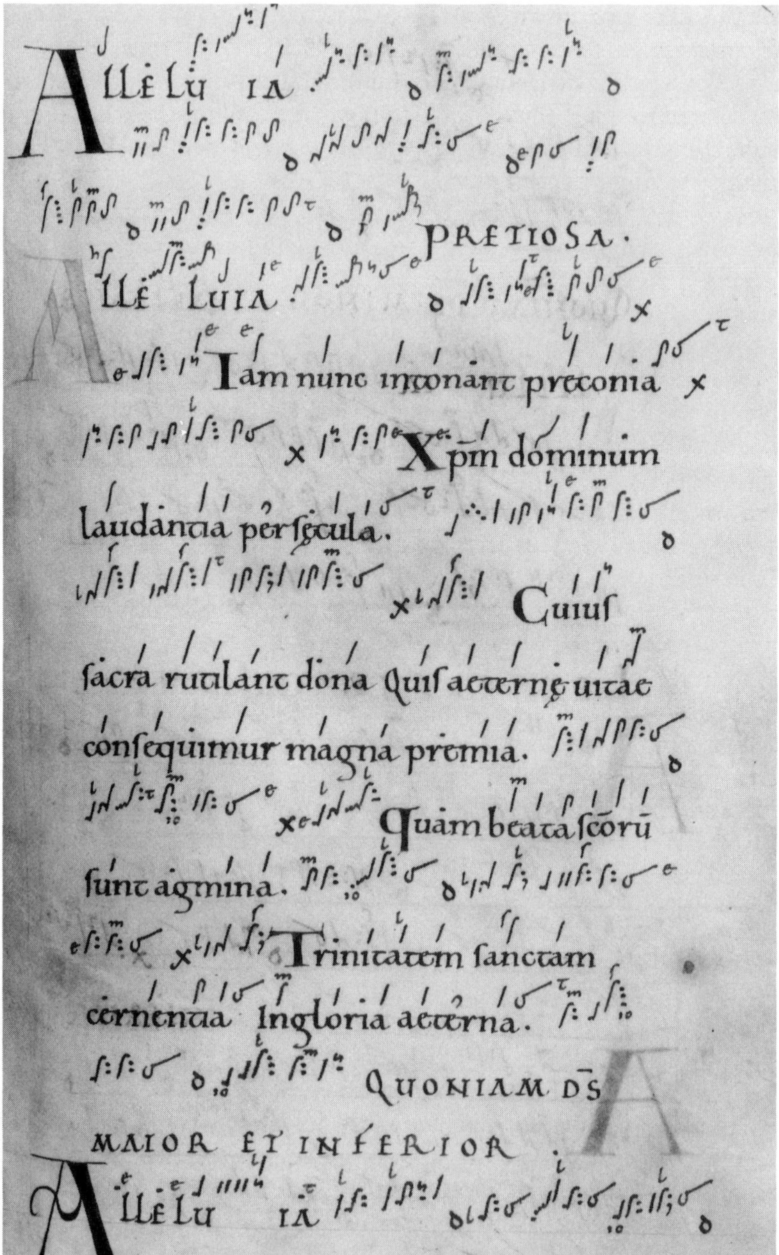

Figure 3.4
A music manuscript showing neumes of the eleventh century. (*Bodleian Library, Oxford Ms. Bodley 775, fol. 125r*)

the first half of the eleventh century. Guido also contributed to music education a system for teaching sight-singing. He either discovered or created a melody for a particular hymn, "Ut queant laxis," in which the first six phrases began on consecutively higher pitches, each separated by a whole tone except the third and fourth, which were only a semitone apart. The syllables corresponding to those pitches were Ut, Re-, Mi-, Fa-, Sol-, and La-; the entire pattern of six tones formed a *hexachord*. Guido taught his students to read the notes of any chant by thinking of the pitches and syllables of the hexachord. The system is called *solmization* after the fifth and third hexachord syllables. (It is still in use, of course, except that the first syllable is now sung as *do* instead of *ut*.)

The hexachord worked well for the pitches from c to a, but then a problem arose. Guido solved this by having his students start with that hexachord, called the "natural" hexachord, and pivot on *sol* (g) to a new hexachord, beginning there with *ut* and thus extending the total range to e'. The process of pivoting from one hexachord to another was called *mutation*. To go still higher one could apply mutation again on c' to produce a natural hexachord an octave above the first, reaching from c' to a', which was about as high as a chant was likely to go. Reversing the process, one could reach to the bottom of the practical range by treating the note c not as *ut* but as *fa* in a hexachord that went down to G.

A hexachord made by mutation from *fa* to *ut* produced a hexachord that reached from f to d'. Obviously the importance of this hexachord was not to increase the range of the system; rather its *fa* produced b-flat. Because the b-flat was written with a curved body, it was called *b mollis* (soft b), and thus a hexachord with *ut* on f was the "soft" hexachord. The b-natural was notated with a square body and called *b durum* (hard b), so the hexachord based on g was a "hard" hexachord. To summarize:

	c	d	e	f	g	a	b♭–b♮	c'	d'	e'
Hard					*ut*	*re*	*mi*	*fa*	*sol*	*la*
Soft				*ut*	*re*	*mi*	*fa*	*sol*	*la*	
Natural	*ut*	*re*	*mi*	*fa*	*sol*	*la*				

The notes of the complete vocal range used in the chant could now be identified as independent points in a scale beginning on G, known by the Greek letter gamma. Any individual pitch would be named by its letter name and the string of hexachord syllables that could be applied to it. As can be seen from the chart above, the pitch g would be G *sol re ut*, and the pitch a would be A *la mi re*. The whole scale was named after the bottom note, gamma *ut*, shortened to *gamut*. Ultimately the gamut was extended at the top all the way to e" (*ela*).

Guido concocted a way to drill his sight-singing students by pointing to the joints of his left hand. Each joint represented a pitch in the gamut. An illustration of the "Guidonian hand," showing the names of the notes in their places, became a common feature of medieval theory handbooks. (Fig. 3.5)

Two important points should be stressed in this summary of the development of chant theory: First, the concepts developed by these early medieval singers and singing teachers have lasted to the twentieth century and have become so ingrained that we take them for granted, an impressive achievement indeed. Second, all these inventions and developments resulted not from acoustical or philosophical abstractions but directly from the needs of church musicians who sought to gain control over their music. Both the concepts and the tools sprang from the creative imaginations and intelligence of practical musicians constantly steeped in music itself.

Later Developments in
the Liturgical Chant

As the body of chant literature became more or less established, the creative impulses of church musicians sought new outlets. It became necessary to find a role for the composer in a situation in which the repertoire was already codified and assumed to be based on longstanding ecclesiastical authority. Composers therefore worked with the body of previously existing music, and took as their task the amplification or glorification of the established chant.

The church's music had evolved by the process of centonization. The basic musical element had for centuries been the melody as a line rather than discrete pitches. It was quite natural, then, that musical composition should be based on already existing music.

A model for composition under these circumstances was ready to hand in the literary technique known as the *gloss*. Authors and scholars quite commonly worked from standard, "classic" texts, such as the scriptures or writings of ancient authors, providing not entirely original literature but running commentary on the given text. The nature of this commentary varied from grammatical analysis to elaboration of arguments, addition of details, and applications of principles. A gloss could be written as interlinear entries within a book, marginal notes, or extended discussions following brief statements extracted from the authority in question. (Plate 1)

The Trope

The musical application of the gloss principle to the chant produced the *trope*. A trope can be defined simply as the addition of words or music or both to an existing chant. More specifically, one might add new words to melismatic

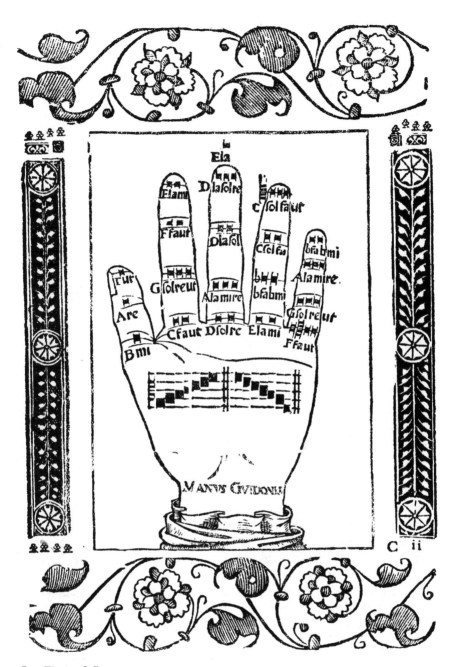

Figure 3.5
Guidonian hand. Such a diagram, showing the position of each pitch of the
gamut on the hand, appeared in many treatises on music in the Middle Ages.
(*The Bettmann Archive*)

passages of a chant, new melismatic material to relatively less complicated passages of text setting, or newly invented passages of words with their own music within an earlier piece. Added words expand or define the preexisting text, possibly to reflect a new theological understanding. The addition of music, by contrast, affects the expressive spirit of the piece, reflecting in the product a greater glorification of God in divine worship, not unlike the addition of embroidery, sculpture, or stained glass to decorate a church building. It is important to note that this method of artistic creation, though it might seem limiting to modern musicians, was entirely characteristic of the medieval mind. It suited perfectly the concepts both of a universal, authoritative liturgy and of the use of melodic lines as the fundamental components of music.

The practice of troping the chant began in about the ninth century and continued to the twelfth. It was applied first to the antiphons of the Mass Proper and later to the Ordinary, when the responsibility for singing the Ordinary passed from the congregation to trained singers. The earliest tropes appear to have been introductory material to be placed before the main body of a chant, but eventually the additions appeared throughout the chant.

A special application of the troping principle was the *Sequence,* which became a complete, independent movement within the Mass. The term is derived from the Latin word meaning "to follow"; what it followed was the Alleluia of the Mass Proper. A ninth-century monk of the Abbey of St. Gall named Notker Balbulus ("Notker the Stammerer") wrote that he had difficulty in memorizing the long, untexted melismas (called *jubilus*) that provided a flourish of praise at the ends of Alleluias. He discovered that when words were added to those melismas the notes became easier to learn. He therefore set himself the task of composing new, high-quality poems to be sung syllabically to the melismas. Such a new composition was sometimes called *prosa.*

Composers soon began to expand the Sequence texts into elaborately structured poetry and even to provide entirely new music, and thus they produced separate movements to follow the Alleluia as another component in the Mass Proper. Seizing their first real opportunity to experiment with musical form in a way that could not be done with the established body of chant music, the composers developed an abstract plan for the form of the Sequence by using rhymed pairs of lines that shared music in the pattern A BB CC DD and so on. The Sequence is thus a milestone in the history of musical form.

One of the first important women composers, the abbess Hildegard von Bingen (1098–1179), excelled in the composition of Sequences. Her Sequence texts are full of rich, mystical imagery, and her music is often quite original. Hildegard's work is especially remarkable because she succeeded in a period in which music in general, and particularly the music of the church, was almost exclusively the domain of men.

The number of Sequences grew rapidly, until eventually there were over four thousand of them. This, of course, proved an unwieldy bulk of material for the singers and planners of the liturgy. Finally all but four—"Victimae paschali laudes," attributed to Wipo of Burgundy (ca. 995–1050), for Easter; "Veni sancte spiritus," attributed to Pope Innocent III (ca. 1160–1216), for Pentecost; "Lauda Sion," attributed to St. Thomas Aquinas (ca. 1225–1274), for Corpus Christi; and "Dies irae," by Thomas of Celano (thirteenth century), for the Requiem Mass—were abolished in the reforms of the Council of Trent (1545–1563).

Liturgical Drama

Another result of the general practice of troping was the development of the *liturgical drama*. The medieval inclination to elaborate and thereby bring more glory to the service led, in about the tenth century, to the acting out of the sung texts.

The earliest instance of this took place in the text of the chants that recount the Easter story. The biblical narrative and, following it, the music in question, took the form of a dialogue between the angels who guarded the tomb of Jesus and the women who came to anoint his body on the third day after his burial. It was perfectly natural to assign the performance to different singers representing the interlocutors. (Fig. 3.6) By the end of the century, Ethelwold, the bishop of Winchester, had written detailed instructions for acting out the dialogue in the Office of Matins on Easter morning. These constitute the first set of stage directions for a liturgical drama, including costumes and props, blocking and gestures, and notes for the actors about the way they should interpret the movement and the vocal performance to convey emotion.

> While the third lesson is read, four brothers robe themselves, one of whom dressed in an alb enters as if for another purpose and discreetly goes to the place where the sepulchre is, and sits there quietly with a palm in his hand. While the third response is being sung, the remaining three come forward, every one dressed in a cope, carrying thuribles with incense in their hands, and hesitantly like people seeking something, come to the site of the sepulchre. For these things are performed in imitation of the angel sitting in the tomb, and of the women coming with spices to anoint Jesus's body. Consequently when the one sitting there sees the three nearing him, just like people straying about seeking something, he begins to sing sweetly in a moderate voice:
>
> *Quem quaeritis in sepulchro, o Christicolae?* [Whom do you seek in the tomb, o dwellers in Christ?]
>
> When this has been sung all through, the three reply in unison:
>
> *Ihesum Nazarenum crucifixum, o caelicola.* [The crucified Jesus of Nazareth, o dweller in heaven.]

Figure 3.6
The music of the trope "Quem quaeritis" from the Sarum rite, in a fourteenth-century manuscript. *(Bodleian Library, Oxford, MS. Rawl. Liturg. d. 4, fol. 131r)*

He answers them thus:

Non est hic, surrexit sicut praedixerat; ite, nuntiate quia surrexit a mortuis. [He is not here; he has risen as he foretold; go, announce that he has risen from the dead.]

At his command the three turn to the choir, saying:

Alleluia, resurrexit Dominus, hodie resurrexit leo fortis, Christus, filius Dei. Deo gratias, dicite eia! [Alleluia, the Lord has risen, today the strong lion, Christ the son of God, has risen. Cry joyfully, thanks be to God!]

This being sung, the seated one as if calling them back sings the antiphon:

Venite et videte locum ubi positus erat Dominus, alleluia. [Come and see the place where the Lord was laid, alleluia.]

Singing these words he rises and lifts the curtain, and shows them the place with the cross gone but with the linen cloths in which the cross was wrapped lying there.[1]

Soon other topics were subjected to similar treatment. The desire to provide equally colorful and dramatic material for Christmas led to plays about shepherds, wise men, and King Herod. Church dramatists did not neglect the possibilities of Old Testament stories or the miracles and parables of Jesus, and eventually they turned to the lives of the saints. They expanded all this material with new action and dialogue (in the vernacular as well as in Latin) and found space for attractive processions and for expounding the morals of the stories. Obviously the church could not accommodate extensive interruptions and texts that manifested little or no reliance on the authority of the scripture or the liturgy. The plays were ordered out of the sanctuaries, the acting was taken over by laymen, and in church courtyards and town squares liturgical drama evolved into, or gave way to, popular mystery and miracle plays.

Questions for Reflection

❖   How important and effective was the establishment of a Catholic musical tradition for the political and ecclesiastical powers in the early Middle Ages? What was its relationship to the establishment of domination by other means such as military or economic force?

❖   How did the liturgical context for any particular piece of church music relate to the style of the piece? How did it affect the musician's or listener's experience of the music?

❖   Who actually sang each portion of the chant in the medieval liturgy? What effects did this have on the general relationship of worship to the common person?

❖   In what ways did the oral and modal tradition affect the composition of music in the chant repertoire? In what ways did the theological position of music in the church affect it?

❖   What evidence exists to indicate how chant was performed in the Middle Ages with regard to tempo, tone color, and dynamics?

❖   What factors might account for the nearly simultaneous establishment of several significant features of liturgical music and musical ideas in the eleventh century? How important were internal musical factors, as opposed to extra-musical, historical factors, in these developments?

Suggestions for Further Reading

Three substantial surveys of medieval music history are John Caldwell, *Medieval Music* (London: Hutchinson, 1978), Richard H. Hoppin, *Medieval Music* (New York: Norton, 1978), and the older book by Gustave Reese, *Music in the Middle Ages* (New York: Norton, 1940). Giulio Cattin, *Music of the Middle Ages I,* trans. Steven Botterill (Cambridge: Cambridge University Press, 1984) deals with both sacred and secular monophonic music.

The standard general reference for the chant, *The Liber Usualis* (latest edition New York: Desclée, 1963) is no longer in print, but is available in many libraries. Willi Apel, *Gregorian Chant* (Bloomington: Indiana University Press, 1958) provides a broad discussion of the repertoire.

On liturgical drama, see O. B. Hardison, *Christian Rite and Christian Drama in the Middle Ages* (Baltimore, Md.: Johns Hopkins University Press, 1965).

Notes

1. Reprinted from William Tydeman, *The Theatre in the Middle Ages* (Cambridge: Cambridge University Press, 1978), 35–36.

4

MEDIEVAL SECULAR SONG AND INSTRUMENTAL MUSIC

Secular Music in the Early Middle Ages

It is impossible to imagine that secular music did not exist during the centuries when the music of the church was in a process of evolutionary ferment. Because of the unstable political situation in the early Middle Ages, however, there was little time or peace for the creation of a sophisticated art-music repertoire in the secular sphere comparable to the repertoire of the chant. Furthermore, since few outside the church could read or had the resources to copy and preserve music in written form, the historical record is naturally biased in favor of the music of the church. Thus, while there was undoubtedly singing and dancing at all levels of society from the lowliest peasantry to the upper class, this music belongs to the oral or folk tradition. It can only be known indirectly by references in literary descriptions, works of visual art, artifacts of musical instruments, and cautious reasoning from traces of it remaining in the European folk music of today.

We can make a few tentative generalizations. The nature of the spoken language must have dominated song; that is, rhythms would have been metrically free and governed by speech rhythm, and melodies were probably modal in the sense that they followed simple basic formulas controlled by the rising and falling inflections of speech. The musical idiom probably did not have the standardization of pitch relationships that developed in church music, where it was important to fit the parts of the liturgy together with musical consistency and to simplify the vast body of melodies so that they could be learned precisely. Dance music would, of course, have differed from song in employing stronger and more regular rhythmic patterns. The instruments used in this music were relatively simple by comparison to those of classical antiquity.

More cannot be surmised. Only after about the year 1000 is it possible to bring secular music into anything approaching the kind of focus with which we can view that of the church.

Latin Songs

In the eleventh and twelfth centuries there arose a class of renegade dropouts from the discipline of clerical studies. These young men typically wandered about from place to place, making their living by their wits (or less honorable means) and often making themselves a general nuisance. They took as their "patron saint" a mythical character named Golias (Goliath) and were known as *Goliards*. Like young male students at liberty in any period, they drank and womanized a good deal, and of course they sang about their exploits. Because they were schooled enough to write, some of their songs have been preserved.

An important collection of this sort of song is the manuscript known as *Carmina Burana* (Bavarian Songs), which dates from the thirteenth century. It contains not only bawdy ballads but also moralistic poetry and some quite sophisticated and touching love songs. Most are in Latin, but a few are in southern German dialect. Unfortunately *Carmina Burana* includes no music that can be read today; a few of the poems have staffless neumes. From other sources that do contain readable music notation, it can be seen that the melodies bear a close resemblance to those their creators had learned in the church. (Carl Orff, the twentieth-century German composer and pioneer in music education, set a number of the *Carmina Burana* songs for chorus, solo voices, and orchestra in a rousing style that evokes the character of the texts quite effectively.)

Another, more elevated type of Latin song also flourished in the eleventh to the thirteenth centuries. These songs reflected serious thoughts and the influence of the Latin of the church and the classical Roman poetry studied in the trivium of the schools. Often the subjects of these songs were religious; though their use was not strictly part of the liturgy itself, some seem to have been used within the sacred service. They are sometimes referred to as *conductus* (from the Latin word meaning "leading"), perhaps because they were employed to accompany action or a procession in the Mass or liturgical drama. A special type was the *planctus* or lament; the oldest one known is on the death of Charlemagne. The music for these songs is related to the musical style of the chant. Because they adopted the rhymed and metered style of poetry, their settings resembled the syllabic underlay and repetitive forms of the hymn and Sequence more than the freer underlay and forms of the proselike movements of the liturgy.

Epics and Minstrels

An important poetic and musical genre was the popular epic sung to entertain medieval listeners with stories of their heroes' escapades. The oral tradition of these long verse narratives, known as *chansons de geste* (songs of deeds), must extend back at least into the Carolingian era. They were performed by *minstrels* who passed them from one to another, undoubtedly enriching and embellishing the stories with each resinging. The earliest surviving written versions date from the eleventh century. The most famous of these is the *Chanson de Roland* (Song of Roland), which tells about the exploits of Charlemagne and his knights battling the Moslem armies in Spain.

The chansons de geste use the vernacular rather than Latin. They are based on stanzas of varying numbers of ten-syllable lines and were probably sung to simple melodic formulas, repeated for each line and adapted to meet the particular needs of unusual lines.

The minstrels who sang these tales often traveled from place to place, performing in court or town square wherever an audience could be found. When they met, they exchanged repertoires, thus spreading the songs throughout Europe. The minstrels cultivated a variety of other skills in addition to singing, including tumbling and juggling, from which they also became known by the alternative French name *jongleurs*. Despite their popularity, they were regarded as socially inferior to merchants, craftsmen, and even peasant farmers.

Troubadours and Trouvères

Beginning around 1100, a new type of lyric poetry set to music arose in the courts of southern France. The aristocracy there found itself relatively at peace; sufficiently wealthy to have leisure time; and educated enough to spend its efforts in artistic, amorous, and literary pursuits. Some of them turned their energies to writing songs. In their own language, Provençal, these poet-composers were called *troubadours* ("finders"). By the middle of the twelfth century such songwriting at the courts had spread to the north of France and to England, where the composers were called by the French name *trouvères*. The common image of a troubadour as a wandering minstrel is, of course, quite mistaken; the troubadours belonged to the upper class of society and composed poetry and music, while the minstrels were found at the lowest social level and were primarily illiterate performers.

Probably the most famous trouvère is England's King Richard the Lionhearted. There is a legend that he was once imprisoned in a secret donjon in Austria and was rescued after being located by his friend and fellow trouvère Blondel de Nesle, who traveled about singing one of Richard's own songs until he heard the captive king answer.

The *canso* of the troubadours and the *chanson* of the trouvères usually dealt with themes of chivalrous love. In the highly stylized courtly manners reflected and supported by the songs of troubadours and trouvères, the love in question was usually that of a young knight for someone else's wife. The lover suffered, pleaded, and ventured deeds of honor for tokens of recognition from the object of his passion. Physical consummation of the relationship was perhaps more dreamed-of than likely, for despite frequent references to sexual intimacy the beloved is often compared with the Virgin Mary in her purity and chastity; intensity of desire always took precedence over its fulfillment. The subject might be treated from any one of a variety of viewpoints; typical formats were the lament (*planh*), a disputation about the fine points of courtly love (*tenso* in the south and *descort* in the north), an amorous encounter of a knight and a shepherdess (*pastorela* or *pastourelle*), and the parting of lovers at dawn (*alba, aubade*). (Fig. 4.1) There were also dance songs (*balada, ballade*), whose lighthearted texts generally took a somewhat explicit seductive approach, mocking the jealous husbands of the women involved.

About five thousand troubadour and trouvère song texts survive, with music for about two thousand, mostly from the later, northern tradition. The melodies are relatively simple, and their pitch organization is very similar to that of ecclesiastical sacred chant. There is no clear rhythmic notation for the vast majority of the repertory, but it is likely that the songs were sung with a more metered rhythm than chant since the texts themselves were poetic ones.

One of the most important contributions of the trouvères was their unprecedented exploitation of the possibilities of musical form. Just as they adopted standardized approaches to their subject matter, they also developed standard poetic designs and musical plans. The internal structures of the stanzas of their songs often rely on recurring melodic phrases, with clear reliance on the distinction between open-ended and conclusive phrase endings. There eventually developed a somewhat standardized stanza structure, consisting of an opening part, or *frons,* made up of a repeated pair of phrases (*pedes;* singular *pes*), followed by a closing section, or *cauda,* of several more or less independent phrases, a pattern that can be outlined as follows:

frons		cauda
a b	a b	X
pes	pes	

Figure 4.1

Gerard Leeu, "Aubade," from *L'Istoire du tres-vaillant chevalier Paris et la belle Vienne, fille du dauphin*. A troubadour sings an aubade in the garden below a lady's window, accompanied by a minstrel. The narrative accompanying this picture tells how the young nobleman Paris and his minstrel entered the garden during the night to sing in the morning for the princess Vienne. (*Bild-Archiv der Oesterreichischen Nationalbibliothek, Vienna*)

The cauda may also incorporate, literally or in varied form, material from the frons, particularly the b part of the pes.

German Court Music

Taking the troubadours as their models, the German courts also produced aristocratic poet-composers, called *Minnesinger* (from *Minne*, the German word for courtly love). True to a general tendency of German culture, their songs, or *Minnelieder*, were inclined to be a bit soberer than those of the troubadours. Many of the texts are explicitly religious in content.

The melodies of the Minnelieder tend to be more angular and inclined to melodic skips than those of the Provençal canso or French chanson, but they also show some influence of the chant. As to rhythm, it is likely that German, which uses stress accents, produced a more regularly metered music than French, which does not.

The predominant form in the Lieder of the Minnesinger was the AAB design, known in German as *Bar* form. The first two sections, which might have several phrases each, were called *Stollen,* and the third section, which also might have several phrases, was called *Abgesang*. The similarity of this plan to that of the characteristic form of troubadour and trouvère songs is obvious.

Stollen	Stollen	Abgesang
A (a b etc.)	A (a b etc.)	B

As in the French repertory, in order to give unity to the entire strophe the Abgesang might share some of the subordinate phrases of the Stollen, particularly the cadential phrase.

Somewhat later (from the fourteenth to the sixteenth centuries) the Minnesinger tradition was preserved and extended by the *Meistersinger,* middle-class composers who organized themselves into guilds. The Meistersinger constructed elaborate rules and complex poetic and musical structures, quite unlike their much more spontaneous forebears. In the nineteenth century, Richard Wagner wrote about these musicians in his music drama *Die Meistersinger von Nürnberg,* which explores the perennial tension between artistic progress and the conservative rules of the artistic establishment.

Monophonic Songs in Other Nations

Italy

Beginning in the thirteenth century there grew up an Italian tradition of popular spiritual songs called *laude*. These are more like folk songs than the sophisticated artistic creations of the troubadours, trouvères, and Minnesinger, although some of them show the same basic principles of form as the northern composers' works. The laude were begun by bands of pilgrims who roamed from place to place doing penance on behalf of the rest of the sinful world and often performing self-flagellation. The laude may have been used either as marching music or as accompaniment to the flagellation itself. In Germany such penitents were called *Geissler,* and they developed their own repertoire of songs (*Geisslerlieder*) parallel to those in Italy.

Spain and Portugal

The Spanish and Portuguese also began to write songs in their vernaculars in the thirteenth century. The most important of these are the collection of *Canti-*

gas de Santa Maria. These cantigas date from the court of King Alfonso X ("the Wise") of Castile and Leon in the second half of the thirteenth century, a court that was also familiar with the songs of the troubadours. They express the popular devotion to the worship of the Virgin Mary, and many recount her miracles, although their primary intention must have been to entertain the court. In structure they often resemble the songs of the trouvères. Among the song types discussed in this chapter, however, the appearance of accurate rhythmic notation is unique to the *Cantigas de Santa Maria,* possibly because of their late date.

Britain

The British Isles had a long oral tradition of song before they produced written music. British musicians developed a wide variety of medieval English lyrics, both religious and secular in character. The bulk of surviving material is somewhat less sophisticated than the repertoire of the continental composers, but the songs compensate for this by the intensity and sincerity of their texts and the simplicity and directness of their music.

Particularly popular in England was the *carol.* Carols were originally dance or processional songs, constructed in several verses that were introduced, separated, and concluded by a refrain called the *burden.* While some purely secular carols existed, most had religious or at least moral texts. Often the texts combined English lyrics with phrases in Latin, reflecting their seriousness of tone. Many carols were associated with festivals, though their connection with Christmas in particular came only later.

Medieval Instruments

Although scoring for specific instruments was not a feature of medieval musical practice, many instruments existed and were used in the music of these centuries. Most of the evidence of instrumental performance comes from extramusical sources, such as depictions in painting and sculpture and references in literature. The following discussion will give only a brief overview of the many instruments available to medieval musicians.

The modern idea of grouping instruments according to families did not exist in the Middle Ages. Instruments were built singly and could be played in any combinations that were available and feasible. The only classification used grouped instruments according to volume and function. Some instruments were loud, or *haut* (French for "high"), and belonged outdoors or in very large halls. Other instruments made a more delicate, soft sound and were called low, or *bas* (French for "low"). (Fig. 4.2)

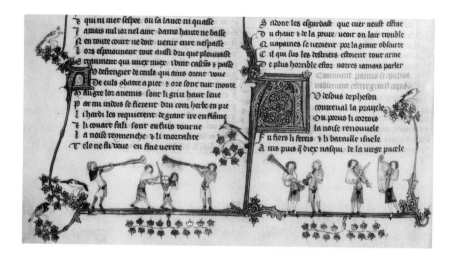

Figure 4.2
Some combinations of medieval instruments, from a fourteenth-century manuscript. Two *haut* combinations are shown—trumpets and drums, bagpipe and shawm—and one *bas* combination—vielle and harp. (*Bodleian Library, Oxford, MS. Bodley 264, fol. 157v.*)

String Instruments

The distant medieval relatives of the ancient lyre or kithara varied a great deal. Some were plucked with fingers or a plectrum, often a bird quill. The *harp,* whose ancestry goes back to ancient Egypt, appears in drawings and carvings from around the time of Charlemagne. It ranked as a royal instrument in Ireland. As the Arabic culture began to be influential in Europe in the Middle Ages, another plucked instrument, the *psaltery,* became popular. The psaltery was a resonating flat wooden box, often triangular or trapezoidal, strung with a number of slightly raised strings running parallel across its surface. The psaltery was also called *canon* from the Arabic *qanun.* The Moorish *ud* became the European *lute* in the fourteenth century. At first the lute was plucked or strummed with a quill. The plucking technique used with these instruments did not, of course, lend itself to the performance of polyphonic music.

The Middle Ages also had bowed string instruments. One, another Middle Eastern export, was the *rebec,* a pear-shaped instrument of which the neck was actually the narrow end of the body. It had three strings. The rebec actually survives today as a folk instrument in southeastern Europe. The French *vielle* or German *Fiedel* had a flat-backed body, a solid, separate neck, and usually five strings. A more complicated cousin of the vielle, the *hurdy-gurdy* or *organistrum,* employed a rosined wheel and a crank instead of a bow to set up the vibration in the strings, and keys along the neck to stop the strings. A particular feature of the hurdy-gurdy was the presence of sustaining drone strings. The earliest versions of this instrument apparently required two players, one to crank the wheel and one to play the keys.

Wind Instruments

The wind instruments of the Middle Ages were at least as varied as the strings. Both the *recorder,* an end-blown flute with a whistle mouthpiece, and the simpler *transverse flute* were used. In the Middle Ages both types would have been made of a simple wooden tube without such "modern" inventions as the metal keys that began to appear in the Renaissance.

Wind instruments with double reeds as vibrators formed the *shawm* family. The shawms produced a loud, penetrating sound with an aggressive nasal tone produced by the reed and a flared bell. Their close relatives are quite common in the music of the Middle East and India today. *Bagpipes* were also known as early as the ninth century, but they were primarily folk instruments. Both shawms and bagpipes belonged to the category of haut instruments.

Brass instruments were apparently not used for art music in the Middle Ages. They were used by heralds and for military signals. Naturally they were considered haut.

Percussion Instruments

Percussion instruments have always existed, and in an immensely wide variety. Bells, cymbals, and drums were known in the Middle Ages. The *kettledrum* came from the Arabian *naker* and was used first in military contexts. A popular combination was the *pipe and tabor,* which were often used to accompany dancing. The tabor, a cylindrical drum, was hung from the player's left arm so that it could be beaten with a stick in the right hand, while at the same time the left hand fingered the three-holed, end-blown pipe.

Organs

The organ dates back to several centuries before the Christian era. Still rare in the time of Charlemagne, organs were given as magnificent gifts from the Byzantine emperors to western kings. Their use in church music dates back at least to the tenth century, and they spread rapidly during the Gothic period. Smaller and more movable versions also existed and functioned in secular contexts. The *positive* organ stood on a tabletop or the floor and generally required two persons to operate it, one for the bellows and one for the keys. The *portative* organ could actually be held by a single player, who operated the bellows with the left hand and played the keys with the right.

The Use of Instruments
in Medieval Music

In the Middle Ages instruments other than the organ belonged to the realm of secular rather than sacred music. The church fathers were opposed to instrumental music in principle, partly because without words music seemed to them no more than idle entertainment and partly because of the association of instrumental music with immoral or licentious activities. When they inevitably encountered the biblical references to instruments, they interpreted them as mere allegories. For example, in the twelfth century Honorius of Autun offered the following gloss on Psalm 150:

> *Praise him with the tympanon and chorus* [i.e., timbrel and dance]. The tympanon is made from skin that has dried and become firm, which signifies unchangeable flesh, made strong against corruption. Therefore praise God because he has made your flesh, once fragile, to be firm and because it will no longer be subject to corruption. . . .
>
> *Praise him with the well-sounding cymbals.* Cymbals shine and resound after they have been forged in the fire. This signifies the bodies of the saints who, after they passed through the fire of adversity, will glisten as the sun and resound eternally in praise of God. . . .
>
> Indeed, through various instruments are signified different orders of those who praise God in Church. . . . The trumpets are preachers; the psalterium those who perform spiritual deeds, such as monks; the kithara those who chastise themselves, like hermits and solitaries. The tympanum is those who have died to their faults, such as martyrs; and the chorus those living harmoniously in the common life, like the canons regular. . . . By these instruments every spirit, that is everything which has spiritual life, praises God; instruments of that sort will resound during the everlasting nuptials of the Lamb, Alleluia.[1]

This does not mean that instruments were never played in the church. Indeed, from the vigorous and repeated censorship of instruments by the authorities we can only conclude that they must have been used at least sometimes.

Even when a piece seems clearly intended for instrumental performance, which is rare, medieval music never specifies the instruments to be used or the way in which they are to be combined with each other or with voices. It is most likely that musicians simply adapted the music to whatever instruments were at hand and could manage the notes. Performances of the same piece must have varied considerably.

Instruments took a variety of roles in vocal music. They undoubtedly doubled the singers' parts, and they may have accompanied voices heterophonically, either in a somewhat more ornamental reading of a melody or in

Figure 4.3
Medieval dancers accompanied by a vielle, drums, and portative organ.
(Bodleian Library, Oxford, MS. Bodley 264, fol. 172v.)

a simple statement of a line while the singer embellished. They may have played drones to support singers, keep them on pitch, and give richness of sound to the music. Although most of the written music seems to have been conceived for voices, instruments could substitute for singers when they were available and singers were not. Instrumentalists may also have provided preludes, interludes, or postludes to vocal pieces. These may have been notated in the manner of refrains within songs or simply improvised by the players.

There survives a small quantity of music actually intended specifically for instrumental performance, the repertoire of dance music. (Fig. 4.3) The most important type of dance was the *estampie*. The estampie, which might be provided with words for singing, was designed as a series of paired, parallel phrases called *puncta*. In this it resembles the form of the liturgical Sequence, of course, suggesting that musicians applied the same manner of formal thinking to both sacred and secular repertoires. A notable feature of the estampie was the use of a harmonically transient or open (in French *ouvert*; in Italian *aperto*) ending on the first statement of each punctum and a stable or closed (in French *clos*; in Italian *chiuso*) ending for its repetition.

The matter of determining instrumentation for performances of medieval instrumental music or of vocal music with instruments may seem frustrating, if not futile. In fact the problems of finding instrumentations for early music provide delightful challenges to the modern player's creativity. There are, of course, historically inauthentic or musically unfortunate scorings. But for the musician who can discover the historical possibilities, learn the techniques of the mechanically relatively simple instruments, and exercise good musical taste and an understanding of the principles of the music itself, there may be many wonderfully effective ways to perform the music. The possibility for variety is one attractive feature of the medieval repertoire.

Questions for Reflection

How can a historian attempt to understand what European secular music was like in the period before the use of notation, or the secular music of the nonaristocratic classes even more recently? What are the limits of speculation based on what is known of notated music of the time? on pictorial or literary evidence? on modern oral traditions in music?

✤ Why did it become necessary to create a new word (*troubadour* or *trouvère*) to distinguish the composer from other types of musicians at a particular point in the development of Western music?

✤ What important historical movements must have affected the spread of the music of the aristocratic classes in France in the twelfth and thirteenth centuries? How might these movements have affected musical style?

✤ How can musicians who want to play medieval music in historically appropriate scorings attempt to discover what was done, since the written music does not specify instrumentation?

Suggestions for Further Reading

Hendrick Van der Werf, *The Chansons of the Troubadors and Trouvères* (Utrecht: Oosthoek, 1972) is an excellent study. R. Briffault, *The Troubadours* (Bloomington: Indiana University Press, 1965) gives a historical survey. An introduction to the Minnesinger repertory, the music itself, and analytical commentary can be found in Ronald Taylor, *The Art of the Minnesinger,* 2 vols. (Cardiff: University of Wales Press, 1968).

On early instruments, see Curt Sachs, *The History of Musical Instruments* (New York: Norton, 1940); Jeremy Montagu, *The World of Medieval and Renaissance Instruments* (Woodstock, N.Y.: Overlook, 1976); and David Munrow, *Instruments of the Middle Ages and Renaissance* (London: Oxford University Press, 1976).

For a good discussion of performance matters, see Christopher Page, *Voices and Instruments of the Middle Ages* (Berkeley: University of California Press, 1986).

Notes

1. Reprinted from James McKinnon, "The Church Fathers and Musical Instruments," (Ph.D. diss., Columbia University, 1965), 239–240.

5

THE DEVELOPMENT OF POLYPHONY

The Significance of Polyphony

The supreme musical achievement of the early Middle Ages was the development of polyphonic texture in music. This new texture reflects in music some of the tendencies of the other arts during the course of the Carolingian (800–1000) and Romanesque (1000–1150) periods. These tendencies—an increase of mass and, in later phases, the proliferation of decoration—were particularly clear in architecture.

The development of composed polyphony, resulting in the displacement of pure melody by multivoiced networks of sound, is an achievement unique to Western music. Much was gained in the creation of polyphony: There was a new sense of depth in the musical texture, and there were increased possibilities for symbolic expression through explicit harmonic relationships. At the same time, the coordination of contrasting lines limited certain elements of style. Rhythm was no longer as free to respond to subtleties in the rhythms of oral language, and melody could no longer be freely ornamented.

Early polyphonic music was referred to by its practitioners and theorists as *organum*. It was formed by adding a new line of music in simultaneous performance with the existing chant, which thus became the *cantus firmus* (fixed song). Because it was built on the foundation of chant melody, it resembles conceptually the architecture of a medieval church, which was constructed on a standard cruciform foundation. Therefore it constituted an application of the principle of the trope, with which it developed almost simultaneously. The idea of troping by superimposition of material on an authoritative text does not differ in essence from the insertion of textual or musical phrases into a chant; in organum the trope is applied simultaneously rather than sequentially.

Carolingian Polyphony

The practice of polyphonic singing evolved from the simple doubling of the chant in octaves or other intervals. It is likely that the first singers of polyphony were inspired by the recognition that men and boys would generally sing the chant in parallel octaves. By the ninth century they had codified this practice and expanded it to include parallel doublings in the other perfect intervals, the fourth and fifth. (It is also possible that the use of the fourth and fifth were inspired by the sound of singing in a large, open sanctuary, where the acoustics reinforced the lower partials of the vocal pitch, creating the effect of parallel voices.) We refer to this simple style as *parallel organum.*

The main surviving sources for this practice are two books dating from about 900, *Musica enchiriadis* (Music handbook) and *Scolica enchiriadis* (School handbook), which give rules for improvising parallel organum. The singers are instructed to begin with the first note of the chant (the melody referred to as *vox principalis*), find the note a fourth or fifth below, and then sing the melody in parallel, beginning on those two pitches (the added lower voice becomes the *vox organalis*). Either or both of these lines may be further doubled at the octave, producing three or four voices.

Parallel organum does not have the effect of true, independent polyphony; it merely adds harmonic color and depth to the line as the overtones of the organal voice combine with those of the principal voice. (Something similar was achieved later in impressionist music with sliding, nonfunctional, tertian harmonies.) In addition to the simple use of parallel motion, however, the sources allow the possibility that the voices will begin in unison, with the *vox organalis* remaining stationary until the *vox principalis* has reached the fourth or fifth above and then proceeding parallel to it and returning to the unison for the cadence of the phrase. We refer to the motion of a moving voice against a stationary one as oblique motion. This procedure already represents an important innovation, since it provides for temporary dissonance leading to consonance and implies the concept of harmonic resolution. It is the first step in the direction of genuine counterpoint. In fact the term counterpoint is derived from the Latin phrase for this kind of homorhythmic relationship of parts, *punctus contra punctum* ("point against point," i. e., note against note).

Romanesque Developments

Free Organum

The next stage in the development of polyphony occurred in about the eleventh century. At this time musicians explored the possibilities of independence of melodic direction between the voices in a style that is sometimes called "free" organum. Contrary motion between voices took an equal place with parallel and oblique motion. The parts still maintained the mostly note-against-note rhythmic lockstep, but they went their own ways with true melodic independence, controlled by the necessity of producing mostly perfect consonances. The parts occasionally crossed, and the *vox principalis* increasingly tended to become the lower of the two parts. The main treatise that gives instructions for this kind of singing is entitled *Ad organum faciendum* (On making organum, ca. 1100). The most important collection of this music is the *Winchester Troper* (ca. 1000), so named because it represents the practice at Winchester Cathedral in England. The extension of the word *trope* to include polyphonic, simultaneous composition shows how closely related organum was to the monophonic trope.

Ultimately parallel motion began to seem stiff and uninteresting, and contrary motion became the norm in polyphonic composition. Obviously, however, the singing of melodically free organum was much more demanding than parallel organum. This accounts for the writing down of the music in manuscripts such as the *Winchester Troper*. For the same reason, such singing had to be restricted to trained soloists, and thus polyphonic music for the next two centuries focused on the solo portions of responsorial chants.

Note-against-note organum provided for the music of the church a feeling of expansiveness comparable to that which the newly attained vertical height of the vaulted, stone-and-masonry roof of Romanesque architecture gave to the church building. (Fig. 5.1) At the same time, the multiplication of voices added a degree of massiveness similar to that of the heavily reinforced walls that supported the vaulting.

Rhythmic Independence

The next new idea in the development of polyphony was to give the contrasting voices rhythmic as well as melodic independence. This was accomplished most notably at the abbey of St. Martial at Limoges in south central France and at the pilgrimage cathedral of Santiago de Compostela in northwestern Spain in the twelfth century. In this style the chant melody chosen to serve as the foundation of the composition moves in relatively slower note values, while the newly composed organal voice proceeds more rapidly, with a proliferation of shorter notes. We might compare this to the interaction of sculpture with architecture in the Romanesque cathedral. As we have just noted, the weight of the vaulted roof required massive support. To give rhythmic articulation and variety to the surfaces of the massive church walls, there was a new blossoming of sculpture; armies of saints lined the walls, and biblical scenes unfolded in the semicircular space or tympanum above the cathedral door. The impulse to decorate a bare surface, whether in cathedral architecture or in

Figure 5.1
Santiago de Compostela in northwestern Spain was one of the most
important centers for religious pilgrimages during the Middle Ages. The
Romanesque cathedral there (1028–1211) illustrates the high, rounded
vaulting of the architectural style of the time. Santiago de Compostela was a
major site for the development of the melismatic style of organum. (*Marburg/
Art Resource*)

the music of the divine service, was a strong one in the mind of the Romanesque artist.

Harmonic Freedom

Florid Organum   Often there are very many notes in the organal voice, or *duplum,* to each note of the chant line. In such compositions, the chant, because of its long-held notes, came to be known as the *tenor* (from the same Latin term used for the repeated tone of a psalm tone, but now used in an entirely new musical context). To distinguish this style from earlier note-against-note organum, we can identify it as *melismatic organum* or *florid organum.* The significance of this new style is that it provided not only rhythmic variety but also harmonic freedom. In general the voices in florid organum are coordinated harmonically by combining in perfect consonances at major structural points, such as at the change of notes in the tenor. Between these points any vertical simultaneity might produce dissonances. Thus the idea of harmonic cadence by means of resolution from the tension of dissonance to the relaxation of consonance was already formed. Unfortunately, since the musical notation of the time had been developed for the more flexible rhythm of the chant, there did not yet exist any method for notating the more precise rhythms required to coordinate the parts in twelfth-century polyphony. This leads to considerable difficulty in interpreting this music, because the only available notational means of indicating the exact coincidences in the voices was by alignment in score format, and it is not always clear today how the parts should be combined.

Discant   A second type of writing in this repertory was the pairing of a chant voice with a duplum in such a way that the two moved in more nearly equal rhythm. This procedure, in which each voice would have a simple or compound neume for each syllable of text, produced a style called *discant* to distinguish it from the florid organum. In discant, the juxtaposition of neumes of unequal numbers of pitches might produce rhythmic combinations of one note against two, three, or more; of two against three; of three against four; and so on. To compensate for this added complexity, the harmony tended to be more limited to perfect consonances.

Gothic Thinking and Style

The next stages in the development of polyphony correspond to the Gothic period in cultural history, lasting from about 1150 through the following century. To understand the nature of musical thought at this time, it is helpful to keep in mind some other manifestations of the characteristic ways of thinking in that era. The crucial concept here is organization, ordering, or coordination.

If it is fair to identify one particular place as central to the Gothic spirit, that place is Paris. By the late twelfth century the French kings (the Capetian dynasty) had consolidated the feudal system so that, unlike other parts of Europe, there existed a relatively centralized French realm, coordinated from the capital city. Thus the political organization had a pyramid structure conceived in layers, with the monarch at the top supported by a number of less powerful lords and so on down to the mass of relatively powerless peasants.

The desire to order learning produced the institution of the university. The teaching masters of Paris formed the university there by joining together to coordinate their disciplines and establish high standards for scholarship. The university grew gradually; an important step was the endowment in 1253 by the cardinal Robert de Sorbon of a resident college of theology with a clear set of organizing statutes. The university as a whole consisted of four faculties, concerned with the liberal arts, law, medicine, and theology.

During the twelfth and thirteenth centuries the works of Aristotle, generally unknown in western Europe for centuries, began to reemerge. They had been preserved by Arabic scholars, so that as European communication with Arabic culture increased in the Middle East during the Crusades and in Spain, the western world rediscovered its own heritage. Important among Aristotle's contributions to philosophy was the idea that knowledge was to be gained by reasoned discourse rather than by faith. The scholars in the twelfth- and thirteenth-century university found that this new understanding challenged much of their learning. Modeling their work on Aristotle, they adopted a new approach to their studies, the dialectical resolution of contradictions by means of debate; it became known as *scholasticism*.

Among the scholars at Paris in the twelfth and thirteenth centuries were such famous thinkers as Peter Abelard (1075–1142) and Thomas Aquinas. Abelard's *Sic et non* constitutes a landmark in the history of thought because it applied the techniques of critical thinking to resolving opposing opinions in matters of religious faith. Aquinas's *Summa theologica* attempted to find a way to coordinate the secular liberal arts and the things of this world with the unknowable world of faith and the divine. The scholastics inevitably threatened the authority of the church, but the force of Aristotle's influence and the strength of their philosophical arguments could not be ignored. The church had to adapt, and to a large extent it did so successfully. It could no longer claim absolute sway over the thinking of its followers, however, and consequently the rise of secular culture, including music, accelerated rapidly from the twelfth century onward.

In the second half of the twelfth century the style of architecture we call Gothic developed, and one of its greatest examples, the cathedral of Notre Dame, rose in Paris. (Fig. 5.2) One of the main characteristics of the style is the

Figure 5.2
The cathedral of Notre Dame in Paris. The church of Notre Dame (begun 1163 and completed in the early fourteenth century) saw the development of rhythmically ordered polyphonic music in the Gothic period. The architecture of the cathedral, its structure clearly ordered by lighter decoration in the higher levels, demonstrates the same sort of Gothic artistic thinking as Notre Dame organum. (*Giraudon/Art Resource*)

increase of height and upward direction of the eye. The rounded arches of the Romanesque cathedral were now raised to a point in the center, which directed the weight downward and thereby reduced the outward pressure on the walls. Most of the remaining outward force was taken by flying buttresses. The pillars and walls no longer needed to be so sturdy and massive, and they were reduced to a relatively fine skeleton. Windows were greatly enlarged, increasing the light inside the edifice, and this also lessened the feeling of weight. The use of stained glass provided decoration and rhythm viewed from the interior, while the exterior was ornamented with biblical sculptures as well as grotesques and functional gargoyles to carry rainwater away from the building.

With its tremendous height, the Gothic cathedral was articulated in vertical layers, the decoration generally growing more and more finely detailed toward the top. The juxtaposition of stylistically articulated levels can be seen on a smaller scale in the three arches over the large west doors of Notre Dame. Each of these arches is really a series of concentric arches (sometimes called orders) decorated with its own sculptured frieze. Such ordered layering became particularly significant for the development of music, as we shall see. Like other Gothic cathedrals, Notre Dame grew over a period of many years (indeed more than most of its contemporaries). As a result its style is far from unified but reflects the changing ideas, tastes, and personalities of generations of builders from the late twelfth to the early fourteenth centuries.

Notre Dame Polyphony

Rhythmic Order in Organum: Leonin

The next important stages in the evolution of musical thinking were worked out by composers associated with the cathedral of Notre Dame. The first composer of polyphonic music whose name we know was Leonin or, in Latin, Magister (Master) Leoninus. Although his music was intended for use in the church, his title clearly indicates that he came from the university community. Leonin produced a collection of organal settings of solo portions of the responsorial chants—that is, the parts of the liturgy (both Mass and Office) sung by trained solo singers—for the major festivals throughout the church year. These polyphonic portions were substituted for the corresponding chant passages, and they alternated freely with regular chanting for the choral segments of the movements in which they would be sung. Leonin's collection was known as the *Magnus liber organi* (Great book of organum), and it is represented whole or in part in four different manuscript books of Gothic polyphony, in libraries in Wolfenbüttel in Germany (two exemplars known as *W1* and *W2*), in Florence (*F*, Fig. 5.3), and in Madrid (*Ma*). The music was apparently composed in the second half of the twelfth century.

Leonin's music marks a definitive step beyond the florid organum of St. Martial and Santiago de Compostela. Specifically, it shows the application

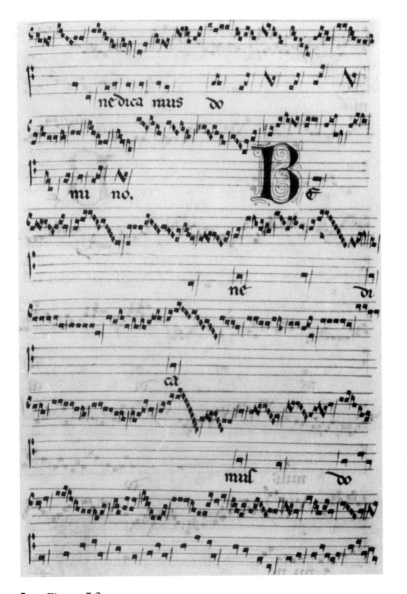

Figure 5.3
A page of the *Magnus liber organi* in the fine Florence manuscript (*F*).
(*Biblioteca Medicea-Laurenziana, Florence*)

of determinate rhythmic relationships to the melodic lines, greatly clarifying the coordination of the polyphonic parts. This is accomplished by means of a system known as the *rhythmic modes.* A composer trained at the university would certainly have studied the principles of poetry, and it is therefore not surprising that such a composer would turn to the well-known organization of long and short syllables grouped in metrical feet. To comprehend the striking new sound of this music, we must understand the basic principles of the Notre Dame system of rhythmic modes.

To apply poetic metrical patterns to music, the Notre Dame musicians presumed that a long note or *long* (Latin *longa,* often abbreviated as L and notated as a square notehead with a tail descending from the right) would be twice the duration of a short note or *breve* (Latin *brevis,* abbreviated as B and notated as a simple, square notehead). The alternation of long and short notes produced "trochaic" (LB, LB, LB, etc.) or "iambic" (BL, BL, BL, etc.) rhythms.

More complex metrical feet, consisting of three durations, were simulated by the use of an extralong long equal to three breves, called "perfect" to distinguish it from the two-breve or "imperfect" long, and an "altered" breve twice as long as a normal ("recta" or correct) breve. This allowed for the "dactylic" rhythm (LBB, LBB, LBB, etc.) and the "anapestic" rhythm (BBL, BBL, BBL, etc.), where the long was perfect and the second of the two breves was altered. Two other patterns were added, the "spondaic," plodding along in of perfect longs, and the "tribrachic," which tripped quickly in groups of three regular breves.

The six rhythmic modes were numbered (like the ecclesiastical modes). They can be summarized and clarified in modern notation as follows:

Mode	Metrical Model	Modal Notation	Modern Notation
1	trochee	LB (L imperfect)	♩ ♪
2	iamb	BL (L imperfect)	♪ ♩
3	dactyl	LBB (L perfect, second B altered)	♩. ♪ ♩
4	anapest	BBL (second B altered, L perfect)	♪ ♩ ♩.
5	spondee	LL (both perfect)	♩. ♩.
6	tribrach	BBB (all recta)	♪ ♪ ♪

It works very well to notate this music in modern notation in $\frac{6}{8}$ time, and that has become the usual way to transcribe the Notre Dame repertoire. In the twelfth and early thirteenth centuries the convention was to indicate each mode by a particular ligature pattern. Thus the singers learned that a three-note ligature followed by a series of two-note ligatures would require rhythmic mode 1, a simple series of two-note ligatures indicated mode 2, and so on. A series of individual longs naturally meant mode 5.

The application of these relatively fixed rhythmic patterns gives an unprecedented physical energy to the music of Leonin. A modal pattern would generally be maintained throughout a substantial passage or a whole organum. Some variety was attained by momentarily combining short values into long ones (*extensio modi*, extending the mode) or subdividing values into shorter ones (*fractio modi*, breaking up the mode).

If the different modes were sung simultaneously in different polyphonic voices, the rhythms would automatically be coordinated with each other. In practice certain combinations were more likely than others. For example modes 5 and 6 coordinate well with any of the others, and mode 2 coordinates better with modes 3 and 4 than mode 1 would.

A further feature of the system is the grouping of modal units into phrases articulated by rests. Such a phrase was called an *ordo* (pl. *ordines*), a term that reminds us of the importance of the concept of order in Gothic art.

In the *Magnus liber organi* the syllabic portions of the chant were generally set with very long, unmeasured notes in the tenor, over which the duplum could elaborate in more or less strict modal rhythm. Quite probably the dronelike notes of the tenor, obviously impossible for a singer to sustain, were taken or at least supported by an instrument; an organ would suit the situation perfectly. When the chant became melismatic, the tenor had to be accelerated in the interest of efficiency. This produced a section in discant style, known as a *clausula* (again indicating the literary training of medieval musicians). A discant clausula demanded modal rhythm in both voices; commonly the tenor adopted mode 5, while the duplum moved in one of the quicker modes.

Perotin

Around the year 1200 a new figure appeared on the Notre Dame scene, one Perotin (Magister Perotinus, in Latin), who expanded and elaborated the music of Leonin.

One of Perotin's achievements was the expansion of the two-voice texture to three and even four parts, creating *organum triplum* and *organum quadruplum*. In this style the tenor maintained unmeasured long notes, while the upper two or three voices generally shared the same modal rhythm. Because these organa were intended for male voices, the organal lines (duplum, triplum, and quadruplum) encompass the same range, often crossing each other. Sometimes they exchange parts with each other in turns; such *voice exchange* extends a passage to two or three times its length without actually requiring the composition of new music. In Perotin's monumental organa tripla and quadrupla, the combination of long, droning tenor notes, the dense polyphonic web of the organal voices, and the hypnotically repetitive modal rhythms produce a magnificent effect; sung in a Gothic cathedral they might be positively overwhelming.

Perotin's second major contribution was the composition of new and more complex discant clausulae to be inserted as substitutions for Leonin's in the music of the *Magnus liber organi*. As we might expect from Perotin, these *substitute clausulae* included three-part as well as two-part scorings. Other stylistic developments also emerged in the clausulae. The fragment of chant melody used in the tenor might be repeated within the clausula. This gives the effect of variations above the repeated tenor melody, and it increases the sense of musical unity. For similar reasons, composers used ordines of the same length throughout the clausula, especially in the tenor, dividing the clausula into a series of short phrases of equal length. The upper voices might follow the same procedure, but as the composers' skill increased, they tended to stagger the ordines in the different voices so that the parts would not have simultaneous rests and the music would not lose its momentum. These experiments with rhythmic and melodic repetition were the forerunners of remarkably complicated musical structures in following generations.

Cadences

The construction of cadences in polyphonic compositions reached an important stage in the thirteenth century. At this time it became conventional to create a sense of finality by moving the voices in contrary, stepwise fashion to the last note. In two parts the cadence required the voices to converge from a third to a unison or to separate from a sixth to an octave (indicated in the following as a 3-1 or a 6-8 cadence). In three parts the outer parts formed the 6-8 cadence, while the inner part paralleled the upper one at a fourth. This gave a $^{6-8}_{3-5}$ progression and produced the perfect consonances of fifth and octave as the last harmony (Ex. 5.1). The expression of cadential feeling in this fashion by contrapuntal contrary motion formed the basis for a variety of later developments and eventually (in the sixteenth century) led to the creation of the powerful authentic cadence.

Example 5.1.

Two- and three-voice cadence forms.

a. The 3-1 cadence in two voices

b. The 6-8 cadence in two voices

c. Cadence in three voices

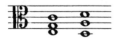

The Medieval Motet

The next stage in the development of polyphonic genres in the thirteenth century was the addition of texts to the upper voices of the discant clausula. This might surprise today's musicians, but it was perfectly reasonable from the point of view of the medieval composer. By the same thought process that led to the textual troping of melismata in the chant, the medieval musician naturally seized on the dupla and tripla of these fragmentary clausulae as material on which to exercise further creative imagination. The modal rhythms of these melismatic lines lent themselves to the application of words that would fit them syllabically, and the ordo controlled the length of the poetic line. The result was that the clausula, originally only a fragment of a liturgical movement, became a complete, self-contained setting of the new text or texts. The piece thus produced was known as a *motet* (from the French *mot*, meaning word). The voice immediately above the tenor was called *motetus*, which is obviously a Latin derivative. A motet takes its name from the text incipits—the first word or words—of each of its voices, working from the top voice to the tenor.

The motet was thus polytextual, with two or three (rarely four) separate melodic lines and as many contrasting sets of words. Two objections immediately come to mind: (1) The conflict of different texts makes them unintelligible in performance, and (2) the motet deviates from the authoritative text of the liturgical tenor. Neither of these issues escaped the church fathers, of course. They were, however, somewhat deflected by the general acceptance of troping as a compositional technique; the first motet texts simply offered a gloss on the text of the tenor. Furthermore, the medieval idea of musical expression did not insist on the close correspondence between musical gestures and text content that we are accustomed to in later music. Indeed it is hardly likely that musicians who worshipped and sang daily in such a stylistically diverse architectural setting as the cathedral of Notre Dame would be distressed by the contrasting modal rhythms, overlapping ordines, and babel of texts distributed among the voices in the thirteenth-century motet.

It did not take long before the motet became separated from its liturgical context entirely, as composers began to set texts that were entirely free of sacred intent. In some cases the text writers even used this genre, born in the church, to attack the church. Though at first the texts were in Latin, later ones employed the vernacular; in some cases the tenor and motetus would be in Latin and the triplum in French, and one text might have sacred content while the other was a thoroughly secular love song. Naturally composers did not merely rely on the existing repertoire of discant clausulae for long; they found more freedom and flexibility in composing new music for the texts of the upper parts. Ultimately even the tenors were newly composed; since such a part would have no liturgical text to name it, it might be called "neuma" or simply "tenor." Presumably it would have been played on an instrument rather than sung.

Perotin and his successors in the thirteenth century also wrote free, nonliturgical polyphonic pieces with only one text and no sacred tenor. These songs, called *conductus,* somewhat resemble the style of discant in two, three, or four voices. Sometimes they were strophic and sometimes through-composed. A common device in the conductus was to signal the close of a primarily syllabic setting with an extensive melismatic passage known as a *cauda* (Latin for tail). Because of the close resemblance between the conductus and a three-part motet in which the motetus and triplum shared the same text, as sometimes happened, this special kind of motet is called a *conductus motet.*

Late Thirteenth-Century Developments

It became a common stylistic feature in the thirteenth-century motet for the triplum to move quickly in short note values, the motetus to proceed a bit slower, and the tenor to march along in stately longs. In a simple form, the distinction would be effected by a triplum in rhythmic mode 6, a tenor in mode 5, and motetus in any of the other modes. This elegantly layered ordering serves the musical function of differentiating the lines more clearly for the listener. As time went on, composers wanted to squeeze even more syllables into the line than the breve would allow, so they created the independent value of the semibreve (SB), written as a diamond or lozenge shape.

A particularly progressive composer in this style was the Frenchman Pierre de la Croix, also known by his Latin name Petrus de Cruce (fl. 1270–1300). In his motets the triplum often pattered along very quickly in strings of rhythmically undifferentiated semibreves, as many as six to the breve (obviously, this requires a free interpretation of the prefix semi). From a literary point of view, this practice meant that in the Petronian motet the effect of the triplum was rather more like prose than poetry. It also forced a general increase in the common duration of all the note values, a kind of rhythmic inflation that continued for several hundred years. The thirteenth-century semibreve is actually the same note we now write as a whole note—the shortest note of Pierre de la Croix's time is the longest note we generally see in the music of the period of common practice.

New Developments in Rhythmic Notation

The motet presented a new and thorny problem for the music theorists of the late thirteenth century: Since the upper voices were syllabic, and one could not write syllabic texts under the compact little ligatures that indicated modal rhythms, how were rhythms to be specified? The solution came from the theorist Franco of Cologne, who wrote an important treatise on the problem, entitled *Ars cantus mensurabilis* (The art of measurable song) shortly after the middle of the thirteenth century. Franco employed four basic duration signs: a double or duplex long (DL), the usual long and breve, and the semibreve. The regular duration of the breve was now called one *tempus* (time); three *tempora* made up a *perfection*. The principal difficulty, of course, was to indicate where longs were to be imperfect (two tempora instead of three) and where breves were to be altered (two tempora instead of one). Franco accomplished this by means of a little vertical line or a dot between notes, indicating the division between perfections. (Fig. 5-4) (Because semibreves related to breves just as breves did to longs, the dot of division could also be used to separate one tempus from another.)

It is easy to see how important Franco's system was. Any rhythms at all could now be notated within the basic triple framework of perfections and tempora. One was not limited to establishing and maintaining a particular mode. In fact, as the reader has probably already guessed, the dot of division is the distant progenitor of the later bar line. Franco's invention certainly ranks as one of the great accomplishments in the history of music theory.

A practical result of the new rhythmic notation was the possibility it offered for making the coordination of lines clear without writing the parts vertically in score format. Since the parts in a motet were rhythmically differentiated—the tenor moving slowly, the triplum rapidly, and the motetus moderately—the slower-moving parts in a score were stretched out over more space than their notes actually required. In the Middle Ages this was a considerable waste, for parchment and even paper were extremely costly. When it became possible to notate the rhythms of the voices without ambiguity, they could be written separately as parts, each filling only the space it actually needed. Commonly the triplum would be written on a left-hand page, the motetus on the right-hand page facing it, and the tenor in a single line across the bottom of both; or if the triplum moved much more quickly than the motetus and contained many more notes, it might occupy an entire page, while the motetus and tenor shared the facing page. This is known as *choirbook* notation.

Hocket

A special device developed in the later thirteenth century was the breaking up of a line between two voices by having them alternate notes and rests. This somewhat curious and even amusing technique was called *hocket* (from the Latin word for hiccup, *hoquetus*). It would provide a moment of lighter and rhythmically sparkling texture within the normal polyphonic style. Hocket continued to be used in the fourteenth century, but it was practically nonexis-

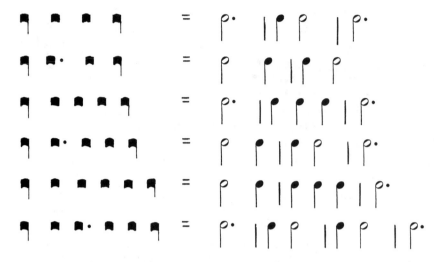

Figure 5.4
Some examples of the effect of the dot of perfection in Franconian rhythmic notation.

tent thereafter until the twentieth. (A passage in the fourth movement of Hector Berlioz's *Symphonie fantastique* and some of the music of Anton Webern are important recent examples.)

Symbolic Values in Medieval Polyphony

Let us consider what is expressed by the polyphonic music we have been discussing. It should be obvious that the expression of the meanings and moods of literary texts was not the primary concern of the composers of polyphonic music up to the thirteenth century. That is not to say that the music expresses nothing. It reflects the general medieval understanding of music's place in human experience. We have seen that music was not considered to belong to the same category of thought as language and literature, the trivium of the liberal arts, at all. It belonged instead to the quadrivium, with the mathematical disciplines and astronomy. Naturally, then, music would be expressive of the ordering inherent in mathematical experience.

We might say that music was expressive in a symbolic sense, as a reflection of the properties of numbers and the stars. The relation of numbers to medieval polyphony is obvious. Harmonic control came from the placement of the perfect consonances on structurally important parts of the ordo. Rhythmically, the music coordinated arrays of contrasting measured durations

Figure 5.5

Cimabue (before 1251–1302), "Madonna Enthroned"
(ca. 1280–1290). The aesthetic approach is symbolic rather
than realistic. The relative sizes of the figures reflect their
importance rather than their location. The throne has an
architectural design, making it represent the church rather
than a real throne. (*Alinari/Art Resource*)

among the various parts. The art of composition was the art of handling numbers.

To the medieval mind numbers symbolized the order of the universe. Boethius had viewed *musica instrumentalis* as the audible reflection of *musica mundana*. In Christian thought divine perfection was reflected in the beauty of numbers and, consequently, in the perfect consonances and rhythmic perfections of music.

In his *Divine Comedy,* the Italian poet Dante Alighieri (1265–1321) framed a world view of his time, intensely concerned with evil and good, hell and heaven, Satan and God, following an elaborately constructed plan based on careful ordering and intricate numerical proportions. On his ascent to Paradise, Dante hears for the first time the music of the spheres. He says (*Paradise,* canto 1),

> When the Great Wheel that spins eternally
> in longing for Thee, captured my attention
> by that harmony attuned and heard by Thee,
>
> I saw ablaze with sun from side to side
> a reach of Heaven: not all the rains and rivers
> of all of time could make a sea so wide.
>
> That radiance and that new-heard melody
> fired me with such a yearning for their Cause
> as I had never heard before. . . .

And Beatrice explains to him that the temporal order is, or ought to be regarded as, a reflection of the divine.

> . . . "The elements
> of all things," she began, "whatever their mode,
> observe an inner order. It is this form
> that makes the universe resemble God. . . ."[1]

Thus in the Middle Ages music's symbolic representation of both natural and divine order, proportion, and harmony constituted the essence of its expressiveness. (Fig. 5-5) This conception underlies Thomas Aquinas's eloquent characterization of music as "the exaltation of the mind derived from things eternal bursting forth in sound."

Questions for Reflection

❖   How was the development and spread of polyphonic music in the eleventh and twelfth centuries a product of travel routes determined by church activities?

✦ How did different cultural, political, and ecclesiastical institutions in Paris around 1200 contribute to the growth of a Gothic polyphonic style?

✦ How many different aspects of contemporary cultural and aesthetic tendencies did the Gothic motet express?

Suggestions for Further Reading

See the general surveys of medieval music cited in the Suggestions for Further Reading for Chapter 3. The polyphonic music of the thirteenth, fourteenth, and fifteenth centuries is surveyed in F. Alberto Gallo, *Music of the Middle Ages II,* trans. Karen Eales (Cambridge: Cambridge University Press, 1985).

For an extensive treatment of the notation of medieval and Renaissance polyphony, see Willi Apel, *The Notation of Polyphonic Music 900–1600,* 5th ed. rev. (Cambridge, Mass.: Medieval Academy of America, 1961). Carl Parrish, *The Notation of Medieval Music* (New York: Norton, 1959) gives a less detailed survey. William Waite, *The Rhythm of Twelfth-Century Polyphony: Its Theory and Practice* (New Haven: Yale University Press, 1954) discusses the interesting rhythmic problems of interpreting early polyphony.

Franco of Cologne's treatise, *Ars cantus mensurabilis,* is excerpted in Oliver Strunk, *Source Readings in Music History* (New York: Norton, 1950).

Notes

1. Dante Alighieri, *The Paradiso,* verse rendering by John Ciardi (New York: New American Library, 1970), 26–27.

6

MUSIC IN THE LATE MIDDLE AGES

The Increasing Secularization of Culture

The Western world was shaken in the fourteenth century by a series of cataclysmic events that contributed to the final collapse of medieval civilization. Perhaps most importantly for musical developments, the church was rocked to its very foundations, and artists, writers, and composers rapidly redirected their attention from the sacred to the secular.

After centuries of great power in both the religious and the secular arenas, the Roman church was threatened both politically and theologically. The monarchs in the north had become stronger, and their rule had grown more ambitious. Both Edward I of England (r. 1272–1307) and Philip IV "the Fair" of France (r. 1285–1314) realized that the exclusion of the church's assets from the tax base reduced the power of the secular government. The church's assets grew steadily, progressively reducing the country's taxable wealth. The kings insisted on their right and need to tax the church's property, but naturally the Pope, Boniface VIII, asserted the separation of the church from the state and the ultimate primacy of ecclesiastical authority. On the home front, challenges came from theologians such as John Wyclif and Jan Hus, who criticized such abuses of ecclesiastical power as the selling of indulgences, by which the wealthy could give money or land to the church in return for a quicker passage to heaven, and the selling of church offices (simony). Finally the church could no longer withstand the pressures. Philip actually captured and humiliated Boniface and soon was able to impose his own will and force the election of his favorite as Pope Clement V.

Clement ruled from Avignon in France rather than from Rome, as did his successors for seventy years from 1309 until 1378 (the so-called Babylonian captivity). This reflected their subjection to the French crown and scandalized the rest of the church. Even after 1378 the situation did not improve, because the church divided into factions, each electing its own pope, until three rivals claimed the office. This Great Schism was intolerable, for the popes blatantly tried to manipulate powerful princes by threats of excommunication. When no one knew which of the bickering popes represented the true church, it was difficult to maintain faith at all. The schism lasted until 1417, when the church fathers met in the Council of Constance and resolved the issue. By then, however, the mortar of faith that had held together the edifice that was the truly Catholic church was eroded beyond repair.

Utterly devastating was the onslaught of the Black Plague beginning in 1348. The Italian writer Giovanni Boccaccio (1312–1353) described the horrors of the disease in the introduction to his *Decameron:*

> . . . at the beginning there began to appear, on men and women alike, either in the groin or under the armpits, certain inflammations, some of which grew like a common apple, others like an egg, some less and others more, which the common people called "buboes." And from those two parts of the body, in a short space of time, this deadly bubo began to appear and come over every part of it. And after that, the character of this disease began to change into black or livid splotches, which appeared in many people on the arms and the thighs and in every other part of the body, in some cases large and sparse, and in some tiny and dense. And, just as the buboes had been at the beginning, these were also a sure sign of coming death. . . .
>
> . . . not only did few recover, but also almost all died within the third day from the appearance of the aforementioned symptoms, some sooner and some later, and generally without any fever or other complication.

Without modern drugs the plague is fatal in 90 percent of cases. The cause of the bubonic plague was unknown, which made it the more fearsome; in fact it was transmitted to humans through rats and the fleas that infested them. The plague entered Europe with returning crusaders and traders from the east and spread like wildfire, especially in the cities, which had grown rapidly as Europe became urbanized. Within a few years several waves of the plague had wiped out at least a third of the total population of the continent (some histories place the death toll much higher).

The psychological and spiritual reactions to this horror were extreme in two directions. Those who believed that the plague represented a divine retribution for the general evils of society (and especially for the abuses in the church) turned to more intense and devout faith. In others fatalism led to indulgence in the most excessive hedonism. Artists found plentiful inspiration in both the sacred and the mundane.

The decline of the church and the rise of secular culture led to the creation of literary masterpieces in vernacular languages rather than Latin. Dante's *Divine Comedy* was the first monumental literary work written in the vernacular. Among Dante's successors, secular topics soon attained the same stature he had established for sacred ones in his essay on heaven and hell. The sonnets of Francesco Petrarch (1304–1374) to his beloved Laura (who became a victim of the plague of 1348) established a poetic form and later provided models to poets and texts to composers. They demonstrate that for literary art secular experience had become as noble as religious. Boccaccio wrote his *Decameron* in the guise of a hundred tales and fables told for their own diversion by a group of young, educated Florentines who had fled to the country to escape the plague. The stories often have earthy subjects and viewpoints that demonstrate the vigor of secular life. In the second half of the century Geoffrey Chaucer (1340–1400) wrote his *Canterbury Tales,* a similar collection to Boccaccio's. That the poet poked fun at the vain and courtly airs of the nun, or at the fat, self-indulgent monk who neglects the Rule of his order to spend his time hunting, shows how far public disdain of the pious had gone. Like Boccaccio, Chaucer did not hesitate to explore the earthly side of human experience.

Ars Nova

The fourteenth century seemed to mark a new level of progress in music, specifically in the realm of the measurement of musical time. This was embodied in the work of Philippe de Vitry (1291–1361), whose career included diplomatic activities as secretary and adviser to several kings of France, as well as an ecclesiastical appointment as Bishop of Meaulx. Educated in the liberal arts at the University of Paris, Vitry became the greatest music theorist of his time. He has been credited with the development of the ideas in the treatise *Ars nova* (The new art, ca. 1322–1323), which has lent its name to the entire century in French music (although the attribution has been questioned). By contrast, the music of the thirteenth century is called *ars antiqua.*

The *Ars nova* treatise contributed a brilliant and radically new approach to the thorny problem of notating the complex rhythms that fourteenth-century composers continually produced. In order to achieve the solution, it was first necessary to reject the fundamental assumption of the preeminence of triple rhythm, an assumption not only deeply entrenched in both principle and practice but also sanctioned by its symbolic value as a sign of divine perfection. Once this conceptual leap was made, however, an entirely original, magnificently effective rhythmic notation became possible. The system is called *mensuration,* which simply means measurement.

The new approach to rhythm first of all gave parity to duple and triple groupings and divisions of all the duration signs. Thus, a long could be divided equally into either two breves or three; a breve could be divided into two or three equal semibreves; a semibreve could comprise two or three minims (M, notated as a diamond-shaped semibreve notehead with a stem). The proportional relationship between longs and breves was referred to by the old term *mode,* and the relationship of breves to semibreves was called tempus (time). If the relationships were two to one, the mode and tempus were regarded as imperfect; if the relationships were three to one, mode and tempus were regarded as perfect. The relationship of semibreve to minim was called *prolation* and classified as either greater (in Latin, *major,* three Ms to one SB) or lesser (in Latin, *minor,* two Ms per SB). To indicate the mensuration, Vitry proposed a system of signatures. A circle indicated perfect tempus, while a half-circle indicated imperfect tempus. The addition of a dot in the center of the signature was added to show greater prolation. Today, of course, we would refer to perfect time and greater prolation as triple compound meter, perfect time and lesser prolation as triple simple meter, imperfect time and greater prolation as duple compound meter, and imperfect time and lesser prolation as duple simple meter. (Fig. 6.1) We still use the open half circle to indicate duple simple meter; we call it "common time."

Once determined at the start of a piece, the mensural proportions remained constant unless a change was indicated in the music. This could naturally be done by a change of mensuration signature, but for brief passages of change to or from triplets red ink was used. With its variety of note shapes, signature designs, and colors, the rhythmic notation of fourteenth-century music manuscripts produced some of our history's most visually attractive scores.

It is important to stress the epoch-making significance of the leap of creative imagination that made possible mensural notation. To abandon the domination of the number 3 in musical rhythm required an intellectual boldness comparable to that of Newton, Darwin, or Einstein. It also depended on the decline of ecclesiastical authority and on an increasing tendency to view music as an autonomous realm rather than a reflection of spiritual or philosophical ideas.

The mensural system fostered the development of a new musical style and technique. It effects a perfect balance between the dominance of triple rhythm in the ars antiqua, with its artificial modes and awkward rules, and the dominance of duple rhythm from the sixteenth to the twentieth century, which demands "extraneous" dots to indicate triple values. The ars nova rhythmic notation is absolutely unbiased toward either 3 or 2, and it made possible the coordination of the most interesting, intricate, subtle, complex rhythmic combinations in Western music up to the present century.

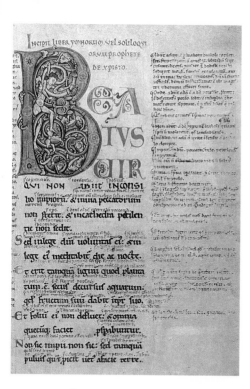

✤ **Plate 1**

Illuminated manuscript with gloss. Here the principle of the gloss is carried out in the margins and between the lines of the main text of the first Psalm. The illumination of the initial *B*, showing a figure struggling out of a tangle of branches, also amplifies the idea of the Psalm, "Blessed is the man who walks not in counsels of the wicked." *(Bodleian Library, Oxford, Ms. Auct. D. 2.4, fol. 1r)*

✤ **Plate 2**

Baude Cordier, *Belle bonne.* The late medieval manneristic style extends not only to the musical aspects of the notation, but to the visual element as well in this manuscript of a love song. *(Giraudon/Art Resource)*

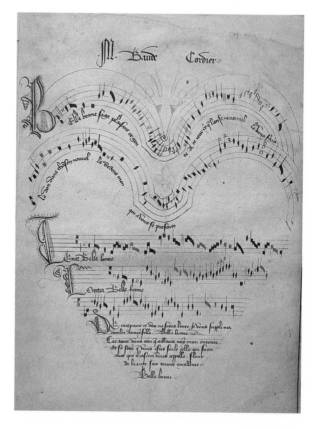

Plate 3

The Limbourg brothers, *Annunciation to the Shepherds,* from the *Très riches heures de Jean, duc de Berry* (1413–16). Though the illustration is of a biblical event, the Limbourgs' inclusion of many everyday details reflects a new, humanistic aesthetic. The angels are shown with lute, drum, music manuscript, shawm or trumpet, and vielle. *(Giraudon/Art Resource)*

❖ **Plate 4**

The angels in the *Adoration* from the Isenheim altarpiece by the German Renaissance painter Mathias Grünewald (ca. 1475–1528) play imaginative instruments, not real Renaissance viols. A visionary but troubled genius who lived in the turbulent period of the Reformation and the German Peasants' Revolt, Grünewald later came to represent an artist's personal struggle with political events as the subject of Paul Hindemith's opera *Mathis der Maler.*

(*Giraudon/Art Resource*)

❖ **Plate 5**

Lavish aristocratic support of the arts in the Baroque led to lavish style, as shown in Peter Paul Rubens's (1577–1640) portrayal of the arrival of Maria de' Medici in France. Maria's wedding in Florence to the French King, Henry IV, had provided the occasion for the composition of Jacopo Peri's opera *Euridice.* After Henry's death she ruled as regent for her son, Louis XIII. Rubens depicted the events of her life in a series of allegorical paintings in this highly ornate style.

(*Musée du Louvre,* © *Photo R.M.N.*)

❖ *Plate 6*
Jacques Louis David (1748–1825), *The Death of Socrates* (1787). The return to the values of classical antiquity in the arts is illustrated in this picture not only by the subject matter, but also by the general restraint in the colors and the symmetrical arrangement of figures around the center point.
(Metropolitan Museum of Art, Wolfe Fund, 1931. Catharine Lorillard Wolfe Collection [31.45])

❖ *Plate 7*
Théodore Géricault (1791–1824), *The Raft of the Medusa* (1818). The picture deals with the Romantic topics of the relationship of man and nature, and death. It depicts and seeks to evoke a variety of complicated emotions, combining grief, fear, horror, and wild hope. The emphasis on the diagonal axes lends a sense of movement rather than stability to the work. *(Musée du Louvre, © Photo R.M.N.)*

Plate 8

J.M.W. Turner (1775–1851), *Childe Harold's Pilgrimage: Italy* (exh. 1832). The different forms of art became closely bound together in the Romantic period. Lord Byron's poem *Childe Harold's Pilgrimage* inspired not only this painting by Turner but also Hector Berlioz's symphony *Harold en Italie* two years later. To all three artists Italy represented not primarily the repository of the classical artistic tradition but a source of Romantic inspiration in its scenery and people. Turner actually exhibited his work with this quotation from Byron:

... and now, fair Italy!
Thou art the garden of the world, the home
Of all Art yields, and Nature can decree;
Even in thy desert, what is like to thee?
Thy very weeds are beautiful, thy waste
More rich than other climes' fertility:
Thy wreck a glory, and thy ruin graced
With an immaculate charm which cannot be defaced.

(Tate Gallery/Art Resource)

✜ *Plate 9*

Claude Monet, *Rouen Cathedral* (1894). This is only one of a series of paintings Monet made of this cathedral's facade in various different types of light at different times of day and night. The impressionist painters were more interested in the sensual impact of light on the eye than in accuracy of detail. Monet's depiction of the cathedral at Rouen obviously does not attempt to help the viewer perceive the symbolic structure or sculptural and decorative elements of the Gothic architecture. Impressionist composers took a similar approach to the sense of hearing.

(Metropolitan Museum of Art, Bequest of Theodore M. Davis, 1915. Theodore M. Davis Collection [30.95.250])

✧ *Plate 10*
Paul Gauguin (1848–1903), *Day of the Gods (Mahana no Atua)* (1894). Gauguin was a leader among the artists at the turn of the century who sought a revitalization of the arts by way of primitivism, as an antidote to the excessive sophistication of the late Romantic and post-Romantic styles. This painting communicates the feeling of a South Pacific culture for its nature gods, while the technique of painting with sharply outlined, flat areas and primary colors gave a simpler and more striking sort of expression than the styles against which Gauguin rebelled. *(oil on canvas, 68.3 x 91.5 cm, Helen Birch Bartlett Memorial Collection, 1926.198. © 1989. The Art Institute of Chicago. All rights reserved.)*

✧ *Plate 11*
Vassily Kandinsky (1866–1944), *Fugue* (1910). Expressionism in painting employed clashing colors that jarred the viewer's sense of sight, and undecipherable shapes that frustrated the rational mind. The abstractness and yet force of expression that resulted led Kandinsky to adopt musical titles for a number of his works, as in this case.
(Solomon R. Guggenheim Museum, New York; Photograph by David Heald)

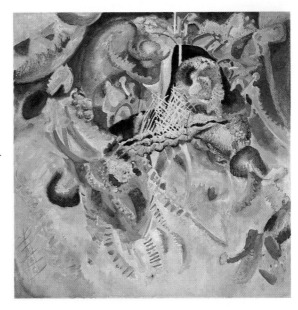

❖ *Plate 12*
Arnold Schoenberg (1874–
1951), *Red Gaze* (1910). In
addition to composing,
Schoenberg was an accom-
plished painter in the
expressionistic style. *Red
Gaze* presents the haunted
face of a psychotically
disturbed personality,
producing the same sort of
effect as did expressionist
music.
*(Municipal Gallery, Lenbachhaus,
Munich)*

❖ *Plate 13*
Pablo Picasso (1881–1973), *Three Musicians* (1921). Artistic objectivity in painting
led to cubism, in which shapes were resolved into simple geometrical figures. This
painting also evokes the artistic past, but in an entirely new way; as in many of
Watteau's paintings from the eighteenth century, the three musicians wear stock
commedia dell'arte costumes—here those of Pierrot, Harlequin, and Domino.
(oil on canvas, 6'7" x 7'3 3/4". Collection, Museum of Modern Art, New York. Mrs. Simon Guggenheim Fund)

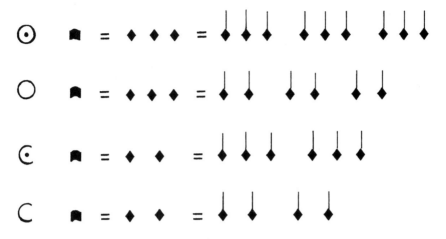

Figure 6.1
The system of mensural notation, showing signatures and the rhythmic combinations each indicates.

Isorhythm

The persistence of delight in numerical combinations that we have already noted in our discussion is evidenced by an elaborate organizational process that was applied to the motet and motetlike compositions in the fourteenth century: the device of *isorhythm* (from the Greek prefix *iso,* meaning "the same"). This term applies to the technique by which a line of polyphonic music, usually the tenor, is organized by serial repetitions of a pattern of rhythmic values. Motet tenors during the thirteenth century had, as discussed earlier, used repetitive ordo rhythms, creating short, reiterated rhythmic figures. We have also observed composers extending tenor melodies borrowed from the chant by simple repetition.

In the ars nova, new complexities were explored. The durational values of the tenor part were laid out in several repetitions of a single, often quite extensive statement called the *talea* (cognate with our word *tally,* meaning "count"). The pitch content could also be set out as several repetitions of a melodic pattern called *color.* The talea and color might have different numbers of units, thereby demonstrating mathematical relationships in sound. For example, Vitry's motet "Garrit gallus/In nova fert/Neuma" has a tenor of seventy-two notes, with a talea of twelve durations and a color of thirty-six pitches. In the piece the talea is stated six times and the color twice. The tenor of the second half of the motet is thus identical to that of the first half.

All kinds of symbolic number relationships could be contrived. Naturally such mathematical subtleties might not be evident to the uninitiated listener; the performer of the tenor, of course, would soon become aware of the talea as he counted the rhythm of his part. The intricate musical structure was not intended to be obvious but was an expression of the composer's love of, and skill in handling, proportion and order. On an abstract and perhaps subconscious level, the isorhythm would give unity and coherence to a large musical construction.

The Roman de Fauvel

A major source of ars nova motets (and for some earlier music as well) is a satirical compilation of music and poetry, the *Roman de Fauvel* (ca. 1316), put together by the poet Gervais de Bus. The *Roman de Fauvel* comprises a series of stories about an imaginary horse or ass named Fauvel; the name is an acrostic derived from the initial letters of the six vices—Flattery, Avarice, Villainy, Variability, Envy, Lasciviousness. (Fig. 6.2) The text mocks many of the evils and hypocrisies of the fourteenth century, not sparing the clergy or the political powers. To say that the texts are irreverent would be an immense understatement; no holds are barred. The extent of disrespect to which the church is subjected indicates the depths to which it had fallen, but the nobility fares little better. (In an altered form, the name of Fauvel survives today in the English expression "to curry favor." The French phrase *étriller Fauvel*—"to curry Fauvel"—and the old English *currayen Favel* became popular expressions to describe seeking gain by hypocritical flattery.)

The *Roman de Fauvel* comprises over three thousand lines of French poetry, and interpolated among them is a variety of Latin and French music. There are monophonic pieces, including Latin liturgical chant, sequences, and conductus, and French trouvère-style and more popular songs. In addition, there are thirty-four motets with Latin, French, or mixed texts, in a variety of styles. They range from the earliest ars antiqua motet type in two voices through contemporary styles, with twenty-three three-voice and even one four-part piece. Several of more advanced pieces are attributed to Philippe de Vitry himself. Thus the *Roman de Fauvel* constitutes a representative musical anthology of polyphonic styles from an entire century or more.

Form in Secular Song

The composers of the fourteenth century wrote many polyphonic love songs, extending the tradition of the troubadours and trouvères. Since they did not

Figure 6.2
A page from the *Roman de Fauvel*. Masked revelers are shown
here playing drums, vielle, and cymbals. (*Bibliothèque
nationale, Paris*)

employ cantus firmi but freely composed all the voices, they developed the
structural procedures of their predecessors to create several standardized designs, known in French as *formes fixes* (fixed forms). The three main formes
fixes are all based on stanzas having the simple musical plan *aab*. A second
common characteristic was the additional presence of a refrain, for which both
text and music were unaltered at each appearance.

The most easily explained of the formes fixes, that of the *ballade,* simply
consisted of stanzas in aab form and a recurring refrain. Thus, indicating the
refrain by the letter C (the use of the capital letter shows that the words as well
as the music return in the refrain), the musical form of a three-stanza ballade
would be outlined

a a b C a a b C a a b C.

Another popular form was the *virelai*. Unlike the ballade, the virelai began with a statement of the refrain (A), and it employed the same music for the refrain as for the end of each stanza (a). As a result, a virelai in three stanzas took the form

A b b a A b b a A b b a A.

A bit more elaborate than the ballade and the virelai was the *rondeau*. The refrain of the rondeau was in two parts (AB) and therefore shared both of its melodic sections with the stanza. This two-part refrain preceded and followed the single stanza, and its first line also interrupted the stanza, giving the form

A B a A a b A B.

Cadence Patterns in the Fourteenth Century

We must now pick up a thread we first discovered in the music of the ars antiqua, the development of the cadence. The 6-8 (or 3-1) and the $^{6-8}_{3-5}$ cadences continued to be used in the fourteenth century, but with new characteristics (Ex. 6.1). Composers had discovered the effect of the half-step, leading-tone motion to the final from below, which gave a much stronger cadential feeling than the modal whole steps from the lower seventh scale degree. Thus, where the seventh note of the mode lay a whole tone below the final, it was raised chromatically to produce a leading tone. This was particularly true of the modes with finals d and g; the f modes naturally have a leading tone, while the situation in the e modes is complicated by the occurrence of a half step above the final. In some cases the penultimate tone at the cadence in the inner part of a three-voice cadence was also sharped, producing a "double leading tone" cadence.

These chromatic alterations were not necessarily notated but could be applied by performers according to convention. Such adjustments were known as *musica ficta*. Musica ficta was also applied in other situations, to avoid melodic and harmonic tritones, for example. Modern editors of medieval music commonly indicate the appropriate places for such alterations by placing accidentals above the notes.

The cadence was also commonly ornamented in the top line by a step down from the leading tone to the tone below and then a skip to the resolution on the final note. The best term for this type of cadence is *escape-tone* cadence. (It is sometimes called a Landini cadence after the Italian composer Francesco Landini, but this is misleading both because many composers used this ornament and because Landini himself did not do so consistently.)

Example 6.1

Development of the cadence.

a. Addition of leading tone to cadence in three voices

b. Double-leading-tone cadence

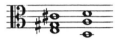

c. Escape-tone cadence

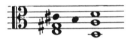

Guillaume de Machaut

The greatest composer of the ars nova was Guillaume de Machaut (ca. 1300–1377). Like Vitry, he worked as secretary to a king, in Machaut's case King John of Bohemia, and at the end of his life held a religious position, as canon at the great Gothic cathedral at Reims. Unlike Vitry, Machaut was not a theorist, but a renowned poet. Some of his secular poetry and music seems to have been the product of a relationship Machaut had while he was in his sixties with a young girl named Peronne, who was also a poet. The two wrote love letters and sent each other poetry for several years.

Machaut wrote a great deal of poetry not set to music, as well as many songs. In this sense he belongs to the trouvère tradition, and he demonstrated his genius in masterfully constructed monophonic and polyphonic songs in the formes fixes.

Machaut composed twenty-three motets, all for three parts. These set both Latin and French texts, and they treat both sacred and secular topics. They were often quite elaborate in design and ingenious in the use of isorhythm. Unlike the polyphonic ballades, rondeaux, and virelais, therefore, the motets seem to have been intended for an elite audience; they show Machaut as a composer's composer.

Machaut's most famous composition is his Mass known as the *Messe de Notre Dame*. It is the earliest surviving setting of the complete polyphonic Mass Ordinary by a single composer. Earlier examples exist of paired Mass Ordinary movements, such as Kyries and Glorias, and of composite Masses;

but the Machaut Mass stands alone in the fourteenth century as a unified multimovement whole, and it is also the longest Mass cycle of the period. The *Messe de Notre Dame* is partly of the type called a *plainsong Mass;* except for its Gloria and Credo, Machaut used a chant melody of an appropriate liturgical movement as tenor for each polyphonic movement.

One immediately notable feature of Machaut's Mass is its density. It is scored in four voices rather than the more common three. This can also be observed in his secular works. The new part is a *contratenor,* occupying the same general range as the tenor. Tenor and contratenor interact; they often cross and also have complicated musical relationships.

The shorter texts of the Mass Ordinary—Kyrie, Sanctus, Agnus Dei, and the closing formula Ite, missa est—are set in motet style, with faster-moving duplum and triplum over steadier tenor and contratenor. Machaut employed isorhythm in a number of passages in these movements, often in quite elaborate fashion and sometimes in all four parts at once. The longer texts of the Gloria and Credo are, for practical reasons, simpler and more nearly homorhythmic.

Machaut was a remarkable figure, and he holds a place of honor as high in the history of literature as in that of music. His significance to our understanding of the musical situation in the fourteenth century lies in the range of his compositions. Because he worked with equal ease and success in both sacred and secular styles, he stands as an excellent representative of the balance and tension that existed between the sacred and secular sides of life in his time.

Mannerism: The Ars Subtilior

French music in the late fourteenth century explored, or rather exploited, the possibilities of ars nova technique to their limits. Musical grace became of secondary importance to elaboration and intricacy. Thus the style, called *ars subtilior* (more subtle art), represents a stage characterized by the term *mannerism.* Mannerism is a recurring phenomenon in the history of music (as well as of other arts). The phenomenon occurs toward the end of the life span of a style when creative artists seem to have attained such great facility with the techniques of the style that indulgence of technique becomes an end in itself.

One manifestation of mannerism in the fourteenth century was the exploitation of the notational possibilities of the mensural system. Composers used every device of the new art to work out what would be the most complex rhythmic relationships between voices in polyphonic texture prior to the twentieth century. In extreme cases the music becomes very difficult to perform, and the proportions are almost impossible to hear. In certain cases the rhythmic notation, with its circles and semicircles, dots and lines, various note shapes, and contrasting ink colors, seems to have been as important visually as aurally. Music was notated on staves drawn in concentric circles, and in one famous case in the shape of a heart (Baude Cordier's "Belle bonne," a love song, of course). (Plate 2)

At the same time, composers tested the limits of chromatic harmony and dissonance. By the end of the century the old modal vocabulary of eight pitch classes (counting the alternative b natural and b flat) had expanded to include the other pitches of the chromatic scale. As long as the music reached an ultimate perfect consonance, composers could try almost any amount of intervening dissonance. The imperfect consonance of the major third functioned as a tolerable temporary sonority for use on rhythmically strong beats, although its acceptance at final cadences remained more than a century in the future.

The Italian Trecento

Polyphony got a late start in Italy. It arose quite suddenly in a relatively sophisticated form in the fourteenth century, or *trecento* as the Italians call it. There had been no practice of composed organum in sacred music to establish a foundation in Italy for the kinds of developments that took place in France. When polyphonic composition did finally appear, it remained generally within the secular sphere. Characteristic of Italian music in the trecento, as in the rest of music history, its grace resides primarily in melody, which, though often elaborate, constantly maintains its vocal character. Italian composers of the trecento did not indulge in either the rhythmic intricacies or the harmonic contortions of their French contemporaries. The greatest of them was Francesco Landini (ca. 1325–1397), a blind organist and song-writer, praised in the literary works of his contemporaries, including Boccaccio.

Italian trecento music is represented in a beautiful manuscript known as the *Squarcialupi Codex*. This elegant anthology, prepared in the fifteenth century, is not always completely accurate in its musical text, but it preserves over 350 of what its compiler must have considered the best or most representative music of the trecento.

One of the leading forms in this repertoire was the *madrigal,* which must not be confused with the more familiar Renaissance madrigal. Trecento madrigal poetry dealt with pastoral or amorous topics and was organized into two or three stanzas of three lines each, plus a refrain or *ritornello* (from the Italian word for "return") of two lines, often in a contrasting meter. This produced a musical structure comparable to that of the ballade in France or the Bar in Germany, though less sophisticated. The madrigal was set in a texture of two voices without a tenor, both parts carrying the same text and sometimes interacting in question-and-answer style or hocket, or even in momentary passages of imitation.

A second common form, the *ballata,* developed later than the madrigal and differs from it in both texture and form. The ballata was scored in three lines, a relatively elaborate vocal melody above two lower parts, tenor and contratenor, that moved in somewhat slower rhythm and may have been played on instruments. This texture is sometimes known as *cantilena.* The form of the ballata shows the influence of the French formes fixes. It consists of a two-line refrain called *ripresa,* a verse made up of two *piedi* of two lines each and a *volta* using the same music as the ripresa, followed by the return of the ripresa. The ballata form might be outlined thus:

ripresa	piedi	volta	ripresa
A B	c d c d	a b	A B

It resembles (unfortunately for modern students) the French virelai.

Another popular type of song was the *caccia.* The Italian word means "chase" or "hunt," and the texts portrayed the outdoor life in realistic fashion. The texture involved two equal voices and a lower part in slower motion. Often the vocal lines depicted the sounds of the hunt with onomatopoeic syllables and appropriate musical gestures. The name of the genre also had a punning meaning, for the upper parts were constructed in canon so that the second voice actually "chases" the first through the piece. In France a similar composition was known as *chace,* and the English later used the term *catch* for a popular type of song. The thoroughgoing polyphonic imitation in the caccia presented a new problem for the composer: Instead of composing the voices successively above the tenor, as had always been the case in cantus-firmus style polyphony, one had to construct the imitative lines simultaneously in order to prevent harmonic disaster. Naturally the lowest voice would then have to be written last rather than first. The tenor, born from the authority of the music of the church, could no longer be conceived as the fundamental and most important voice in the texture; it had become merely an accompaniment to the vocal melody above.

The rapid growth of secular culture in Italy that we mentioned earlier in discussing the literary works of Petrarch and Boccaccio was thus paralleled in music. By the sixteenth century Italy would become the center of European musical culture. First, however, a general upheaval, already begun in the fourteenth century, completely reshaped the careers and the ideas of artists and musicians and, indeed, created one of the great divides in the history of Western culture.

English Polyphony

Before leaving the fourteenth century, we must take note of some peculiarities of polyphony in England during this period. The English had adopted French styles in the thirteenth century; indeed, one of the great sources of the Notre Dame repertoire, the manuscript *W1*, came from St. Andrews in Scotland. The genres of conductus and motet are represented among the "Worcester fragments" (so named because this type of composition seems to have been centered in Worcester), which date from the thirteenth and fourteenth centuries.

Another genre appearing in the Worcester fragments, the *rondellus*, exploits the principle of voice exchange as the basis for somewhat extended compositions. We have already encountered the use of voice exchange in Notre Dame organa of the Perotin style, but the technique became especially developed in England. In the rondellus, all the parts have the same material, but segments of this material are presented in different orders in the various voices, so that each idea is passed around among them. There might also be an independent bottom line consisting of a repeated phrase called *pes* (Latin for "foot").

Gymel and English Discant

English musical style differed from continental music in its use of simple rhythms and homorhythmic texture, a taste for the imperfect consonances of the third and sixth, and reticence about the free use of dissonance. These tendencies were exploited in two special types of polyphonic singing used in England in the late Middle Ages. The simpler of these was *gymel*, in which an improvised second voice was expanded from an existing part in the course of a polyphonic composition, usually (at least in earlier examples) requiring the other polyphonic parts to drop out. (The improvisation required singers to employ the technique of "sighting," in which they mentally visualized their notes on the staff with the notated line.) The other type of English polyphonic singing, which was known as *English discant*, employed three voices in predominantly homorhythmic texture. In English discant the cantus firmus characteristically lies in the middle voice; the counter, which runs below it, may form octaves, sixths, fifths, thirds, and unisons with it; the third voice rides above the cantus firmus and has a tendency to parallel it at the fourth. An unusual but characteristically English sound results when the cantus firmus in the middle is paralleled by the counter at the lower third and the upper voice at the fourth, producing consecutive $^6_3$ sonorities. In such contexts, the imperfect intervals no longer seem merely subsidiary to perfect ones but are clearly valued for their full sonority.

Secular Music: Rota

Little strictly secular music has survived from England in the fourteenth century. The most remarkable example is the famous *rota* "Sumer is icumen in." The rota resembles the rondellus, except that instead of beginning together the upper voices have staggered entrances, producing canonic imitation. "Sumer is icumen in" contains four canonic upper lines and two bottom lines that relate by voice exchange. The resulting polyphonic construct is extremely sophisticated for its time (perhaps as early as the end of the thirteenth century). It is also noteworthy for the constant presence of thirds in its harmonic structure, which gives it a strikingly advanced sound.

The English predilections for straightforward, easily followed rhythms and for the richness of the imperfect consonances reveal a musical aesthetic based more on empirical, sensual values than on symbolic, intellectual principles. This would have considerable influence on the future of music throughout Europe.

Questions for Reflection

✣   What advantages did Vitry's rhythmic notation system have over the system that preceded it? What advantages might it have over that used for the music of the period of common practice?

✣   In the perspective of their careers in general, what place did music have in the lives of Philippe de Vitry and Guillaume de Machaut?

✣   How did the music and musical thinking of the fourteenth century challenge traditional assumptions about music? In general what ideas did it threaten?

✣   What individual traits of music in France, Italy, and England in the fourteenth century reflected national tastes or cultural tendencies that extend through the history of those nations beyond that century?

Suggestions for Further Reading

For the treatise *Ars nova,* see the translation by Leon Plantinga in *Journal of Music Theory* 5 (1961), 204–223. Other fourteenth-century treatises, including the discussions of the new notation in France by Jean de Muris and of the somewhat different Italian system by Marchetto da Padua, as well as the conservative attack on the new notation by Jacob of Liège, are excerpted in Strunk, *Source Readings in Music History* (New York: Norton, 1950).

Gilbert Reaney, *Guillaume de Machaut* (London: Oxford University Press, 1971) is a good biography of this important composer.

7

THE RISE OF THE RENAISSANCE

Renaissance Humanism

The increasing secularization of culture in the fourteenth century produced the movement we know as the Renaissance. In contrast to the Middle Ages, the Renaissance freed the imagination from authority, specifically from the dogma of the church. There arose a new conviction that solutions to problems and the achievement of personal fulfillment could come from human intellect and effort rather than only from divine revelation or grace. This new movement is referred to as *humanism*.

By the fifteenth century the role and power of the church had declined sharply. Even after the Council of Constance had mended the Great Schism in 1417, the church never entirely regained its authority, although it staved off the inevitable crisis of the Reformation for another century. Despite its continued political and economic importance, it had lost its domination over the manner of thinking in Western culture; the period of reliance on ecclesiastically sanctioned authority for understanding had come to an end.

No longer satisfied to build their ideas on the foundation of scripture and the authority of the church, the humanist artists and thinkers of the fourteenth and fifteenth centuries returned to the pre-Christian civilization of Greek and Roman antiquity for models and for confirmation that a European culture need not depend on the Christian religion. Petrarch, for example, actively sought out and rediscovered important documents of the classical philosophers and writers. Many ancient treatises were published and circulated in translation. Sculptors and architects modeled their work on the statues and temples of Greece and Rome. In this sense, the humanist movement could justifiably be considered a "renaissance," or rebirth of classic culture, in relation to which the intervening period seemed a "middle" or "dark" age.

Especially influential was the reemergence in the fifteenth century of the works of Plato. As we noted in discussing Gothic thought and the scholastics, Plato had been eclipsed in the twelfth and thirteenth centuries by Aristotle. But with the patronage of the Medici family, who ruled the city of Florence, Marsilio Ficino (1433–1499) translated all of Plato's works into Latin, and they were avidly studied throughout Europe. The pursuit of a higher Reality, a goal clearly derived from Plato's thought, became an important quest for the Renaissance. But this higher Reality was to be pursued outside the divine revelation of Christianity, within humankind itself. Pico della Mirandola (1463–1494), another Florentine, penned an "Oration on the Dignity of Man," citing in his argument for a view of humanity as a great miracle not only Judeo-Christian scripture but also ancient classical and Arabic sources. The purpose of philosophy and art for the Renaissance humanists no longer consisted in winning salvation after death, but in *virtù*, personal success and honor achieved through the cultivation of one's own talents and personal fulfillment in this life. In 1434 the architect Leon Battista Alberti (1404–1472) wrote, addressing the young men of his family,

> But if anyone wants to investigate diligently what most exalts and increases families and what maintains them at a high level of honor and of happiness, he will clearly perceive that men most often bring about each of their own good conditions and each of their bad ones; nor, indeed, will he attribute to any material thing such power that he would ever judge *virtù* to be worth less than fortune when it comes to gaining praises, greatness, and fame.

In consequence of this belief that persons are the masters of their own fate, there grew up a new and pervasive optimism about mankind itself.

As the times changed, people began to take a new view of the world. Empiricism replaced authority, and firsthand observation became the principle of knowledge and art. As a result, long-held beliefs about the nature of earth and heaven collapsed. Christopher Columbus's conviction that the earth was round so overpowered the received assumption that one could fall off the edge that he staked his life on it in the attempt to establish a new route to the Orient. The astronomical observations of Copernicus (1473–1543) shattered the crystalline heavenly spheres in which the stars and planets had been supposed to rotate about the earth.

The humanist artists also looked at their world in an entirely new way. Instead of seeing things as symbolic of divine order, and objects as material for glorification of the house and word of God, they viewed the world as they experienced it. In the fourteenth century the visual arts had already become more realistic. The fourteenth-century Italian painters, particularly Giotto di Bondone, learned to give their figures shape and depth. (Fig. 7.1) They began

Figure 7.1
Giotto di Bondone (ca. 1267–1337), *Madonna with the Infant Jesus, Saint, and Angels* (ca. 1305–1310). Giotto pioneered a newly realistic style of painting, giving tangible shape and texture to his figures. (*Alinari/Art Resource*)

to paint the textures of skin and clothing in a sensuous manner so that the viewer could imagine the feel of the surface.

Renaissance humanist artists also recognized the importance of an approach that relied on direct, individual observation of nature. Leonardo da Vinci (1452–1519), in his *Treatise on Painting,* wrote, since you know, painter, that you cannot be good if you are not a universal master at imitating by your art all the qualities of the forms that Nature produces—which you will not know how to do if you do not see and portray them in your mind—therefore, when you are walking through the countryside, turn your judgment to various objects, and look by turns at one thing and then another, making a selection of various such objects, culled out from those that are less good. . . .

He also stressed careful observation and accurate portrayal of people in real life:

take delight in watching studiously those who talk together with gestures of their hands. If you are personally acquainted with them, get close to them and hear what leads them to make such gestures as they do. . . . Pay attention to those who laugh and those who cry, observe those who shout with rage, and likewise all the conditions of our minds. Observe social manners and note that it is not appropriate . . . for a master to act like a servant, nor a little child like an adolescent or likewise as an old man who can barely support himself; do not make a peasant's gesture like one that should belong by custom to a nobleman, nor the strong man's like the weak one's, nor prostitutes' gestures like those of honest women, nor men's like women's.

Also new and significant in Renaissance painting was the use of proportions to reflect visual perspective rather than symbolic organization. The sizes of figures in medieval art had established their hierarchical rankings, and the persons depicted did not necessarily seem to relate to one another in actual space, but people in Renaissance paintings began to relate as equals even though they appeared for the moment in different planes. Settings provided realistic contexts for figures, rather than extraneous ornament. Balance and symmetry of planning, not an ecclesiastically grounded cosmology, now fulfilled the artist's human urge to create order.

Perhaps most influential of all for music, the Renaissance produced a new interest in literature, for in writing one might find a means of self-expression. This meant the elevation of the trivium in the educational system from its former modest position as the first and most elementary part of schooling (grammar school) to a position of honor. Responding to the demand for more and more copies of books, in the 1450s Johannes Gutenberg (ca. 1395–1468) developed the technique of printing from movable type. The Venetian printer Aldus Manutius (1449–1515) produced editions of the Greek and Latin philosophers, poets, and dramatists, as well as of the great Italian literature. The spread of literature increased the rate of literacy and, in turn, the possibility for original thought in response to what had been written in the past. Literature became closer to music; the modern conception of music as belonging to the same class of endeavors as literature (the humanities) has its roots here. As we shall see, musicians became deeply committed to words as the new basis for musical composition.

The Hundred Years' War and English Music on the Continent

In 1337 King Edward III of England asserted his claim to the French throne of Philip VI. This precipitated the beginning of the Hundred Years' War, which lasted from 1338 until 1453. The fighting laid waste to much of France, and even during periodic truces bands of momentarily unemployed mercenary soldiers lived off the land, pillaging farms and towns. For a number of years, much of France was actually under English control. The French finally found a rallying point in Joan of Arc, and their determination was only intensified by her capture and execution by the English in 1431. Still the war dragged on for over two decades. Such a political upheaval would not normally be conducive to a great flowering of the arts, for there was little leisure or money to spare when patrons of the muses became patrons of Mars. Yet in an unexpected way the Hundred Years' War affected the development of musical styles, for it carried musicians from one region to another, effecting a cross-fertilization that might not have occurred otherwise.

The English brought their music to France with them, and the characteristic sound of English polyphony became very popular with the continental composers. In 1441–1442 a French poet, Martin le Franc, wrote in his *Le Champion des dames* about the music of his countrymen before and after the influence of the English:

Tapissier, Carmen, Césaris
Not so long since did sing so well
That they amazed all of Paris
And everyone who there did dwell.
But their discant did not possess
A melody of such delight—
They tell me, who can bear witness—
As G. Dufay and Binchois write.

For they now have a novel way
Of making brisk, sweet combinations
In music soft, or loud and gay,
In ficta, cadences, mutations,
They have put on the countenance

Of Englishmen, like Dunstable,
So that a wondrous elegance
Makes their song glad and notable.

The "countenance of Englishmen"—le Franc uses the French phrase *contenance angloise*—must have meant the English concentration on the imperfect consonances and avoidance of dissonance, also termed *panconsonance.* These mellifluous sonorities, so totally unlike the complicated harmonies of the French mannerists of the late fourteenth century, conquered and held the ears and imaginations of the French while the English armies attained only a temporary grasp of the land.

John Dunstable

The composer John Dunstable (ca. 1390–1453) may have gone to France with the English regent in Paris, the Duke of Bedford; at least his music crossed the channel at this time. Dunstable was one of the greatest composers England has produced. He was probably educated in the great tradition of the medieval liberal arts, for he appears to have been active as a mathematician and astronomer. His great motet "Veni sancte spiritus/Veni creator spiritus" proves that he mastered the French techniques of cantus firmus composition as well as the esoteric mathematical intricacies of isorhythm and proportion. At the same time, he had such control of the harmony that even in the older style he could maintain the English panconsonant sound.

The panconsonant style must have appealed to the musicians on the continent because of the new humanist willingness to admit sensuous attractiveness as at least the equal of symbolic meaning in judging the value of music. Given time to pursue the implications of humanist ideals, the French composers might, of course, have turned in this harmonic direction on their own. As it happened, however, at the same time that Renaissance ideas filtered into France from across the Alps, English armies and their music invaded from across the channel and presented them with a sound that responded to the needs of the burgeoning cultural movement. This happy coincidence produced a quite rapid revolution, which Le Franc could aptly describe as "putting on the countenance of Englishmen."

The New Style on the Continent

The composers whom Le Franc cites as representatives of the "novel way" of composing were associated by patronage with the territory of Burgundy, which included a large area of what is now northeastern France and the Low Countries. Their style has often been called Burgundian for this reason, though their travels and the dissemination of their music also spread their ideas in France and Italy. Burgundy was ruled by dukes who were related to the French royal family but generally avoided direct involvement in the Hundred Years' War, preferring to play the English and French against one another to their own advantage. Because they did not deplete their resources in militaristic adventurism, they were able to cultivate a fabulous court, a center for music and other arts. (Fig. 7.2) The elaborate and affected styles of dress we often associate with the noble lords and ladies of fairy tales—peaked hats with veils and shoes with long, curled toes—stem from this period. At one especially lavish court banquet a huge pastry shell was presented, from which two dozen musicians played; hence came the "four-and-twenty blackbirds baked in a pie" of the nursery rhyme "Sing a song of sixpence."

But the legacy of the Burgundian dukes went far beyond fairy tales and nursery rhymes. They gathered to the protection of their court at Dijon some of the greatest artists and musicians of the fifteenth century. The Duke of Berry, brother to Duke Philip the Bold of Burgundy (r. 1364–1404), commissioned a breviary that ranks as one of the art masterpieces of the time, the so-called *Très riches heures du duc de Berry* (1413–1416), which opens with illustrations by the brothers Limbourg representing the months of the year. The miniature paintings depict scenes of everyday life in nature, using beautiful color and amazing attention to detail. The religious pictures throughout the book also incorporate everyday scenes and depict specific locations within the Burgundian territories. (Plate 3)

Guillaume Dufay

Most important of the musicians with ties to Burgundy was Guillaume Dufay (ca. 1400–1474). Dufay was a singer and churchman rather than a courtier; he was affiliated with the cathedral at Cambrai from the time he was a boy chorister. He must have been well-educated, and he certainly traveled widely. He spent considerable time in Italy, including several different periods of service as a singer in the papal choir in Rome. While in Italy he also came to know some of the great noble patrons of the arts in the Renaissance.

Sacred music is prominent in Dufay's output, but the weakening of the centripetal force of the church in the face of humanistic trends is also evident in these works. Dufay followed Dunstable, writing motets in the cantus firmus style that made use of isorhythm and mathematical proportional relationships but also employed the new sonorities of imperfect consonances. By this time four-part texture was common, and the four voices were known as *superius, contratenor altus* (or simply *altus*), *tenor,* and *contratenor bassus* (or *bassus*), Latin versions of the Italian terms we still use. The addition of the contratenor bassus below the fixed tenor was a great advantage to composers, for it allowed freedom to create harmonic sonorities from the lowest voice up. The

Figure 7.2
Among the artistic leisure pursuits of the fifteenth-century aristocracy was tapestry weaving. This section of a three-part tapestry from Chaumont shows cornetti, a portative organ, harp, lute, and singers. *(Cleveland Museum of Art, Gift from Various Donors by Exchange, 60.176)*

symbolic value of the cantus firmus as a foundation gave way to the desire for appealing vertical sounds.

One of Dufay's masterpieces in the fifteenth-century manner of handling the medieval motet framework is the magnificent motet "Nuper rosarum flores/Terribilis est locus iste," composed for the dedication of the dome of the cathedral in Florence. (Fig. 7.3) Dufay's motet tenor is laid out in four isorhythmic segments with mensural changes at each statement, in the proportions 6:4:2:3, which may have been intended to correspond to the proportions used in the architectural dimensions of Brunelleschi's dome. The use of a chant tenor (taken from the Mass for the Dedication of a Church) and the use of isorhythmic technique look backward to the Middle Ages. The harmonic language, based on the pervasive sound of thirds, is progressive.

Another new style in church music that also shows the increasing independence from medieval cantus firmus polyphony is the use of a paraphrased

Figure 7.3
The great Cathedral of Santa Maria del Fiore in Florence was begun in 1294, but the late thirteenth-century builders of the body of the cathedral had left unsolved the problem of constructing the unprecedentedly huge dome that had been called for. The brilliant architect Filippo Brunelleschi (1377– 1446) solved this problem with great ingenuity, and the construction was completed in 1436. Guillaume Dufay's motet "Nuper rosarum flores/ Terribilis est locus iste," for the cathedral's dedication, employs in its music proportions resembling those of the architectural design. (*Alinari/Art Resource*)

chant melody as the top voice in a polyphonic setting. In this type of piece the chant is handled freely, often with added notes to grace the simple, existing line. Two lower parts, moving in slower rhythm than the upper melody, but both at approximately the same pace, accompany the top voice. The distinction in style between these accompanying parts and the melody in the top voice suggests performance of the lower lines by instruments. The texture is that of the cantilena style used in the secular Italian music of the preceding century. Humanism had obviously made subtle inroads into even the sacred repertoire.

The composers of the so-called Burgundian school, including Dufay, also adapted the principle of English discant, but they now placed the chant in the topmost line. The method was to transpose the cantus to a relatively high pitch and arrange a bottom voice to accompany it in sixths and, at cadences especially, at the octave. A middle voice would simply be improvised by singing from the chant line but a fourth lower, so that the whole texture produced a polyphonic succession of $\frac{6}{3}$ and $\frac{8}{5}$ verticalities. The technique was called *fauxbourdon* (false bass). Pure homorhythm could be varied by giving the lowest voice a certain degree of independence, and the chant melodies were commonly paraphrased in a subtle fashion. Fauxbourdon verses were often used in alternation with chanted verses of hymns to provide variety; this manner of performance is known as *alternatim.*

The gradual veering away from the ecclesiastical authority of liturgical practice and the creation of a purely man-made order is further evidenced in the *cantus firmus Mass.* Unlike the plainsong Mass of Machaut, Masses in the fifteenth century began to rely on a single cantus firmus for all their movements. This undermined the liturgical integrity of the Mass in favor of purely musical unity. Sometimes the cantus firmus for all the movements was taken from some ecclesiastical melody, but Dufay realized that once the liturgy had been abandoned there was no absolute need for a sacred cantus firmus, and he thus employed secular tunes. He wrote one of his most famous Masses on the tenor of his own secular chanson "Se la face ay pale" (If I have a pale face). Another unifying device Dufay employed was to begin all the movements of the Mass with the same opening idea, a *motto* or *head motive.*

Dufay wrote fine secular music as well as sacred. Among these works are chansons in the traditional formes fixes and cantilena texture. Often there are extensive untexted, virtuosic passages in the melodic top voice, which suggests the use of instruments along with the singer, as well as in the lower voices. The forms are often more expansive than those of the earlier composers, for the sections tend to have several poetic lines each. What is really new about them, however, as in Dufay's sacred works, is their harmony, which exploits the imperfect consonances.

Gilles Binchois

The Binchois mentioned by Martin le Franc was Dufay's contemporary Gilles Binchois (ca. 1400–1460). Unlike Dufay, Binchois was not a cleric (Fig. 7.4), and he naturally left relatively little sacred music. He was, in fact, a soldier, as well as a singer in the Burgundian ducal court. His chansons are particularly noteworthy for the gracefulness of their melodies.

Polyphonic Cadences

One stylistic move that would have important effects later in the history of music was experimentation with the polyphonic cadence. The $\frac{6}{3}\text{-}\frac{8}{5}$ cadence was still common, but during this time composers also tried other possibili-

Figure 7.4
Guillaume Dufay and Gilles Binchois, portrayed in a manuscript of *Le Champion des dames,* in which they are praised by Martin le Franc as the finest composers of the new fifteenth-century style. Dufay is depicted in ecclesiastical robes with an organ, while Binchois, who excelled in secular music, is dressed as a courtier and has a harp. (*Bibliothèque nationale, Paris*)

ties. The harmonic combination of the second and seventh degrees of the mode in the penultimate harmony could be brought into closer correspondence with the lower partials in the overtone series, and thereby made to sound particularly attractive, by placing a bass note a fifth below the second degree (i. e., a major third or tenth below the raised seventh). This produced a $\frac{5}{3}$ verticality just before the second and seventh opened out to the octave on the final (Ex. 7.1a). In three voices this presented the problem of what to do with the bass voice on the last note, and one solution was to carry it up an octave to make the fifth of the concluding $\frac{8}{5}$ harmony. This is sometimes called the *octave-leap cadence* (Ex. 7.1b).

Example 7.1

Development of the cadence.

a. Addition of bass tone to major sixth before cadence

b. Octave-leap cadence

c. Authentic cadence in four parts

The bass could, of course, also rise a fourth or fall a fifth to the final as the stepwise upper parts moved outward, tripling the final at the cadence. This bass motion was more likely to occur, however, in a four-part setting, where the altus now commonly sustained the fifth of the mode in both cadential harmonies, and, of course, the final harmony still contained only perfect intervals, that is, octaves and fifths (Ex. 7.1c). It will easily be seen that what thus evolved from the old two-part contrapuntal cadence is the authentic cadence in four voices. It must not be overlooked, however, that the two basic cadential voices continuously maintained their dominance over the feeling of cadence throughout the thirteenth, fourteenth, and fifteenth centuries. Good voice leading at cadences continued to rely on this procedure until the twentieth century.

This period of Burgundian leadership was a transitional one, but it was extremely important in the history of Western music. During a period of turmoil in France, Burgundy was in a position to provide the nexus for interaction among French advanced compositional technique, English sonoral beauty, and Italian humanism. No longer truly medieval nor yet part of the mature Renaissance, early fifteenth-century polyphony provides an outstanding example of how music history incorporates both the interaction of music with general political and cultural history and the progress of purely musical ideas.

Questions for Reflection

❖   Why was the cultural division between the Middle Ages and the Renaissance greater than any other break between historical periods since the beginning of the Christian era?

❖   How did the travels of important individual musicians affect the history of music in the fifteenth century?

❖   How did the aesthetic meaning and musical function of the cantus firmus in polyphony differ in the Renaissance from its meaning and role in the music of the Middle Ages?

Suggestions for Further Reading

For an overview of the Renaissance, see Friedrich Blume, *Renaissance and Baroque Music* (New York: Norton, 1967). A historical survey can be found in Howard M. Brown, *Music in the Renaissance* (Englewood Cliffs, N. J.: Prentice-Hall, 1976). More detailed is Gustave Reese, *Music in the Renaissance* (New York: Norton, 1959).

Excellent studies of individual composers are Margaret Bent, *Dunstaple* (London: Oxford University Press, 1980), and David Fallows, *Dufay* (London: Dent, 1982).

8

THE HIGH
RENAISSANCE

The Growth of the Renaissance
Musical Style in the North

While the composers of the period of Burgundian leadership planted the seeds of a new musical style for the Renaissance, the growth of the style to its maturity belongs to the northwestern region of Europe that comprises modern Belgium, Luxembourg, the Netherlands, and part of northern France. When it was no longer a battleground for French and English armies after 1453, this region was better able to cultivate the arts. By the end of the fifteenth century composers from this region dominated musical style all over Europe, and their leadership lasted until well into the sixteenth century. These composers may be grouped together as a Franco-Netherlands school, though, of course, their music manifests a variety of local and personal traits.

Johannes Ockeghem

The musical patriarch of these composers was Johannes Ockeghem (ca. 1420–1496), a singer, composer, and director at the royal court in Paris. He had been a student of Dufay and possibly also of Binchois, and his own pupils and imitators were legion.

Ockeghem often followed the tradition of cantus firmus composition, particularly in some of his Masses. His motets sometimes also employed paraphrased chant material in the upper voices. The chansons, of which we have about twenty, frequently rely on the formes fixes.

Ockeghem's fascination with the arcane aspects of compositional technique can be observed in his use of *canon*. In this case the term does

107

not mean a roundlike composition, as it generally does today, but goes back to its original denotation and simply means a rule or instruction for realizing several parts out of only one that is notated. Such an instruction might produce contrapuntal imitation, but that was only one of the aspects of the canon in the middle and late fifteenth century. For example, the canon could tell the performer to sing a given line backward at the same time it was sung forward (*per motu contrario*, "by contrary motion"; also called *cancrizans*, "crab motion"), to omit rests in the derived part, or to use rhythmic augmentation or diminution. The only limit on the possibilities was the ingenuity of the composer. Ockeghem's masterpiece of canonic writing is his *Missa prolationum,* in which the voices sing the same melodic material under different mensural signatures. Often the canons were given as verbal conundrums, so that the performer would have to puzzle out the riddle first and then solve the musical problem. This sort of musical game playing fulfilled the natural desire for intellectual challenge in a new way that superseded the medieval reliance on isorhythmic treatment of a given tenor.

In his more forward looking pieces Ockeghem abandoned preexisting material and conventional forms in favor of a freer, more empirical technique. This had been tentatively tried by some of his predecessors, but through his efforts it grew into the style of the future. Particularly in motets Ockeghem used a texture of four or five voices, all employing essentially the same melodic style; there is little attempt to relate the contrapuntal lines to each other. The voices all sing the same text, presenting it one grammatical phrase at a time, so that the result is a through-composed structure. The risk in this style is lack of coherence either in textural or formal terms. Musical unity arises from the grammatical sense of the words, of course, and from the long, flowing melodic writing that elides one phrase section into another so that choppiness is always avoided. Typical for this composer is the use of dense scoring in a relatively low register. (Ockeghem himself was a bass.) The somber thickness of the sound combines with the seamless, continuous flow of the lines to give the music a character that some listeners describe as mystical.

Jacob Obrecht

Younger than Ockeghem and more progressive in compositional style was Jacob Obrecht (1452–1505). In several respects Obrecht's works are typically clearer for the listener than Ockeghem's. For one thing, the textures in his music are more transparent, partly because there are frequently passages where not all the available voices sing at once, and partly because they do not concentrate as much on the low registers. The melodic lines are more sharply defined; the phrases are more strongly directed and lead to more frequent cadences. As a consequence the structural sections are shorter and more easily grasped. Obrecht also integrated the lines with each other by occasional passages in which a gesture introduced in one voice is then imitated in another. Each of these style traits became characteristic of the music of the High Renaissance in general.

Josquin des Prez and the Ars Perfecta

The greatest of Ockeghem's successors, and one of the greatest composers in Western music, was Josquin des Prez (ca. 1440–1521). A native of northern France, Josquin traveled to Italy, and, like Dufay, entered the most elevated circles of Italian Renaissance culture. The cities in which he worked included Milan, where he was a member of the cathedral choir and later served the powerful Sforza family; Rome, where he sang in the papal choir; and Ferrara, where he became *maestro di cappella* (music director) to the Este family. Between the periods of work in Rome and in Ferrara, Josquin spent some time in France, probably including a term at the royal court in Paris. He spent the last years of his life in the Netherlands region, where he held a church post. His contemporaries considered Josquin the master composer of the current style. Martin Luther wrote, "Josquin is master of the notes, which must express what he desires; on the other hand, other choral composers must do what the notes dictate." His genius in music was likened to that of Michelangelo in architecture, painting, and sculpture. He was apparently a strong-willed artist, for the agent of one of his prospective patrons advised hiring Josquin's talented contemporary Heinrich Isaac (ca. 1450–1517), who was "able to get on with his colleagues better and composes new pieces more quickly." "Josquin," the agent reported, "composes better, but he does it when it suits him and not when one wishes him to."

Certainly Josquin had an unprecedented mastery of scoring and harmony. The sound ideal for the Franco-Netherlands composers was that of an unaccompanied vocal ensemble in four, five, or occasionally six or more equal parts. Josquin's compositions achieve transparency of texture by holding each voice part to a particular range. The ranges of adjacent voices relate approximately as the ambitus of corresponding authentic and plagal modes; that is, the tenor has about an octave beginning a fourth or fifth above the bottom of the bass range, the alto lies about an octave above the bass, and the soprano about an octave above the tenor. There is little crossing of parts to confuse the listener's ear.

Josquin's handling of harmony was highly polished. The imperfect consonances were accepted anywhere except at final cadences, so that the rich $\frac{5}{3}$ and $\frac{6}{3}$ sonorities were heard throughout. Equally important, dissonance was treated with great care. Dissonances were restricted to suspensions and passing tones on rhythmically weak beats.

Josquin not only achieved perfect control of these aspects of the Franco-Netherlands style but also thoroughly integrated the contrapuntal lines and matched the musical structure precisely to the text. The techniques he developed became those of the entire following century and have been called the *ars perfecta* (perfect art).

The problem of vertical coherence among the parts in polyphonic texture was solved by pervasive use of contrapuntal imitation, commonly called *fuga.* For each text phrase the composer constructed a melodic idea that could be carried through all the voice parts in turn. This *point of imitation* would conclude and give way to another. Thus the contrapuntal lines were audibly related to each other. To provide contrast for the passages in fuga, or for special emphasis, some phrases might be set homorhythmically in the manner called *familiar style,* the different voices declaiming the words simultaneously.

Each point of imitation generally concluded with some form of cadence corresponding to the punctuation of the text. Strong grammatical divisions, such as the ends of sentences, might be expressed by the authentic cadence progression and a rhythmic caesura; weaker punctuations could be handled by a more transitory conclusion, such as an incomplete cadential progression or the elision of text segments by allowing a new point of imitation to begin before the preceding one had concluded. The result of this was a sectional plan in which more and less sharp divisions were interspersed at the same rate as in spoken or written language, and this gave an overall sense of balance between continuity and articulation in form.

The importance of the text to the composer cannot be overemphasized. As we have just discussed, both the melodic ideas and the structure of the music derive from the text. Josquin stands out above his predecessors for the naturalness with which his melodic points of imitation reflect the words. Rhythm and melodic inflection in the music always respect the sound patterns of the spoken phrase. Such abuses of the text as rests between syllables of a word or at inappropriate places in the phrase are rigorously avoided. In some instances Josquin, and composers who followed his lead, also generated melodic ideas by depicting the meanings of the words—a mention of height or rising motion evoked an upward gesture in the melodic pitches, for example—but these devices are relatively subtle. Some writers in the sixteenth century referred to the thoroughgoing sensitivity to the relation between words and music as *musica reservata,* perhaps "reserved" in the sense that it was addressed to connoisseurs who would appreciate such subtleties. This area of composition gave a fruitful field for later generations.

In his Masses Josquin also provides models for compositions based on sources other than the text itself. Since the composer had to set the Ordinary of the Mass again and again, he would soon exhaust the melodic inspiration the words could provide. Thus he would look elsewhere for ideas. In some cases this meant simply taking points of imitation, as an earlier composer might have taken a cantus firmus, from the chant repertoire; this method produced the great *Missa Pange lingua,* based on the melody of Thomas Aquinas's important hymn. The two *Missae L'homme armé* are similarly contrived, but from a popular song that was also used in this way by numerous others. Somewhat more esoteric was the derivation of melodic material from solmization. The *Missa La sol fa re mi* takes its melody from a musical pun on a favorite phrase of one of Josquin's patrons (*Lascia fare mi*, Italian for "Leave it to me"). The process of *soggetto cavato* (subject carved out) could produce musical readings of any words by matching the vowels with those of the hexachord syllables; Josquin turned the name of his patron Duke Ercole of Ferrara into the Latin "Hercules dux Ferrariae" and then "carved out" the vowels to get the hexachord syllables *re ut re ut re fa mi re* to provide the subject for another Mass.

A further technique for obtaining musical material was simply to appropriate substantial sections of an existing piece, adjusting the notes, reordering segments, and making any other changes necessary to underlay the Mass text. This was called *contrafactum* (compare the word *counterfeit*) or *parody* (from the Greek prefix *para-*, meaning "akin to," and root *aeidein*, meaning "to sing"), but it did not have the modern connotation of an inferior imitation or mockery. In fact, to parody a work of another composer could be regarded as a means of paying homage to him. Josquin's *Missa D'ung aultre amer* and *Missa Malheur me bat* parody chansons by his respected predecessor Ockeghem. Naturally, when a motet or secular song was parodied to create music for a Mass, the original intimate relation between words and music disappeared. By way of compensation, the composer of the parody generally contributed increased musical complexity, perhaps by more thorough use of imitation or by the addition of one more voice part to the texture.

The Ascendancy of the Northern Style

During the last two decades of the fifteenth century and the first two of the sixteenth, composers who came from northern France and the Low Countries not only achieved the most polished manner of composition but also spread it through the whole of Europe. A typical composer's biography includes a youthful period of training in the north followed by a sojourn in Italy. In maturity the composer might rise to the peak of the profession in either of those two places or might travel still further to serve as musician to noble patrons in some other region who wished to have the best of Renaissance musical culture at their own courts. Heinrich Isaac managed to juggle a schedule that included work in Florence, where he served not only the church but also Lorenzo (the Magnificent) de Medici, and in Austria and Germany under the patronage of the Holy Roman Emperor Maximilian I. The younger composer Adrian Willaert (ca. 1490–1562) went from the Netherlands by way of a fine training at the royal court in Paris under Jean Mouton (ca. 1470–1522) to Italy, where he followed Josquin's trail to Rome, Ferrara, and Milan and then became maestro di cappella at the great Basilica of St. Mark in Venice, arguably the most prestigious directorship in sixteenth-century Europe.

The ascendancy of the northern region in music means more, however, than merely that these composers had more success and fame than those of other nations. The compositional technique practiced by Josquin's contemporaries and perfected by him came to be the basis for all the styles of the following generations through the sixteenth century. As the technique was taken over by Willaert, it was codified in turn by his pupil (also a later director at St. Mark's), the Italian Gioseffe Zarlino (1517–1590) in his treatise *Le istitutioni harmoniche* (Harmonic institutions, 1558), which became the classic composition text of the century. The strength of the northern style, which we must now call the cosmopolitan Renaissance style, can be explained on several different grounds.

In the preceding chapter we noted that the empirical appeal to the senses rather than to symbolism justified the adoption of imperfect intervals as consonances. It also caused the minimization of dissonance in a panconsonant harmonic syntax. For similarly empirical reasons, the medieval preeminence of triple rhythm, with its implication of divine perfection, steadily yielded to the more natural, "human," duple rhythms of the heartbeat, respiration, and walking.

An interesting comparison might be made between the development of perspective in painting by fifteenth-century artists and the equal-voiced texture of High Renaissance music. (Fig. 8.1) As was remarked earlier, the relative size of figures in medieval art typically indicated their comparative importance and had nothing to do with the way in which they might interact in actual space. This corresponds to the hierarchical rhythms of the cantus firmus, motetus, and triplum in a thirteenth- or fourteenth-century motet. With the rise of humanism artists no longer wished to express symbolic relations in an abstract view; they wanted to show the world from their own viewpoint. In perspective painting figures are understood to be the same size even though they appear foreshortened according to their distance from the observer. They might potentially relate to one another as equals, despite their momentary situation in different visual planes. High Renaissance equal-voiced texture adopts a comparable approach: The different voices occupy different spaces, but they are of equal value, and the listener's attention is free to hear the entire texture or to pass among them as they take up points of imitation.

We have also emphasized the importance of the text in music. Among other things, this forced the abandonment of the polytextual, cantus firmus–based, medieval type of motet, in which the texts could not be understood. From the late fifteenth century on, the term *motet* denotes a setting of a Latin, sacred (or at least serious) text other than the Ordinary of the Mass. The

Figure 8.1

The Virgin on the Throne with the Child and Two Angels, by the Flemish
painter Hans Memling (ca. 1430–1494), an approximate contemporary of
Ockeghem. The use of perspective and the view of the outdoor scene behind
the figures add to the realism and humanism of the painting. The angels in the
foreground hold a vielle and a harp. *(Scala/Art Resource)*

freedom from the cantus firmus allowed clear declamation and flexible interpretation of the words, so that the rich poetry of the Renaissance humanist writers could be fully appreciated in music. The following generations of the sixteenth century became fascinated to the point of fixation with the possibilities for relating music to literary texts and explored this relationship in a variety of facets.

Music for Social Use in the High Renaissance

Among the effects of the Renaissance on music was a rapid increase in the demand for secular repertoire. The growing power and wealth of the nobility gave them at least equal footing with that of the church for patronage of the arts. More important, the invention of an efficient method of printing had the same effect on music as it had already had on literature. The first publication of music from movable type was released by Ottaviano de Petrucci (1466–1539) of Venice in 1501. This publication, *Harmonice musices odhecaton A,* consisted of a collection of Franco-Netherlands-style chansons. (The Greek term *odhecaton* means "one hundred songs," but actually there were only ninety-six.) It is significant that the *Odhecaton,* as it is sometimes known, contained secular music. The needs of churches did not suddenly change; they could still be met by manuscript copies as they had in the past. Petrucci sensed that there was a large new market for secular part-songs, and his guess turned out to be accurate. *Odhecaton A* had to be reprinted in 1503 and 1504, and the sequels *Canti B* and *Canti C* appeared immediately. Soon other printers followed Petrucci's example, making music available to less wealthy households throughout Europe; most important among these were Pierre Attaingnant (ca. 1494–1552) in Paris and Tylman Susato (ca. 1500–1560) in Antwerp. The demand for more music for this commercial market immediately affected composers by reorienting their efforts toward secular genres. In addition, their compositional styles now had to respond to the abilities, tastes, and imaginations of a new class of singers, primarily amateurs seeking domestic amusement.

Music was regarded as so important a leisure occupation for the educated classes in the High Renaissance that one appeared uncouth if one could not participate in musical discussions and diversions. Baldassare Castiglione (1478–1529) described the ideal Italian aristocrat in *Il cortegiano* (The courtier) in 1528. He recommended that the courtier learn to sing a part in polyphonic songs, know something of string instruments, and particularly be able to sing with the accompaniment of the lute. He also stressed that this noble paragon should be so skillful that he could sing or play, as he did everything, with a certain *sprezzatura* or nonchalance that would suggest that he could toss off the most difficult tasks with careless ease. In his *A Plaine and Easie Introduction to Practicall Musicke* (1597), the English composer, theorist, and music publisher Thomas Morley (1557 or 1558–1602) began with a humorous, quasi-dramatic dialogue between two brothers (probably not noblemen but upwardly mobile members of the middle class), one of whom has been so embarrassed by his ignorance of both music theory and practice that he has resolved to study the art before he presents himself again in polite society:

> POLYMATHES: Stay, brother Philomathes, what haste? Whither go you so fast?
>
> PHILOMATHES: To seek out an old friend of mine.
>
> POL: But before you go I pray you repeat some of the discourses which you had yesternight at Master Sophobulus his banquet, for commonly he is not without both wise and learned guests.
>
> PHIL: It is true indeed, and yesternight there were a number of excellent scholars, both gentlemen and others, but all the propose which then was discoursed upon was music.
>
> POL: I trust you were contented to suffer others to speak of that matter.
>
> PHIL: I would that had been the worst, for I was compelled to discover mine own ignorance and confess that I knew nothing at all in it.
>
> POL: How so?
>
> PHIL: Among the rest of the guests, by chance master Aphron came thither also, who, falling to discourse of music, was in an argument so quickly taken up and hotly pursued by Eudoxus and Calergus, two kinsmen of Sophobulus, as in his own art he was overthrown; but he still sticking in his opinion, the two gentlemen requested me to examine his reasons and confute them; but I refusing and pretending ignorance, the whole company condemned me of discourtesy, being fully persuaded that I had been as skilful in that art as they took me to be learned in others. But supper being ended and music books (according to the custom) being brought to the table, the mistress of the house presented me with a part earnestly requesting me to sing; but when, after many excuses, I protested unfeignedly that I could not, every one began to wonder; yea, some whispered to others demanding how I was brought up, so that upon shame of mine ignorance I go now to seek out mine old friend Master Gnorimus, to make myself his scholar.[1]

It was for such amateur musicians as these that the sixteenth-century composers produced myriad secular compositions, ranging in content from ribald rhymes to sophisticated sonnets and in musical style from lively, popular dance tunes to complicated intellectual masterpieces.

Regional Variations of the Cosmopolitan Style in Secular Music

After the peak of its influence in the early decades of the sixteenth century, the international style of the northern composers became a point of departure for a variety of regional substyles in secular genres. The music of the composers who remained in the Low Countries did not change rapidly, and therefore it soon became more conservative than that of other areas. Their chansons retained the smooth, panconsonant, polyphonic flow and continuously unfolding rhythm of the motet.

The French Chanson

In France a special kind of approach to sung texts affected the compositional style of the chanson. As illustrated by the works of Paris court composer Claudin de Sermisy (ca. 1490–1562), the French focussed on the clear and accurate declamation of the poetic syllables. In attempting to treat the words with perfect clarity, the composers favored familiar-style treatment, with all voices articulating the syllables simultaneously. A simplified or schematic realization of the natural speech rhythms of the language determined durational values. With poetic texts of consistent line construction, this yielded predictably patterned phrases and therefore in some cases a dancelike character. So many French chansons began with a dactylic (long-short-short) rhythm that that rhythmic gesture became a recognizable trademark of the genre.

Another technique in sixteenth-century French chansons, the use of musical onomatopoeia, recalls the fourteenth-century caccia and chace. Particularly notable for this device is Clément Janequin (ca. 1485–1558), who asked his singers to create clever and amusing sound effects. His "La guerre" illustrates a battle; "Le chant des oiseaux" is a catalogue of different birdsongs.

English Music

After the end of the Hundred Years' War, England drew back across the English Channel and became somewhat isolated from the development of the cosmopolitan musical style on the continent. We have relatively little secular music from England at this time, though it was certainly cultivated at the court; Henry VIII himself composed some songs. Carols continued to be popular. The English style did not achieve the sensitivity to text or the structural coherence of the French and Netherlandish music of Josquin's time and later; the use of imitation to relate the contrapuntal lines to each other occurs less pervasively. In addition, English music is much more likely to break into extended melismas than the music on the continent.

German Music

The song practice of Germany appears more closely bound to the past than that of other areas. As we have mentioned before, the monophonic tradition of the Minnelied was continued by the middle-class Meistersinger, who formed themselves into a musical guild like the well-established craft guilds and with rigorous dedication preserved in their Lieder the old form of the Bar. The greatest of the Meistersinger, Hans Sachs (1494–1576), pursued the profession of master shoemaker in Nürnberg as well as composing a large output of words and music. Nearly three centuries after his death he reappeared as the central character of Wagner's *Die Meistersinger von Nürnberg.*

The secular polyphonic compositions of the German Renaissance, also called Lieder, stuck to an older style. They commonly rely on a preexisting tune in the tenor voice, presented in relatively slow-moving note values. In numerous cases there was a pair of voices in canonic imitation. Three-part scoring was still common, though a freely composed bass gave the harmony independence from the cantus firmus. A popular device was to combine several different popular song melodies into a single composition to produce a *quodlibet* (Latin for "whatever you like").

The Italian Frottola and Madrigal

In the period of the advent of the Franco-Netherlands style, Italy already had a popular musical genre, the *frottola.* These songs used vernacular poetry and dealt with amorous or satirical topics. Their settings were straightforward and syllabic, in familiar style, with orientation toward the top voice. They may have been sung as part-songs by several voices or performed by solo voice with instruments taking the lower parts. Characteristically their rhythms were strongly patterned in the manner of dance music. The harmony was simple and diatonic. Structurally the frottola adopted strophic form in several verses. Native composers naturally dominated in this light genre, but Josquin did not disdain to try his hand at it when he was in Italy. The old spiritual lauda, now given a polyphonic texture, provided a religious counterpart of the frottola, similar in style but generally a bit less lively, as suited its content.

In the second quarter of the sixteenth century there arose in Italy one of the great genres of social music making, the *madrigal.* The madrigal was sophisticated vocal chamber music and a high-class art form, unlike the more popular frottola. The emergence of the madrigal depended on the convergence of three different factors: the polyphonic chanson style brought by the northern composers to Italy, the demand for music to be used in social contexts by wealthy and educated amateurs, and the cultivation of excellent poetry by the Italian Renaissance writers. The sonnets of Petrarch from the fourteenth century inspired humanist poets of the sixteenth century to imitate and excel the father of Italian vernacular love poetry.

In the first stage of the history of the madrigal, immigrant northern composers took up Italian poetry and graced it with their own musical style. The madrigals of Jacques Arcadelt (ca. 1505–1560), a Flemish composer who for a time led the papal choir in Rome, provide good examples. These madrigals are quite simple and restrained, using almost exclusively syllabic text settings and diatonic harmony. They resemble the Franco-Netherlands motet, except that, like the contemporary Parisian chanson, they are somewhat inclined to use familiar style rather than fuga, which gives them a more defined rhythmic sense. The music reflects with great sensitivity the declamation, grammatical structure, and verse structure of the poetry. Its generally diatonic idiom and natural vocal lines obviously were intended to meet the needs of amateur performers. Somewhat more complex are the madrigals that Adrian Willaert composed in Venice at approximately the same time that Arcadelt was writing.

By the middle of the century the madrigal had increased in expressivity and complexity. The poets began to explore a more impassioned poetic tone, and composers matched them with increased musical sophistication; the leading composer of this more sophisticated stage in the madrigal was Cipriano de Rore (1516–1565), Willaert's immediate successor as maestro di cappella at St. Mark's. In this second period of the madrigal's development, melodic gestures and rhythm increasingly imitated images of gesture and motion in the poetry. Harmonic evocation of moods grew more common: The general resolution of the church modes into the broad classes of major and minor began to take place, and composers recognized the optimistic expressive tendency of the major and the depressed character of the minor modes. Chromaticism was also exploited for expressive reasons.

Word painting was especially cultivated, following Aristotle's dictum (*Poetics*) that art should consist of a *mimesis* (imitation) of life. In some cases the word painting was reserved to the readers of the parts, as when short note values, requiring black noteheads, were used to express darkness, or two semibreves on the same pitch, by that time drawn as round rather than diamond-shaped notes, appeared when the text mentioned the lover's eyes. This "eye music" (sometimes called by the German name *Augenmusik*) obviously would mean nothing to an audience, but the madrigal was addressed to the singers, and an audience was not really anticipated. A look at Rore's madrigals makes it clear that performers who sang these pieces at sight with any degree of the *sprezzatura* that Castiglione demanded of the courtier must have worked hard at their musical skills.

The Poetic Model for Musical Expression

We have several times emphasized the importance of texts for composers of the Renaissance. It is no exaggeration to say that one cannot possibly understand what is going on in a piece of sixteenth-century music unless one first understands the text.

The aesthetic by which this connection manifested itself in the Renaissance can be appropriately identified as poetic. By imitating the rhythmic and inflective patterns of the text, the musical points of imitation reinforce the delight in beautiful sound patterns that makes poetry musical. The periodization of the musical structure according to the lines of the text similarly lends the music a pace that imitates that of poetry. Most of all, the employment of musical mimesis of word meanings to generate musical ideas captures in the most vivid and concrete fashion the idea of the poetic image.

Zarlino made this clear in *Le istitutioni harmoniche*. He cited Plato as his authority for the principle:

> the harmonies ought to accompany the words, for this reason: Although it was said . . . , according to Plato's opinion, that melody is made up of speech, harmony, and rhythm, and that in such a combination one of these things should not take precedence over another, nevertheless he places speech before the other parts, as the principal thing, and the other two parts as those that serve it.

He also stressed that word meanings are to be reflected in harmony and choice of mode:

> For if in speech . . . matters may be dealt with that are happy or sad, or serious and also without any seriousness, or similarly chaste or lascivious, it follows that we must also select a harmony and a rhythm suitable to the nature of the matters that are contained in the speech, so that from the combination of these things, mixed together with proportion, there will result a melody suited to the subject matter.
>
> . . . One will know best how to do this when he has paid attention to what I have written . . . and has considered the nature of the mode in which he wants to write his song. He should do his best to accompany each word in such a way that, where it denotes harshness, hardness, cruelty, bitterness, and other similar things, the harmony will be similar to it—that is, somewhat hard and harsh, but in such a manner that it is not offensive; likewise, when any of the words expresses weeping, sadness, grief, sighs, tears, and other similar things, that the harmony will be full of sadness.

And both declamation of the words and grammatical sense must also be considered:

> we should be sure to suit the words of the speech to the melodic figures in such a manner, with such note values, that nothing barbarous is heard—as in a case when a long syllable in the vocal line has to be declaimed on a short note, or, on the other hand, a short one has to be declaimed long. . . .

. . . Likewise, one should be careful not to separate any parts of the speech from each other with rests, as some not very intelligent people do, as long as the clause or any part of it is not finished in such a way that the sense of the words is complete. And one should not make a cadence—especially one of the main ones—and not put in a rest longer than that of the minim, if the sentence is not complete, . . .

The significance of this for the history of music aesthetics is enormous; it brought about one of the great dividing points of music history. The aesthetic break between the Middle Ages and the Renaissance was deeper than that between any of the periods that followed, until our own era. While until the fifteenth century music was governed by numbers and religious symbolism, after the fifteenth century it was governed by words and literature. The medieval composer was an architect in tones; the Renaissance composer became a musical poet. When music gave up its mathematical affiliations for poetic ones, it became no longer symbolic but expressive. It no longer mirrored the perfection of divine order but embodied the experience of mankind. It became, in short, humanist.

So long-lasting was this new outlook that the link between literature and music remained indissoluble until the twentieth century. This complementary relationship produced a great variety of aesthetic interpretations, but never between about 1500 and 1900 was the fundamental assumption abandoned that, as the English writer Henry Peacham (ca. 1576–1643) put it, music is "a sister to poetry."

Questions for Reflection

✤   Compared to earlier periods how strongly did national taste, the predilections of particular patrons, and the personalities of composers affect the style of music in the late fifteenth and sixteenth centuries?

✤   How did the printing of music affect musical style in the sixteenth and following centuries? Were there any ways in which music printing might have had a negative impact on music?

✤   In what ways did the relationship of music to words increase the vitality of music in the sixteenth century? What might music have lost in exchange?

✤   It has been said that the Renaissance invented the artist, as opposed to the artisan (see Chapter 23). What does this statement mean for the musician and for music?

Suggestions for Further Reading

Excerpts from the writings of Morley and Zarlino can be found in Oliver Strunk, *Source Readings in Music History* (New York: Norton, 1950); see also Thomas Morley, *A Plain and Easy Introduction to Practical Music*, ed. Alec Harman (New York: Norton, 1973), and Gioseffe Zarlino, *Le istitutioni harmoniche*, Part 3, *The Art of Counterpoint*, trans. Guy A. Marco and C. V. Palisca (New Haven: Yale University Press, 1968) and Part 4, *On the Modes*, trans. Vered Cohen and ed. C. V. Palisca (New Haven: Yale University Press, 1983).

An important book on secular vocal music in the High Renaissance is James Haar, ed., *Chanson and Madrigal, 1480–1530* (Cambridge: Harvard University Press, 1964). Alfred Einstein, *The Italian Madrigal*, rev. ed. (Princeton, N.J.: Princeton University Press, 1971) is a standard work. A more concise survey is Jerome Roche, *The Madrigal* (New York: Scribner's, 1972).

On Josquin des Prez, see Edward E. Lowinsky and Bonnie J. Blackburn, eds., *Josquin des Prez: Proceedings of the International Festival-Conference Held at the Juilliard School at Lincoln Center in New York City, 21–25 June 1971* (London: Oxford University Press, 1976).

Notes

1. Thomas Morley, *A Plain and Easy Introduction to Practical Music*, ed. Alec Harman (New York: Norton, 1973), 9.

9

INSTRUMENTAL MUSIC IN THE RENAISSANCE

The Place of Instruments in Renaissance Music

From a philosophical point of view, instrumental music might seem to hold a difficult position in the Renaissance. Since the relationship of words and music dominated Renaissance musical thinking both in aesthetics and composition, instrumental music might have been pushed into the background as a kind of awkward stepsister to vocal music. As in any age, however, musicians did not let mere philosophy hamper their imaginations or quell their creative urges. Players took out their instruments every day without stopping to worry about how music achieved its beauty, structure, or expressive value in the absence of words. And there were interesting developments in the abstract world of textless music that influenced the future in many ways.

Renaissance Instruments

The classification of instruments into *haut* and *bas* types continued from the Middle Ages into the Renaissance. New in the sixteenth century was an incipient sense of planned scoring. The homogeneous sound of vocal a cappella music was reflected in the grouping into choirs of instruments of a single type but different sizes and ranges. This system still affects the way composers think about timbres and plan instrumentation.

Consorts

Builders constructed matched sets of instruments, forming a *chest* or, in actual performance together, a *consort.* One could purchase a set of recorders, for example, that would allow the playing of four-part compositions for soprano, alto, tenor, and bass.

There were two types of double-reed instruments. One was the old, loud shawm family, generally used outdoors. The other type, much softer and more suitable for indoor playing, was the family of *crumhorns* (from the German *krumm,* meaning "crooked"). The crumhorn differs from the shawm in three prominent respects: Its bore is cylindrical rather than conical; its reed is enclosed inside a wooden cap rather than being held directly in the player's mouth; and the end is not broadly flared but curves outward in a graceful arc. (Fig. 9.1)

All in all, the types of woodwinds and the variety of tone colors available was considerable. The *schreierpfeife* resembled shawms but had capped reeds. There were also two major types of bass reed instruments, belonging to the type with a tube that folded back on itself, a group known as *kortholts.* One was the *racket,* which had its length compacted inside a small cylinder held between the player's hands. The other, known as the *dulcian* or *curtal,* was a simpler predecessor of the modern bassoon. The transverse flute continued to be used from the Middle Ages throughout the Renaissance and on to the present.

Prominent in the brass and lip-vibrated class is the *sackbut,* predecessor of the modern trombone. The sackbut had a narrow bore and a gently flared bell and consequently made a much softer tone than the trombone. Often combined in consorts with alto, tenor, and bass sackbuts was the *cornett* (in Italian, *cornetto;* in German, *Zink*). As its name suggests, the cornett was, at least at first, simply a small animal horn; holes were drilled along its length so that it could be fingered like a recorder, shawm, or crumhorn, and a cup mouthpiece was placed at the small end. Later cornetts were made of wood. The sound of the instrument is quite restrained, not at all like the brassy brilliance of the modern trumpet. It was used to accompany choral music, because its sound seemed well matched to the sound of the voice.

The Renaissance bowed string instruments, or *viols,* also came in chests. Viols differ from the instruments of the modern violin family in several important respects; in fact they are related to the guitar in certain ways, for they have six strings, a fretted fingerboard, and a flat back. In addition, the shoulders of the viol are much more sloped than those of the violin, viola, and cello. The treble viol sat upright on the player's lap. The larger ones were held between the player's legs and consequently were known in Italian as *viola da gamba* or "leg viol." (Fig. 9.2) A double bass viol, called *violone* in Italian, was also used,

Figure 9.1
A set of crumhorns.

and it is the legitimate ancestor of the modern double bass. By the end of the sixteenth century the violin, with its more penetrating tone and greater flexibility, began to come into use.

Broken Consorts

While much music was played by homogeneous consorts of instruments, there was also the possibility of a mixed or "broken" consort comprising instruments of various families, within the constraints of the *haut/bas* dichotomy. The players were practical, and the indication of specific scorings simply was not a component of Renaissance musical style. By the end of the sixteenth century in England, however, there was a standard broken consort grouping, which included one or more recorders, both plucked and bowed string instruments, and keyboard instrument.

Plucked Instruments

A variety of plucked string instruments were available. The lute and all its relatives were now plucked with the fingers of the right hand rather than with a plectrum as in the Middle Ages. This made possible the performance of polyphonic music by a single player. Large, low-pitched lutes, or *archlutes,* included the *theorbo* and *chitarrone.* The *vihuela,* ancestor of the modern guitar, dominated the scene in Spain.

Figure 9.2
Treble and bass viols.

Keyboard Instruments

The Renaissance was the period in which keyboard instruments other than the organ arose. Mechanically simplest of these was the *clavichord,* the strings of which were touched by metal tangents attached directly to the backs of the keys. The clavichord has a very small, intimate tone. The *harpsichord* is more practical as an instrument to be played for an audience or in ensembles. Each of its keys activates a *jack,* which holds a plectrum made of quill. The result is a relatively brilliant and strongly articulated sound. The *virginal,* a small, box-like harpsichord with strings running at right angles to the keys, was popular in England. The organ, of course, continued to be used in the church, but it was largely replaced by the harpsichord in secular contexts.

Tablature

Vocal polyphony in the Renaissance was usually read from part-books, each singer having only his own line, as modern instrumental ensemble players generally do, rather than the full score that today's choral singers use. This arrangement was also employed in consort music. For solo playing, such as on the plucked strings, part-books were, of course, impossible, and score notation was impractical. A special notation called *tablature* was developed particularly for lute and vihuela players.

Rather than giving the player a graphic picture of the musical sound (like the pitches on a staff) or a symbolic indication of the tones (such as the note shapes that indicate duration), tablature instructs the player where to place the fingers. (Modern guitar chord diagrams employ the same principle but with much less precision.) The basic principle of tablature was to show the reader a picture of the six strings as six horizontal lines and assign a letter or number to each fret on the neck of the instrument. The player stopped the string at the fret corresponding to the letter or number placed on that line and plucked that string. Rhythm would be indicated by stems and flags placed above the tablature. (Fig. 9.3) Tablature is, of course, eminently practical, but it is extremely difficult if not impossible to imagine simply by looking at the notation what the music sounds like. One must play the music to reveal the musical lines and their polyphonic interplay.

The use of tablature was also adapted for keyboard players. However, they sometimes read from a two-staff score or, occasionally, from a larger score showing each of the polyphonic parts (*partitura*).

Instruments and Vocal Music

It was common in the fifteenth and sixteenth centuries to perform vocal works with instruments. The instruments might simply double parts as they were sung. This allowed those without vocal gifts to participate in secular, domestic music making. In churches, although the a cappella sound remained the ideal, the choral lines were regularly supported by the organ, sackbuts, and other appropriate instruments.

Sometimes in polyphonic vocal music instruments played some lines while singers took others. This might happen simply because players were available and vocalists were not, and details such as the absence of a singer should not deter the performance of a song with, for example, only a viol on the bass line. As we have remarked before, numerous pieces seem to call for the combination of solo voice and instruments, though such a scoring is not specified. Among these are the cantilena-style chansons of the Burgundian composers, the Italian frottole of the early sixteenth century, and some of the sixteenth-century French chansons. As the sixteenth century continued, more pieces were specifically written for combined voices and instruments, so that we have a wealth of music for solo voice and lute; some songs for voice and keyboard; and, especially from England, consort songs for singer and viols.

Instrumental Adaptations of Vocal Music
and Genres

The richness of the vocal music literature invited instrumentalists to adapt that music for their own use. They certainly played from the singers' part-books to

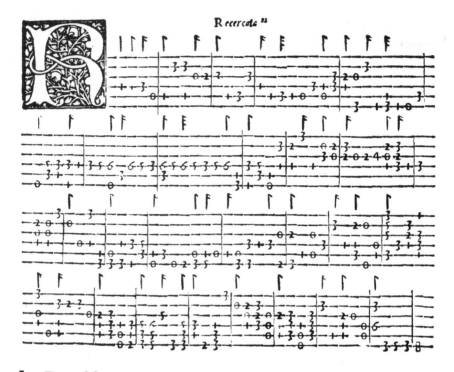

Figure 9.3
A ricercar for lute, notated in tablature. (*Francesco da Milano,* Intavolatura de viola o vero lauto. *Naples, 1536*)

supplement their own repertoire. To adapt the music to their instruments or make it more attractive they composed transcriptions of vocal pieces. This was especially common among lute and keyboard composers and players.

For original works the composers took the vocal genres as their models. The instrumental *ricercar* (from the Italian for "to seek out," cognate with "research") imitated the motet in treating contrapuntal points of imitation one by one in a succession of dovetailed periods. The *canzona* was modeled on the French chanson, with much use of familiar style and even the characteristic opening dactylic rhythm of the vocal genre. Of these two types, the ricercar was more complex and serious, while the canzona was livelier and more lighthearted.

English musicians developed a unique and rather peculiar adaptation of a vocal source in instrumental music. Apparently composers especially liked a particular phrase from the *Missa Gloria tibi trinitas* of one of their greatest native sons, John Taverner (ca. 1490–1545). That phrase was the setting of the words *in nomine* from the statement "Benedictus qui venit in nomine Domini" in the Sanctus. Transcriptions of the passage and new pieces using the melody as a cantus firmus were so numerous that they amount to an entire genre of instrumental pieces known simply as *In nomine*.

The grounding of much Renaissance instrumental music in vocal style and vocal genres reflects how far advanced vocal music was beyond instrumental music. The words themselves had solved basic problems of musical sense and structure for vocal music. By adapting the vocal genres to their own use, instrumentalists took advantage of the musical structures at which composers of vocal works had previously arrived. There were new problems with this approach, however. The sense of musical ideas generated by word meanings or by the natural diction of phrases and sentences did not necessarily carry over convincingly into abstract tone-patterns in instrumental ricercars and canzonas. Even more perplexing was the difficulty of achieving structural coherence without a text, for the through-composed approach to form threatened to leave instrumental music merely wandering from one musical point to another without logical connections.

Instrumental Genres

Dances

As it was in the Middle Ages, dance music was a very important type of purely instrumental music in the Renaissance. Such pieces might be either practical ones actually intended to accompany dancing or independent pieces created by using the patterns of dance music in a stylized fashion. (The latter approach is not different in concept from Chopin's in his composition of waltzes, polonaises, and mazurkas for the piano.) A popular dance type in France during the fifteenth and sixteenth centuries was the *basse danse;* it was also common in Italy, where it was called *bassadanza*. This was a smooth, gliding dance for couples, generally using some form of triple rhythm. (Fig. 9.4)

Often Renaissance dances come in pairs that match a slower dance with a faster one. In Italy the bassadanza was replaced by the slow *passamezzo,* which was paired with a vigorous fast dance called *saltarello*. In France the slow dance came to be known as *pavane,* while the more animated one was the *gaillarde*. The passamezzo and pavane most commonly used duple meters, while the saltarello and gaillarde had compound meters and exploited hemiola. These dances were also popular in England as *pavan* and *galliard*.

The pairing of pieces in this fashion is significant, for it demonstrates that the instrumental musicians had begun to deal with the problem of shape and direction in a multisectional musical construction. Variety and contrast are provided by the different rhythmic characters of the dances, while their order offers a sense of forward motion and climax.

Figure 9.4
Renaissance dancers accompanied by shawms. (*Bibliothèque nationale, Paris*)

Variations

Another popular instrumental type was the variation set. Composers often treated song tunes or dances in series of variations. Because dances typically had standard phrase lengths corresponding to the prescribed sequences of steps, it was not so much their tunes that were varied as their harmonic plans or conventional bass patterns. The techniques of variation naturally exploited the idiomatic capabilities of the instrument for which the set was composed and the virtuosity of the composer or performer.

The variation set also manifests the need of instrumental composers to come to grips with problems of coherence and variety that composers of vocal music did not have to solve. In a series of variations the twin principles of unity and contrast are both applied effectively. A master composer could produce a sense of large-scale shaping by organizing many short variations into groups and by employing a rhythmic or textural crescendo toward the end of the set.

Instrumental Pieces in the Style of Improvisations

Improvisatory pieces formed another class of instrumental compositions. The rise of virtuoso technique, especially on lute or vihuela and on keyboard instruments, led to the creation of many such works. These pieces might bear titles such as *fantasia,* reflecting the untrammeled freedom of the imagination exercised in the composition, or *toccata* (Italian for "touched," usually referring to the keys of a harpsichord or organ), implying that the piece featured facile fingering. The term *ricercar* also appears for such improvisational pieces, as well as for the polyphonic, "vocal" type discussed earlier. In Spain such compositions were known as *tiento* (from *tentar,* "to feel out").

Players often used such improvisatory pieces to introduce more structured instrumental or vocal pieces. Such a piece might be called *intonazione,* which suggests that its purpose was either to provide the pitch for a performance or to check the intonation of the instrument itself before starting another, more formal number. Other common titles were *prelude* and *preambulum,* simply indicating that the piece was to be played before something else.

Naturally there was relatively little concern for principles of musical form within these improvisatory pieces. Nevertheless, the combination of such a free introduction with another, more systematically constructed piece constitutes an important contribution of the Renaissance instrumental composers and players to the development of musical form after the sixteenth century.

Questions for Reflection

❖   What elements of Renaissance instruments and instrumental practice are closest to those of the Middle Ages? Which anticipated later instrumental usage in the period of common practice?

❖   What are the advantages and disadvantages of tablature notation compared to the standard notation instrumentalists use today?

❖   How would Renaissance humanistic thought and sound ideals have changed the practice of instrumental music in the church compared to such practice in the Middle Ages?

❖   What ideas did vocal music contribute to instrumental musical structures and processes in the Renaissance? What did dance contribute?

Suggestions for Further Reading

For discussions of Renaissance instruments, see the Suggestions for Further Reading for Chapter 4. On early keyboard music, see Willi Apel, *The History of Keyboard Music to 1700*, trans. Hans Tischler (Bloomington: Indiana University Press, 1972).

Investigations of performance problems include J. A. Bank, *Tactus, Tempo, and Notation in Mensural Music from the Thirteenth to the Seventeenth Centuries* (Amsterdam: Annie Bank, 1972); Andrew Hughes, *Ficta in Focus: Manuscript Accidentals 1530–1450* (Rome: American Institute of Musicology, 1972); and Howard Mayer Brown, *Embellishing Sixteenth-Century Music* (London: Oxford University Press, 1976).

10 THE REFORMATION

The Background of the Reformation

The turmoil in the Catholic church that had been growing for centuries finally came to a crisis in the sixteenth century. The institution of the church had somehow held together despite its leaders' obvious abuses of money, political power, and morality. However, these abuses could last only as long as thought was founded on the authority the church claimed. The rise of humanism and the emphasis on independent thought in the Renaissance inevitably led to doubts and arguments that would challenge the church itself. Scholars who read the classics in the original languages also read the Bible in the original Hebrew and Greek and discovered ideas there that contradicted received doctrine. In the competition between authority and the scholar's own reading and reason, the latter naturally prevailed.

The immediate cause of the catholic church's downfall was the selling of indulgences, which allowed wealthy sinners to ease their journey to heaven in the next life by paying money to the church in the present one. Martin Luther (1483–1546) read the New Testament letters of the apostle Paul and found in them the doctrine that no amount of human merit could offer salvation, but only the grace of God. He exposed indulgences as the basest kind of extortion, serving to fill the coffers of Rome rather than to promote salvation. Luther's posting of his famous *Ninety-five Theses* on the door of the collegiate church at Wittenberg in 1517 turned out to be the point of no return in the church's slide from absolute power.

The Reformation also had roots in the growing sense of nationalism in Europe. The papacy had long been a prize held alternately—during the Great Schism, simultaneously—by Italy and France. The northern and eastern parts of Europe, as well as England, naturally resented this and, quite reasonably, saw in it a form of foreign political oppression. Thus when the theological attack on the Roman church came, it quickly found support among the general populace in these spiritually disenfranchised areas. The bloody German Peasants' Revolt was a product of political frustration combined with the Reformation's spiritual inspiration. (Plate 4) Henry VIII, unable to obtain from the pope an annulment of a fruitless marriage, declared spiritual independence from Rome in the 1534 Act of Supremacy and made himself head of the Church of England.

Consequently, both the Roman church and the reformed church were quickly fragmented. There were followers of Luther in Germany and Scandinavia; groups led by Jean Calvin (1509–1564) and Swiss reformer Ulrich Zwingli (1484–1531) in Switzerland, the Netherlands, Scotland, and parts of Germany; and pockets of more radical Anabaptists in many areas. For the history of music this meant the growth of a variety of practices and musical styles and repertoires. Each denomination had its own ideas about music, which sprang from the theological position and musical inclinations of its leadership.

The Music of the Lutheran Reformation

Martin Luther's original intention was not to divide the church but to reform it from within. He had come from the Roman Catholic tradition and never doubted the value of music in religious life and liturgy. He himself was a music lover and amateur musician; he played the lute and the flute. He also strongly endorsed the use of music in the education of young people. Luther's main concerns about worship itself were the church's exclusion of the common person through its emphasis on secretive, mysterious rites; its vast and complicated liturgy; and its stubborn insistence on the use of Latin rather than the language of the people. To respond to this concern, Luther contrived a new liturgy in 1526. The *Deutsche Messe* (German Mass) was modeled on the Gregorian liturgy and music, but it was simplified and translated into the vernacular. Even this was intended not as a replacement for the Latin Mass, but only as an alternative to it for use in smaller churches.

Luther promoted hymns for congregational and devotional singing. These hymns in the Lutheran tradition are known as *chorales*. The chorale actually consists of a strophic text and a melody. Luther took on the task of writing some chorale texts himself; his most famous is "Ein' feste Burg ist unser Gott" (A mighty fortress is our God). He may have composed the music for this and some other chorales. He also had an important musical collaborator in Johann Walter (1496–1570). Published collections of Reformation chorales appeared as early as 1524. In German music the chorales took on an importance similar to that of the chant in music prior to the Reformation. (Fig. 10.1)

Figure 10.1
Two pages from a German chorale collection of 1533. As the woodcut indicates, the music shows the first stanza of a Christmas chorale: "We should praise Christ, the son of the spotless maiden Mary, as far as the sun shines and reaches to all the ends of the earth." The chorale was adapted from the Gregorian hymn "A solis ortus cardine," sung at Lauds on Christmas morning. (*Staatliche Lutherhalle, Wittenberg*)

The chorale melodies were sometimes brand-new compositions by the reformed composers. The need for a large quantity of music on short notice, however, also led to the borrowing or adaptation of Gregorian melodies with, of course, German words. The Latin Easter Sequence, "Victimae paschali laudes," for example, was parodied in this fashion to create the Lutheran chorale "Christ lag in Todesbanden" (Christ lay in death's bonds); the Advent chorale "Nun komm, der Heiden Heiland" (Now come, the nations' savior) came from the Latin hymn "Veni, redemptor gentium" (Come, redeemer of the people). In their search for melodies the chorale writers also turned to vernacular secular songs. The Lied "Innsbruck, ich muss dich lassen" (Innsbruck, I must leave thee), already set in two different polyphonic versions by Heinrich Isaac, was given a sacred text beginning "O Welt, ich muss dich lassen" (O world, I must leave thee).

Although the chorales were monophonic, composers naturally arranged them in polyphonic settings. Following the tradition of the secular polyphonic Lied, some of these had the chorale melody in the tenor voice, surrounded by other free parts. Alternatively the chorale melody was placed in the topmost voice and the other voices matched it in familiar style. This type is known as *cantional* setting. Such pieces were suitable for performance by congregation and choir, the congregation singing the melody while the choir provided the full polyphonic texture. For trained singers in choirs there were soon settings in motet style, comparable to the Latin motets of the cosmopolitan tradition that continued in the Catholic churches of the time. In such a *chorale motet*, the points of imitation were derived from the consecutive phrases of the chorale. Each phrase was then treated separately in fuga or familiar style, with a periodic structure just like that of the motet.

The Calvinist Reformation

In Switzerland, France, the Netherlands, and Scotland, the Reformation looked primarily to Jean Calvin for its authority. Unlike Luther, Calvin was not musical. In fact he was suspicious of music, having the same sort of reservations about its popishness that the early Christian fathers had expressed toward the pagan associations of music in their own time. Like the early church leaders, too, Calvin laid greater emphasis on the words of church music than on the music itself. Moreover, Calvin was generally more strongly opposed to the Roman liturgy than Luther, and he aimed to create a worship service more oriented toward preaching than toward prayer, praise, and the Eucharist.

Calvin considered banishing music from the worship service altogether, but he ultimately compromised by allowing the congregation to sing monophonic psalms. No polyphonic singing was allowed in church, and nonscriptural songs were banned altogether. Thus the Calvinist Reformation did not produce a body of new hymn texts comparable to the chorales of the Lutherans. Instead, the Huguenots, as Calvin's French followers were commonly known, created rhymed, metrical translations of the biblical psalms into vernacular poetry. These were sung to tunes often adapted from the chant or from secular music.

Although only unison singing was permitted in public worship, simple polyphonic settings were permissible for private devotional use in Calvinist homes. As the Lutherans had Johann Walter, Calvin's movement found a musical leader in the Frenchman Louis Bourgeois (ca. 1510–1561). Bourgeois set many of the psalm melodies, treating them like the French chansons of the period, syllabically in simple rhythms and in predominantly familiar style. There were also some more sophisticated, motetlike arrangements.

The psalms and their music appeared in published form in collections called *psalters*. The psalters spread this repertoire very widely. The first Calvinist collection was published in 1539 in Strasbourg, and the first complete collection of all 150 psalms appeared in Geneva in 1562. In the meantime an important collection called *Souterliedekens* (little psalter songs) was released in the Netherlands in 1540. In Germany there were already psalm settings (including some monophonic ones by Hans Sachs), and the first complete Lutheran psalter dates from 1553, but the French psalms in translation became much more popular and helped expand the chorale repertoire. As the Calvinist movement spread to the British Isles, psalters appeared in English; the collection of Thomas Sternhold and John Hopkins, known simply as "Sternhold and Hopkins" (1562), is a classic of the genre.

The Calvinist psalters are the forerunners of all modern hymnbooks in America. The Pilgrims brought with them the *Ainsworth Psalter* (1612, Amsterdam), and the first native American psalter was the famous *Bay Psalm Book,* published in Massachusetts in 1640. Many of the tunes of the early sixteenth century are still used today; certainly the best known of all must be the tune called "Old Hundredth," to which almost all American Protestants sing the Lesser Doxology, "Praise God from whom all blessings flow."

The Reformation in England

As has already been mentioned, the Reformation in England was as much political as theological. Henry VIII rejected the political authority of Rome, including the right of the pope to uphold or annul an English king's marriages, and finally took to himself spiritual as well as secular authority in his realm.

The religious history of England during the Tudor period is one of alternation between Reformation austerity in the Calvinist manner and returns to the Roman church. In 1534 Henry VIII separated the English church from the Roman, and after his death reform was continued in the name of his young son Edward VI, who ruled from 1547 to 1553 and died before his sixteenth birthday. There followed a return to Roman Catholicism under Queen Mary, who had strong Catholic ties, since she was the child of Henry's first marriage and the wife of King Philip II of Spain. She, in turn, died in 1558. Her sister, Elizabeth I, achieved the final separation of the Anglican from the Roman church.

The English liturgy was similar to the Roman but was translated and in some ways reformed. It included only two daily services derived from the Divine Office, Morning Prayer (from Matins) and Evening Prayer (from Vespers). These might be composed musically as either *Great Services,* if the composer treated the setting in elaborate polyphonic and melismatic style, or *Short Services,* if the music was simple, syllabic, and in predominantly familiar style. The Holy Communion, which corresponds to the Roman Mass, is less important for music than the Roman Mass or the Anglican Morning and Evening Services.

In English music a polyphonic setting for performance by the choir is called an *anthem* (a corruption of *antiphon*). A *full anthem* employs a cappella

choral voices in a through-composed setting with phrase-by-phrase polyphonic treatment of the text, in the same manner as the Latin motet. A *verse
anthem* opposes solo singers accompanied by instruments against the choir.

The Counter-Reformation

The reformers' success finally forced the Roman Catholic church to attend to
the sad state into which some of its activities had declined. The process of
reform from within the Catholic church is known as the Counter-Reformation.
Pope Paul III called the college of cardinals together at Trent (in northern Italy)
to review and reform all aspects of the life of the church. The Council of Trent
lasted eighteen years (1545–1563), and of course music was only one of the
many items on its agenda.

The particular musical concerns of the Council of Trent were the same
ones that had worried the early church fathers and the contemporary Protestant reformers. They were disturbed by the complexity of the liturgy, secular
styles and practices that had crept into worship through the centuries, the use
of instruments in the service, and the obscuring of the liturgical words both by
careless singers and by composers who neglected words in favor of elaborate
music.

One clear action that the council took was to strip the Sequence out of
most Mass Propers. Of a total of over four thousand Sequences, they left only
four, "Victimae paschali laudes" for Easter, "Veni sancte spiritus" for Pentecost,
"Lauda Sion" for Corpus Christi, and "Dies irae" for the Requiem Mass.

On the details of musical style there was considerable debate. The most
conservative cardinals seriously wished to forbid all polyphonic music in the
church, turning the calendar back eight centuries. Fortunately more musical
heads prevailed. There was no precise legislation of a style, but some general
principles emerged: Sensualism, gratuitous elaboration, and virtuosic technique were to be avoided, and, above all, the words were to be made clear.

The actual effect of this reconsideration of music and these guidelines was
the espousal, informally at least, of the Franco-Netherlands panconsonant
motet style as the particular style of Roman Catholic church music. Ideally the
music was to be sung a cappella or with very discreet support from the organ.
There would be no highly expressive dissonance or sensual, dancelike
rhythms, and melodic lines would be singable by nonvirtuoso choristers. Most
of all, a syllabic text underlay and familiar-style texture would clarify the
words.

Palestrina

The model composer of the music of the Counter-Reformation was Giovanni
Pierluigi da Palestrina (ca. 1525–1594), who worked at St. Peter's in Rome. He

adopted the Franco-Netherlands technique and worked it into a rich, highly polished language, with minimal dissonance and gently pulsing rhythmic flow that seems to wrap the listener in a blanket of mystical peace. So masterful was Palestrina's handling of the style that his name later came to be practically synonymous with the ars perfecta of sixteenth-century counterpoint.

Indeed Palestrina's reputation was such that he became the subject of a popular legend. According to an often-repeated but unlikely story, Palestrina deserves credit as the savior of polyphonic music in the Catholic church at the Council of Trent. It is said that as the council was debating the fate of polyphony, they heard Palestrina's *Missa Papae Marcelli* (Mass for Pope Marcellus). The clarity of its text and beauty of its music convinced them that banning polyphony not only was unnecessary but also would eliminate a force of great beauty and power from worship.

Tomas Luis da Victoria and Roland de Lassus

Palestrina represents the conservative side of the music of the Counter-Reformation. There was, however, a more impassioned type of Catholic faith, which guided the Spaniard Ignatius of Loyola (1491–1556) to found the Society of Jesus, or Jesuits, who adopted an aggressive missionary program and took as their particular responsibility the expansion of human knowledge. For a musical interpretation of this experience, we can turn to the works of the Spanish composer Tomas Luis da Victoria (ca. 1549–1611). Victoria studied in Rome with Palestrina, but his style is much more expressive or madrigalistic than Palestrina's. The rhythms are less smooth, for instance, and chromatic and dissonant harmonies highlight the intensity of emotion in the words.

Another important Catholic composer, Roland de Lassus, or, as he styled himself in Italian, Orlando di Lasso (ca. 1532–1594), was the last great Netherlands composer to follow the well-worn path to Italy and then north again. He wrote with perfect fluency in the secular styles of his native region and Italy, and, after serving in Munich, in that of the German Lied. His motets were gathered into a monumental collection under the title *Magnum opus musicum*. Among his other sacred works are Masses and motet-style settings of the stories of the Passion of Christ from all four Gospels. Lassus's sacred music seems more aggressive than Palestrina's; its stronger melodic profiles and greater variety and contrast show perhaps less spirituality but more spirit.

Faith, Music, and the Power of Words

Each of the special sets of musical concerns of the different denominations of Christianity that appeared in the sixteenth century inspired a different approach to composition. Though some of the reformers (and counterreformers)

supported music more enthusiastically than others, the production of important musical ideas and repertoires in each movement demonstrates the power
of music as a force in religious experience.

As in the secular realm, the importance of words to sacred music can
hardly be overstressed. Whether they were principally concerned with the
intelligibility of words in Latin (the Council of Trent) or in vernacular languages (the northern reformers), with the danger of music as a distraction
from the sacred words or as a sensual pleasure (Calvin), or with the attempt
to find the right musical style to set the proper tone for the words of worship
(Palestrina) or make the specific sense more vivid (Victoria), theologians and
composers inevitably found their attentions focused on texts.

However, the words presented to the composers of sacred music not only
problems but also opportunities and inspiration. The English Catholic composer William Byrd (1543–1623), who wrote music for both Roman Catholic
and Anglican services, expressed the problems and the joy of sacred words in
the dedication to his *Gradualia* of 1605–1607:

> For even as among artisans it is shameful in a craftsman to make a rude
> piece of work from some precious material, so indeed to sacred words in
> which the praises of God and of the Heavenly host are sung, none but
> some celestial harmony (so far as our powers avail) will be proper. More-
> over in these words, as I have learned by trial, there is such a profound
> and hidden power that to one thinking upon things divine and diligently
> and earnestly pondering them, all the fittest numbers [i.e., tones] occur as
> if of themselves and freely offer themselves to the mind which is not
> indolent or inert.[1]

Questions for Reflection

❖   How do Luther's and Calvin's theological positions on music in the
church echo earlier traditions of thought about music and religion?

❖   What stylistic aspects of Lutheran church music can be attributed to
German national tastes and traditions in music? What stylistic characteristics
of Lutheran and Calvinist church music account for the survival of numerous
sixteenth-century works into the twentieth century?

❖   How can William Byrd's position as composer for the Anglican church be
reconciled with the fact that he remained a Roman Catholic?

Suggestions for Further Reading

An important study of the music of the Lutheran church is Friedrich Blume, *Protestant Church Music* (New York: Norton, 1974). On English Reformation music, see Peter LeHuray, *Music and the Reformation in England, 1549–1660* (London: Oxford University Press, 1967).

The classic study of the Palestrina style is Knud Jeppesen, *The Style of Palestrina and the Dissonance*, 2d ed., trans. Edward Dent (London: Oxford University Press, 1946).

For concise biographical and critical discussions and good bibliographies for Byrd, Lassus, Palestrina, and Victoria, see *The New Grove High Renaissance Masters* (New York: Norton, 1984), which presents updated versions of the articles from *The New Grove Dictionary of Music and Musicians* (London: Macmillan, 1980). Some good individual studies are Paul Nettl, *Luther and Music*, trans. Frida Best and Ralph Wood (Philadelphia: Muhlenberg, 1948); Jerome Roche, *Palestrina* (London: Oxford University Press, 1971); Jerome Roche, *Lassus* (London: Oxford University Press, 1982); Edmund H. Fellowes, *William Byrd*, 2d ed.(London: Oxford University Press, 1948). A comprehensive study of Byrd's works can be found in the three-volume set *The Music of William Byrd*: Vol. 1, Joseph Kerman, *The Masses and Motets of William Byrd* (Berkeley: University of California Press, 1981); Vol. 2, Philip Brett, *The Songs, Services and Anthems of William Byrd* (in preparation); Vol. 3, Oliver Neighbour, *The Consort and Keyboard Music of William Byrd* (London: Faber, 1978).

Notes

1. Oliver Strunk, ed., *Source Readings in Music History* (New York: Norton, 1950), 327–328.

11

THE WANING OF THE RENAISSANCE

Italian Music at the End of the Sixteenth Century

The madrigal continued to be the most important genre for Italian secular music in the late sixteenth century. Palestrina and Lassus each composed many excellent examples. Palestrina's madrigals resembled his sacred music in holding to a conservative style. Lassus, who also contributed to the repertoire of French chansons and German Lieder, excelled in a wide variety of styles; his madrigals are more lively and colorful in their treatment of the text.

Following the advances made by Rore (discussed in Chapter 8), Luca Marenzio (1553–1599) brought to its peak the use of texts as the inspiration and shaping force for the madrigal. In his works one can discover a clear textual reason for practically every musical detail. Some of his most effective madrigals set the ardent and sensuous love poems of his contemporary Torquato Tasso (1544–1595). Marenzio's work has been considered the culmination of the madrigal style.

The theatrical entertainments performed in the Italian courts were important sources of poetry for composition. During the sixteenth century these entertainments included plays, often elaborately staged. It became common to provide between the acts of plays a brief diversion in the form of an *intermedio* (pl. *intermedi*) or entr'acte. These usually portrayed ancient heroic or pastoral stories in pantomime and dance, with polyphonic musical accompaniments and songs. Pastoral plays with music also became popular as embellishments to grand state occasions, noble weddings, and the like. They were particularly popular and lavish in the city of Florence. Everywhere they were taken seriously as artistic works; the verses of such important poets as Tasso and Battista Guarini (1538–1612) served as texts for many of the madrigalists.

143

The increasing sophistication of composers was paralleled by the increasing virtuosity of singers. It was common for singers of polyphonic compositions, like players of instruments, to improvise embellishments or "divisions" in their musical lines. When individual singers performed with lute, keyboard, or a consort of viols, the freedom to demonstrate their vocal ability was even greater. Notable for their vocal feats were several gifted women who sang at the ducal court of Ferrara in the last decades of the sixteenth century; the most famous of these virtuosas were Lucrezia Bendidio (1547–1583), Laura Peverara (ca. 1545–1601), and Tarquinia Molza (1542–1612). The music written for the Ferrarese women by the court composer Luzzasco Luzzaschi (1545–1607) shows that they excelled in extremely rapid passagework over impressively wide vocal ranges.

Still another aspect of the style of the late Italian Renaissance was the classification of vocal ensemble pieces into various specific categories. Compared to the madrigal, which tended to be compositionally complicated and more serious, the Italians had the *canzonetta,* which was lighter in mood, likely to be for a smaller group of voices, and simpler to sing. The *balletto* was a dance song and featured lively, strongly metrical rhythms and a recurring refrain, which often used the nonsense syllables *fa la la.* A *villanella* was a popular song, characteristically employing a much less sophisticated type of poetry than the madrigal. It was commonly satirical or amorously suggestive in its content, mocking the madrigal's lofty intentions. The villanella would be deliberately simple and even crude in technique; familiar-style texture in only three parts was normal, as was the deliberate use of such musical faux pas as parallel fifths for humorous effect.

Late Renaissance Mannerism

As was the case at the close of the Middle Ages, some artists at the end of the Renaissance exaggerated their expressive technique to the point of mannerism, and composers were no exception. In the visual arts, mannerism was manifested to evoke a particularly powerful emotional response through exaggeration and distortion that departed from the earlier Renaissance ideals of moderation and purity of design. These features are particularly noticeable in the works of the painter El Greco (1541–1614), whose career is associated with the deeply spiritual religious inspiration of post-Counter-Reformation Spain, where Saint Teresa of Avila (1515–1582) and Saint John of the Cross (1542–1591) had their mystical visions. (Fig. 11.1)

In literature there was a comparable style in the impassioned amorous sonnets of Tasso, which carry the genre beyond the subtlety and refinement of Petrarch to express strongly sensual attraction and unbridled ardor. (Fig. 11.2) Perhaps the closest English parallel would be the metaphysical and amorous sonnets of John Donne (1573–1631), which are full of extravagant imagery.

Figure 11.1
El Greco (1541–1614), *Christ on the Cross with Landscape*. El Greco's work exemplifies late Renaissance mannerism in painting. The figure is elongated and distorted, conveying the tortured content more effectively than would a purely realistic depiction. (*Cleveland Museum of Art, Gift of the Hanna Fund, 52.222*)

Mannerism in music found its most forceful expression in the highly idiosyncratic madrigals of Carlo Gesualdo (ca. 1560–1613), Prince of Venosa. For Gesualdo the actual meanings of the words were less important than the generally wrought up emotional condition of the speaker. He particularly

Figure 11.2
In this painting, known as either *Allegory of Music* or simply *The Musicians* (ca. 1594–1595), Michelangelo da Caravaggio (1573–1610) seems to suggest the sensual surfeit of late Renaissance expression. (*Metropolitan Museum of Art, Rogers Fund, 1952. [52.81]*)

seized on the expressive potential of chromatic harmony, and he selected highly passionate (though not always poetically polished) texts to give himself the opportunity to explore the most striking melodies and harmonic progressions. Gesualdo's works often use chromatic vocal lines that are difficult if not impossible to explain within the old syntax of the modes, and they abound in unusual successions of harmonies, especially those that create cross-relations between the parts. The madrigals of Gesualdo pressed the rules of composition as laid down in Zarlino's *Le istitutioni harmoniche* to their limits. Nevertheless, Gesualdo did not explicitly abandon the principle of cautious handling of dissonance.

The Italian Style in England

After its long period of isolation from the developments of Renaissance style on the continent, England was suddenly brought up to date by the 1588 publication by Nicholas Yonge (d. 1619) of a collection of translated Italian madrigals entitled *Musica transalpina.* The English composers took up the Italian genre with alacrity. They were abetted in this by the simultaneous flowering of Tudor poetry, for this was, of course, the era that produced Shakespeare. Books of madrigals, as well as the other Italian types of music, adapted into English as *canzonets* and *balletts,* came out through the remainder of the Elizabethan period and even for several years thereafter. An important anthology of contributions by twenty-four madrigalists, *The Triumphs of Oriana* (1601), was dedicated to Queen Elizabeth, which shows how highly esteemed this type of composition had become. Each of the texts includes a passage in praise of Oriana (a pseudonym for Elizabeth).

A particular expressive mannerism in English polyphony of this period is the simultaneous cross-relation. To express intense feeling the English composers characteristically called for the sounding of a pitch in its natural and its sharped or flatted form. The result is the bizarre clash of an augmented or diminished unison or octave. This procedure stretches the rules of consonant counterpoint, of course. It is explained from a theoretical point of view by the observation that in these cases the higher version of the pitch is presented in a line that leads upward, while the lower version proceeds downward. Thus the momentarily grating sonority is justified by the strongly directed linear motion.

France

At the end of the Renaissance the French produced a mannered approach to the direct treatment of poetic syllables in music that we have already noted in their secular chansons and in the Calvinist psalm settings. The principal exponent of this was the poet Jean-Antoine Baïf (1532–1589), who established the Academy of Poetry and Music in 1570. Baïf attempted to apply ancient Greek and Latin meters to the French language to create a *vers mesurée,* a somewhat artificial plan that produces a rather stilted result quite unlike the natural French language. The task of setting this verse to music fell to the composers of the academy, among whom was the talented Claude LeJeune (1528–1600). The strict application of Baïf's principles, making long syllables twice as long as short ones, produced a *musique mesurée* in which all the voices moved together in homorhythmic fashion. This could, of course, have been deadly dull, but because the syllable lengths do not predictably add up to consistent musical groupings, the effect is of freely changing meter, and some of the settings achieve a graceful elegance.

The creation of academies to exert rational control over different fields of endeavor became a characteristically French tendency. We shall observe this again in the seventeenth century.

A uniquely French genre was the *vaudeville* (from *voix de ville,* meaning "town voice") or city song. The vaudeville was a kind of simple, strophic song, performed either by vocal ensemble or, perhaps more commonly, by solo singer and lute. (The sixteenth-century vaudeville has none of the connotations the word carries in the tradition of American popular theater entertainment.) Vaudevilles were commonly used for dancing.

The vaudeville was superseded by the more sophisticated *air de cour* (court song), which first appeared in 1571 and continued into the seventeenth century. The *airs de cour* were often based on the musique mesurée approach to rhythm. The scoring called for solo voice with lute.

The Venetian Style

Before leaving the Renaissance, we must take note of a special development associated particularly with the city of Venice. In the course of the fifteenth and sixteenth centuries Venice developed into one of the most important commercial cities in Europe. As the northeastern port of Italy, it was a major point on land and sea trade routes between Europe and the East. An oligarchy, Venice was governed not by individual noblemen, but by a council made up of members of the wealthy merchant class. The city rapidly became both extremely rich and, compared to other Italian cities, secure. In contrast to the practice in other cities, the arts were more a civic privilege than a tool for the self-indulgence or self-aggrandizement of the nobility.

One of the great musical centers of Europe in the sixteenth century was Venice's basilica of St. Mark. We have already met some of its celebrated maestri di cappella, Willaert, Rore, and Zarlino. The basilica has several galleries, in which were placed separate organs; it became the focus for the development of a special type of scoring that used multiple choirs antiphonally to create a stereophonic effect. (Fig. 11.3) This polychoral technique, sometimes called *cori spezzati* ("spaced-out choirs"), was not entirely new, of course, since it followed the venerable practice of antiphonal singing in the church; nor was it necessarily limited to St. Mark's. It gained popularity, however, from its use by Willaert, who also applied it in the secular realm in some of his madrigals. By the end of the century the polychoral style had become well established.

St. Mark's organists Andrea Gabrieli (ca. 1510–1586) and his even more talented nephew Giovanni Gabrieli (ca. 1553–1612) mastered the polychoral technique. They generally used broad, simple rhythmic gestures and a good deal of familiar style scoring to support and clarify the musical dialogue. The separate choirs join at some moments, particularly at the conclusion of a piece, to give a massive dynamic climax. Giovanni Gabrieli carried the polychoral design into his 1597 canzonalike, eight-part instrumental piece headed "Sonata pian e forte," which is also notable for having the first occurrence of specific indications of dynamic contrasts throughout a musical work. (The term *sonata* here, by the way, is not yet established as the designation of a

Figure 11.3
The basilica of St. Mark in Venice, begun in 1063, was the site of important experiments in polychoral composition in the sixteenth century. The galleries had space for two different organs and different vocal or instrumental ensembles. *(Alinari/Art Resource)*

particular genre; Gabrieli probably thought of the work as a canzona and simply meant the heading literally: "played soft and loud." The forte and piano indications refer to passages where both four-part choirs play together (forte) or either choir plays alone (piano). This work also pioneered in the scoring of specific instruments, calling for one ensemble made up of a cornetto and three sackbuts and another including a violino and three sackbuts.

The Significance of Late Renaissance Styles

The development of a wide variety of national, local, and individual styles in the late sixteenth century may be regarded as evidence that the principles and techniques of the Renaissance had reached a point of crisis. The ideal of a highly polished musical *lingua franca* that had permitted the cosmopolitan style in music to be lauded as "ars perfecta" had given way to the experiments and exploitations of particular aspects of the style by individual composers or schools of composers. They had inherited an elegant and refined cosmopolitan language. Though their ideas were extremely imaginative and their composition skillful, they certainly left Renaissance music in a riot of idiosyncratic interpretations.

As we begin to examine the music of the seventeenth century, though, we shall discover that the new approaches of these composers comprised the seeds of an altogether new style. The Italian madrigalists' desire for a greater intensity in musical expression, the French academics' insistence on clarity through simple texture and strictly text-based rhythm, and the Venetian abandonment of the ideal of homogeneous sound in favor of contrasts in scoring and dynamics, were harbingers of essential elements of a new musical language.

Questions for Reflection

❖   How did nonmusical events in history contribute to the formation of late-Renaissance musical styles? What purely musical forces shaped the development of those styles?

❖   What aspects of the national character of Italy and France are embodied in the particular musical styles developed in each of those countries in the late Renaissance?

❖   Would it be justifiable to regard the history of musical style in the Renaissance as having roots, main stem, and branches, like a plant? Why or why not?

Suggestions for Further Reading

The end of the Renaissance is discussed in the general studies listed in the Suggested Readings for Chapter 7. For the late madrigal, see also the Suggested Readings for Chapter 8. Two sources focussing on the English madrigal are Edmund H. Fellowes, *The English Madrigal Composers,* 2d ed. (London: Oxford University Press, 1948), and Joseph Kerman, *The Elizabethan Madrigal* (New York: American Musicological Society, 1962).

Biographies of individual composers include Denis Arnold, *Marenzio* (London: Oxford University Press, 1965); Glenn Watkins, *Gesualdo: The Man and His Music* (Chapel Hill: University of North Carolina Press, 1973); Egon Kenton, *The Life and Works of Giovanni Gabrieli* (Rome: American Institute of Musicology, 1967); Denis Arnold, *Giovanni Gabrieli and the Music of the Venetian High Renaissance* (London: Oxford University Press, 1979).

12 THE ARRIVAL OF THE BAROQUE

Rationalism

The humanistic direction of the Renaissance led to the movement in philosophy known as rationalism. To the philosophers of the seventeenth century it was essential that reason supersede received authority not only from the church but also from antiquity or any other source. Francis Bacon (1561–1626) articulated the rationalist philosophical premise in 1620:

> Man, the administrator and the interpreter of nature, does and understands only as much as he has observed, in reality or the mind, of nature's order: he neither understands nor can do any more.

René Descartes (1596–1650) systematically pursued the rigorous application of reason in the service of philosophical understanding in his *Discourse on Method* of 1637. In his *Meditations* (1641) Descartes forced himself to abandon the authority of the church and scripture and of earlier philosophy, and even the evidence of his own senses—every presupposition except reason itself. Beginning with the only verifiable truth he could think of, "Cogito, ergo sum" (I think, therefore I exist) he reconstructed the world.

A different sort of rationalism, rooted in the premise that only material things are real, led the Englishman Thomas Hobbes (1588–1679) to develop a political philosophy that viewed social organization as a means of mutual protection against the purely selfish instincts of human individuals. Hobbes concluded that a strong absolutist monarchy was justified not by the divine right of kings but because it was the most effective means to assure social stability.

It would be an exaggeration to think that rationalism constituted the sole philosophical viewpoint of the seventeenth century. The French philosopher Blaise Pascal (1623–1662) offered a view of the human condition that argued for faith, not reason, as the way of fulfillment. Baruch Spinoza (1632–1677) attempted to synthesize reason and empiricism, human intellect and human will, and Nature and God.

Aesthetic Considerations

The musical period from about 1600 to about 1750 has come to be known as the Baroque era. This is a somewhat unfortunate name. The term, borrowed for music from art history, was originally applied to the arts with a derogatory implication: It means overly ornamented, distorted, bizarre, eccentric, or even grotesque. Like the term *Gothic* used for the period beginning in about 1150, it is based on the viewpoint of a later generation that had different aesthetic values. There certainly is a strain of exaggeration and lavish ornamentation in some Baroque art, literature, and music. We find such characteristics, for example, in some of the paintings of Peter Paul Rubens (1577–1640), with their women voluptuous to the point of fatness, surrounded by chubby cherubs or cupids. (Plate 5) The expansive richness of some of the verbal pictures in John Milton's (1608–1674) *Paradise Lost* (1667) leave a similarly ornate impression, as in this description of the angel choirs of heaven:

> . . . all
> The multitude of Angels with a shout
> Loud as from numbers without number, sweet
> As from blest voices, uttering joy, Heav'n rung
> With Jubilee, and loud Hosanna's filld
> Th'eternal Regions: lowly reverent
> Towards either Throne they bow, and to the ground
> With solemn adoration down they cast
> Thir Crowns inwove with Amarant and Gold,
> Immortal Amarant, a Flowr which once
> In Paradise, fast by the Tree of Life
> Began to bloom, but soon for mans offence
> To Heav'n remov'd where first it grew, there grows
> And flowrs aloft shading the Fount of Life,
> And where the river of Bliss through midst of Heavn
> Rowls o're *Elisian* Flowers her Amber stream;
> With these that never fade the Spirits Elect
> Bind thir resplendent locks inwreath'd with beams,
> Now in loose Garlands thick thrown off, the bright
> Pavement that like a Sea of Jasper shon

Impurpl'd with Celestial Roses smil'd.
Then Crown'd again thir golden Harps they took,
Harps ever tun'd, that glittering by thir side
Like Quivers hung, and with Praeamble sweet
Of charming symphonie they introduce
This sacred Song, and waken raptures high;
No voice exempt, no voice but well could join
Melodious part, such concord is in Heaven.

(Book III, lines 344–371)[1]

Perhaps the most extravagant of all the arts in the Baroque period was interior design, which featured sculpture and painting that crowded walls and columns with a riot of figures. Often these figures hardly seem able to stay in their places but are so crowded that they emerge into the room and intrude into the viewer's space.

The artists of the seventeenth and early eighteenth centuries would not have identified these "baroque" qualities as their aesthetic purpose, however. Indeed, it would be a gross misrepresentation to characterize all the art of the time as sharing these traits. The quiet domestic scenes painted by Jan Vermeer (1632–1675) and the intense visions of Rembrandt van Rijn (1606–1669) are quite different from the works of Rubens. The styles of the French comedic dramatist Molière (Jean Baptiste Poquelin, 1622–1673) and tragedians Pierre Corneille (1606–1684) and Jean Racine (1639–1699) could hardly be said to resemble that of Milton in any way. Like artists of all times, those of this period thought of themselves as "modern." They must have seen more variety among their styles than later historians, whose purpose is to impose some order on this century and a half.

If required to identify a particular way in which their aesthetic intention had turned away from that of the High Renaissance, the artists of the so-called Baroque era probably would have stressed the understanding of how the work was to affect the observer, reader, or audience. Unlike the artists of the fifteenth and early sixteenth centuries, they intended not simply to depict or imitate (Aristotelian mimesis) reality in an aesthetically satisfying manner, but to impose a particular state of mind on the audience. The quality of the work of art depended on how strongly it affected the observer or listener. To sense the importance of this, one need only view Gianlorenzo Bernini's sculpture of the Ecstasy of St. Theresa of Avila for the Cornaro Chapel. The figure is totally abandoned to the moment of religious transport. (Fig. 12.1)

The Doctrine of Affections

In the seventeenth-century view of human experience states of mind were known as *affections,* passions, or humors. The rationalist Descartes explored these affections in his 1649 treatise *The Passions of the Soul.* The affections are

Figure 12.1
The hallmark of Baroque artistic expression is consuming passion, as in
the sculpture *St. Teresa in Ecstasy* for the Cornaro Chapel (1645–1652) by
Gianlorenzo Bernini (1598–1680). St. Teresa abandons herself to passion as
an angel pierces her heart with the arrow of divine love. The surrounding
decoration displays the Baroque love of ornament. (*Alinari/Art Resource*)

quite static, not much like the fluctuating feelings we now call emotions. (Fig. 12.2) There are six basic affections: love, hate, joy, sorrow, wonder, and desire; any others must be compounded from these.

Descartes gave a physiological explanation for the affections that seems rather quaint today, based as it is on the application of rational argument in total disregard for any scientific study of anatomy. In his theory Descartes said the affections depended on bodily fluids known as *humors* (hence the use of this term as a synonym for affections), which controlled one's state of mind according to whether they were watery or thick and whether they rose to the head or flowed downward. Particularly important for aesthetics was the belief that the consistency of the humors, and consequently the passions, could be altered by external stimuli. Thus a work of art ought to provide a stimulus that would change the humors to produce the intended affection; a painting, a poem, or a piece of music should make the viewer, reader, or listener feel joy, for example, not merely depict a joyful occasion or figure.

This doctrine of the affections clearly has something in common with the Greek doctrine of ethos. They are not the same thing, however, any more than the doctrine of the affections is identical to the Renaissance idea of mimesis or to the understanding of emotional expression in the nineteenth century. The doctrine of ethos insists that through the work the artist changes the character of the audience, while the doctrine of the affections somewhat more modestly grants the artist power only over the audience's present state of mind.

Generally then, when we refer to the period of music history from 1600 to 1750 as Baroque, we should do so without intending to criticize the music as gaudy or overly ornamental. *Baroque* has become merely the conventional term for all the music of that era, much of which is not particularly "baroque" at all. If we wish to think of the music according to its place in general cultural history, we might refer to it as the music of the period of rationalism. If we wish to use a general term to capture the aesthetic views of the period, we might call it the period of affective expression. In any case, it is important to keep in mind that the Baroque era lasted for a long time and, like other periods, actually includes a wide variety of different styles, some that thrived simultaneously and others that arose by historical evolution.

The Florentine Camerata

In the 1570s in Florence there was a group of intellectuals, including some musicians, who met in the home of Count Giovanni de' Bardi (1534–1612) to discuss the art and philosophy of the ancients and their application to contemporary culture. They are known as the *camerata* (from the Italian word *camera,* "a room," since they met in a private room rather than a public place; the

Figure 12.2
Baroque opera was more a matter of rhetorical expression of the affections than true drama. The characters in this scene from a Baroque opera performance painted by Pietro Domenico Olivero express simple affections by standard rhetorical gestures: the young girl, sorrow; the father, haughty sternness; the young man, humble petition. (*Museo Civico di Torino*)

English cognate is, of course, *comrades*). Among these men was Vincenzo Galilei (late 1520s–1591), a lutenist and singer (and, incidentally, the father of the great scientist Galileo Galilei), who, in a treatise entitled *Dialogo della musica antica e della moderna* (Dialogue on ancient and modern music, 1581) presented a critique of the sixteenth-century polyphonic technique, based on aesthetic grounds developed from the theories of the Greeks. He objected to polyphonic text settings because he felt that they created confusion rather than clarity in interpreting the affections (he commonly uses the phrase *concetti dell'anima,* or "conceptions of the soul") that the words intended to express. He wrote,

> if the practice of music . . . was introduced to mankind for the purpose and aim that all the wise alike agree in saying—which is that it originated, firstly, for no other reason than to express with greater effectiveness the conceptions of their soul in celebrating the praises of the gods, of the genii, and of the heroes, . . . and, secondly, to impress them with equal force into the minds of mortals for their profit and comfort—then it will be clear that the rules observed by the modern contrapuntists as inviolable laws, as well as those others that they so frequently use by choice and to demonstrate their know-how, will all be directly opposed to the perfection of the best and true harmonies and melodies. . . .
>
> . . . the nature of the low sound is one thing, that of the high another, and that of the intermediate . . . is different from the one and the other of these. Similarly . . . fast motion has one property, slow another, and moderate . . . is far from the one and from the other of these. Now, these two principles being true, which they certainly are, it can easily be concluded from them . . . that singing in consonance in the manner that the modern practitioners use is inappropriate. For consonance is nothing other than a mixture of high and low sound, which (as you have already understood) strikes the sense of hearing inoffensively, or delightfully, or most sweetly.

Galilei continued by arguing that while the polyphonic style may sound very elegant, it does not genuinely convey the passions to the hearer:

> There is nobody who does not regard the variety of these [i.e., Zarlino's] observances as excellent and necessary means to the simple delight that the sense of hearing takes in the variety of harmonies. But for the expression of conceptions they are pernicious, for they are useful for nothing except to make the ensemble varied and full, and this is not always, indeed is never, suited to the expression of any conception of the poet or orator. . . . Consider each rule of the modern contrapuntists in its own right, or, if you wish, all of them together. They intend nothing but the delight of the sense of hearing—if it is possible to call that true delight. There is no book at hand for them that speaks, nor that thinks or ever thought, of such an invention as the means by which to express the conceptions of the soul and to impress them with the greatest possible effect on the minds of the hearers; . . .

He further ridiculed the mimetic manner of dealing with poetic texts:

> Lastly I come, as I promised, to the treatment of the most important and principal part of music, and this is the imitation of the conceptions that

are drawn from the words. . . . Our practical contrapuntists say, then, or hold to be certain, that they have expressed the conceptions of the soul in suitable fashion and have imitated the words whenever, in setting to music a sonnet, a *canzone,* a *romanzo,* a madrigal, or any other text in which there is found a line that says, for example, "Bitter and savage heart, and cruel desire," which is the first line of one of Petrarch's sonnets, they have made many sevenths, fourths, seconds, and major sixths among the parts when they are sung, and created by means of these a rough, harsh, and graceless sound in the ears of the hearers. . . . At other times they will say they are imitating the words when among the conceptions of these there are any meaning "to flee" or "to fly," which they will declaim with as much speed and with as little grace as anyone can imagine. And in texts that have said "to disappear," "to be reduced," "to die," or actually "exhausted," they have made the parts break off instantaneously with such violence, that instead of inducing any of these affections, they have moved the listeners to laughter, and at other times to contempt. . . . When they have said "alone," "two," or "together," they have made a solo, two, or all together sing with unusual elegance.

Finally, Galilei offered his own principles for musical expression:

Then they wonder that the music of their time does not create any of the notable effects that ancient music created; where, on the contrary, the former is so far from the latter and so deformed—indeed its opposite and its mortal enemy, as has been demonstrated and will be demonstrated even more. They would, rather, have more to be amazed about if it did create any [such effects], since it possesses no means to enable it to think of them, much less achieve them, its purpose being nothing other than the delight of the sense of hearing, and that of the other kind [ancient music] being the production in another person . . . of the same affection as in one's self.

. . . if they want to understand the way [to express the affections in music], I am happy to show them where and from whom they can learn, without much effort or nuisance—indeed, with the greatest enjoyment— and here it is. When for their amusement they go to the tragedies and comedies that the buffoons act, they should sometimes give up their unrestrained laughter, and instead be so gracious as to observe in what manner one peaceful gentleman speaks with another—with what kind of voice as regards highness and lowness, with what volume of sound, with what sort of accents and gestures, how he declaims with regard to speed and slowness of motion. They should pay a little attention to the difference that occurs among all these cases: when one of them speaks to one of his servants, or one of these with another; they should consider what happens when a prince is discoursing with one of his subjects or vassals, when with a supplicant who is making an entreaty; how an enraged man speaks, or an excited man; how the married woman; how the young girl; how the simple child; how the clever prostitute; how the man in love when he talks to his beloved in order to get her to give in to his wishes; how those who lament; how those who shout; how the timid man; and how those who exult with happiness.

What Galilei proposes, therefore, is that in order to express the affections of the speaker, the music should imitate not the poetic images themselves but the manner in which an actor spoke in assuming a particular role and creating a particular affection. This approach led to a new Baroque aesthetic for music, following the model of oratory rather than that of poetry. The new composers adapted to their musical compositions the principles they found in the already well-developed and familiar study of rhetoric. They discussed musical forms as if they paralleled the sections of a public speech, and they classified musical gestures as "figures" in the same fashion that one would list the figures of speech (simile, metaphor, hyperbole, and so on).

From his correspondence with the Roman scholar Girolamo Mei (1519–1594), Galilei learned that the music of the ancient Greeks was not polyphony but *monody* (from the prefix *mono-*, plus the root *aedien,* meaning "to sing"). This fit in well with Galilei's own reservations about the conflicting melodic gestures among the voices in a polyphonic composition. Moreover, he already had experience with the Renaissance lute song. He proposed that the new music should consist of a single vocal melody line with accompaniment by lute or keyboard instrument, a compromise between returning to bare monophony and the confusing complexities of counterpoint. Thus, out of an aesthetic theory came the justification for the idea of *homophonic* texture.

Monody and the Basso Continuo

By the time Galilei wrote his treatise, there were several models in the polyphonic repertoire that already approached the homophonic conception. The traditions of solo singing included the polyphonic cantilena-style settings of fourteenth- and fifteenth-century songs, and the practice of singing frottole to familiar style accompaniment played on the lute or other instruments. Of course in the flexible performance practice of the time practically any polyphonic piece could be taken up by one voice and instruments, whether or not that was the original intention.

The solo song tradition with which Galilei was most directly acquainted was that of the Italian Renaissance *aria,* a simple formulaic setting for voice and lute (or similar accompaniment) in familiar style that was used to sing poetic texts in a variety of standard forms. Since Italian poetry employed lines of conventional lengths, mostly seven or eleven syllables, the melodies of these arias could be repeated for stanzaic poems in strophic fashion. They might also be transferred from text to text, for they did not attempt to interpret word meanings. The aria formulas generally had a simple harmonic style, sometimes no more than an alternation among a few $\frac{5}{3}$ harmonies, and clear, declamatory rhythmic character. Singers and players would have improvised variations in the repetitions of the phrases according to their taste and skill.

Galilei himself wrote some arias, but he was not a very distinguished artist. The composer who most deserves credit for putting the camerata's ideas into practice in the solo song is Giulio Caccini (ca. 1550–1618), whose collection *Le nuove musiche* (New music, published in 1602) demonstrates the full potential of monodic song. Caccini's preface to *Le nuove musiche* makes clear that his aim was what Galilei had espoused, "to move the affect of the soul." He expressed concern with the accurate performance of his songs and thus left us a document that explains some of the ornamental figures of early Baroque performance practice: free melismatic *passaggi;* the *accento,* a run up to a note from a third below; a dynamic shaping of a single sustained note that he calls *esclamatione;* the *trillo,* at that time a rapid reiteration of a pitch; and the *gruppo,* which is equivalent to the later trill on two adjacent notes (Ex. 12.1).

Example 12.1

Vocal ornaments of the early Baroque, from Caccini's *Le nuove musiche.*

The songs of *Le nuove musiche* are of two sorts. There are several strophic arias, continuing the tradition of the sixteenth-century genre. There are also madrigals in monodic style. The madrigals owe to the polyphonic Italian madrigal a free form derived from the divisions of the text. Of course these through-composed songs are more likely than the arias to interpret the words; they are also more inclined to apply a florid, virtuosic style that is impossible when the same music has to suit a number of different verses equally well.

The most important new aspect of these monodic madrigals and arias is the nature of their accompaniment. Caccini took pains to explain the somewhat new notation he used for the keyboard (or possibly lute) accompaniment. He gives only a bass line, with numbers to indicate to the player what intervals above those notes are to be filled in to flesh out the supporting part. This practice, which dominated music throughout the entire Baroque period and continued into the nineteenth century, is known as *basso continuo* or *thoroughbass*. (It is so pervasive that the great German music historian Hugo Riemann was inclined to label the period the "basso continuo era.")

This approach to writing accompaniments was not a new invention of Caccini's. It evolved from a shorthand of Renaissance church organists who often assisted choirs by playing along with the lowest line of the vocal parts, doubling the bass when it was present, the tenor when the bass dropped out, and so on. This was called *basso seguente* (following bass). To be still more helpful, the organist might supply other details, such as the top line, the entrances of points of imitation, or important notes of the harmony. The numbers were added to bass lines beginning in the 1590s, though they remained optional, so a basso continuo part might be either *figured* or *unfigured*.

The basso continuo part might be played on a single instrument that could perform chords, such as a harpsichord or organ or a lute or theorbo. To highlight the bass line, however, it was more effective to double that part on a linear bass instrument. In the early part of the Baroque period the viola da gamba and violone were probably the most common companions for the keyboard or lute in continuo bass playing. By the end of the period the cello had generally supplanted the viol. Wind instruments such as bassoons or trombones could also play continuo parts.

The basso continuo represents a significant step in a new direction. It produced a polarized musical texture between melody and bass lines with independent functions. The bass line provided a harmonic foundation and consequently gave up some of the melodic flow that it had shared with the other parts in polyphonic music. Meanwhile, the top voice melody became freer to undertake rhetorical expressive figures and virtuosic ornamental gestures.

Concertato

Essential to the style of Baroque music is a new sound ideal. In opposition to the (at least theoretical) model of the homogeneous sound of an a cappella vocal ensemble that dominated the Renaissance, Baroque composers favored a scoring that featured contrasting timbres. The term commonly applied to this sort of scoring is *concertato,* or, in English, *concerted*.

The use of the term apparently began as a way of indicating that a vocal piece was doubled in performance by instruments; a motet or madrigal might be "concertato" with organ or viols. As we noted earlier, the exploitation of contrast in scoring was a particular hallmark of the Venetian composers of the late sixteenth century. It is not surprising, therefore, to find the first appearance of pieces actually called concertos in Giovanni Gabrieli's 1587 publication of some polychoral settings for multiple choirs and instruments by his uncle Andrea. From the beginning of the seventeenth century, the term *concertato* implies any use of contrasting voices or instruments with separate functions, from solo songs with keyboard continuo accompaniment to large, multimovement instrumental works with one or more soloists and orchestral ensemble.

Seconda Prattica

One of the very important factors in the break between the Renaissance and Baroque musical styles was their different approaches to dissonance. It will be remembered that the ideal in the Renaissance was the panconsonant treatment of harmony codified in 1558 by Gioseffe Zarlino in his *Istitutioni harmoniche*. Zarlino prescribed a very cautious handling of dissonant tones, limiting them to unaccented passing tones and suspensions. The late sixteenth-century mannerists had carried the style to its limit by exploiting chromaticism but had not explicitly abandoned the principles of the panconsonant harmonic language. At the turn of the century, however, the very premises of the style were challenged.

In 1600 the theorist G.M. Artusi (ca. 1540–1613) published a very strong attack on some recent madrigals by the rising composer Claudio Monteverdi (1567–1643). In his essay, subtitled *Delle imperfezioni della moderna musica* (On the imperfections of modern music), Artusi provided score examples that showed several different passages from Monteverdi's music in which various striking and (according to the rules of Renaissance counterpoint formulated by Zarlino) totally impermissible dissonances occurred, including accented passing tones and neighboring tones as well as the unprepared dissonances, appoggiaturas and escaped tones. Monteverdi, at the time maestro di cappella to the Duke of Mantua, responded briefly to Artusi five years later in the foreword to his *Fifth Book of Madrigals*. He wrote simply,

> Do not be surprised that I am giving these madrigals to the press without first responding to the attacks that Artusi has made against a few minor details of them; for, being in the service of His Most Serene Highness of Mantua, I am not master of that time which such a thing would require of me. I have, nevertheless, written the reply to make it known that I do not create my things by chance, and as soon as it is rewritten it

will emerge into the light, bearing on the front the title *Seconda Pratica, o Perfezioni della Moderna Musica* [Second practice, or perfections of modern music]. At this, perhaps, some will be astonished, not believing that there is another practice besides that taught by Zarlino; but they may be sure that, as far as the consonances and dissonances are concerned, there is also another consideration, different from the established one, which, to the satisfaction of both reason and sense, justifies modern composing. And this I have wished to say so that this term "second practice" in the meantime may not be taken over by anyone else, and also so that the ingenious may in the meantime consider other, secondary things having to do with harmony, and believe that the modern composer builds on the foundations of truth.

He never published the promised reply, but his defense was amplified by his brother Giulio Cesare Monteverdi in 1607 as an appendix to a set of Claudio's pieces called *Scherzi musicali.* This essay explains that dissonances forbidden by the older style—*prima prattica* (first practice) or *stile antico* (old style)—are justified in the new music by the affections suggested by the words. This principle is defended on the basis of the ancient Greek authors, who included words as an integral component of music, and by appealing to the precedent of the expressive madrigals of Rore, Marenzio, Gesualdo, and others. Artusi had, of course, omitted the words from the examples he had published (though he actually did anticipate this defense).

Thus this new harmonic style, to be called seconda prattica or *stile moderno,* operates on the fundamental premise that the text or expressive intention controls the details of the music. It can be perceived wherever the harmonic syntax of the former style is disrupted. Consequently a decisive difference between Renaissance and Baroque music is the treatment of harmony. Not surprisingly, in view of the emphasis on rhetoric as the model for expression, applications of nonharmonic tones in music were explained as "figures" of musical discourse.

Expression of New Ideas in New Styles

As was suggested earlier, the rupture between the Middle Ages and the Renaissance was much greater than that between the Renaissance and the Baroque. The close relation between literary and musical art is common to both. What changed was the manner in which this relationship was understood and employed in music.

The change from the Renaissance to the Baroque reflects first of all a change in aesthetic thought. Instead of attempting to reflect poetic sound, structure, and imagery in music, Baroque composers sought to induce certain powerful affections in their listeners. The understanding of the manner in which this was to be achieved changed from a poetic, mimetic model to a rhetorical one.

The sound of the music was affected in several ways. The homophonic texture of an expressive solo line and basso continuo accompaniment replaced the polyphonic style. The concertato sound ideal of timbral contrast rather than homogeneity dominated the new music. The panconsonant sonority of Renaissance music was superseded by the seconda prattica's free use of dissonance to increase the affective force of the composition.

Questions for Reflection

✤   How does the change from Renaissance to Baroque in the history of musical style compare to the change from the Middle Ages to the Renaissance?

✤   How are the rational and passionate components of music experience kept in balance or synthesized in Baroque artistic and musical thought and style?

✤   How does the basso continuo texture relate to earlier textures in the history of music?

Suggestions for Further Reading

An excellent overview of the Baroque period in music history can be found in Friedrich Blume, *Renaissance and Baroque Music* (New York: Norton, 1967). Two fine surveys are Manfred F. Bukofzer, *Music in the Baroque Era* (New York: Norton, 1947), now somewhat dated, and Claude V. Palisca, *Baroque Music*, 2d ed. (Englewood Cliffs, N.J.: Prentice-Hall, 1981).

Detail on the Florentine camerata may be pursued in Claude V. Palisca, *The Florentine Camerata: Documentary Studies and Translations* (New Haven: Yale University Press, 1989). The preface to Caccini's *Le nuove musiche* is available in Oliver Strunk, *Source Readings in Music History* (New York: Norton, 1950), and in the excellent edition of *Le nuove musiche* by H. Wiley Hitchcock (Madison, Wis.: A–R, 1970).

Giulio Cesare Monteverdi's amplification of Claudio Monteverdi's *seconda prattica* is included in Strunk, *Source Readings in Music History*. Biographies of Claudio Monteverdi are Leo Schrade, *Monteverdi, Creator of Modern Music*

(New York: Norton, 1964); Denis Arnold, *Monteverdi*, rev. ed. (London: Dent, 1975).

Notes

1. John Milton, *The Complete Poetry of John Milton*, ed. John T. Shawcross (New York: Anchor, 1971), 307.

13 THE EARLY BAROQUE

Three Styles

In 1649 the Italian musical scholar Marco Scacchi (ca. 1600–1697) wrote in a letter to a German composer a list of musical styles that were current in the first half century of the Baroque period. He subsumed all the different types of vocal music under three general headings: *stylus ecclesiasticus* (church style), *stylus cubicularis* (chamber style), and *stylus theatralis* (theatrical style). Each had its own place, and each possessed its own compositional characteristics. Naturally the church style was the most conservative of the three and the theatrical style the most progressive. A good deal of variety was possible within each classification, however, and cross-fertilization among the styles was recognized. In the present chapter we shall consider the music of this period under Scacchi's headings, though not in the same order in which he treated them.

The Creation of Opera

In earlier eras of music history, music had been combined with drama in the service of religion—in the ancient Greek dramas, for example, and in medieval liturgical drama. The more these dramatic types became independent of religious connections, however, the more they focussed on action and speech rather than music.

During the Renaissance composers had written *madrigal dialogues* in the form of conversations between characters; for example, the poet may speak to his own heart or to the god of love (Amor, Cupid). Sometimes the distinction between the interlocutors was reflected by a division of the singers into two groups. There were also *madrigal comedies,* series of polyphonic ensemble songs that traced a brief comic story.

The action in such musical dramas naturally unfolded solely in the imaginations of the singers and listeners, for an ensemble of singers cannot, of course, sensibly act out a single speaker's role. Such a drama is closer to a radio play than to a staged production in a theater. Orazio Vecchi's *L'Amfiparnaso* (1597), the most famous madrigal comedy, was published with woodcut illustrations to help the singers visualize the action.

In addition, the intermedi and pastoral dramas provided texts for many madrigalists. These productions set the stage, so to speak, for the early development of opera.

The Florentine camerata, with its intense interest in the art of ancient Greece, predictably gave much attention to the Greek drama. From Rome, Girolamo Mei informed the Florentines that he believed that the Greeks had sung their dramas throughout. Now the achievement of the monodic texture provided a practical solution to the problem of singing actors. Taking their subject matter from the Greek stories that were already commonly used in the pastorals, the Florentine composers experimented with a new type of musical drama, sung and acted throughout, and created the opera.

First Experiments in Opera

The first opera was a production entitled *Dafne,* which was created in 1594 and staged in 1598. The libretto was written by the poet Ottavio Rinuccini (1562–1621), and the music was primarily the work of the composer and singer Jacopo Peri (1561–1633). Unfortunately only fragments of *Dafne* have survived. In 1600, however, on the occasion of the wedding of Maria de' Medici of Florence to Henry IV of France (an extravagant occasion, also commemorated in paintings by Rubens), Peri and Rinuccini teamed up again and created the first genuine opera that survives intact, *Euridice.* Appropriately, it recounts the story of Orpheus, the great singer of Greek myth, and how through the power of his music he attempted to recover his dead wife Euridice from Hades. Peri probably sang Orpheus's role himself. (Caccini, one of the more competitive personalities in music history, soon joined the operatic movement. He managed to force a few numbers of his own composition into Peri's *Euridice* and also brought out a complete setting of the same libretto.)

It is fortunate for music history that Peri wrote about his composition in a foreword to the opera when it was published the next year. He explained there that in *Dafne* and *Euridice* he had abandoned the former lyrical style of singing and adopted a more speechlike style. This new declamatory style, which Caccini called *stile rappresentativo,* is now generally called *recitative.* Peri identified its rhythms as falling between those of natural speech and those of singing. In examining the music, we find that the melodic inflections are similarly guided by considerations of affective speech more than by meaning. The texture is, of course, basso continuo homophony.

One of the most striking features of Peri's music, to which he devoted considerable attention in his foreword, is the way in which he used harmony. The bass line was given the responsibility for underscoring the stresses in the text, which it accomplishes by the timing of harmonic changes. The harmonies between the vocal line and the bass are often freely dissonant, which creates a sense of forward motion through the phrase between one stressed, consonant harmony and the next. Thus Peri achieved a type of seconda prattica based not directly on emotional tensions but on the nature of speech itself.

Emilio de' Cavalieri (ca. 1550–1602), the director who staged the first performance of Peri's *Euridice,* can also claim some of the credit for the early development of opera. His sacred, somewhat idealized drama *Rappresentatione di anima e di corpo* (Representation of the soul and the body) was produced in Rome in 1600. It might be regarded as the first opera, since its libretto was actually set to music throughout, but its allegorical nature diminishes its dramatic character. Its score deserves recognition as the first printed score with figured bass. Cavalieri also claimed for himself the invention of the stile rappresentativo; his dialogue does not show the true recitative style, however, but is relatively lyrical and measured in its rhythm. Cavalieri also did not explore the advanced harmonic possibilities of the seconda prattica for affective expression.

Orfeo

The first true masterpiece of opera was Monteverdi's *Orfeo,* composed in Mantua in 1607. In this his first opera, the composer demonstrated that he could be as skillful and imaginative in an extended dramatic work as he could be expressive and experimental in the madrigal. He and his librettist Alessandro Striggio (ca. 1573–1630) adopted the same Greek story that Peri had used in *Euridice,* but Monteverdi achieved a more effective reconciliation of the dramatic usage of the recitative style with the need for purely musical interest. As a matter of fact, much of the design of Monteverdi's *Orfeo* seems to have been modeled on Peri's opera. Monteverdi expanded the plan, however, in both breadth and depth.

The opera opens with a brilliant "Toccata" for an instrumental ensemble, a model for the later opera overture and for the use of instrumental pieces to help articulate dramatic action. *Orfeo* is also one of the earliest examples of specific instrumentation indicated by a composer. Monteverdi assigns particular instruments throughout the opera for particular expressive purposes.

Some important dramatic choices that became normative for opera through the next three centuries are already established. The composer uses recitative to carry the dramatic action and dialogue. Closed songs in symmetrically conceived forms are used to set the general mood; at this date these commonly take the form of strophic or varied strophic songs, sometimes with instrumental *ritornello* passages between the stanzas. The occurrence of dance rhythms indicates that dancing was part of the staging.

One important song in Orfeo is Orpheus's "Possente spirto," which he sings to enchant Charon, the guardian of the entrance to Hades. The song is a set of variations, and Monteverdi published it with two versions of the solo vocal part, one highly ornamented. This gives us some insight into the performance practices of singers in that time. (The successive stanzas of "Possente spirto" also employ a series of changing instrumental accompaniments.)

Developments in Italian Opera

Opera soon spread to still more cities in Italy. The smaller courts competed with each other in staging operas as lavishly as their finances would allow. Two major cities in particular pursued unique directions, guided by their own characters.

In Rome it was quite natural that librettists and composers would explore subjects from sacred rather than ancient Greek sources. Cavalieri's *Rappresentatione di anima e di corpo* had anticipated this tendency. A prominent example from a slightly later stage was *Sant'Alessio* (1632), the life of Saint Alexis, by Stefano Landi (ca. 1590–1655).

In 1637 the city of Venice, with its tremendous wealth and characteristic sense of commercial enterprise, became the first city to open a public opera house that sold tickets and operated on the basis of profit. It soon had several competing theaters. This was an almost unique situation in the seventeenth century; only Hamburg (another commercial port city, which might appropriately be considered the Venice of Germany) followed this lead. Monteverdi, who moved to Venice in 1613, became one of the city's leading opera composers.

Stylistic Trends

Some noteworthy stylistic trends gradually formed in the Italian opera. First among these was the tendency to concentrate increasingly on solo singing. Choruses, which had been very important to the early operas of Peri and Monteverdi, gradually exited the stage. The two styles of solo singing, parlando dialogue and lyrical song, diverged more and more. Monteverdi's last opera, *L'incoronazione di Poppea* (The coronation of Poppea), employed free and rapid shifts from one style to another for rhetorical effect, even within a single sentence. In the works of his successors, however, beginning with those of Francesco Cavalli (1602–1672) and even more in the case of the operas of Antonio Cesti (1623–1669), the styles became increasingly compartmentalized into more extended passages of recitative, each leading to a separate, closed *aria*. The recitative became rapid and not especially melodic. With lyrical contours and musically conceived form, the aria momentarily arrested the action, providing emotional expression and musical gratification.

There were two principal aria styles. The so-called *bel canto* (beautiful singing) type used generally syllabic settings and relatively slow motion (usually in triple meter), which gave the singers the opportunity to let the vocal sound resonate. The contrasting type was a florid style featuring rapid coloratura passages; it showed off the performer's vocal agility. The structures of these arias also became somewhat standardized into two patterns. One model was the variation, either in strophic form or with a melody unfolding over a short ostinato bass formula. The other was the symmetrical ternary design, which, as we shall discover, later evolved into an elaborate, large-scale scheme.

Like the chorus, instrumental pieces became less and less important, with the exception of the opening number. In *Sant'Alessio* Landi had raised the curtain with a structure that was quite successful, a two-part plan comprising a slow, homorhythmic opening followed by a fast, canzona-style section.

In the middle of the century the plots of some of the operas became rather complex. Subplots, sometimes involving comic characters, mingled with the main action. This trend jeopardized the dramatic integrity of the libretto, to be sure, but it offered greater entertainment value.

Also important to the entertainment value of opera was the component of sheer spectacle. Designers and builders contrived fabulous sets, including onstage waterfalls and fountains, back-lighted scenery, and fire-breathing monsters. Machinery made possible almost instantaneous scene shifts, gods descending from the clouds, and the like. When we remember that these machines were operated by manual labor, we must admire the ingenuity of their designers. On the other hand, the use of open flame lighting accounted for a large number of theatre fires in the seventeenth and eighteenth centuries.

Vocal Chamber Music

Marco Scacchi included in the category stylus cubicularis, or chamber style, all secular vocal music other than opera. He identified within this category three different types, according to their scoring.

The first type of chamber music was the vocal ensemble song in the tradition of the sixteenth-century madrigal, which was intended for a small group of singers, presumably singing one to a part and without instrumental assistance. Such pieces continued to be composed, published, and sung after 1600, of course.

Claudio Monteverdi's books of madrigals had no accompaniment through most of Book 5. Beginning with the last six numbers of Book 5, however, basso continuo accompaniment was provided, and it was added for a reissue of Book 4. Such pieces would fall into Scacchi's second subcategory, solo or ensemble works with continuo, as would, of course, the solo arias and madrigals of Caccini's *Le nuove musiche*.

The third subcategory of chamber music comprised pieces with additional independent instrumental parts in the concertato manner. (Fig. 13.1) Such parts might function as accompaniment to the voice, but they were particularly useful to provide introductory or interludelike sinfonias and ritornellos, and to make pictorial or affective contributions in quasi-dramatic songs. A masterpiece of this type is Monteverdi's dramatic madrigal "Il combattimento di Tancredi e Clorinda," published in Book 8 (1624). In setting to music Torquato Tasso's touching story of the tragedy of the crusader Tancred who unknowingly fights and kills his beloved Clorinda, Monteverdi employed not only the two characters and a narrator but also a string ensemble that depicts the action and, through the use of written-out, measured tremolos that Monteverdi called *stile concitato* (agitated style), the affective experience of the characters.

Texture and Form

In the stylus cubicularis the composer was more likely to be concerned with problems of musical coherence than in the stylus theatralis, where the action provided a strong sense of direction and a counterfoil to the music. This resulted in special treatments of both texture and form.

The purely monodic texture of the new music offered more clarity than the interwoven sound of polyphonic music. On the other hand, monodic singing left a significant gap in musical interest. It therefore became popular to compose and sing duets with basso continuo accompaniment, where two voices could provide sufficient contrapuntal interaction to maintain interest, yet preserve a degree of clarity.

Composers cultivated a variety of forms as well. As we have noticed, Caccini's *Nuove musiche* had incorporated two different forms: the madrigal, which adopted a free form controlled by text as its Renaissance predecessor had; and the aria, a simple strophic song. Also common was the use of free melodic variation over repeated ostinato bass formulas (Ex. 13.1). Some of these bass lines lasted an entire strophe; two popular ones were the *romanesca* and *ruggiero*. Such forms are called *strophic variation*. Alternatively, the bass might be shorter, lasting only a few measures. Two types of pieces that use this procedure are the *chaconne* and *passacaglia*. A very common bass was the descending minor tetrachord (two whole steps downward followed by a half step), which might be disguised by octave transfer or by chromatic passing motion. This became a standard device for indicating the affection of sadness, and it is sometimes called the *lamento* bass.

Figure 13.1
Pieter de Hooch (ca. 1629–1677), *The Music Party* (ca. 1665). The
Netherlands painter here shows a group of seventeenth-century musicians
with instruments, forming an ensemble to make chamber music for their own
enjoyment. Here are a recorder, lute, and violin playing with the singer, who
keeps time with her right hand. A bass viol rests at one side. (*Cleveland
Museum of Art, Gift of the Hanna Fund, 51.355*)

Early in the seventeenth century the term *cantata* (sung) was applied to
works in strophic variation form and sometimes to those in other forms as
well. Soon this designation came to mean a multisectional piece using contrasting singing styles, and it took on quite different implications.

Sacred Music

In Scacchi's classification all church music is subsumed under the category
stylus ecclesiasticus. As in the case of chamber music, however, the theorist
recognized several different types of this music.

Example 13.1

Standard bass patterns of the early Baroque.

The first three actually belong to the sixteenth century but continued into the seventeenth and even the eighteenth. The primary ecclesiastical style was the polyphonic, a cappella, Netherlands-style motet and Mass. In this type of music the counterpoint was still strictly controlled by the rules of panconsonance laid out by Zarlino. This style might also have been known as prima prattica, stile antico, or, perhaps more commonly, *stylus gravis* (Latin, serious style). It became so thoroughly identified with sacred music that the sound of this harmonic and contrapuntal manner in a secular piece could serve as an allusion to the church and sacred matters. A second subtype of the ecclesiastical style was the polychoral scoring of the Venetian tradition. A third group was made up of works in the polychoral style but with concertato instruments. Scacchi takes for granted that this music still uses the harmonic language of the stile antico.

The Sacred Concerto

The final and most progressive type of church music identified by Scacchi was the *sacred concerto*. In this type the modern style is applied to the composition of motets; in other words, the sacred concerto developed from the Renaissance motet in the same way that vocal chamber music with basso continuo arose from the sixteenth-century madrigal. The first composer to publish monodic pieces under the designation "concerto" was the Italian Lodovico Grossi da Viadana (ca. 1560–1627), whose *Cento concerti ecclesiastici* (One hundred church concertos) appeared in 1602. These concertos—motets for one, two, or three voices with an unfigured basso continuo—still employ the simple conservative harmonies of the stile antico. Because of their harmonic restraint they constitute only a tentative step into the new period.

In 1613 Monteverdi left Mantua for Venice to assume the duties of mae-stro di cappella at St. Mark's Cathedral, following in the footsteps of Willaert, Rore, and Zarlino. He composed equally brilliantly in all styles, of course, but it was most significant that the hero of the seconda prattica should be brought to the most prestigious church music directorship in Europe. He had proved his mastery of the stile antico in a parody Mass based on a motet by the early sixteenth-century Netherlands composer Nicolas Gombert (ca. 1495–1560), but his other sacred music did not neglect the affective possibilities of the *stile moderno,* and he may be said to have brought sacred music definitively into the Baroque aesthetic. For example, his setting of the Office of Vespers, published with the Mass in 1610, employs the monodic texture with basso continuo and demands extreme virtuosity from the solo singers.

In the north the new style in sacred music found its greatest composer in Heinrich Schütz (1585–1672), who worked primarily in Dresden. From 1609 to 1612 Schütz visited Venice to learn from Giovanni Gabrieli, and he went to that city again in 1628–1629 to absorb the newer manner of Monteverdi. He established a synthesis that combined the monodic style and affective aesthetic of the Italians with the German language and taste. Schütz's most important music is sacred, including both Lutheran and Roman Catholic works. His three collections of *Symphoniae sacrae* (Sacred symphonies) follow Gabrieli's *Sacrae symphoniae.* During the period when Germany was embroiled in the Thirty Years' War, he was compelled to write for more limited forces and produced *Kleine geistliche Concerten* (Little sacred concertos) with equal success.

Among Schütz's sacred music are some quasi-dramatic, multimovement works, an Easter oratorio, a Christmas oratorio, *Die sieben Worte Jesu Christi am Kreuze* (The seven words of Jesus Christ on the cross), and the Passions according to Matthew, Luke, and John. These works reflect the apparently irresistible influence of the Baroque love of the dramatic on the music of the church.

Oratorio

The *oratorio* developed from the motet and sacred concerto, as an outgrowth of the musical settings of biblical texts in dialogue. In this, it was as natural a development as the liturgical drama of the Middle Ages. It is not easy to distinguish the moment at which the first fully developed oratorio appeared. Such pieces were variously called motet, dialogue, concerto, cantata, and *histo-ria.* As the composers' imaginations led them to develop the interaction be-tween characters and to portray dramatic events in music, these pieces could no longer be incorporated into the liturgy. They were performed in a prayer hall adjoining the church sanctuary, which was called *oratorio* and gave its name to the genre sometime around 1640.

The stories of the oratorios were taken from the Bible, especially from the Old Testament, which is rich in dramatic episodes. Modern poets filled in details and invented new dialogue to add length and interest. If the text was in Latin, as was the case in the early oratorios, the work was an *oratorio latino*; if it was in Italian (or another language in another country), it was an *oratorio volgare*. The general tendency was for the oratorio latino to be in prose, incorporating the words and following the style of the Bible, while the oratorio volgare was commonly in poetic verse. It became common to divide the action into two large sections, like the acts of a play or opera.

The action was not staged as in opera but was narrated by a singer known as *testo* (text) or *historicus*, and this became a crucial distinction between opera and oratorio. While most of the singing fell to the narrator and the solo singers who took the lines of the individual characters in the story, there was a greater use of chorus than in opera, for the mechanics of bringing a chorus onto an operatic stage did not inhibit the creator of the oratorio. Thus the oratorio allowed more variety and contrast in vocal sound than the opera did, partially compensating in this way for what the oratorio lacked in costumes, stage design, and movement.

The oratorio became very popular among devout lay Christians, especially in Rome. It could even serve as a substitute entertainment during Lent when the opera houses were closed in deference to the penitential season.

The composer most responsible for the early establishment of the oratorio was Giacomo Carissimi (1605–1674), who worked primarily in Rome. His works were mostly composed for a society of devout laymen, the brotherhood of the Sanctissimo Crocifisso (Most Holy Crucifix) at the elite, upper-class Church of San Marcello. Such societies were one result of the aggressive Jesuit movement in the period following the Counter-Reformation.

Seventeenth-Century Instrumental Music

In his list of musical styles Scacchi did not include purely instrumental genres at all. Nevertheless, the early seventeenth century was an important period for the development of instrumental music, which steadily gained importance in musical life. Several instrumental genres were at a crucial transitional stage between the Renaissance and the mature forms of the late Baroque, and significant changes took place.

The rich variety of instruments available to composers in the early seventeenth century is displayed in the three-volume book *Syntagma musicum* by the German composer, theorist, and organist Michael Praetorius (1571–1621). Praetorius also suggested imaginative ways of using instruments in performances of sacred vocal music to create contrasts of scoring.

It is of primary importance to observe that the early Baroque maintained the types of instrumental music known to the Renaissance. A number of new factors in musical thinking came together, however, to direct those older forms along new paths. These include the doctrine of the affections, the concertato principle, the new harmonic language, and ideas about abstract musical form.

The Ricercar

Around the turn of the century, composers must have begun to realize that the ricercar, which had been the most advanced instrumental genre of the sixteenth century, had an inherent problem. In taking the motet as its model, it adopted a free form consisting of a series of interlocking sections based on various points of imitation; but while a motet made sense of the free form through the meaning in its text, the textless ricercar risked giving the impression that the music wandered aimlessly from one point to the next.

The solution to this problem, achieved in the ricercars and other similar works such as the keyboard *fantasia,* was to concentrate on working out one point of imitation or *subject* through an entire piece. Besides providing unity to the piece, this use of one predominant idea was in keeping with the Baroque aesthetic assumption that an entire piece or movement should be governed by a single affection. In order to provide variety, the subject might be altered at each new polyphonic *exposition* by such techniques as rhythmic augmentation or diminution, and it might be accompanied by several different countermelodic ideas in turn. The pervasive use of a single subject (in this early period usually limited to a single tonal area) gave coherence to extensive compositions.

The Sonata

The canzona developed along what we might consider the opposite path to that of the ricercar. Endangered by the same potential undirectedness as the ricercar, the canzona tended to fall apart into short, contrasting sections that maintained interest more through contrast than through unity. The result was the rise of the *sonata* (meaning "sounded," i.e., "played"; compare *cantata*). Ultimately the divisions between the sections of the sonata resulted in the formation of clearly distinguished movements. These were related by contrasting tempos, generally the alternation of slow and fast. The individual movements later grew to have their own internal forms.

While the ricercar and fantasia continued as thoroughly contrapuntal types, the sonata was more modern and adopted the texture of one or a small number of melodic parts accompanied by basso continuo. (Fig. 13.2) For the

Figure 13.2
Keyboard instruments, with their role of playing basso continuo in all sorts of music, grew immensely in importance during the Baroque period. This harpsichord dates from 1618; it was built by the Amsterdam craftsman Andreas Ruckers the Elder. (*Musik Instrumenten Museum, Staatliches Institut für Musikforschung Preußischer Kulturbesitz, Berlin*)

same reason that the chamber vocal duet was popular, the texture of two solo instruments and continuo thrived in the sonata. This texture is commonly called *trio texture,* and a sonata that employs it is a *trio sonata.*

The violin family of instruments, which could more easily handle the demands of the florid Baroque style, began to replace the Renaissance viols in the seventeenth century. Most trio sonatas call for two violins, keyboard, and cello. Other combinations of instruments are also possible, such as recorders, flutes, and oboes on the upper lines and bassoon on the bass part.

Sets of Variations

The construction of sets of variations offered composers a simple but effective way to achieve both unity and variety in musical form during this early period in the growth of instrumental music. Such sets were often called *partita,* since they were made up of many *partes.* Variations sometimes explored the possibilities available in ornamenting a given melody. Another type of variations borrowed the same harmonic formulas used for vocal dance songs in strophic variation form, such as the romanesca and ruggiero. Still another type, especially suited for Lutheran church organists, employed a chorale melody as a cantus firmus, stated either straightforwardly or with melodic embellishment, around which other parts wove the series of variations. Such a practice naturally produces a *chorale partita*. Early examples appear in the 1624 collection *Tabulatura nova* by the organist Samuel Scheidt (1587–1654), who served the court at Halle in Germany. This collection also contains variation sets based on secular melodies. The title *Tabulatura nova* refers to the appearance, unusual at that time, of polyphonic parts written out in open score to show clearly the contrapuntal interplay of voices. In fact Scheidt's notation is not tablature at all.

Dance Music

Like the Renaissance the Baroque era produced a great deal of dance music and stylized pieces based on dance music. The individual dances tended to adopt a binary form with two halves roughly equal in length and separated by a strong cadence, each half commonly repeated.

The practice of pairing slow and fast dances was gradually extended to more movements, forming a *suite*. Suites loosely followed a simple plan of contrasting tempos and rhythmic characters. There might be a free piece by way of introduction, sometimes labeled *prelude*. The opening dance movement was now the *allemande,* in duple rhythm at a moderate tempo and with a characteristic anacrusic beginning. This was followed by a *courante,* faster and using triple or compound rhythms. After this pair there would often be a *sarabande,* featuring triple meter with a distinctive agogic stress on the second beat of the measure and a very slow tempo. The remainder of the suite was quite flexible and might include various other dance types. Among these the *gigue* eventually emerged as the favorite choice for the final movement, since its fast compound rhythm lent a brilliant touch to the end of a suite. The rational planning of the multimovement shape of the suite—particularly the ordering of allemande, courante, sarabande, gigue—became more or less standard in Germany after about 1650 due to the influence of the keyboard suites of Johann Jacob Froberger (1616–1667). In France and England there was more flexibility. In Italy the suite idea was used in the various movements of the sonata but was not much pursued as an independent type.

One possibility in the suite was to have the movements share some fundamental musical idea, so that they constituted a manifestation of the theme-and-variations principle. The dance suites in Johann Hermann Schein's (1586–1630) important collection *Banchetto musicale* (1617) illustrate the variation process. The allemande was given a regular duple statement followed by a strict variation in triple meter. In addition, the variation principle was employed more flexibly in a general sharing of the allemande's motivic material by the pavane-galliard pair and the courante that comprise the remainder of the suite. A consequence of this is that the term *partita,* which could identify a variation set, sometimes also denoted a suite.

Improvisatory Instrumental Music

Improvisatory types of pieces continued to be used during the Baroque era, especially by keyboard players. These improvisatory pieces were often entitled "toccata" or "prelude." In such works the free, virtuosic passagework might be paired with contrapuntal sections resembling fragments of ricercars or canzonas.

Questions for Reflection

❖   What historical factors led to the distinction between church, chamber, and theatrical styles in music in the early seventeenth century? How have more recent periods of music history maintained or forsaken the separation of styles by social function?

❖   In what sense is the music of Baroque opera dramatic? In what senses is it not truly dramatic?

❖   For what kinds of singers were the Baroque monodic madrigal, aria, and cantata intended, and how would the social contexts in which they were likely to be performed differ from the usual situations in which they are most often heard today? How does that difference affect the singer's and hearer's experience of the music?

❖   How did the effects that the Thirty Years' War had on music compare to those of the Hundred Years' War? Is it possible to generalize about the effects wars have on the development of music or the arts in general?

❖   How did the appearance and development of the oratorio differ from or resemble that of the medieval liturgical drama?

❖   What factors in the early seventeenth century contributed to the increasing importance and sophistication of purely instrumental music?

Suggestions for Further Reading

A standard history of opera is Donald J. Grout, *A Short History of Opera,* 2d ed. (New York: Columbia University Press, 1965). The early history of opera is outlined in Robert Donington, *The Rise of Opera* (London: Faber and Faber,

1981). A translation of Peri's preface to *Euridice* can be found in Oliver Strunk, *Source Readings in Music History* (New York: Norton, 1950).

The authoritative work on the oratorio is Howard E. Smither, *A History of the Oratorio* (Chapel Hill: University of North Carolina Press, 1977–1987), of which the first volume deals with the period under consideration in this chapter. One biography of Schütz is Hans Joachim Moser, *Heinrich Schütz,* trans. C. F. Pfatteicher (St. Louis: Concordia, 1959).

David D. Boyden, *The History of Violin Playing from Its Origins to 1761* (London: Oxford University Press, 1965), and Willi Apel, *The History of Keyboard Music to 1700* (Bloomington: Indiana University Press, 1972) give valuable information on the development of instrumental music in the early Baroque.

14 THE HIGH BAROQUE

French Opera in the Seventeenth Century

The Background

The musical situation in France in the second half of the seventeenth century differed from that of other countries and periods. By way of historical background it is important to note that in the Thirty Years' War France had succeeded in asserting its integrity against the Hapsburg Holy Roman Empire. The efforts of the French prime minister, Cardinal Richelieu (1585–1642), established the idea of the modern nation-state and centralized the government under the absolute rule of King Louis XIII (r. 1610–1643). After Louis's death there was a decade's delay before his son came of age, during which Louis XIII's wife, Anne of Austria, acted as regent, aided by her prime minister Jules Mazarin (1602–1661), an Italian. Louis XIV took the reins of government in 1653 and ruled until 1715. He strengthened the absolutist monarchy and cultivated a brilliant court life in his new palace at Versailles. (Fig. 14.1) Of course music had an important place in the court, and its development was powerfully affected by the political situation.

Within the area of cultural affairs the French kings took up the tradition of academicism that we have already noted in the Renaissance with Baïf's *Académie de poésie et de musique*. In the seventeenth century official academies were founded under royal sponsorship. The first was the *Académie française*, set up in 1635 under Richelieu to study and cultivate the *belles lettres*. Its greatest figures were the dramatists Corneille and Racine, who brought the genre of stage tragedy from the Greek models up to the present. There followed in 1648 an *Académie royale de peinture et de sculpture*, and, under Louis XIV, a whole series of new academies, for dance, graphic arts, the sciences, music, and architecture. The *Académie royale de musique* was established in 1669. The purpose of

Figure 14.1
Louis XIV's magnificent palace at Versailles naturally included an opera theater. *(Giraudon/Art Resource)*

these academies was to set up and maintain high intellectual and artistic standards and a French national style. In practice the result was partly to shape all these activities according to the court's own interests and tastes and partly to maintain an intellectual, rationalistic manner in French art. As a result

French Baroque music tended to be more Apollonian than that of other nations at the same time.

France had a special tradition of court entertainment in the form of the *ballet de cour*. The ballet of the early seventeenth century was not a stage production performed by professionals but a participatory art form with the courtiers themselves as the dancers. Following a quasi-dramatic plan, the ballet combined dance with instrumental music, spoken narrative and dialogue, airs and ensemble singing, and all the trappings of dramatic spectacle: costumes, sets, and machines. In several different ballets, including a spectacular ballet of 1653, the *Ballet de la nuit,* the young King Louis XIV was presented as the sun, the allegorical center of the universe; the nickname "Sun King" stuck with him, for it seemed to reflect not only his glory but also the way in which French society radiated from the royal court and the manner in which the nobility revolved around its center. The ballet exerted a powerful influence on the development of opera in France; the fact that it occupied the place that opera sought to invade led to the inclusion of a considerable quantity of dance in French opera when it did arise.

The Beginnings of French Opera

Not surprisingly, opera first appeared during Mazarin's premiership. He brought several operas from his homeland for performance at the French court in the 1640s. The French did not find the Italian style congenial to their taste, however, and soon attempted to produce a national operatic style of their own. The librettist Pierre Perrin (ca. 1620–1675) criticized the Italian manner in his preface to the *Pastorale d'Issy* of 1659, written by him and composed by Robert Cambert (ca. 1628–1677). The Italian opera was too long, he claimed, its recitatives monotonous, its poetry stilted, and the words of the arias unintelligible; furthermore, the Italian castrati "horrified women and made men snicker." Perrin was granted the royal privilege to establish the academy for music, which meant that he held a monopoly on opera in France.

Perrin soon lost the academy to the Florentine expatriate composer Jean-Baptiste Lully (1632–1687). Lully had come to Paris in 1646, and he rose rapidly to prominence through his skills in both art and politics. He was, in fact, perhaps the most successful schemer and manipulator among all the great composers in the history of music. French music in the second half of the seventeenth century and even beyond was largely dominated by the powerful influence of Lully.

From 1653 Lully was instrumental composer to Louis XIV. As a member of Louis's orchestra known as the *Vingt-quatre violons du roi* (the King's twenty-four strings), Lully was impatient with existing performance practices, including general lack of discipline and the inclination of the players to embellish their own parts freely, without regard for the ensemble. In 1656 he established the rival *Petits violons* (Little strings), with first sixteen and later twenty-one players. With this group Lully set new standards for discipline and ensemble. The simplicity of his style appealed naturally to French aesthetic taste, and the two groups were reconciled in 1664.

In the meantime, Lully also served in the ballet. He was a dancer from 1653, when he danced beside Louis in the *Ballet de la nuit,* until 1663, and he became superintendent of music in 1661. With the comic playwright Molière, Lully created *comédies-ballets* between 1663 and 1672. These productions combined the traditions of the Italian pastoral operas and the French ballet de cour and laid the groundwork for a fully developed French type of opera. When he bought the license for the Académie de musique from Perrin in 1672, this position and several royal patents gave Lully practically complete control of musical life in France.

The culmination of Lully's musical style came in the operas that he called *tragédies lyriques,* on which he collaborated with the librettist Philippe Quinault (1635–1688). These productions, which followed the classical plan of five acts, adopted classical mythological plots replete with laudatory references to the great nation of France and its king. They took from the French ballet tradition a considerable quantity of dancing, more participation of the chorus than the Italian opera of the same period, and lavish machinery and sets.

Musical Style in French Baroque Opera

The music of the solo singing in French opera tends to make the distinction between the recitative and the aria less obvious than in Italian opera. The recitative does not patter along so rapidly, and in good French tradition it is quite carefully measured according to the requirements of diction. As a result the scores often show rather flexible barring. The *airs* derive their style more from the simple air de cour than from the Italian aria. While they are more metrically regular than the recitative, they are still simple and generally syllabic.

Instrumental music in Lullian opera had the usual functions of accompanying singing and articulating the dramatic action, and naturally it also supplied dance accompaniments. An influential contribution to the history of instrumental form was the *French overture,* which found a particularly satisfactory manner of treating the opening of a large-scale musical work. The overture began with a slow and stately passage in homorhythmic style, generally featuring dotted rhythms. There followed a faster, lighter, commonly fugal section, and there might be a brief return to the opening style at the end. Following the practice of the Vingt-quatre violons du roi, French string orchestral writing is in five parts and thus is weightier than Italian scoring, which typically has only four or even as few as three parts. The French also preferred plenty of wind instruments; they had a particular liking for the nasal double-reed sound.

English Music in the Seventeenth Century

The First Stuarts

In the first half of the seventeenth century England was under the rule of the Stuart kings James I and Charles I. In the field of church music the Anglican Services and the full and verse anthems of the late Renaissance continued to develop. The secular vocal repertoire moved from polyphonic madrigals toward accompanied solo song. In instrumental music keyboard dances and variations and ensemble fantasies were predominant. The court had a tradition somewhat comparable to the French court ballet in the *masque,* a variety entertainment with recitatives, songs, choruses, dances, and costumes. No less a literary figure than John Milton contributed to the genre in the masque *Comus* (1634), written in collaboration with the composer Henry Lawes (1596–1662). Because there was also a thriving theater, incidental music for plays was especially cultivated, and opera did not make an immediate impression.

The Commonwealth

During the period of Cromwell's Commonwealth (1649–1660) the Puritan ideals of the Roundheads deeply affected the English arts, especially music. The musical influence of the flamboyant court cultures of the European continent was severely limited. Because the musical establishments of the Cavalier court and church were disbanded, domestic music held a significant place, and the smaller, simpler genres, such as song, appear more prominent in the music history of the period. The theater, whose morals the Puritans considered highly suspect, was aggressively suppressed. Musical concerts, however, were not banned, and under that guise plays could be given with a great deal of inserted music. The result seems a bit artificial and patchworklike in retrospect, but such hybrids kept English theater alive.

The Restoration

After the Stuart Restoration with the accession of Charles II to the throne in 1660, music was revived in both court and church. The earlier English traditions of secular masques and sacred Services and anthems were resumed, and the influence of Italian and French styles began to be felt in earnest.

In sacred music the anthem developed a mature Baroque style. The choral sound that emerged during this time has a uniquely English character, in which concentration focusses on clear, idiomatic declamation of text in a predominantly homophonic texture. In verse anthems the solo sections generally resemble the simpler, declamatory French style rather than the ornate Italian manner. Still heard occasionally are expressive simultaneous cross-relations inherited from the English composers of the late Renaissance.

Henry Purcell (1659–1695), the leading English composer in the last part of the century, was born just in time for the Restoration and worked as both a royal and a church musician, holding the posts of composer to the king's violin ensemble and of organist at the royal court and at Westminster Abbey. In his short life he served three kings: Charles II, James II, and William III.

Opera did not become a truly native genre in England. *Venus and Adonis* (1684 or 1685) by the composer John Blow (1649–1708), though it was fully composed in music, was called a masque and included court participants. Purcell's masterful short opera *Dido and Aeneas* (1689), written for a girls' school, is atypical. More representative is the "semiopera" *The Fairy Queen* (1692), in which an abbreviated and adapted spoken version of Shakespeare's *A Midsummer Night's Dream* provides the framework for a series of brief, unrelated masques. The effect is certainly that of a curious mish-mash by modern standards, but the work has the virtue of combining the art of England's greatest playwright with that of one of its finest composers. Purcell's music in these theatrical compositions shows his love of the English choral anthem, perhaps some influence of the French in the approach to declamation in recitative, and a gift for the Italian style of operatic solo singing. Especially noteworthy are the arias constructed as variations over a repeating ground bass, a type at which Purcell ranks with the greatest of all seventeenth-century composers.

Composers in the ages of court patronage had much to do that was temporary and practical. Court composers of this period produced many fine occasional pieces, which unfortunately are not suitable for our common performance situations in the twentieth century. Such works include Purcell's *odes* and *welcome songs* to celebrate such events as royal arrivals, weddings, and birthdays. They combine solo and choral settings with much fine music but have texts that often depend on the specific occasion for which they were composed. The odes for St. Cecilia's Day, honoring the patron saint of music, are more practicable.

Among Purcell's instrumental works are keyboard and ensemble pieces. The polyphonic fantasy or *fancy* for viols still had a public, though the Italian sonata with basso continuo was increasing in popularity.

Italian Opera

Toward the end of the seventeenth century Italian opera developed a sharply defined style. Its general characteristics are often associated with the southern city of Naples, though they were by no means exclusive to composers working there. The leading composer of the Neapolitan opera was Alessandro Scarlatti (1660–1725). Scarlatti had come to Naples from Rome, and while he did not create the style, his works represent its culmination.

The change of approach during the century is striking. Largely due to the efforts of the librettist Apostolo Zeno (1668–1750), the plots were tightened up, the mixture of serious and comic material was sorted out into separate scenes, and eventually, in order to raise the literary level of the genre, the comedy disappeared, leaving the genre we know as *opera seria*.

A thinning and sorting process also took place in the music. The standard orchestral opening number, known in Italy as *sinfonia* rather than overture, usually was the only purely instrumental element as dancing declined. The sinfonia consisted of three rather independent movements in contrasting styles and tempos, ordered fast-slow-fast. The use of choruses was abandoned almost entirely, as was most ensemble singing, so that the opera became a chain of alternating recitatives and arias.

The style of recitative became simpler, employing rapid, free rhythms and limited melodic contours. Most of the recitative was supported only by the basso continuo, which tended to play at a very slow harmonic rhythm; this type was called simple recitative (in the nineteenth century it came to be known as *secco*, or "dry"). The entire string ensemble might be used for special effects, giving the scoring known as *accompagnato*. Segments of recitative in which still more passion was to be expressed, as often occurred at the end of a recitative passage, might be set in *arioso* style, with more melodic interest and generally a more rapid continuo motion.

The arias grew increasingly florid and virtuosic. As a consequence of the Baroque commitment to maintaining the governing affection by musical means throughout a piece, each aria normally adopted a particular affective style based on characteristic melodic-rhythmic figures. Thus, a "rage" aria might have wide-ranging scales and arpeggios, a heroic aria could employ trumpetlike motives, a mournful one would use chromatic motion and "sighing" slurs, and so on.

By the end of the century the closed form adopted by most arias was ternary form. This led to the full-fledged *da capo* aria structure. In this plan there were two large, contrasting parts, the second followed by a return to the first indicated simply by the marking "da capo." The first part opened with an instrumental *ritornello* in the main key, establishing the aria's affective content. A section for the solo singer followed, setting out the first half of the aria's text, departing from the opening key and proceeding to another. In this contrasting key came a return of the instrumental ensemble with ritornello material. Then followed a second solo section that repeated the text of the first solo section, modulating back to the main key. Finally the part closed with a return to the ritornello, again in the main key. The second large part, containing the second half of the aria text, was predominantly the province of the singer and featured further key contrast. In outline, the form operated as follows:

Part 1					Part 2	Part 1 da capo
	Text A		Text A			Text B
Rit.1	Solo A1	Rit.2	Solo A2	Rit.3		Solo
Main key	_____	New key	_____	Main key		Other key(s)

Important here is the coordination of textual and thematic material with a harmonic plan and scoring to create a musical design that operates on several · levels simultaneously. This became an increasingly important process through the eighteenth century.

Free embellishment of the musical line by solo performers was inherent in Baroque performing tradition, and especially so in the da capo aria. The vocalist was expected to ornament the return of the first large part of the piece to the limit of his or her skill, though within the sense of the music and the words. The technical virtuosity of these singers was undoubtedly impressive. The greatest of the singers were the castrati, whose beautiful boy soprano voices were preserved by surgery, and who grew to great physical strength and imposing size and presence without their voices changing into the usual masculine register. The castrati took the heroic roles in the Italian opera, to the shock or amusement of audiences from other nations. They were the masters of vocal technique, but later, as they and the music for which they were suited went out of fashion, their skills were no longer taught.

With the practice of improvised embellishment, we naturally find composers and critics complaining of tasteless self-indulgence on the part of many a prima donna and primo uomo. An amusing satirical treatise on the subject, *Il teatro alla moda* (The fashionable theater) by the composer Benedetto Marcello (1686–1739), indicates that opera was often controlled by the singers, their protectors, the special-effects crew, and the animal trainers, rather than by the librettist and composer, who, in turn, knew nothing of each other's business. At its best, however, the Italian opera of the period offers glorious vocal music based on the evocation of powerful passions.

The Cantata and Other Vocal Chamber Music

Vocal chamber music continued to thrive and develop in the High Baroque. The most sophisticated type was the cantata. As the genre evolved, it tended more and more to form a series of articulated movements, alternating recitatives and arias. The texts became like monodramas for solo voice with basso continuo, possibly obbligato instruments, or even small orchestral ensembles. As would be expected, the forms of the arias duplicated those of the opera.

Cantatas had their greatest success in Italy, but they were also popular in all the other nations of Europe.

Smaller vocal pieces also existed. Simple strophic songs or one-movement, closed-form arias had a market especially among middle-class amateur musicians. (Fig. 14.2) These pieces generally do not pretend to the status of high art, but there are occasional delights among them. Lute-accompanied settings were eventually supplanted by those with basso continuo. In France the air was still cultivated. England got some fine songs from Purcell and other composers. The German burghers' wives and daughters sang continuo-Lieder and *Arien* that characteristically extolled moral virtues.

German Musical Genres

In the second half of the seventeenth century Germany was more influenced by French and Italian music than influential on the music of those countries. The French and Italians had never looked to Germany for musical leadership, but German composers often imitated the styles of music developed in France and Italy, and they traveled to those countries to learn the latest musical techniques, as we have already seen in the case of Schütz.

In northern Germany at this time there arose ideas and styles that were peculiar to the region. The dominance of Lutheranism there helped create a musical culture quite different from those of the Catholic-dominated regions.

The music of the Lutheran church occupies an impressive place in the history of the development of vocal music in Baroque Germany. In addition to chorale arrangements and solo pieces and ensembles for several voices with basso continuo, the sacred concerto developed into a sophisticated multi-movement construction. The leading composers of this repertoire were Dieterich Buxtehude (ca. 1637–1707), who served as organist in Lübeck in the far north of Germany, and Johann Pachelbel (1653–1706), who worked in central Germany and was therefore more influenced by Italian styles, including the Venetian polychoral tradition. The largest of their works combined sections for full choir; passages for one, two, or sometimes three solo singers; and instrumental ensemble or basso continuo accompaniment. The repertory of chorale melodies sometimes provided thematic material, and chorales could appear as cantus firmus (generally in the top voice) or in imitative treatment.

Keyboard Music

In the field of keyboard music the German church organists, among them Buxtehude and Pachelbel, entered their heyday in the seventeenth century. The needs of the service led to the cultivation of chorale settings for organ. To introduce congregational chorale singing they employed the *chorale prelude*, a

Figure 14.2
Gabriel Metsu (1630–1667), *The Music Lesson* (1659). The figures have been playing lute and bass viola da gamba. The young woman and the music master flirt while the viol player retunes his instrument. (*Metropolitan Museum of Art, Gift of Henry G. Marquand, 1890. Marquand Collection. 91.26.11*)

statement of the chorale melody as a cantus firmus, supported by independent material devised to produce an affection in keeping with the chorale text. A successful manner of handling this type of composition was to integrate the cantus firmus with the rest of the texture by giving the main melody in relatively long notes in one line—commonly the soprano or tenor—and introducing each of its phrases by motives from the chorale presented in imitative texture in the other parts. This technique is known as *Vorimitation* (fore-imitation, or pre-imitation). It has already been mentioned that chorales could provide the basis for variations in the chorale partita, a type especially culti-vated by Georg Böhm (1661–1733) of Lüneburg, where Johann Sebastian Bach gained some of his early experience. An elaborate fugal setting of chorale-derived subjects produced the *chorale fantasia* or *chorale fugue*. All such works based on preexisting melodies fall into the classification of *gebunden* (bound) forms.

Of course the organists also explored genres that were *frei* (free). Among these were the descendants of the now-familiar improvisatory preludes and toccatas. These were often combined with fugal composition, either by alter-nation of virtuosic sections with more rigorous imitative contrapuntal ones or by the pairing of separate movements in the two contrasting styles. Such pieces did not form part of the church service, but they were commonly played before or after the worship itself.

Musical Drama

Germany's native musical drama in the years around 1700 was the *Singspiel,* a type that employed spoken dialogue and a vocal style more like that of song than that of the elaborate aria. The princely courts mostly preferred to import Italian opera. As mentioned earlier, Hamburg followed Venice in opening a public opera theater in 1678. The most important composer there was the music director Reinhard Keiser (1674–1739), whose stage works in both Italian and German are the best of the period.

The Development of Instrumental Forms and Idioms

In the course of the seventeenth century the increasing interest in instrumental music independent of vocal contexts or models led to the development of idiomatic styles associated with individual instruments. The violin family was fully developed and became the usual core of instrumental ensemble group-ings. Players achieved a technique that allowed the performance of lines that vastly exceeded the range, flexibility, and speed limits of earlier melodies based on vocal ideals. (In turn the singers' techniques began to imitate those of instruments, and in much mature Baroque vocal music the tables have been turned so that music for voices adopts an instrumental idiom.)

The concertato ideal led to the exploitation of a wide variety of instrumen-tal colors. Most of the orchestral instruments began to approach their modern forms, though they all continued to evolve over the next couple of centuries. The Baroque composers freely employed recorders and flutes, oboes and bassoons, trumpets and timpani, as well as strings and keyboard instruments. Also available were horns (still associated with the hunt), trombones (often used to support choral singing in churches), and various other instruments, from the old viols and lute to the mandolin.

Style Developments in Instrumental Music

The rise of instrumental music also required musical structures that would maintain attention through a balance of unity and contrast and would have a satisfactory coherence and overall form. These goals were reached in different ways in various genres. To generalize we can offer several broad observations. The idea of the domination of a movement by a single affection created a high degree of unity within any movement, for the affection should be produced by concentration on one expressive musical figure, which would give focus and also provide an insistent rhythm and melodic motive throughout the movement. Contrast was likely to be produced by concertato scoring or by the so-called *terraced dynamic* changes that imitated concertato effects.

A most significant and far-reaching discovery was that musical shape could be created by departure from and return to a main key area. Further, these departures and returns could be articulated by melodic events and scoring changes. These procedures at last compensated for the absence of the coherence provided to vocal music by a text. We now turn to a consideration of the application of these ideas in various instrumental genres.

Fugue

In the first half of the century the *fugue* had already been anticipated by the use of a single subject throughout an imitative polyphonic ricercar or fantasia. In instrumental fugues of the mature Baroque (and, by extension, in vocal ones as well) the subject's profile became progressively sharper in both rhythm and pitch contour than the smooth, lyrical material of the motetlike ricercar. In addition to giving the subject a stronger musical design, this profile also lent a clearer affection to the fugue as a whole. Manipulation of the subject in the course of the piece took a variety of forms. Inversion of the pitch contour was common. Somewhat less frequent, but not by any means rare in the later Baroque, was the use of rhythmic augmentation or diminution.

With regard to the harmonic design of the fugue, one important step was the normalization of the *tonal answer,* whereby the second voice, entering at the fifth scale step from the first, could be adjusted so that it stayed within the main key rather than immediately establishing a new one of its own. The exposition now served not only to introduce the subject and the various polyphonic voices but also to establish the harmonic center for the fugue.

Once the key center was asserted, the fugue could depart from it, achiev-ing forward motion and tension. The modulation might use free material or fragmentary motives from the subject in an *episode*. Having arrived on a new pitch level, the fugue could attain temporary stability at that point by a return of the subject or an entire exposition. This process could be repeated in several stages, ultimately resuming the key area of the opening. At the conclusion composers learned to increase the cadential climax by *stretto,* rapidly overlap-ping imitative entries of the subject. They also reinforced the sense of har-monic stability through the use of a *pedal point.*

It is impossible to overemphasize that fugue is not a form or even in the strict sense a genre. While the separate keyboard fugue perhaps comes to mind most readily when we speak of *fugue,* the term applies equally to ensem-ble music for instruments or voices. Fugue is, in fact, simply a technique or set of techniques that can be used in achieving a satisfying musical product in contrapuntal texture. The devices discussed briefly here represent the most common means by which composers worked out problems of musical con-struction in imitative polyphonic pieces or movements in the Baroque period and later. They may be present or absent in any work identified as a fugue, or in many works, movements, or passages that do not bear such a designation.

The Suite

Stemming from the Renaissance dance pairs, the suite was the first multimove-ment genre in instrumental music. In German suites from about the middle of the seventeenth century on, the appearance of dances in the order allemande, courante, sabarande, and gigue became normative, though by no means uni-versal. The advantage to that sequence was, of course, that it provided contrast between adjacent movements, as well as progression from slower to faster movements. Other movements might be added. One such movement was the prelude, which was not in dance style; it might be in the free manner of the improvisatory solo prelude, or it might imitate a French opera overture. If the suite did adopt the usual plan, the other movements most often came after the sarabande. They might include additional allemandes or courantes, *bourrées, gavottes, minuets,* or a number of other dances.

Unity was provided over the entire span of the suite by the use of a single key throughout. To the Baroque composers and writers on music, the different dances, with their proper rhythmic styles, embodied different affections. The German theorist Johann Mattheson (1681–1764) gave a list of the affections of the dances in his *Der vollkommene Capellmeister* (The complete music direc-tor, 1739): The affection of the minuet was "moderate gaiety"; that of the gavotte, "jubilant joy"; of the bourrée, "contentedness"; of the courante, "hope"; of the sarabande, "ambition"; and of the gigue, a variety of passions ranging from anger to flightiness.

In France, the term *ordre* was used in preference to the word *suite.* The ordre might incorporate not only the standard types but also free pieces, and the scope of the genre increased to take in large numbers of movements. The French composers were also fond of identifying their pieces by people's names (real or fictional) or by titles indicating affective content, rather than simply by dance nomenclature. This French school reached its climax in the keyboard ordres of François Couperin "le grand" (1668–1733). The greatest member of a family of important musicians, Couperin served both the church and the royal court of France and authored an important treatise on keyboard playing, *L'Art de toucher le clavecin* (The art of playing the harpsichord, 1717). Among the topics discussed in this treatise is the use and proper performance of the embellishments or *agréments* that the French applied to the notes of the music. They indicated these agréments by a wide variety of signs written above, below, or adjacent to the notes of their otherwise generally simple-looking melodic lines. The question of *goût* or good taste was a matter of great concern in regard to ornamentation, as in all matters of French music, art, and life in general at this time. Books of keyboard pieces frequently included tables of agréments and discussions of their proper use.

Of course suites could be composed for any medium. In the early seventeenth century the solo suite for lute was common. As time passed, the harpsichord began to dominate the genre. Even other solo instruments, such as the viol or cello, could be given suites. With the rise of French opera, the practice of excerpting dances from stage works to make multimovement orchestral suites developed, and before long composers began to write original suites for orchestra. Since these usually started with an overture, the French term *Ouverture* was sometimes applied to the entire suite.

All of the standard Baroque dances unfolded in binary form, a plan that had already begun to appear in the Renaissance. Each dance was constructed in two main parts, and each part was repeated. The first part moved away from the main key center and cadenced in a related but contrasting area. The second half began at that point and cadenced in the opening key again. This practice is of immense significance, for it represents the beginning of the principle of tonal departure and return, tension and relaxation, that was to underlie the development of musical form for the next two centuries.

The Mature Baroque Sonata

In Italy the suite did not catch on as it did in the northern countries; instead the most important multimovement instrumental genre was the sonata. As we have noted, the genre evolved from the fragmentation of the Renaissance canzona into separate movements. The term *sonata* identified any work in contrasting movements, usually for one or more instruments with basso continuo, and later for keyboard solo.

The sonata presented its own peculiar set of challenges and rewards. Among these were the development of idiomatic instrumental writing, the sustaining of purely musical interest, the achievement of musical shape based on unity and contrast, and the evocation of a convincing expression.

The archetype for instrumentation in the sonata was scoring for one or two violins and basso continuo, though naturally a wide variety of combinations of linear instruments was available. The violin's idiom offered greater range and flexibility than the older vocal models, and more access to chromatic harmony than the wind instruments of the time. As we have already noted, the most popular and effective combination was the trio sonata scoring with two upper parts and continuo (four players in all), for this created textural interest through the interplay of the upper lines. A sonata for solo melodic instrument and continuo constitutes a *solo sonata* (three players).

The Italian Baroque musicians recognized two classes of sonatas, the *sonata da camera* or chamber sonata, and the *sonata da chiesa* or church sonata. The terms clearly refer to the originally intended use of the pieces, and the types differed in style accordingly.

The sonata da camera was the Italian interpretation of the suite principle; it was a suite in all but name. It comprised a set of dance movements, often including an *allemanda*, a *corrente*, a *sarabanda*, and a *giga*. A prelude might be attached at the beginning. The sonata da chiesa differed from the sonata da camera in not employing dances, though in some cases the rhythmic idioms of the dances and their binary forms are nevertheless evident in the music. Fugal writing is much more likely to turn up in the church sonata than in the chamber sonata.

While the sonata da camera, because of its use of dance styles, was unsuitable for performance in church, the sonata da chiesa could certainly be played in a secular setting. Thus in both function and style the da camera and da chiesa types overlapped to some degree, and many sonatas do not fall clearly into one category.

Arcangelo Corelli   As the Baroque era reached its height, the outstanding composer in the genre of the sonata was Arcangelo Corelli (1653–1713), who had been trained in Bologna, which was then the leading center for violin playing. Corelli worked in Rome for some of the great musical patrons there, including the church San Luigi dei Francese; Queen Christina of Sweden, for whom he directed *academies,* as concerts were commonly called; and the Cardinal Pietro Ottoboni, with whom Corelli formed a close personal friendship such as was practically unknown between noble patrons and composers in any era. His published sonatas include five sets of twelve sonatas each: opp. 1 (1681) and 3 (1689) comprise trio sonatas da chiesa; opp. 2 (1685) and 4 (1694), trio sonatas da camera; and op. 5 (1700), solo sonatas da chiesa and da camera. Opus 5 is important because an ornamented version of its violin parts was published in 1711, giving evidence of the virtuoso practice of the time. Corelli achieved a stellar reputation, and in the later eighteenth century he was regarded as the first composer to belong to the "modern" era.

What made Corelli's music so effective was that it established a new harmonic syntax. Analysis of his sonatas reveals that he employed a remarkably limited repertory of phrase complexes. The essential element is the pervasive pairing of the two upper lines in counterpoint of thirds and sixths, leading to cadential unisons or octaves. These intervals are frequently obscured because they are embellished in a variety of ways by the application of different figures; one of these, the chain of suspensions, seems almost a cliché in Corelli's works. Below the fundamentally parallel motion of the upper lines, the continuo bass works in contrary motion. Because there is a limit to the ways in which this can be handled in the approach to a cadential unison or octave, Corelli's music plays the same few harmonic patterns over and over. His imagination saves these from growing tiresome, of course, and the very convincing counterpoint produces harmonic cadence formulas that give the music an unprecedented sense of forward direction. These progressions—and it is now for the first time that the word *progression* becomes genuinely appropriate to describe how harmony works—seemed so strong that they were adopted as natural and inevitable by following generations. Soon they became the basis of an entire theory of harmony, but that belongs to a later chapter.

Concerto

In the late seventeenth century composers began to exploit the concertato principle in adapting the ensemble sonata for performance by a larger orchestral ensemble, thereby producing the *concerto*. The German composer Georg Muffat (1653–1704), who had trained under Lully and later absorbed Corelli's style in Italy, described in the foreword to his *Auserlesene Instrumental-Music* (Selected instrumental music, 1701) several different ways of playing his concertos, depending on the availability of ensembles, ranging from a trio (that is, four players) to a large, mixed group:

> If you are lacking string players, or want to try out these concertos with only a few, you can form a complete little trio, with everything that is necessary at any time, out of the three following parts: Violin I concertino, Violin II concertino, and Basso continuo and Violoncello concertino. . . . Then it is to be observed that, besides *piano* and *forte,* at T. (Tutti) all the players should play forcefully, but at S. (Solo) softly and gently. . . .

> If, however, still more players are available, you will want to add to all the aforementioned parts the three other ones, namely, Violino primo, Violino secundo, and Violone or Harpsichord of the concerto grosso (or large choir), and to assign to each part, as your numbers and good judgment dictate, either one, two, or three players. . . .

> When among your musicians there are some who are able to play and modulate the French oboe or shawm agreeably, you can get the best effect

by using two of these instead of the two violins, and a good bassoon player . . . to form the concertino or little trio in certain of these concertos; . . .

Muffat's instructions give us a good impression of the flexibility and practicality that governed scoring choices in these years. More importantly Muffat describes something like a sonata in which from time to time the parts are doubled, tripled, or quadrupled by additional players, who then drop out and return according to directions in their parts. The small solo group, which plays throughout, is called *concertino,* and the full ensemble, which reinforces certain passages, is the *tutti* (all) or *concerto grosso* (big concert). Other composers identify the complete group as *ripieno* (full). The work is then called "concerto" or "concerto grosso." Another option is to have only a single solo player with intermittent support from the ripieno, in which case the concerto is a *solo concerto.* There were also *ripieno concertos,* without soloists but exploiting various combinations within the full ensemble. It is important to note that the size of the orchestra seems to range up to a dozen or perhaps, at the very most, twenty players. These concertos were intended for private wealthy homes, not for the large concert halls of the nineteenth and twentieth centuries.

Giuseppe Torelli　Naturally a composer would wish to take advantage of the concertato alternation of soloistic and full sound to create a logically organized musical form. The Bolognese composer Giuseppe Torelli (1658–1709) pioneered in this. The concerto typically had three movements, alternating fast, slow, and fast tempos. For the first and third movements Torelli developed a rational, systematic plan by which the contrast of tutti and solo sections could be coordinated with other elements of musical design. The ripieno played harmonically stable ritornello passages, while the soloist or concertino group supplied modulatory episodes with more virtuosic melodic material. The first and last ritornelli would, of course, be in the home key; the other ritornello or ritornelli took place in contrasting keys. The structure of a simple movement would follow an outline such as this:

Ritornello		Ritornello		Ritornello
Ripieno	Solo	Ripieno	Solo	Ripieno
Main key	——	Contrast key	——	Main key

It is now clear that the large-scale da capo opera aria of Alessandro Scarlatti applies the same ritornello plan to the vocal genre.

Antonio Vivaldi　The greatest master of the Italian Baroque concerto was Antonio Vivaldi (1678–1741) of Venice. Vivaldi presumably learned to play the violin from his father, a musician at St. Mark's basilica. He studied for the priesthood and was ordained, but ill health and his musical vocation kept him from an active pastoral career. From 1704 he worked as a teacher, composer, and music director for the Ospedale della Pietà, one of several orphanages that Venice maintained for the illegitimate female progeny of the sailors who put in to port there. The girl orphans became fine musicians, and the Ospedale fielded a large orchestra of from twenty to twenty-five players. Vivaldi composed many concertos for the concerts they presented. In fact he left over five hundred concertos. He composed much other music, too, both church music and operas. (He also traveled all over Europe to produce his operas, much to the frustration of his employers at the Ospedale.) Nevertheless, it was Vivaldi's concertos that made his lasting reputation.

Vivaldi built on Torelli's foundation. Though they maintained the same structural basis, the individual movements of his concertos were longer and more elaborately developed than those of his predecessor. The slow movements in particular are unprecedentedly sophisticated.

Perhaps most important, however, was Vivaldi's approach to the composition of the ritornellos. He invented material that was perfectly suited to the tonal function demanded of it. A typical Vivaldi ritornello opens with a bold, memorable gesture that focusses closely on the main key. Then that key is reiterated through some strong motivic material, and finally the tonal center is hammered home by clearly defined Corellian cadential patterns. The sharp definition of the material and the strength of its grip on the key allowed Vivaldi to abbreviate the ritornello at subsequent appearances, thereby tightening the form. This principle of inventing thematic or motivic material for a specific purpose in relation to harmonic structure became crucial in the eighteenth century. The employment of a variety of melodic and figurational ideas in the same movement, rather than concentrating on a single affective figure throughout, led away from the Baroque rhetorical aesthetic and toward new possibilities for musical style.

The appeal of the concerto to Baroque taste was natural. It embodied the principle of contrast that was essential to musical thought in the period. Its soloistic flair certainly suited the taste for dynamic, rhetorical expression. And it indulged the Baroque appetite for ornamentation and for virtuosic display. It also satisfied the desire for a large, rationally articulated artistic design based on both unity and contrast. As the opera was the Baroque vocal genre *par excellence,* the concerto was the ideal Baroque instrumental genre.

Questions for Reflection

✛   How did political structure affect musical life and how did processes of musical thinking and style resemble political structures in late seventeenth-century France, England, Italy, and Germany?

✤   Why would it be appropriate to describe a large Baroque opera aria as a concerto movement for voice? What significant differences are there between the two structures?

✤   How did the ideas of affective expression and of key center support large forms in instrumental and vocal music in the high Baroque?

Suggestions for Further Reading

Two fine books on French Baroque music and musical life are R. M. Isherwood, *Music in the Service of the King: France in the Seventeenth Century* (Ithaca, N.Y.: Cornell University Press, 1973), and James R. Anthony, *French Baroque Music from Beaujoyeulx to Rameau* (New York: Norton, 1978).

For the history of English music in the High Baroque, see Edward J. Dent, *Foundations of English Opera* (Cambridge: Cambridge University Press, 1928), and Christopher Dearnley, *English Church Music, 1650–1750* (London: Barrie & Jenkins, 1970). The most comprehensive study of Purcell is Franklin B. Zimmerman, *Henry Purcell: His Life and Times,* 2d ed. (Philadelphia: University of Pennsylvania Press, 1983).

For the history of Italian opera, see the Suggestions for Further Reading for Chapter 12. A biography of Alessandro Scarlatti is Edward J. Dent, *Alessandro Scarlatti: An Introduction to His Operas* (Berkeley: University of California Press, 1979). Marcello's *Il teatro alla moda* is excerpted in Oliver Strunk, *Source Readings in Music History* (New York: Norton, 1950).

On church music in Germany, see Friedrich Blume, *Protestant Church Music* (New York: Norton, 1974). An excellent study of Buxtehude is Kerala J. Snyder, *Dieterich Buxtehude, Organist in Lübeck* (New York: Schirmer, 1987).

The following books discuss the various genres and forms of instrumental music in the Baroque period: Alfred Mann, *The Study of Fugue* (New York: Norton, 1965); William S. Newman, *The Sonata in the Baroque Era,* 3d ed. (New York: Norton, 1972); Arthur Hutchings, *The Baroque Concerto,* 3d ed. (London: Faber, 1973). Studies of important instrumental composers of the Baroque era include Wilfred Mellers, *François Couperin and the French Classical Tradition* (London: Dobson, 1950); Marc Pincherle, *Corelli: His Life, His Music,* trans. H. E. M. Russell (New York: Norton, 1968), and *Vivaldi, Genius of the Baroque,* trans. Christopher Hatch (New York: Norton, 1957); Walter Kolneder, *Vivaldi,* trans. B. Hopkins (Berkeley: University of California Press, 1971).

15

THE END OF THE BAROQUE ERA

The Character of the Late Baroque Era

In the third decade of the eighteenth century there began to appear changes in musical thought and style that supplied the roots of a new era. Yet through the middle of the century the styles of Baroque music continued to be employed by several prominent composers, whose contributions rank as the greatest masterpieces of the period. In the present chapter we shall consider some of these composers and some of their works.

For the most part, the composers to be discussed here did not create new genres. Instead they explored and expanded the types of works already established by the end of the seventeenth century: in vocal music the opera, oratorio, sacred concerto, and cantata; in instrumental music the fugue, suite, concerto, and sonata. They brought these genres to high levels of sophistication, polish, and intensity. This is by no means to imply that they were unoriginal; each had a strong personal style that could be stamped on the now fully developed Baroque forms, and each is clearly recognizable in his music.

As we have observed, the conclusions of the Middle Ages and the Renaissance were marked by a mannerist stage in which composers seemed to take such delight in the techniques of the style that technique became an end in itself. It is not entirely appropriate to apply the term *mannerist* to these late Baroque composers, though their compositional technique was often impressive in its own right. Only in some of the late works of J. S. Bach do we find something like mannerism in its true sense, but there the genuineness and profoundness of commitment to affective content give the music a sincerity that entirely prevents its seeming merely to revel in technique. **203**

Opera Seria—Handel and Others

With the works of Alessandro Scarlatti the Baroque opera seria had reached a stage of full development, but the genre remained extremely popular among the European aristocracy right through the middle of the eighteenth century. Italian composers continued to write in this style, of course, and they and others spread it to centers outside Italy.

Among these composers the greatest was George Frideric Handel (1685–1759). Unlike most musicians of that time, Handel was not from a particularly musical family, but his talent and desire led him away from the professional career that his father had hoped he would follow. As a youth he abandoned his university studies and went to Hamburg, where he learned about opera under Reinhard Keiser and began to compose his own operas. At the age of twenty-one he traveled to Italy, as was only natural for a budding young opera composer, to absorb the Italian style firsthand. There he met Corelli and soaked up the influence of Alessandro Scarlatti, polishing his style not only in opera but also in sacred music, secular cantatas, and instrumental genres. He was also able to get operas of his own composition produced in some of the major Italian theaters.

By 1710 Handel had established a considerable reputation and accepted the offer of the position of music director at the elector's court in Hanover. He immediately got permission to spend the 1710–1711 opera season in London, where, there being no national operatic tradition, Italian opera seria was a lively fad. He had tremendous success, making a great impression on the English, as London in turn did on him. After returning to Hanover for a year he obtained a second leave of absence and returned to England, where he stayed for the rest of his career. In 1714 Queen Anne of England died and the elector of Hanover succeeded to the English throne as George I, so Handel was once again the subject of his former master.

The German composer continued for a number of years to have a fine career in offering Italian opera to English audiences. His output in the genre totals forty operas. The greatest of these and the one most likely to be heard today is *Giulio Cesare* (1724), a loosely historical treatment of the story of Julius Caesar and Cleopatra. From 1720 to 1728 these works were produced under the patronage of the king himself, through the Royal Academy of Music, an institution with a name obviously adapted from that of the opera in Paris.

Handel's operas show both mastery of the conventions of the Italian opera seria and imaginative handling of those conventions. Many of the arias are fine representatives of the standard da capo structure; however, some modify the form in original ways, varying the rigidly predictable structures. Sometimes the motivation for these variants seems to be simply the elimination of excessive repetitions, but they are also often responses to the specific dramatic situations.

After a decade and a half, however, the English audience was clearly finding the opera seria distant and artificial. The language was foreign, the mythological and classical plots were naturally not as familiar to the increasingly middle-class musical public as to the Italian courts of that era, and the unnaturalness of the castrato voice encountered the same objections from the English that the French had raised several decades earlier. The great satirist Joseph Addison had already attacked the Italian opera style in 1711 in the famous journal *Spectator* when Handel first went to England. He found the elaborate stagings ridiculous and the librettos contrived and circumlocutory.

In 1728 the Royal Academy of Music failed due to poor management of both financial and personnel matters. At that very moment there happened to be available an alternative form of entertainment to which the audiences flocked. This was *The Beggar's Opera,* concocted by the English dramatist John Gay (1685–1732) and the German composer and theorist Johann Christoph Pepusch (1667–1752), who spent most of his career in England. It was the first of the new genre *ballad opera,* which combined spoken dialogue with simple songs accompanied by basso continuo. Ballad opera offered a variety of appeals to the London middle class: the plots, often featuring political satire, and characters were taken from contemporary life; the words were in the vernacular; the music was simple and the tunes catchy; and, of course, it did not use castrati. Much of the music was actually borrowed or parodied from existing popular songs.

Obviously Handel could not give up his own style to write ballad opera tunes. Between 1729 and 1734 he and a partner collaborated in running a New Royal Academy, but this also failed. For three more years he tried once more. Now, however, the remaining opera-going public was divided between Handel's theater and a rival company, the Opera of the Nobility, which featured the Italian composer Nicola Porpora (1686–1768). Handel composed a few more operas, but it was clear that the flame of Italian opera in England was flickering its last. The competition eventually drove both companies to the verge of bankruptcy. Porpora saw which way the wind was blowing and fled back to greener pastures in Italy. Handel, however, was by this time a naturalized citizen and felt England to be his true home.

One of the centers of Baroque opera in Germany was Dresden. Porpora spent some time there after the debacle in London, though he worked mostly in Italy. Among the most admired opera seria composers in Italy and Germany in the eighteenth century was Johann Adolf Hasse (1699–1783), who like Handel left Germany for Italy to study in his formative years. He served as music director to the elector of Saxony in Dresden between 1730 and 1763 (with some extended periods in Italy during those years), and thus became to Germany rather like Handel was to England. His work is closely associated with that of the greatest late-Baroque opera librettist, the Vienna court poet Pietro Metastasio (1698–1792), who achieved a kind of final polishing of the conventions of Baroque operatic dramaturgy.

The Metastasian opera libretto extolled rationalism and the absolutist political system in a highly stylized dramatic structure. Dialogue took place in simple recitative, leading to a character's expression in an aria of his or her affection of the moment. Characters were alloted numbers of arias according to carefully developed schemes of theatrical hierarchy, and typically each aria was placed so that the character could immediately make an effective exit. Such conventions seemed stiff and artificial to later, more naturalistic critics; yet each convention had its basis in reason, and the emphasis on solo arias rather than interaction between characters in ensembles arose inevitably out of the aesthetic in which rhetorical expression was the model for music.

The opera on the continent remained the property of the aristocracy, so Hasse was never confronted with the sort of crisis that Handel experienced in London. At the end of his life Hasse went to the brilliant court of Vienna, where a new era in the history of musical style was soon to reach its climax.

The Intermezzo

As has already been noted, under the influence of the librettist Apostolo Zeno the Italians had dropped comic episodes from their operas in the late Baroque. In the first part of the eighteenth century, comic relief was provided by entirely separate works performed between the acts of the opera seria. Such a comic musical entertainment was called an *intermezzo*.

The standard opera seria had three acts; as a result the intermezzi usually had two. Their plots were simple, set in the present day, and often slapstick. The characters and action derived from the stock comic situations used in *commedia dell'arte,* a popular Italian street theater genre that had thrived in the sixteenth century. Usually the story revolves around a clever young woman who gets the better of a bumbling old man. The literary style of the texts was deliberately unsophisticated. The music of the intermezzi included simple recitatives, da capo arias, and ensembles for the solo singers. The solo parts were in true Italian operatic style, not at all like the songs of the English ballad opera; they could demand very competent singers. Unique to the intermezzo was the employment of the bass voice; basses did not appear in opera seria. (The taste of the time found the idea of a bass singing music in the Italian operatic idiom inherently ludicrous.) Accompaniment for the intermezzo was provided by a reduced orchestra in a simpler style than in opera seria.

Intermezzi were sometimes concocted by *pasticcio* (patchwork) out of several existing works, and many are anonymous. It was not unusual for fine composers to write these comic dramas themselves, however; Hasse, for example, made a contribution to the genre. The most famous and historically important intermezzo is *La serva padrona* (The maid mistress, 1733) by Giovanni Battista Pergolesi (1710–1736).

Opera in France

It is impossible to exaggerate the length of the shadow cast by the colossal figure of Lully on French opera throughout the remainder of the Baroque period. Evidence of this can be found in the operatic career of the French composer Jean-Philippe Rameau (1683–1764). Rameau began as a composer of keyboard pieces in the tradition of Couperin and established himself as a theorist with his important *Traité de l'harmonie* (Treatise on Harmony, 1722). His real ambition was to succeed in the field of opera, but he was unable to make any headway. He was severely handicapped by his reputation as a theorist, for the public was deeply suspicious of music that might be academic and dull. Moreover, in Paris one needed influential friends in high places in order to get ahead. When Rameau was nearly fifty, he finally received the support of the greatest musical patron in France, the fabulously wealthy and powerful Alexandre-Jean-Joseph Le Riche de la Pouplinière. As La Pouplinière's household music master and composer, Rameau gained the opportunity to produce his first opera, *Hippolyte et Aricie,* in 1733. This was followed by the tremendously successful exotic opera-ballet *Les Indes galantes* (The elegant Indies) two years later, securing his position. Rameau continued to compose operas, opera-ballets, and later comédies-ballets, raising the operatic genres to a new level of quality unmatched by his immediate predecessors.

Rameau had his detractors, however, who launched against him one of the greatest polemical attacks in the history of music. They held up Lully, now dead fifty years, as the standard for French opera, and became known as Lullistes. They claimed that Rameau's works were dense in texture and academically abstruse. He and his supporters, the Ramistes, insisted that his music maintained rather than deserted the ideals of Lully. From a twentieth-century perspective his writing certainly sounds like it continues the Lullian tradition with considerable grace and with the addition of the progressive harmonic syntax of the post-Corellian era. Ironically, in a later operatic argument, when the conservative French felt their national style threatened from the outside, Rameau became the hero of the great French tradition.

Handel and the Oratorio

Once it became clear to Handel that he could no longer expect to continue his career primarily as a composer of Italian operas, he turned his attention to a new field with greater promise, the oratorio. Before coming to England Handel had written Latin church music, both sacred and secular cantatas in Italian, oratorios in Italian and German, and even a few German sacred concertos (now lost). During his first two decades in England he wrote occasional English anthems in the style of his adopted country. Thus he was well equipped to undertake a major turn in his oeuvre toward the oratorio.

Oratorios appealed strongly to the tastes of the rising English bourgeois audience. They did not have the artificialities of the opera, especially the use of castrati and the complicated sets and stage machinery. They were written in the English language, and the subjects, instead of coming from ancient Greece and Rome, were taken from the Bible, a source intimately familiar to the middle class. They had over opera the further advantage that they used the chorus, partaking of the already popular English choral tradition.

Handel's oratorios usually take their stories from the dramatic narratives of the Old Testament, including the heroic story of *Esther* (1732, originally a masque), the captivatingly human characters of King Saul and David (*Saul*, 1739), the epic saga of the Exodus (*Israel in Egypt,* 1739), the tragedy of *Samson* (1741), the excitement of Israel's battles for independence (*Judas Maccabeus,* 1746), the judgment and glory of *Solomon* (1749), and the moving tale of *Jephtha* (1751), already used by Carissimi. The best-known of the oratorios, *Messiah* (1742) is somewhat atypical in that it has no dramatic plot line as such. There were nonbiblical topics, as well, such as *Semele* (1743) and *Hercules* (1745).

In some ways the oratorios resemble the opera seria. They adopt the three-act plan of the opera, they use solo recitatives for dialogue and arias for the great dramatic expressions of individual characters. Their overtures are typically in the format of the French overture. The use of the chorus is the hallmark of the genre, however, and the chorus is used much more than in the contemporary Italian oratorio. Handel modeled his oratorio choruses on the magnificent English choral anthem style. The choruses provide affective commentary, participate in the action as masses of people such as armies, and even offer narration. In the use of madrigalistic pictorialism, the chorus can set the scene with a vividness that compensates for the absence of staging and actual scenery.

The performers were drawn from two main sources. The solo singers came from the theatrical and opera stages. There were no castrati (some of the male roles were handled by women, however), and basses took serious leading roles. Excellent choruses could be drawn from the English church choirs; the choir for the first performance of *Messiah* was made up of the combined choirs of two Dublin churches.

Germany

While the many German courts of the eighteenth century largely resembled those of Italy—with private instrumental ensembles, church music, and operas—another musical world also existed. This was the civic music program, operating in the cities and towns that were not the domains of dukes, princes, and electors. These cities employed town musicians for various functions, including grand ceremonial occasions; often took the responsibility for music in the city churches; and governed schools in which music was taught. To take charge of the management of these programs, the municipal authorities employed a *Kantor*. Many fine composers, directors, and teachers found employment under this kind of public patronage. Probably the most prominent and successful of them all was Georg Philipp Telemann (1681–1767).

As a young man, Telemann went to the city of Leipzig to study law. He soon became a prominent musical figure in the city, starting a collegium musicum for his fellow students (Fig. 15.1), later taking on the directorship of Leipzig's opera house, and serving as a church organist. His prominence understandably rankled the Kantor there, Johann Kuhnau (1660–1722). After Telemann left Leipzig he held two court positions, in Sorau and Eisenach. From 1712 he was director of music for the city of Frankfurt, and in 1721 he accepted a similar position at the great city of Hamburg, arguably the most prestigious such post in Germany. When Kuhnau died in 1722 Telemann was eagerly recruited by the Leipzig city fathers, and though he was not free to take the job, he succeeded in using the offer as a bargaining chip to enhance his role in Hamburg. He added the directorship of the Hamburg Opera to his work load from 1722 until it closed in 1738.

Telemann's works include a few operas, but the strongest impression one gets from an overview of his output is the sense of the immense demand on the Kantor for practical music. In meeting his church obligations he produced more than a thousand sacred cantatas, a substantial number of oratorios, and other sacred music. For various occasions and general use there are choral and solo vocal pieces. Among the instrumental music are French-style orchestral overtures, concertos, sonatas, and keyboard pieces. In all this music, the style leans away from intense affectiveness and contrapuntal complexity, and concentrates on directness, simplicity, and transparency. This does not simply explain how Telemann was able to produce such a vast quantity of music but also reflects his sensitivity to a change in musical taste that anticipated the coming of a new era.

Johann Sebastian Bach

The composer in whose work the art and technique of Baroque music attained its consummation was Johann Sebastian Bach (1685–1750). Like all composers in the periods in which the patronage system operated, his music was inextricably bound to the practical situations in which he worked. Thus we can understand some aspects of his creativity in terms of his biography. At the same time, however, Bach seems to have felt a special vocation to produce the

Figure 15.1

A collegium musicum provided a forum for the performance of Baroque secular concert music in many towns. The collegium musicum was often associated with the university. Today many universities have early music ensembles known as collegium musicum. (*Germanisches Nationalmuseum, Nürnberg*)

most thoroughly developed works possible in nearly every genre (except opera) of the era of which he was to see the end. For that reason, he stands out among even the fine composers with whom he was contemporary.

Bach's Early Career

Bach came from a family that produced many musicians, and to a large extent his career was rather routine. He was the son of a town musician in the relatively small town of Eisenach. Both his parents had died by the time he was ten, and he lived for the next five years with his brother, an organist in the town of Ohrdruf. At fifteen he went to Lüneburg, where he sang in the choir of the Michaeliskirche in return for a free education at the school attached to that church. In Lüneburg the young Bach must have taken advantage of Georg Böhm's presence to learn the best of the great German organ tradition. He also traveled to Hamburg to hear another important organist, Johann Adam Reinken (1623–1722).

At the age of eighteen Bach began his professional career as a musician. After a few months as a minor court musician in Weimar, he found a church organist's position in the town of Arnstadt. In 1704 he took a leave of absence to go to Lübeck to hear Buxtehude's music, staying three times as long as he had permission to. The situation in Arnstadt was unhappy in various ways, and in 1707 he left for a similar job at Mühlhausen.

The music that Bach wrote during these first years consists, as we would expect, mostly of organ pieces for his own use. He experimented with the *gebunden* genre of organ pieces based on chorale melodies, and his skill as a player is abundantly evident from his free pieces such as toccatas and preludes. He was also competent in fugal writing, though the fugues of this period seem somewhat loose compared to those he crafted later in his life. At Mühlhausen Bach also had occasion to write sacred concertos (or, as they are more commonly but inaccurately known, "cantatas") for special liturgical occasions. These works show that he already had a well-developed style in choral and solo vocal writing.

The Court of Weimar

In 1708 Bach progressed to a new style of musical life, taking an appointment at the court of the duke in Weimar. His main duties were again as organist, and he must have played chamber music as well. In 1714 he was promoted to the position of Konzertmeister. Italian sonatas and concertos became available to the Weimar court orchestra, and Bach copied and transcribed works of Vivaldi, becoming in the process familiar with the latest Italian instrumental style. He soon began to write original works in the Italian manner, including trio sonatas for the two manuals and pedals of the organ. At Weimar Bach also wrote a number of cantatas.

Although in general Bach's music was practical and intended to satisfy the immediate needs of his job, he launched a project in Weimar that shows another side of his musical personality. This was the *Orgel-Büchlein,* a collection of chorale arrangements for the organ, based on a systematic organization keyed to the liturgical calendar. These settings were intended to incorporate affective interpretation of the chorales' content in their figuration, together with the most polished contrapuntal technique. Of the projected 164 pieces in the set, Bach completed only 45. Though unfinished, the *Orgel-Büchlein* constitutes the first of numerous systematic compilations of pieces Bach made that embody the essence of particular Baroque styles and genres.

The Court of Cöthen

Bach left the service of the Duke of Weimar in 1717 for the court of the very musical prince at Cöthen. Here Bach served for six years as Kapellmeister, and his duties were in the secular rather than the sacred sphere. In the realm of vocal music Bach composed occasional secular cantatas at Cöthen but no church music. He wrote a good deal of his chamber and orchestral music during this time, including concertos (the well-known collection of six Brandenburg Concertos was assembled to represent his work in this area when he was seeking to move again) and at least two of his orchestral suites (Ouvertüren) in the French style.

From the Cöthen years there is also a considerable quantity of keyboard music. His eldest son, Wilhelm Friedemann Bach (1710–1784), was old enough to begin to study music, and Johann Sebastian put together a graded series of pieces that would teach both musical principles and performance technique: His *Clavier-Büchlein* (Little keyboard book, 1720) for Wilhelm Friedemann Bach includes little dance pieces, early versions of the inventions and sinfonias, and some of the preludes and fugues that were incorporated into the first book of the *Well-Tempered Clavier* in 1722. Later came a similar collection of easy pieces, the *Anna Magdalena Bach Notebook*, named for Bach's second wife.

These didactic collections gave Bach the opportunity to create systematically arranged anthologies of model pieces. The inventions and sinfonias are organized according to all the usually practicable keys in the unequal temperaments of the time (those with no more than four sharps or flats), from C major up the scale to B minor. When he came to the preludes and fugues, Bach adopted the still-new idea of equal temperament and wrote one in each of the twenty-four major and minor keys of the chromatic scale. Each piece has its own, unique affective character and compositional style, and at the same time they are arranged in an abstract pattern to form a clearly planned whole.

The City of Leipzig

In 1723, after the city fathers of Leipzig were unsuccessful in attracting as Kantor either Telemann or several of their other choices, they settled on Johann Sebastian Bach. His Cöthen prince's interest in music had waned, so Bach accepted the position, which he retained until his death. His responsibilities in Leipzig were numerous and varied. He was associated with the St. Thomas Church and School, where he taught Latin as well as music, and supervised the music for four churches and special music for civic occasions. (Fig. 15.2)

The church music in Leipzig was a complicated affair. At the smallest church a unison choir of boys led the service. At the next larger church a four-part choir sang simple settings of chorales. At the two largest churches there were either elaborate polyphonic motets or full-scale concerted cantatas, switching back and forth between the two churches on alternate Sundays. Thus Bach had to produce a cantata every week. His immediate concern was

Figure 15.2
The St. Thomas Church and School where Bach worked for much of his
career were the subject of this pencil drawing by the nineteenth-century
composer Felix Mendelssohn. Mendelssohn helped launch the revival of
Bach's music, and he led the campaign to construct the Bach monument, also
shown here. (*Mendelssohn-Archiv, Staatsbibliothek Preußischer Kulturbesitz,*
Berlin)

to compose a repertoire of these cantatas to update the choir library. He did
this fairly regularly over the first years of his tenure in Leipzig, so that there
were several complete cycles for the entire liturgical year. Two of these cycles
were completed in 1723–1724 and 1724–1725, another from 1725 to 1727,
a fourth in 1728–1729, and a final one over several years beginning in 1729.
Two hundred cantatas have survived, but a number are known to have
been lost.

The musical force for the cantatas included a small choir and orchestra.
Bach pleaded with the authorities for three singers on each of the four parts,
and intended generally from one to three players on each orchestral instrument, giving a choir of twelve and an orchestra of around twenty. The instrumentalists came partly from the school and partly from the city band.

The typical plan for a cantata included six movements: an opening chorus, a solo recitative, and an aria or duet, all sung before the sermon; then another recitative, another aria or duet, and a chorale, in the second half of the service. Other movements might be added. The first movement is sometimes an elaborate arrangement of a chorale (often the same chorale that concludes the cantata) in concerted style. The poetry for the free or "madrigalistic" movements and recitatives of the cantatas (i.e., those not based on the chorales) was by contemporary poets; two of the most important were Erdmann Neumeister (1671–1756) and Christian Friedrich Henrici (1700–1764), who wrote under the pseudonym Picander.

In addition to cantatas, Bach's sacred vocal music includes motets based on either biblical or chorale texts, Latin Mass settings (still used in the German church at that time), and oratorios. The so-called Christmas and Easter oratorios were constructed from cantatas and are not in the usual dramatic vein of oratorios.

Bach's greatest oratorios are the Passion oratorios based on the gospel narratives of John (1724) and Matthew (1727). They should be thought of as belonging to Good Friday in the liturgical cycles with the Sunday cantatas. They combine the scriptural texts with chorales and free, meditative arias, duets, and choruses. Bach adapted the free texts for the *St. John Passion* from the poetry of B. H. Brockes (1680–1747), which Handel also set; those for the *St. Matthew Passion* came from Picander. The narration is taken by a tenor in the role of the evangelist or gospel author, and it and the dialogue are sung in recitative. The chorus is used for crowd scenes (*turba*) and the disciples, as well as for reflective chorales and madrigalistic choruses. The solo singers also provide comment and reflection in arias and duets. The musicians for the *St. Matthew Passion* include two choirs and orchestras as well as solo singers.

In 1729 Bach added to his busy schedule the directorship of the collegium musicum that Telemann had founded. This allowed him to turn again to secular orchestral and chamber music. He used works from Cöthen, but he also composed new pieces, including two more orchestral suites, concertos for the harpsichord, and sonatas. He led the collegium musicum until 1737.

Bach's Culmination of Baroque Styles

By about 1730 it must have been clear to Bach that the Baroque aesthetic and style embodied in his music were soon to be replaced by a new kind of musical thought. He had composed in all the Baroque genres except opera, for which he had never had a need in the professional positions he held. At Leipzig his available practical repertoire was now substantial, and he had thoroughly learned the ins and outs of the musical organization for which he was responsible. All these factors help to explain a number of rather special works and collections that he produced during the 1730s and 1740s. These works seem to be deliberately intended to serve as paradigmatic models of the styles of Baroque music, laid out according to clear governing plans, following in the pattern that Bach had set for himself in the *Orgel-Büchlein* and the *Well-Tempered Clavier*. (The second book of the *Well-Tempered Clavier* actually belongs to this period.)

The first of these paradigmatic collections comprises the four parts of the *Clavierübung* (Keyboard practice). The first part was a set of six partitas (suites) for harpsichord, collected and published in 1731. The second part (1735) combines representative harpsichord pieces in two contrasting national styles, a French overture and dance suite placed side by side with an Italian concerto. The third part (1739) represents the German organ heritage in a collection of chorale preludes framed by a great prelude and fugue. The fourth part (1741–1742) is a set of thirty variations, the so-called *Goldberg Variations,* of which every third one is a canon at a particular interval, that is, at the unison, the second, the third, and so on.

Bach's great paradigmatic vocal work is the so-called B-minor Mass. This was assembled in about 1747–1749 out of existing pieces. The B-minor Mass cannot be regarded as a liturgical work, partly because the Lutheran church did not use the full Latin Mass, and partly because it is too huge to be practicable. Rather, it collates movements in the various styles of sacred vocal music, from the old-fashioned stile antico to the most brilliant concertato scoring. The layout of the traditional Mass serves as Bach's grand framework, but even within individual movements the subdivisions are logically and symmetrically conceived.

Three sets of chorale-based organ pieces also belong in the category of Bach's paradigmatic collections. The first is a group of eighteen chorales mostly composed in the Weimar period but assembled in around 1747 to demonstrate a variety of approaches. The second is a set of six chorales arranged from cantata movements and published in 1748 or 1749 by Schübler. The third collection was written on the occasion of Bach's election in 1747 to the Society of the Musical Sciences and consists of five canonic variations on the Christmas chorale "Vom Himmel hoch."

In 1747 Bach paid a visit to his second son, Carl Philipp Emanuel Bach (1714–1788), who was employed as harpsichordist to the flute-playing Prussian King Frederick II (Frederick the Great) at the royal court in Potsdam, near Berlin. On that occasion J. S. Bach was given a fugue subject, purportedly invented by Frederick, on which to improvise at the piano. After his return to Leipzig Bach wrote out the three-part "ricercar" he had improvised, added a six-part ricercar, a trio sonata for flute with violin and continuo, and ten canons, all based on the "royal theme," and dedicated the set of pieces to the king under the title *Musical Offering.*

Following the idea of a monothematic collection that he had already used in the "Vom Himmel hoch" variations and the *Musical Offering,* Bach began his most technically complex composition, *The Art of Fugue* in the late 1740s, leaving it not quite complete at his death. The plan of the collection was to proceed systematically through the art of fugal composition, from simple fugues up to a quadruple fugue, one of whose four subjects was formed from the musical notes B-A-C-H (B indicating B flat, and H indicating B natural in German), and not neglecting strict canons at various intervals. Bach died before the publication could be completed, so that the end of the quadruple fugue is missing and the final structure imperfect. Nevertheless, it ranks as the greatest practical study of contrapuntal technique in the history of music.

Questions for Reflection

❖   How were Handel's and Bach's responses to changing musical tastes different?

❖   How did the French and Italian attitudes toward their national operatic styles reflect their different national interests and their political situations in the late Baroque period?

❖   In what ways did the different balances of influence among the social classes affect music in England, France, Germany, and Italy at the end of the Baroque era?

❖   In what ways would it be appropriate to consider the music of the composers discussed in this chapter "mannerist"? Why might the term seem less appropriate for this music than for that at the end of the Middle Ages or Renaissance?

Suggestions for Further Reading

Paul Henry Lang, *George Frideric Handel* (New York: Norton, 1966) is an excellent biography. Otto Erich Deutsch, *Handel, a Documentary Biography* (New York: Black, 1955), presents the composer as revealed in contemporary documents. Handel's operatic career is discussed in Winton Dean, *Handel and the Opera Seria* (Berkeley: University of California Press, 1969).

On Rameau, see Cuthbert Girdlestone, *Jean-Philippe Rameau: His Life and Work*, rev. ed. (New York: Dover, 1969).

The most up-to-date material on Bach appears in Christoph Wolff et al., *The New Grove Bach Family* (New York: Norton, 1983); also recommended is Karl Geiringer, *Johann Sebastian Bach* (London: Oxford University Press, 1966). For a good impression of the composer in his context, see Barbara Schwendowius and Wolfgang Dömling, eds., *J. S. Bach: Life, Times, Influence* (Kassel: Bärenreiter, 1976).

16 NEW CURRENTS IN THE EARLY EIGHTEENTH CENTURY

Departure from the Baroque

It is convenient to assign the end of the Baroque period to the death of Bach in 1750, but it is essential to realize that one musical period does not end and another begin in such a sharply articulated fashion as that date suggests. Bach was already regarded as something of a throwback, out of step with the latest developments, during his own time.

New styles established themselves in the second quarter of the eighteenth century that would have continuing influence through the remainder of that century and beyond. Among these the most important was the unwillingness of younger composers to bind themselves to the sort of insistent concentration on a single affection that characterized Baroque, rhetorical musical expression. A more flexible, varied approach to the single piece or movement appealed to the new taste. In addition, there was an increasing desire for clarity and transparency in structure, partly for purely aesthetic reasons and partly as a reflection of a less-sophisticated musical audience, the growing middle class.

Musicians were also exploring new theoretical principles that would remain in force through the nineteenth century. The tonal system, already incipient in the music of the High Baroque, was worked out and firmly established. The use of tonality in formal planning and the articulation of tonal form by details of the musical surface began to produce new principles of design.

The Development of the Tonal System

By the end of the seventeenth century the successions of harmonies that composers were using had settled into patterns that are familiar to us from the standard musical repertoire. Especially in the music of the Bolognese instrumental composers and in the Italian opera, though also in other repertoires and in other regions, the syntax of chord progressions had become focussed on a few models that entirely dominated the music. This harmonic idiom appears very strongly in the sonatas and concertos of Corelli, and as a consequence he was commonly acknowledged by the eighteenth century to be the first "modern" composer.

Through the first two decades of the eighteenth century, composers, theorists, and music students still based their work on the principles of intervallic consonance and dissonance that had supported the polyphonic textures. Even in the homophonic style based on the basso continuo, a harmony was identified by its bass note and the intervals above it. The tonal idiom had, however, been arrived at empirically out of the combination of contrapuntal motion among voices, particularly the interaction of two upper voices in trio texture and the opposition of the bass.

The theory of functional, tonal harmonic progressions was not developed until Rameau wrote his *Traité de l'harmonie* in 1722. Rameau's observations of harmonic practice led him to an entirely new perspective on harmony: Instead of viewing a chord as a combination of various intervals above a bass note, he regarded it as a permutation of a harmonic abstraction built in thirds—a *triad*. Thus, for example, Rameau would not view the harmony with c as its bass note and e′ and a′ above it in the older manner as a type of harmony based on C but as a version of the triad founded on A. As a result Rameau also had to articulate the concept of harmonic *inversion* and to distinguish the *root* or fundamental bass of a triad from the actual sounding bass tone.

This idea of the triad, inversion, and root offered a totally new perspective on harmony, with great potential for clarifying the way in which chord progressions work. It explained, for example, why the same tones in the construction e′-g′-c″ do not function in the way they do in the construction e′-g′-b′: The triad, identified by its root and not the bass note, offers the consistent index of how the tones in the harmony will function. This gave Rameau the key to a theory of *functional harmony*. In the *Traité de l'harmonie* Rameau argued that a particular progression of chord roots seemed to control the flow of the music of his time. He gave the name *tonic* to the harmony of closure, that built on the first note of the scale; the name *dominant* to the triad that most strongly led to the tonic, built on the fifth scale degree; and the name *subdominant* to the triad constructed on the fourth scale degree. Once the functions of triads within a key had been identified, *modulation* could be explained. A triad that could appear in two different keys could be used as a pivot from one to another by treating it as having one function when it arrived and another when the music moved on.

An especially controversial aspect of Rameau's approach was his insistence that melody should be derived from harmony. Until this time the vertical element in music was primarily conceived as the product of simultaneous tones in horizontal melodic lines. Rameau suggested that the composer should have in his mind the progression of harmonies and that the melody should derive from those harmonies. This procedure would have important results. First, it supported the inclination of melody to clarify harmonic content (as was the case in Vivaldi's characteristic ritornello themes), an important element of the style of the later eighteenth century. Secondly, the tendency of melody to proceed in vocal fashion, mostly in stepwise motion, became weaker, while the outlining of triads and the resulting emphasis on a more instrumental skipping motion increased.

The directing of phrases by simple harmonic progressions led to a slowing down of harmonic rhythm in general. In Baroque music the rate of harmonic change was likely to be the beat. In the later eighteenth century it was more likely to be the measure. A phrase would then generally consist of only a few harmonies, over which a melody could unfold.

The Galant Style

In France

During the first decades of the eighteenth century music moved away from the grandiloquence and intensity of the rhetorical expression of the Baroque toward lightness and pleasing decorativeness. It is only natural that this style is associated particularly with France, where intellectual control, combined with the national inclination not to take life or art too seriously, had always tempered the Baroque. A common term for this new aesthetic outlook is the French word *galant*, which implies elegance, charm, intimacy, grace, clarity, and naturalness—all the very opposite of the Baroque style. This new ideal appeared in the different arts around the end of the reign of Louis XIV, who died in 1715, and continued well into the era of Louis XV (1710–1774). It is particularly apparent in painting and interior decoration, where it is sometimes known as *rococo*, from the ornamental shell designs or *rocailles* that commonly appeared on walls. (Fig. 16.1) The French painters Jean-Antoine Watteau (1684–1721) and his follower François Boucher (1703–1770) represent the style in the visual arts. (Fig. 16.2) In music, the galant manner can be heard in the *ordres* of François Couperin and the suites of Rameau.

Figure 16.1
Germain Boffrand's interior decoration of the Salon de la Princesse in the
Hôtel de Soubise is an example of the rococo style with its light and delicate
type of decoration. (*Giraudon/Art Resource*)

The first mark of the musical galant is its general lightness of texture.
There is clearly a single melodic part without any pretense of counterpoint,
and accompanying harmonies are voiced sparingly. In general this music
has a considerable degree of rhythmic flexibility that is quite different from
the steady rhythmic pulsation we associate with Baroque music. Decorative
surface ornamentation is applied to the simple melodic line in the form of
agréments. Forms are simple: the binary dance structure, or the rondeau with

Figure 16.2
The galant style of music in the eighteenth century was characterized by charm and sentiment. Jean Antoine Watteau (1684–1721) shows this aesthetic in his paintings, such as "Mezzetin" (ca. 1719). The character here, dressed in Italian *commedia dell'arte* costume, seems lost in pensive sentimentality. (*Metropolitan Museum of Art, Munsey Fund, 1934. 34.138*)

a recurring refrain that keeps the music from launching ambitious expeditions.

Outside of France

The galant style was not regarded in the eighteenth century as the exclusive domain of the French. The German flutist and theorist Johann Joachim Quantz (1697–1773), writer of an important treatise on flute playing and music in general, the *Versuch einer Anweisung die Flöte traversière zu spielen* (Essay on a method of playing the transverse flute, 1752), used the term *galant* to describe the keyboard works of the Italian composer Domenico Scarlatti (1685–1757). Scarlatti, the son of the famous Italian opera composer Alessandro Scarlatti, is known mainly for his keyboard music, though he also composed in other genres. When Handel had visited Italy in 1706–1710 the two young composers engaged in a performance competition, Handel winning for his organ playing while Scarlatti was the victor at the harpsichord. In 1719 Scarlatti became keyboard master to the Portuguese princess Maria Barbara, who in 1728 married the crown prince of Spain and took Scarlatti with her to Madrid, where he spent the bulk of his career.

The most influential works in Scarlatti's output were the keyboard pieces that he called *essercizi* and that are usually known as sonatas today. Each consists of only a single movement, but in the earliest manuscripts they often seem to be grouped by key in pairs or groups of three. These pieces are usually in the binary dance form.

We shall see that binary form grew to be the most important structure of the music of the Classic period. Scarlatti's contribution to the form is a new degree of clarification in the structure. There is a tendency in his pieces for a contrasting key to be firmly established near the middle of the first part and for the new key to remain strongly stable until the repeat sign at the end of the part. Likewise, in the second half the tonic returns in the middle and the music remains harmonically stable thereafter. Thus each part of the two-part design is subdivided at the arrival of a key. The arrivals are characteristically strongly set up by a full or half cadence.

Scarlatti profited from the example of the Italian instrumental music of the preceding generation in devising melodic material that clearly serves a harmonic function. It is often possible to identify the various ideas within a piece as particularly contrived to establish a key, provide contrast, or bring about a stable cadence. Often the second sections of the two parts of the form, beginning with the tonal arrival (the contrasting key in the first part and the tonic in the second part), are the same except for the necessary transposition. This gives unity to the movement by demonstrating the parallel between the two parts through a musical rhyme and produces the effect of resolution into the tonic of the material originally associated with the region of tonal tension.

French and Italian Operatic Comedy

Among the genres that appealed most successfully to the new eighteenth-century audience was the comic opera. We have already seen how in Germany the Singspiel coexisted with Italian opera in Hamburg under Reinhard Keiser, and how in England the ballad opera had displaced the Italian opera during Handel's career. Characteristic of these genres was a contemporary setting and action, the use of the vernacular, spoken dialogue rather than recitative, and more modest musical demands and production values.

In Italy, at about the same time that the intermezzo was developed to provide comic relief between acts of the opera seria, there grew up an independent comic operatic genre, the *opera buffa*. Like the intermezzo and the comic genres of England and Germany, the opera buffa was a national response to the current demand for a less artificial, more immediately appealing genre. It also took its plots from contemporary situations. Like the intermezzo, the opera buffa adopted a two-act division and employed stock characters and situations. It was considerably longer and called for a larger cast than an intermezzo, however, so it could stand on its own as an evening's entertainment. Unlike the ballad opera and Singspiel, opera buffa maintained the recitative and called for a more elaborate style of vocal singing (though not, of course, as flamboyant as the style of the Baroque opera seria).

La Guerre des Bouffons

One of the great controversies in music history was the argument that took place in the eighteenth century over the relative merits of French and Italian musical styles. This disagreement came to a head in the 1750s, when it was a hot item for debate among critics in various journals and pamphlets. The direct cause of the conflict was the appearance in Paris in 1752 of a troupe performing Italian opera buffa, in particular Pergolesi's *La serva padrona*.

Some of the French audience found the Italian vocal style a positive revelation. In comparison to the French air, with its syllabic text setting and frilly agréments, the Italian aria featured both a more natural *cantabile* style and greater virtuosity in florid writing. Since in the Italian melismas the ornamental aspect was written into the line rather than added by small symbols, the detail seemed better integrated into the whole.

On the other hand, the supporters of the French style found the lively Italian melodic style busy and artificial, while their own music seemed to them simpler and more natural. They adopted as their hero Rameau (who had himself been attacked in the 1730s as having abandoned the true French tradition going back to Lully). The entire debate became known, punningly, as the *Guerre des bouffons* (War of the buffoons).

No less a figure than the great French philosopher Jean-Jacques Rousseau (1712–1770) engaged in this polemical battle. He took the Italian side. He reported an amusing experiment he had undertaken to determine the relative merits of the two styles by consulting an impartial observer:

> I saw in Venice an Armenian, an intelligent man who had never heard any music, and before whom there were performed in a single concert a French monologue [from Rameau's *Hippolyte et Aricie*] that begins with this line:
>
> Temple sacré, séjour tranquille
>
> and an aria by Galuppi [the Italian opera composer Baldassare Galuppi (1706–1785)] that begins with this one:
>
> Voi che languite senza speranza.
>
> Both of these were sung, the French one in mediocre fashion and the Italian one badly, by a man accustomed only to French music and at that time very enthusiastic about that of M. Rameau. I noticed in the Armenian during the French song more surprise than pleasure; but everybody observed from the first measures of the Italian aria that his face and his eyes softened, he was enchanted, he gave up his soul to the impressions of the music, and, even though he understood the language only slightly, the mere sounds caused him noticeable delight. From that moment on no one could make him listen to any French air.

Rousseau even composed a dramatic musical piece himself, *Le Devin du village* (1752). This work is an example of *opéra comique,* a genre defined partly by its light subject material and partly by its use of unaccompanied spoken dialogue rather than the recitative of the French tragédie lyrique or the Italian opera. Opéra comique filled a position in France similar to that of the Singspiel in Germany or the ballad opera in England, though its music was more polished than that of the latter.

The empfindsamer Stil

The galant style, whether in a French or Italian manifestation, did not, of course, satisfy the artistic inclinations of all musicians in the first half of the eighteenth century. To those who sought depth of expression from music, it must have seemed particularly flimsy and unfulfilling. The desire for a more profound emotional statement in art belongs characteristically to the German spirit, and so it should not be surprising that a rival approach was cultivated there. The center of this movement was the city of Berlin.

The usual term for this aesthetic approach is the German word *Empfind-samkeit,* which is translated as "sensibility" or "sentimentality." The term implies that the feelings expressed are somewhat naively emotional. We refer to the idiom of this music as the *empfindsamer Stil* (sentimental style). In order to achieve the expression of sentiment, the composers adopted and often exaggerated some of the more obvious affective gestures of the Baroque. But in contrast to Baroque music, a single movement might have these gestures in profuse variety rather than concentrating on a single affect throughout a movement. This is an important new conception, that emotional experience is not made up of static passions but of constantly fluctuating feelings, and that, by extension, a musical work might combine widely different styles in free juxtaposition.

Carl Philipp Emanuel Bach

One of the greatest composers of the *empfindsamer Stil* was Carl Philipp Emanuel Bach (1714–1788), the second son of J.S. Bach. He had been taught by his father; indeed he proudly claimed that his father had been his only teacher, but his style represents a completely different generation. C.P.E. Bach worked for the Prussian king Frederick the Great in his palace, Sans Souci, at Potsdam near Berlin from 1738 to 1768. Frederick played the flute, and C.P.E. Bach's most important duty was to accompany the king in chamber music.

The king's flute teacher was Johann Joachim Quantz. In his treatise on playing the flute, which discusses not only the technique of flute playing but also such matters as the standard musical forms and genres of the late Baroque, as well as style and expression, Quantz was particularly concerned to distinguish the Italian from the French style. He concluded that the great virtue of German music was that it took something from each of those nations and struck a balance between them. He does not seem to have recognized the *empfindsamer Stil* as a specifically German type, and indeed his own music tended to use a galant idiom.

The king's tastes were guided by those of his mentor and consequently did not suit C.P.E. Bach, who also found himself underpaid and underappreciated. In 1768, when Telemann (who was C.P.E. Bach's godfather) died, C.P.E. Bach succeeded to the position of music director and Kantor in Hamburg.

In addition to his musical compositions, which included keyboard pieces, concertos and sonatas, symphonies, songs, and church music, C.P.E. Bach wrote a book on keyboard playing, the *Versuch über die wahre Art das Clavier zu spielen* (Essay on the true manner of playing the keyboard, 1753). In this book he took for granted the ideals of the *empfindsamer Stil,* particularly stressing the flexibility of music to move quickly from one emotional state to another, quite unlike the Baroque concentration on a single affect at a time:

A musician cannot move others unless he too is moved. He must of necessity feel all of the affects that he hopes to arouse in his audience, for the revealing of his own humor will stimulate a like humor in the listener. In languishing, sad passages, the performer must languish and grow sad. . . . Similarly, in lively, joyous passages, the executant must again put himself into the appropriate mood. And so, *constantly varying the passions* he will barely quiet one before he rouses another.[1] (Emphasis added.)

Charles Burney (1726–1814), an English writer on music who traveled widely and met most of the important musicians of the eighteenth century, visited C.P.E. Bach in 1773. His description of the composer's playing suggests that Bach took the expression of feeling very seriously:

. . . he grew so animated and *possessed,* that he not *only* played, but looked like one inspired. His eyes were fixed, his under lip fell, and drops of effervescence distilled from his countenance.[2]

The *empfindsamer Stil* is easily recognized in practice, even in instrumental music, where there is no text to clarify the expressive content. Many of its gestures come from operatic recitative. Particularly tear-jerking in the melodic language are the frequent descending-half-step motives and lines broken up by gasping rests. Angular, unvocal lines may also appear. Chromaticism and surprising chord progressions are common in the harmony. Rhythm may be treated with a great deal of flexibility; the most extreme manifestation of this is the keyboard fantasy, in which entire pieces may be written without bar-lines.

Keyboard Instruments

Particularly suited to this sentimental expressiveness was the clavichord, which allowed more subtle and immediate dynamic control than the harpsi-chord. Because the clavichord operates on the very simple principle of key and tangent as a direct connection between finger and string, the force on the key was precisely reflected in the loudness of the tone. Moreover, a subtle increase and decrease of pressure on the key could give a waver to a sustained pitch that resembled most delightfully the singer too caught up in sentiment to control the voice. The problem with the clavichord was that its sound was so diminu-tive that it could hardly be heard throughout a large room, and it was quite incapable of producing a genuinely loud tone.

The need for a more powerful but still dynamically flexible instrument was met by the recently invented piano. The new instrument had been created by the Italian instrument maker Bartolomeo Cristofori (1655–1731) around 1700 and took its name from the fact that it played both "piano e forte." The early version of the modern piano is now sometimes distinguished by the use of the full name *pianoforte,* or *fortepiano.* C.P.E. Bach would have played instruments by the important German organ builder Gottfried Silbermann (1683–1753).

Song

Such expressive sentimentality in vocal music became clearest in the Lied, which flourished in the middle-class parlors of Germany in the eighteenth century. The earliest examples of the new style were merely parodied from simple, keyboard dance pieces by the addition of words to the melody line. A group of composers known as the *First Berlin School* (including C.P.E. Bach), cultivated the keyboard-accompanied Lied with new concentration. They espoused an uncomplicated style that expressed simple feelings in a manner that would appeal to the German burgers and their wives and daughters. Many of the poems they set belong to a literary sentimental style that begs for musical treatment in *empfindsamer Stil.* This movement also produced the sentimental novel, which began to thrive in the early eighteenth century and culminated in a style known as *Sturm und Drang* (storm and stress), which exploited raw emotion.

Structure in Early Eighteenth-Century Instrumental Music

At this point it will be helpful to introduce a means of outlining musical forms. The foundation of form is its tonal plan, so we shall place that on the lowest level in our diagrams. The tonic will be indicated by the Roman numeral I (i in minor keys) and other harmonies or tonal areas by their appropriate numerals. When it is necessary, letter names of keys will appear to identify them specifically. We shall use capital letters in the second half of the alphabet to identify melodic ideas. Standard letter abbreviations include *P* for themes associated with the principal key, *S* for themes associated with the secondary key, and *K* for themes associated with cadencing. Nonthematic material, such as is often used for transitional or cadential passages will be identified, if necessary, by small letters (*t, k*). New material introduced in the second part of a binary form will be designated by *N.*

To express the typical structure of the simplest binary dance form such as might be found in a movement from a Baroque suite, we might draw the following diagram:

```
Part 1        ‖ Part 2        ‖‖
P        :‖:P'       :     ‖‖
I      V ‖         I        ‖‖
(or i    III‖        i)‖‖
```

(In general the alternative of the relative major key as a substitute for the dominant in minor key pieces in this structure can be taken for granted and will not be included in future diagrams.)

The subdivided binary form of a one-movement sonata by Domenico Scarlatti, where the arrival of the dominant in the first part and the return of the tonic in the second part are assigned parallel material, can be expressed in schematic form as follows:

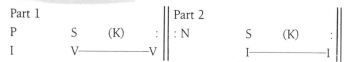

```
Part 1                    ‖ Part 2                    ‖‖
P      S    (K)    :‖ : N      S    (K)    :‖‖
I      V————————V ‖       I——————————I ‖‖
```

Of particular importance in the later part of the century was yet another modification, in which the return of the tonic key in the second part is signaled by the return of the same material that established the tonic at the opening of the form. There is then a stable section at the end, adapted from the first part in such a way that no modulation occurs. This is generally known as *rounded binary* form. It can be outlined thus:

```
Part 1      ‖ Part 2            ‖‖
P      :‖:         P       :     ‖‖
I      V‖      I———————I ‖‖
```

These various treatments of the basic binary plan are found throughout the instrumental works of the composers of the galant movement. They continued to be employed in the dance movements from which they evolved, of course. They also predominated in other instrumental pieces, particularly in Italy but also in northern countries.

Developments in Instrumental Music

Among the works of composers in the generation following Domenico Scarlatti, the keyboard sonata comprised a piece in several movements in contrasting tempos. Each movement was likely to adopt some variant of the basic binary form. Following Scarlatti's lead, composers increasingly used thematic events to highlight the tonal plan. Changes of texture—from melody-and-accompaniment style to chordal scoring, imitative writing, and bare octave passages—similarly helped articulate passages of establishment of the tonality, modulatory transition, cadence, and so on. The multimovement keyboard sonata became very important in the history of music after the middle of the century.

As the middle of the eighteenth century approached, an important development in instrumental music was the rise of the independent *sinfonia,* which grew into the symphony. The genre originated in the opening sinfonia of the Italian opera and therefore followed the three-movement layout of that model. The leading center for the early independent sinfonia was the city of Milan, and the most noteworthy composer was Giovanni Battista Sammartini (1701–1775), a church composer, organist, and teacher. A Sammartini sinfonia was typically scored for string orchestra. A common ensemble might have from three to seven first violins, three to five seconds, one to three violas, one or two each of cellos and basses, and a harpsichord to play basso continuo. The harpsichord player usually led the performance.

Like the keyboard sonata, the sinfonia profited from the success of the late Baroque composers in coordinating musical styles and dynamics with tonal structure. A bold opening in chordal or unison style established the key of the opening or closing of a section in a binary sinfonia movement just as it would in a ritornello in a Baroque concerto. Busier, more contrapuntal passages suited the tonally unstable transitional areas. Lyrical, cantabile scoring lent itself to slow movements.

Progress in the genre of the sinfonia was not limited to Italy. The German composers in the 1740s at the brilliant court of Mannheim, capital of the Palatine region in central Germany, contributed particularly to orchestral scoring. The orchestra at Mannheim became the most polished ensemble in Europe at that time, especially under the direction of Johann Stamitz (1717–1757). Charles Burney wrote of the Mannheim orchestra:

> I found it to be indeed all that its fame had made me expect: Power will naturally arise from a great number of hands; but the judicious use of this power, on all occasions, must be the consequence of good discipline. Indeed, there are more solo players, and good composers in this, than perhaps in any other orchestra in Europe; it is an army of generals, equally fit to plan a battle, as to fight it.[3]

The Mannheim orchestra was a large one for its time. According to a list of personnel there in 1756, Stamitz and his colleagues had at their disposal four flutes, two oboes, two bassoons, four horns, twelve trumpets (kept at court for heraldic purposes, of course, and not used in such quantity in the sinfonia), two timpani, twenty violins, four violas, four cellos, two basses, and the harpsichord.

Burney's remarks on the Mannheim orchestra also give attention to Stamitz's use of dynamics:

> Since the discovery which the genius of Stamitz first made, every effect has been tried which such an aggregate of sound can produce. It was here that the *Crescendo* and *Diminuendo* had birth; and the *Piano*, which was before chiefly used as an echo, with which it was generally synonymous, as well as the *Forte,* were found to be musical colours which had their *shades,* as much as red or blue in painting.[4]

Burney's remark about Stamitz's originality in the use of dynamics refers to orchestration as well as simply the indication of the markings *crescendo* and *diminuendo* in the score. Stamitz developed the technique of scoring a rise in pitch coordinated with an increase in loudness, textural density, and the number of participating instruments. A sustained passage of such a crescendo is sometimes referred to as a "Mannheim steamroller."

In melodic style the Mannheim group tended to employ regular series of rather square, four-measure phrases. However, they thoroughly understood the principle of choosing appropriate styles for the different needs of the various parts of a tonal form. One particular thematic type that was favored for establishing the principal key in a fast orchestral movement was the rapid rising arpeggio, or "Mannheim rocket."

The form of the Mannheim type of sinfonia tends to reflect the ritornello practice of the Baroque concerto and not simply the straightforward binary form used in Milan. Also more characteristic of the German than the Italian composers was the addition of an internal movement in the form of a minuet. Stamitz was the first composer to insert the minuet consistently. This development may reflect the influence of the orchestral suite on the sinfonia, or it may come from opera, where at this time a minuet was commonly used for the first music at the opening of the curtain after the introductory sinfonia. The four-movement sinfonia became the standard pattern after 1750.

Questions for Reflection

❖ In what ways do the galant style and empfindsamer Stil differ, and what aspects of musical thinking do they share?

❖ How were the new ways of musical thinking in the first part of the eighteenth century responses to social changes during that period?

❖ In what way did tonality's function in the developing binary form in the early eighteenth century differ from its function in the earlier forms of mature Baroque music?

Suggestions for Further Reading

Rameau's *Treatise on Harmony* is available in an English translation with annotations by Philip Gossett (New York: Dover, 1971). Quantz's treatise is published in English as *On Playing the Flute*, trans. Edward R. Reilly (New York: Schirmer, 1966). C.P.E. Bach's keyboard treatise is published as *Essay on the True Art of Playing Keyboard Instruments*, trans. William J. Mitchell (New York: Norton, 1949). The latter two treatises are excerpted in Oliver Strunk, *Source Readings in Music History* (New York: Norton, 1950), as are some of the documents from the guerre des bouffons. For a collection of a number of important writings on musical aesthetics of the period, see Peter le Huray and James Day, eds., *Music and Aesthetics in the Eighteenth and Early Nineteenth Centuries* (Cambridge: Cambridge University Press, 1981).

An excellent biography of Scarlatti is Ralph Kirkpatrick, *Domenico Scarlatti*, new ed. (Princeton, N.J.: Princeton University Press, 1983).

The development of the sonata in the eighteenth century is surveyed in William S. Newman, *The Sonata in the Classic Era* (Chapel Hill: University of North Carolina Press, 1983).

Notes

1. Carl Philipp Emanuel Bach, *Essay on the True Art of Playing Keyboard Instruments*, trans. and ed., William J. Mitchell (New York: Norton, 1949), 152.

2. Charles Burney, *An Eighteenth-Century Musical Tour in Central Europe and the Netherlands*, ed., Percy A. Scholes (London: Oxford University Press, 1959), 219.

3. Ibid., 34–35.

4. Ibid., 35.

17 THE EARLY CLASSIC PERIOD

The Enlightenment

The cultural movement into which the music of the second half of the eighteenth century must be placed is called the Enlightenment. In all fields there was a tendency toward intellectualism. In France a group of thinkers under the leadership of Denis Diderot (1713–1784) compiled the *Encyclopédie* (between 1747 and 1765) to codify contemporary knowledge. The *Encyclopédie* also embodied a philosophical ideal of unprecedented freedom of thought. The climax of philosophy in this period was Immanuel Kant's (1724–1804) *Critique of Pure Reason* (1781), which examined the possibilities and limits of rational thought.

In the spheres of politics and economics, old assumptions were challenged by new ideas. In *The Social Contract* (1762) Jean-Jacques Rousseau argued that government should arise from the general will of the people rather than be imposed by a small class at the pinnacle of an artificial social hierarchy, a revolutionary proposition that influenced the American and French revolutions in 1776 and 1789–1792. In his treatise *The Wealth of Nations* (1776), Adam Smith (1723–1790) espoused a laissez-faire economic system free from government restraints.

The Enlightenment in the sciences replaced the older Rationalist approach with a more empirical one, appealing to direct observation and experimentation rather than to mere reflection in isolation. Carl Linnaeus (1707–1778) set up the framework for a system of biological classification that would suggest new ways of thinking about the organic world. Antoine Lavoisier (1743–1794) founded quantitative chemistry and thereby brought scientific research into a new phase.

The practical application of the intellect to technological problems led to new inventions. The field of electricity was explored by Benjamin Franklin (1706–1790) and the Italians Luigi Galvani (1737–1798) and Alessandro Volta (1745–1827). The invention of an efficient steam engine in 1769 by the Scottish inventor James Watt (1736–1819) made possible the Industrial Revolution.

The Classic Outlook

The term *Classic* is commonly employed to characterize the music of the second half of the eighteenth century. Like some other terms used to label musical style periods, this one was not used by eighteenth-century musicians to characterize their own music, and it must be understood that the term embodies elements of truth but also must be taken with a grain of salt.

In the broadest usage a classic work of art is one that is a model or sets a standard. Such a work has a universal or timeless appeal, perhaps in a variety of senses. For example, the works of Shakespeare are classics of the late Renaissance theater, and the poems of Walt Whitman are classics of nineteenth-century American literature. Palestrina's polyphony was the classic model for the panconsonant contrapuntal technique, while Corelli's sonatas were classics in the eighteenth century.

The adjective *classic* in any context also suggests a relation to classical antiquity; a style of art considered classical should have general qualities also commonly regarded as belonging to the culture of the Graeco-Roman era. Of course the ancients produced a tremendous variety of artistic expressions, and the culture of Rome differed in many ways from that of Greece. The qualities that are usually known as classic, however, are those of the Apollonian spirit. Among these are clarity and simplicity; symmetry, balance, and order; and objectivity. The most important formulator of the classic aesthetic in eighteenth-century art was the German archaeologist Johann Joachim Winckelmann (1717–1768), who studied the artifacts unearthed at that time in Pompeii and Herculaneum. Winckelmann wrote a *History of Ancient Art* (1764) that was widely read in the last third of the century, in which he characterized the art of classical antiquity as bearing "noble simplicity and quiet grandeur."

This Apollonian viewpoint certainly affected some artists in the period between about 1760 and 1800, notably the French painter Jacques Louis David (1748–1825), whose *Oath of the Horatii* (1784), *Death of Socrates* (1787; Plate 6), and *Lictors Bringing to Brutus the Bodies of his Sons* (1789) not only take their topics from ancient history but also feature great nobleness of content, quietness of color, and control of design. This movement in the visual arts is generally known as neoclassic, to differentiate it from the ancient classic period.

Figure 17.1
The Parthenon in the Acropolis of Athens. Symmetry and simplicity of design
were the characteristics of Greek art that seemed most important to
eighteenth-century artists reacting against the Baroque and rococo styles.
(Marburg/Art Resource)

The use of models from ancient times can be seen most clearly in architecture. In Paris the French architect Germain Soufflot (1709–1780) constructed a church (1755–1792) dedicated to Sainte Geneviève based on the Pantheon in Rome. In America Thomas Jefferson (1743–1826) designed the Virginia State Capitol (1785–1796) in Richmond based on the proportions of an ancient temple. (Figs. 17.1, 17.2)

The movement toward a more objective approach in art was not limited to the visual arts. English writer Alexander Pope (1688–1744), in his 1735 *An Essay on Criticism,* used carefully balanced couplets to argue for artistic control:

'Tis more to guide, than spur the Muse's steed,
Restrain his fury, than provoke his speed;
The wingèd courser, like a gen'rous horse
Show most true mettle when you check his course.

With classical references, Pope emphasized that to evaluate artistic works we must understand the contexts from which they arose:

Figure 17.2
Thomas Jefferson, the Virginia State Capitol in Richmond. Jefferson was clearly influenced by the design of ancient Greek temple architecture (cf. Fig. 17.1). *(Virginia Division of Tourism)*

You then whose judgment the right course would steer,
Know well each ANCIENT'S proper character;
His Fable, Subject, scope in ev'ry page;
Religion, Country, genius of his Age:
Without all these at once before your eyes,
Cavil you may, but never criticize.

And he urged reliance on models from classical antiquity:

Be Homer's works your study and delight,
Read them by day, and meditate by night;
Thence form your judgment, thence your maxims bring,
And trace the Muses upward to their spring.[1]

One example of the eighteenth-century desire to achieve control and order was the *Dictionary* of the English language created by Samuel Johnson (1709–1784) in 1775. Johnson's dictionary standardized English usage, which had been quite flexible until the eighteenth century.

As a rule the literature of the eighteenth century belongs to the intellectual realm of prose, rather than the effusive and expressive domain of poetry.

Particularly successful was social criticism and satire, which reflected the Enlightenment interest in social and political reform; Jonathan Swift (1667–1745) in *Gulliver's Travels* (1726) and *A Modest Proposal* (1729), and Voltaire (François Marie Arouet; 1694–1778) in *Candide* (1759) attacked the comfortable self-satisfaction of the age with ruthless pointedness sharpened by their impressive wit.

It could hardly be expected that the music of the second half of the eighteenth century would return to models of ancient times in the same way as art and literature. Too little remained of the music of classical Antiquity to provide composers such models as were available to David, Soufflot, and Pope. What could be done had largely been tried by the creators of monody and the opera a century and a half earlier. The effects of the true classicizing movement in music appear directly only in some rethinking of the opera. Nevertheless, a deep-rooted desire for clarity and formal symmetry, for the most part only subconsciously inspired by ancient ideals, also pervaded the music of the period.

The Situation of the Musician

The patronage system that had operated since the Middle Ages continued to support most musicians in the late eighteenth century. As political power and wealth centered on several great capitals, musical developments also focussed on those cities. By 1750 the Prussian capital of Berlin had already established its musical position in the style of Empfindsamkeit, and after the death of Frederick the Great in 1786 his nephew Frederick William (r. 1786–1797), who played the cello, continued to patronize music. In Austria the Holy Roman Empire's capital, Vienna, became the center of an international musical style during the period of Frederick the Great's persistent rival Maria Theresa (1717–1780) and her son Joseph II (r. 1780–1790). Paris in the days of Louis XV (r. 1715–1774) and Louis XVI (r. 1774–1793) continued to cultivate a brilliant artistic life. In Russia, following the reforms and Europeanization begun by Peter the Great, Catherine the Great's (r. 1762–1796) capital at St. Petersburg generally imported western European composers.

Other, smaller court cities also cultivated music, of course. In Salzburg, Austria, the prince-archbishop maintained a fine musical establishment in the context of a glittering rococo architectural milieu. Germany had active musical establishments in the electoral courts; particularly important were Mannheim and Munich. The Italian peninsula remained politically fragmented, and sections of it were controlled by foreign powers (Spain in the south and Austria in the north). However, its cities kept up their musical life in opera, church, and court. In England, where the merchant class controlled a large portion of the wealth, culture was directed more toward commercial enterprise.

The patronage of a wealthy aristocracy had mixed effects on the musician. Its main advantage was a degree of personal security; the court musician was housed, fed, and clothed (albeit in a servant's livery). There was no lack of musical opportunity, and working in close association with a fairly stable group of colleagues gave musicians the chance to interact to their mutual profit. On the other hand, the position of the musician carried the relatively low social status of a household servant. Moreover, the musician was at the mercy of the desires and tastes of the patron. As has already been mentioned, C.P.E. Bach chafed under this situation at Berlin, and soon other composers would challenge the patronage system in an attempt to attain artistic independence.

With the continuing rise of the bourgeoisie and the progressive relocation of the wealth of Europe from the aristocracy to the middle class, new musical institutions and situations arose. The public opera house—developed in Venice a century earlier and later attempted in Hamburg—became a more common phenomenon. Public concerts, generally called *academies,* began to occur, with tickets sold by subscription in advance. A new profession appeared, that of the impresario, who arranged concert series in a number of cities. This gave composers an alternative way to make a living. Among the early successful impresarios were some who were also important composers. In London from 1764 Johann Sebastian Bach's youngest son, Johann Christian Bach (1735–1782) and Karl Friedrich Abel (1723–1787) put together an important series of concerts. In Paris François-Joseph Gossec (1734–1829) directed the *Concerts spirituels,* which began in 1725 and lasted until the revolution, and the *Concerts des amateurs* from 1769. In Leipzig Johann Adam Hiller (1728–1804) led a series of concerts that from 1781 were known as the Gewandhaus Concerts and became one of the longest-running such concert series.

Another newly profitable enterprise was the composition of music for publication. Music publishing had, of course, constituted an active industry for over two hundred years, yet the market did not yet bear tremendous mass production. Even as recent a composer as J.S. Bach published very little of his total output. Composers' first obligations had been to their patrons and to practical needs; the audience for published music had been limited, and commonly the publication of music had depended on a special occasion or on a dedication to a noble patron in expectation of financial remuneration. In the course of the eighteenth century, however, there began to grow up a large enough consumer class to encourage composers to try to earn a decent living from works composed for the public.

One genre that particularly depended on the commercial market was the Lied, which flourished in sheet music and domestic periodicals. Even the leading composers in the large genres contributed to the song repertoire, and minor composers began to find the Lied a field with some potential for specialization. The simple, popular aesthetic ideal and style espoused by the Berlin composers made their Lieder spiritually sympathetic and stylistically familiar to the German bourgeois public.

The turn away from reliance on patronage affected musical style. The composer was no longer guided by the practical needs of the nobleman's daily life, and he was increasingly free to explore his own imagination rather than compose to the patron's taste. He confronted a new opportunity to express his own most personal or profound artistic thoughts. In attempting to please the public, however, he subjected himself to a different kind of influence. The aristocratic audience had been musically and artistically knowledgeable, often fairly well trained musicians themselves. We have mentioned that Frederick the Great played the flute and his successor Frederick William II the cello; Maria Theresa appeared as a singer in her younger days. The nobility thus constituted an audience of *Kenner* or connoisseurs. The middle-class public appreciated music in a less-sophisticated manner. Many among them were not musicians themselves; they were instead *Liebhaber* or amateurs. Their preferences naturally ran to music that was simpler in compositional detail and more striking in effect.

Contrasting Careers for Classical Musicians: Haydn and Mozart

It is useful to consider as examples of the benefits and disadvantages of the patronage system the careers of the two greatest composers of the Classic era—Franz Joseph Haydn (1732–1809) and Wolfgang Amadeus Mozart (1756–1791)—between the 1750s and about 1780.

Franz Joseph Haydn

Haydn was born in a small village in the Austro-Hungarian territory into a not particularly musical family. As he showed musical talent, he was sent to study with a musical relative and in 1740 entered the choir of St. Stephen's Cathedral in Vienna. The cathedral exploited its boy choristers' abilities but did not reward them with much in the way of education; thus, when Haydn lost his voice in 1750, he found himself on his own in the great capital and very poorly equipped to support himself. However, Vienna offered him the chance to rub shoulders with some fine musicians and other important figures, including the court poet and librettist Metastasio, who lived in the building where Haydn had a garret room. Haydn managed to study privately for a time with the opera composer Nicola Porpora, in whose house he served as a valet, and he gained some fluency in the galant style. Without patronage, however, he nearly starved, for he could earn very little money by private teaching and playing. In 1759 he was finally discovered by Count Ferdinand Morzin of Bohemia, who made Haydn his Kapellmeister and offered him his first decent living. Unfortunately, Morzin disbanded his musicians for financial reasons in 1761.

Haydn then gained a position with the wealthy Esterhazy family, close relatives of the imperial family in Vienna. Prince Paul Esterhazy made him vice-Kapellmeister and put him in charge of most of the household music, with an ensemble of sixteen players. When Prince Paul died in 1762, the new prince, Nicholas, expanded the palace orchestra to thirty. In 1766 the old Kapellmeister died, and Haydn gained full authority over this substantial musical establishment. Soon after this the prince moved from his fine palace at Eisenstadt to Esterhaza, a fabulous new country palace that rivaled Versailles in splendor. It was described, perhaps by Prince Nicholas himself, as follows:

> The castle is in Italian style . . . surrounded by a beautifully proportioned stone gallery. Most valuable are two rooms used by the prince. One of them contains ten Japanese panels in black lacquer adorned with golden flowers and landscapes, each of which cost more than a thousand florins. The chairs and divans are covered with golden fabric. There are also some extremely valuable cabinets and a bronze clock that plays the flute. In the second room, richly adorned with golden ornaments, is another gilded clock with a canary on top that moves and whistles pleasant tunes when the clock strikes, as well as an armchair that plays a flute solo when you sit on it. The chandeliers are made from artistically wrought rock crystal. In the library there are seventy-five hundred books, all exquisite editions, to which novelties are being added daily. It also contains numerous manuscripts and many excellent old and new engravings by the best masters. The picture gallery is liberally supplied with first-class original paintings by famous Italian and Dutch masters which fill the eye of the connoisseur with delight and admiration.[2]

The music at Esterhaza did not all take place in the prince's chambers in the palace. There were, in fact, two different opera theaters on the grounds.

> In an alley of wild chestnut trees stands the magnificent opera house. The boxes at the sides open into charming rooms furnished most luxuriously with fireplaces, divans, mirrors, and clocks. The theater holds four hundred people. Every day, at 6 P.M. there is a performance of an Italian *opera seria* or *buffa* or of German comedy, always attended by the prince. Words cannot describe how both eye and ear are delighted here. When the music begins, its touching delicacy, the strength and force of the instruments penetrate the soul, for the great composer Herr Haydn himself is conducting. But the audience is also overwhelmed by the admirable lighting and the deceptively perfect stage settings. At first we see the

clouds on which the gods are seated sink slowly to earth. Then the gods rise upward and instantly vanish, and then again everything is transformed into a delightful garden, an enchanted wood, or, it may be, a glorious hall.

Opposite the opera house is the marionette theater, built like a grotto. All the walls, niches, and apertures are covered with variegated stones, shells, and snails that afford a very curious and striking sight when they are illuminated. The theater is rather large, and the decorations are extremely artistic. The puppets are beautifully formed and magnificently dressed; they play not only farces and comedies, but also *opera seria.* The performances in both theaters are open to everyone.[3]

Haydn thus had substantial responsibilities and a tremendous amount of work. He had to provide regular *Tafelmusik* (dinner music), two academies (concerts) every week, the music for the regular and the marionette opera, and sacred music for the princely worship services. Moreover, Prince Nicholas himself was an avid player of the *baryton,* a fretted, bowed string instrument related to the old viola da gamba. For this peculiar instrument Haydn composed at least a hundred and twenty-five trios for the prince to play with his hired musicians.

The advantages of Haydn's situation are clear: He had a good ensemble of players who were under his own discipline and played together day and night; he had no lack of opportunities for which to compose; his Croesuslike patron attracted to Esterhaza the finest musicians in Europe and audiences of noble connoisseurs. It is clear from the report above that the name of Haydn became famous enough to be included as one of the attractions of the palace. On the other hand, the composer's imagination was necessarily channeled according to the prince's needs and tastes, so that when baryton trios and puppet operas were called for Haydn had to spend his efforts on those; in addition, he complained of his isolation at Esterhaza, away from a musical center where he could have been inspired and challenged by frequent hearings of the latest compositions of his best contemporaries. As he himself once put it, he was "forced to become original." Haydn continued to work at Esterhaza until after Prince Nicholas's death in 1790, and thereafter remained officially the Kapellmeister of the Esterhazy family.

Wolfgang Amadeus Mozart

Mozart's situation was quite different from Haydn's. His father, Leopold Mozart (1719–1787), was employed as a violinist and court composer by the prince-archbishop of Salzburg and was the author of an important treatise on violin playing, the *Versuch einer gründlichen Violinschule* (Essay on a fundamental violin course, 1756). Wolfgang was a musical child prodigy who began both playing and composing at a very early age and was supported (and sometimes driven) by his father's high ambitions for him. In 1762, when Wolfgang was just six years old, Leopold presented him and his sister "Nannerl" (her real name was Maria Anna, and she was two and a half years older than her brother) at the electoral court in Munich and at the court of the Empress Maria Theresa in Vienna. The following year Leopold took the two children on a tour to Paris and London. Wolfgang's first published compositions, four sonatas for keyboard and violin, appeared in Paris in 1764. In London he met and learned from Johann Christian Bach, some of whose keyboard sonatas he later transcribed into small concertos.

After 1766 the Mozarts used Salzburg as their home base—Leopold was by this time deputy Kapellmeister and Wolfgang held the title of honorary court concertmaster—and made a series of visits to Italy so that Wolfgang could absorb the Italian style and try to widen his reputation. The first of these trips lasted from 1769 to 1771. They met the leading Italian sinfonia composer Sammartini and the opera composer Niccolo Piccinni (1728–1800) in Milan. Wolfgang studied counterpoint with the renowned theorist and teacher Padre Giovanni Battista Martini (1706–1784) in Bologna. They gave concerts in any city where it was possible, and Mozart even managed to compose his first Italian opera seria, *Mitridate, rè di Ponto,* and see it successfully staged in Milan. Leopold and Wolfgang made two more journeys to Italy in 1771 and 1772–1773.

In 1772 a new archbishop was installed in Salzburg, Count Hieronymus Colloredo. For Colloredo, whose court naturally needed liturgical music, Mozart wrote a quantity of Masses, other sacred settings, and sonatas da chiesa in Baroque trio scoring. However, the archbishop and Mozart could not agree on the proper role of the court musician. Mozart knew his own genius and was inclined to insist on respect and a certain degree of freedom, while Colloredo wished to hold his youthful court concertmaster to the position and duties of a servant. Particularly irksome to Colloredo were the Mozarts' continual requests for liberty to travel. Mozart was off to Vienna in 1773 and to Munich to stage an opera in 1775. By 1777 Mozart's discontent in Salzburg and ambition for his career was so great that he asked to be dismissed from the archbishop's service. He and his mother traveled to Mannheim and Paris, hoping to find a good new position, but none was offered. His mother died in Paris in the midst of the journey, and Mozart had to see her buried there and send the news to his father. He returned to Salzburg, where he was granted a new and somewhat higher paying position as court organist.

The new situation turned out not much different from the former one. Mozart's relationship with Count Colloredo did not really improve, and by 1781 things had come to a crisis. After a particularly acrimonious confrontation, Colloredo fired Mozart and had his steward literally kick the young composer out of the room. This colorful event took place in Vienna, and Mozart, now free from service, resolved to establish himself in that city, making his living by teaching and by giving concerts until he could find patronage.

Thus, in sharp contrast to Haydn, Mozart pressed the limitations of the patronage system to their extreme. He managed to travel widely and to absorb the influences of the different national styles of all the important musical capitals of Europe, and he challenged the position of the musician as mere lackey to a noble court. Ultimately the system could no longer tolerate such independence, and he was ejected from it.

Comic Opera in the Early Classic Period

As the opera buffa matured, it increased in sophistication. Unlike the serious opera, it featured ensemble singing in which the rhetorical expression of the affections gave way to musical working out of the conflicts between characters. This ensemble writing culminated particularly in the act finales, in which as many characters as possible appeared on stage at once. The dramatic action could then come to a climax in a number that would also be musically satisfying. Among the best of the Italian composers was Piccinni, who brought to the opera a fine sense of musical form adapted to dramatic needs and a more interesting texture in which the orchestra gained some independent appeal.

The finest opera buffa libretti were written by Carlo Goldoni (1707–1793). Besides the craftsmanship of his texts, which brilliantly met the needs of the composer, Goldoni contributed a more thoughtful tone to the stories. The characters increasingly took on flesh and blood, and the situations turned away from mere farce and toward social comment and sentimental or semiserious situations. The designation *opera buffa* seemed inappropriate for these more-sophisticated comic operas, and the term *dramma giocoso* was applied.

Haydn wrote operas for the theaters at Esterhaza, but he did not really consider opera to be among his true fields of expertise. Mozart, on the other hand, composed operas throughout his life, both seria and buffa, as well as Singspiel. His first opera buffa was *La finta semplice* (1769), based on a Goldoni plot, and almost simultaneously came a Singspiel, *Bastien und Bastienne*, derived from Rousseau's opéra comique *Le Devin du village*. Mozart's first opera seria, *Mitridate, rè di Ponto* of 1770 has already been mentioned. These works and the others that followed in the 1770s are well crafted but not highly original. They demonstrate Mozart's early grasp of the contemporary styles of dramatic music and a good sense of the demands of the stage and the singers.

Opera Seria and Opera Reform

The Classic inclination toward simplicity and naturalistic expression also began to take effect within the opera seria after the middle of the century. Composers began to take steps to modify the artificial conventions of the opera. More and more often they gave up the static da capo aria structure and consequently reduced the possibility of the singers ornamenting ad libitum. The distinction between recitative and aria gradually lessened because increasingly the recitative was accompanied rather than secco and because the cadences at the ends of recitatives, and even in some cases arias, were not always clearly articulated but elided with the following material. The orchestra and chorus were given more to do, with the result that the opera seemed less a chain of individual singers pouring out their passions like orators. These changes came about gradually, and conventions of the Baroque opera can certainly be found throughout the Classic period.

The most remarkable opera reformer was Christoph Willibald Gluck (1714–1787), a native of Bohemia (what we now call Czechoslovakia). Gluck left his homeland for Italy to absorb the musical style of that country, much as Handel had done thirty years earlier. In Milan between 1737 and 1741 he came under the influence of Sammartini, and he stayed in Italy until 1745. Then he traveled, meeting Handel in England in 1746. In 1752 Gluck settled in Vienna under imperial patronage. There he worked closely with the Italian librettist Raniero Calzabigi (1714–1795), a very progressive dramatist (and one of the earliest literary figures on the continent to appreciate the achievements of Shakespeare). The collaboration of these two men produced several remarkable works, notably *Orfeo ed Euridice* (1762), a retelling of the myth that had so inspired the early Baroque opera composers, and *Alceste* (1767), which took up a subject already tackled by Lully. Both of these operas sound quite unlike the usual Italian operatic fare of the period. The vocal lines are much simpler, the forms are less static, and the orchestration is more interesting. The classicizing process is clearly at work here.

Gluck provided an explicit outline of his aims in the dedication essay he wrote for *Alceste* in 1769. He said first that he was committed to keeping musical considerations in second place to dramatic ones:

YOUR ROYAL HIGHNESS! When I set out to create the music of *Alceste*, I proposed to remove from it completely all those abuses, introduced either by the mistaken vanity of singers or by the excessive complaisance of composers, that have for a long time disfigured Italian opera and turned the most splendid and most beautiful of all spectacles into the most ridiculous and offensive. I thought to restrict music to its true function of serving poetry through expression and through the situations of the story, without interrupting the action or smothering it under useless, superfluous ornaments, . . .

He took back control of the vocal parts from the singers who had indulged themselves in self-aggrandizing virtuosity in the old da capo aria form:

> I did not want, therefore, to stop an actor in the greatest heat of the dialogue to wait for an annoying *ritornello,* nor to hold him up in the middle of a word on a favorable vowel in order to display in a long *passaggio* the agility of his beautiful voice, nor to wait for the orchestra to give him time to regain his breath for a cadenza. I did not believe it my duty to rush rapidly through the second part of an aria, which might be the most impassioned and important part, so as to have space to repeat literally four times the words of the first part, and to finish the aria where perhaps its sense does not end, so as to make it easy for the singer to demonstrate that he can capriciously vary a passage in so many fashions; in summary, I have tried to eliminate all those abuses against which for a long time good sense and reason have clamored vainly.

Echoing the neoclassic ideals of the archaeologist Winckelmann, whom he probably met in Italy, Gluck wrote,

> I believed, then, that my greatest effort ought to be concentrated on seeking a beautiful simplicity; and I have avoided making display of difficulty at the expense of clarity; . . .

And he did not neglect to credit his collaborator Calzabigi:

> By good fortune, the libretto—in which the famous author, conceiving a new level of drama, had substituted for florid descriptions, superfluous paragons, and sententious, cold moralizing the language of the heart, strong passions, interesting situations, and an ever-changing spectacle—suited itself marvelously to my intention. Success has justified my maxims, and universal approval in such an enlightened city has clearly demonstrated that simplicity, truth, and naturalness are the great principles of the beautiful in all works of art.

"Simplicity, truth, and naturalness" were the watchwords of the neoclassic movement, and especially of the theories of the French *philosophes.* It should not be surprising, therefore, that Gluck's works had even greater success on the Parisian opera stage of the second half of the century than in Vienna, where tastes still tended to the decorative galant style. Indeed the increased importance of chorus and orchestra in Gluck's operas had its basis in the French tradition. In the 1770s Gluck arranged, translated, and revised versions of both *Orfeo ed Euridice* (1774) and *Alceste* (1776) for the French audiences, and he also composed several major libretti in French, traveling to Paris to supervise the productions.

Following the challenge of the Italian style during the *Guerre des bouffons* in the 1750s, the French were eager to adopt a new style that would both satisfy their national proclivities and offer an aesthetic program that would counter the popularity of the Italian manner. Gluck's works and his theories provided exactly what the French wanted, and the operatic battles were joined once more. Piccinni was adopted as the paragon of the Italian style, and the *Guerre des Gluckistes et des Piccinnistes* was on. Piccinni got the worst of it. This is not surprising, since the Gluckistes had a more clearly reasoned platform and therefore at least a stronger debating position when the struggle took place in the journals rather than in the theater. In addition, of course, Gluck's party could appeal to French nationalism—an odd appeal, to be sure, backed up by the work of a Bohemian composer trained in Italy, but no more surprising than Handel's earlier success with Italian opera in England.

While Gluck's operas and theories embodied fine aesthetics, they had few immediate imitators. The stripped-down simplicity of the most classicizing passages did not meet the need for at least some degree of showiness and brilliance in the operatic genre. Gluck's austere style appealed to the intellect, and though it was interesting it was not sufficiently entertaining to support a broadly based new style. However, his theories about the proper relation between the libretto and the music were long-lasting and, as we shall discover, were taken up later in the history of operatic aesthetics. Mozart, who was in Paris during the controversy between the Gluckistes and Piccinnistes, stayed clear of the fighting. We shall discover his particular point of view on the aesthetic position of music and libretto in the opera in the next chapter.

Instrumental Genres and the Sonata Plan

Music in the Classic period depended on a considerable degree of convention in structure and style. This reliance on convention, looked down on by the romantics of the nineteenth century, offered considerable advantages that we should not neglect to observe. For one thing, it allowed the production of large quantities of music that, even when it did not reflect genius, met a high standard of craftsmanship and ensured audience appeal. More importantly it fostered a cosmopolitan style that permitted composers a wide audience to whom any work within the musical *lingua franca* would be accessible.

One of the areas in which convention prevailed during the Classic period was the formulation of a fairly standardized overall outline for various types of instrumental music. We may refer to this outline as the *sonata plan*. It applied to solo, chamber, or orchestral works by a variety of titles, with certain characteristic variants. In broad outline it consisted of several self-contained, contrasting movements, unified around a single tonality. The following discussion describes and places in context the most important instrumental genres of the period.

The Symphony

The symphony assumed predominance in the instrumental repertoire, replacing the concerto and orchestral suite that had held this position in the Baroque era. It constitutes a sonata-plan work for orchestra. The orchestral ensemble for the Classic period was not fixed but varied considerably. Its core was the four-part string group—two violin sections, violas, and cellos and basses playing from the same line—totalling from about sixteen to as many as forty players for the largest and most important standing orchestras. The woodwinds included one or two flutes, a pair of oboes, and a pair of bassoons; two clarinets might appear, usually as alternatives to the oboes. A pair of horns was common; at Mannheim there were two pairs. Two trumpets and a pair of timpani might be incorporated in particularly brilliant works. The role of the winds gradually developed during the early Classic era from mostly supplying sustained harmonies and occasionally doubling the violins' melodic line to playing fully independent parts. The orchestra was commonly led from the keyboard. The original sources often provide a continuo part for harpsichord or piano, though this was usually no longer necessary to complete the harmony and is often omitted in modern performances of this repertoire. As a violinist, Johann Stamitz led the Mannheim orchestra from the concertmaster's position, but his works also include figured bass parts.

The sonata plan may be understood best if we begin by examining it as it was expressed in the symphony. After 1750 the symphony normally has four movements. The first movement is generally longest and somewhat serious; it adopts a fast tempo, though it may be prefaced by a slow introduction after the manner of the Baroque French overture. The second movement is slow and may either be in the sentimental vein of the empfindsamer Stil or cantabile, like a graceful aria. It is very likely to be in the subdominant or, in minor-key works, the submediant, representing a relative relaxation in intensity in comparison to the other movements. Third comes a minuet movement, derived from the Baroque orchestral suite and actually consisting of two binary-form minuets (the second called *trio*), the first returning after the second and played without its repetitions. The finale is fast and light to provide a brilliant, optimistic conclusion.

The String Quartet

Similar to the symphony in design is the *string quartet,* which replaced the Baroque trio sonata as the chamber music genre par excellence for the Classic period. Early quartets often employ two violin parts and place the viola line in octaves with the cello, which suggests that the trio texture with basso continuo gave way only in stages, first by the substitution for the keyboard part of mere doubling of the bass. Haydn's early quartets, written in the 1760s, provide examples of this texture. It is also possible that the early quartet allowed the option of using multiple players on each line *ad libitum,* which creates a small string orchestra, rather than only one player on each part.

The sonata plan for the quartet is usually identical to that of the symphony. In some instances, two minuet movements are included, one preceding and the other following the slow movement.

Because the sound of the string quartet is rather spare and transparent, it depends more on structure and texture for its appeal than do other genres. During the early Classic period composers could employ two textural possibilities besides the older, triolike scoring. They could give the first violin the lead and let it carry almost all the melodic interest while the other three parts together functioned as its accompaniment. This gave the music a very transparent texture and placed minimal demands on the amateur performers for whom some of this literature was intended. It also gave virtuoso violinists opportunities to shine even in intimate settings; Haydn's quartets op. 9 (ca. 1769) and op. 17 (completed 1771), for example, have quite technically advanced first violin parts that would have been played by the Esterhaza violinist Luigi Tomasini (1741–1808). Composers also explored the possibilities of more rigorous four-part counterpoint, creating fugal movements in a post-Baroque style. Haydn worked with this approach in the finales of three of the six quartets of op. 20 (1772).

The Keyboard Sonata

After 1750 the fortepiano became more fully developed and replaced the harpsichord as the instrument of choice. Its ability to create dynamic effects helped make it popular. The piano sonata offered the composer a market for publication, since the drawing rooms of the middle class demanded a steady supply of such music. It also appealed to composers because dynamic effects could be made to reinforce musical structure. The keyboard solo sonata adopted the sonata plan, usually in only three movements, omitting the minuet.

The sonata for keyboard with violin also had a vogue in this period. Significantly, such pieces did not derive from the Baroque solo sonata with basso continuo, in which the violin had held the dominant musical interest. They were created by adding a violin part to an essentially self-sufficient keyboard sonata. The violin's roles in this repertoire were generally to double the right-hand melodic line of the piano part, to add fullness to the harmony in an accompanimental function, and occasionally to lend a countermelodic interest. This type of scoring created a double market for the music, for the pieces could be played either with or without the violin. The piano trio, for piano, violin, and cello, developed in a similar manner. The cello parts in early examples usually do no more than reinforce the bass lines of the piano parts.

The Concerto

The Classic period inherited the Baroque concerto genre and adapted it to the new style. The concerto grosso declined in importance, but the use of multiple featured solo players was preserved in the *sinfonia concertante*. The sinfonia concertante is sometimes described as a symphony with passages for soloists but will be better understood as a genuine concerto with concertino groups. Many sinfonie concertante were composed and played in the late eighteenth century, but the genre as a whole did not fare well through the nineteenth century's emphasis on the star soloist, and few are played in the modern standard orchestral repertoire.

More important were solo concertos, which were written for most of the available instruments, for various occasions, and for particular players, but of which those for violin or piano stand out. The masterpieces of the genre are the piano concertos of Mozart, who used these works to present himself as both composer and performer.

The concerto and sinfonia concertante both adopt the three-movement version of the sonata plan. Since their predecessor was the Baroque concerto, unlike the symphony they did not absorb a significant influence from the suite, and they consequently do not commonly include a minuet.

The Divertimento

A very important and common genre in the eighteenth century was the *divertimento*, which was composed for less formal entertainment situations in noble households rather than for concert presentations. The title *Divertimento* was given to specific pieces, but the term may also be used to cover a variety of subtypes with various titles. Among these are the French *Serenade* or Italian *Serenata* and the German equivalent *Nachtmusik*, all suggesting a piece to be played in the evening. One also encounters the title *Cassation*, which is of uncertain derivation; it might indicate a piece to be played out of doors, from the German *Gasse*, meaning "street." The ensembles called for in divertimenti vary considerably, from string quartets to wind ensembles or full orchestras, which reflects that they were generally written for specific occasions and the players who happened to be at hand.

The divertimento was more closely related to the suite than to the other instrumental genres mentioned here. It is likely to have more than four movements, sometimes many more. Moreover, these movements are likely to incorporate dances, not only minuets but also gavottes, bourrées, and the like.

The Sonata Form and Its Variants

One of the finest creations in the history of musical structure is the conventional form developed in the Classic period for large movements within sonata-plan works. This form, sometimes known as *sonata form* and sometimes as *sonata-allegro form,* deserves special consideration, partly because of its effective and flexible conception and partly because it is popularly so misunderstood. It was used almost universally for opening movements in the symphony, quartet, and sonata; with certain common adaptations it was employed in slow movements and finales; and in a special form it was also used in the concerto and sinfonia concertante.

Harmonic Plan

The sonata form is defined first of all by its harmonic plan, which is an expansion of the well-established rounded binary form. It therefore has two main parts, the first establishing a principal key and modulating to a contrasting key (dominant or relative major), and the second returning to the tonic. Both the arrival of the new key and the return to the tonic are strongly confirmed by a considerable period of activity and a firm cadence in those tonal areas. The two parts of the structure are therefore divided into two sections each: Part 1 contains the principal key area with the departure from it, followed by the secondary key area; part 2 begins with the modulatory passage and concludes with the passage from the return of the principal key to the end.

Thematic Plan

The tonal plan of the sonata form organizes a series of thematic events, which in turn articulate the crucial moments in the harmonic outline. As in the usual rounded binary form, the establishment of the tonic at the beginning and its return in the second part are related and reinforced by the use of the same thematic material (P) at both points. In addition, the arrival of the secondary key area is also correlated with a clear thematic statement; this may be a contrasting theme (S) or, less commonly but not by any means rarely, the same theme as that used to set up the principal key (P used as S, in which case the form is sometimes regarded as a "monothematic sonata form"). Other important sections may also be identified with particular melodic material, transitions (T, or t if the material cannot appropriately be thought of as thematic), and closings (K or k). In general the passage following the return to the tonic in part 2 incorporates all the main thematic ideas of part 1, so that everything is ultimately resolved into the tonic key. Thematic activity in the often very brief third section remains quite unpredictable and irregular; eighteenth-century musicians commonly called this section "fantasy."

Outline of Sonata Form

Sonata form, in its most characteristic manifestation, can be outlined as follows:

Part 1			Part 2		
Section 1	Section 2		Section 3	Section 4	
P (T, t)	S (K, k)		"fantasy"	P (T) S (K)	
I	V————V		modulatory	I————I	

A monothematic sonata form would be outlined in the following manner (note that section 4 does not require two full statements of the P material, since one statement provides the necessary resolution):

Part 1			Part 2		
Section 1	Section 2		Section 3	Section 4	
P	P		"fantasy"	P	
I	V————V		modulatory	I————I	

For movements in minor keys where, as is common, the S material appears in the relative major key rather than the minor dominant, there are two possibilities for the return of the tonic, depending on the character of the S material. If the material can effectively be transformed into minor, section 4 can be entirely in the tonic minor. Otherwise section 4 can shift to the parallel major when S arrives:

Part 1			Part 2		
Section 1	Section 2		Section 3	Section 4	
P (T, t)	S (K, k)		"fantasy"	P (T) S (K)	
i	III————III		modulatory	i————i	
				or i——I—I	

Application of the Form

It must be stressed that the sonata form is extremely flexible, not a mold into which composers poured thematic ideas. The form of any movement is precisely the form of that particular movement, and its classification as an example of sonata form means only that it shares the characteristic tonal design of Classic form, organizing and articulated by thematic events.

The composers of the late eighteenth century recognized that they were using this large-scale binary structure consistently by convention for major instrumental movements. They did not use the term *sonata form*; it was an invention of nineteenth-century theorists looking back at the repertoire of Classic works and attempting to describe them in an orderly fashion. Also anachronistic are three familiar terms used to identify units within the form.

Part 1 of the sonata form was later called *exposition;* sections 3 and 4 were dubbed *development* and *recapitulation,* respectively. The odd positioning of these terms in relation to the sonata scheme as we have observed it reveals the source of the confusion: The later theorists regarded the form as if it were based on thematic rather than tonal organization, and the design consequently appeared to be ternary instead of binary. Of course, from this point of view actual pieces are likely to seem harmonically unimaginative and, frequently, thematically exceptional; but understood as the musicians who wrote and played them did, the harmonic plan appears in its proper place as a well-conceived convention to be employed in varied ways limited only by the imagination of the composer.

Adaptations of the Form

As was noted earlier, one common adaptation of the sonata form for first movements was to preface the main form with an introduction. This introduction employed the slow tempo and stately rhythm of the Baroque French overture, and it often featured chordal texture and dotted rhythms. The slow introduction generally appears only in symphonies and larger divertimenti; it did not particularly suit the nature of the quartet, sonata, or concerto.

In slow movements the third section might be omitted, the cadence in the dominant at the end of part 1 serving as a dominant preparation for the immediate return of the tonic. The result can be diagrammed as follows:

Part 1		Part 2	
Section 1	Section 2	Section "4"	
P (T, t)	S (K, k)	P (T) S (K)	
I	V————V	I————I	

For a lighter movement, such as a finale, the sonata idea often combines with the rondo principle. In the Classic rondo the theme presented at the beginning in association with the tonic key (the rondo theme) returns several times in the tonic, its appearances separated by contrasting episodes in contrasting keys. In the so-called sonata-rondo the P material returns like a rondo theme, and the tonic recurs with it, but the overall tonal plan incorporates some of the tonic-dominant opposition of the sonata form:

P (T, t)	S	P(!)	"fantasy"	P (T, t)	S	P
I	V	I(!)	other key(s)	I	I	I
			or modulatory			

The Classic concerto produced a special treatment of the sonata form that applied the ritornello principle developed in the Baroque concerto to the general plan of the sonata. The sonata form was articulated by the addition of tutti ritornellos to establish the key at the beginning and to provide satisfactory closings at the ends of both parts 1 and 2. For the bulk of the movement, the soloist took the lead and the orchestra provided support. The two parts were not repeated.

Rit.	Part 1		Rit.	Part 2		Rit.
	Section 1	Section 2		Section 3	Section 4	
Tutti	Solo		T	S		T
	P (T, t)	S	K	"fantasy"	P (T, t) S	K
I—I	I	V	V—V	modulatory	I	I—I

In this way the tonal structure of the sonata form is articulated not only by the thematic events but also by the changes in scoring. It should be easy to see how the young Mozart arranged keyboard sonatas of older composers, such as J.C. Bach, as concertos. At its simplest, this merely required the composition of the ritornellos and the scoring of orchestral support for the existing keyboard sonata.

As in the Baroque period, the eighteenth-century soloist was actually a member of the tutti, playing with the orchestra in the ritornellos. A violinist would naturally join the first violins as section leader when not taking a solo role, and a keyboard player would lead the tutti as continuo player. Opportunities for soloistic virtuosity in the concerto sonata form came in the playing of embellished versions of material presented in simpler fashion by the orchestra, but even more in the transitional passages and in section 3, where thematic presentation is less important and the unstable harmonic situation is explored in idiomatic passagework. Within the final ritornello it also became common to let the orchestra pause after a tonic $^6_4$ chord and allow the solo player to insert an improvised *cadenza* to show off his or her technique and creative imagination. After the cadenza, which conventionally ended on a dominant chord and a trill, the orchestra returned for a brief closing passage reiterating the tonic.

Expression and Function

Like form, expression was governed by a certain degree of convention in the Classic period. The second half of the eighteenth century inherited from the Baroque a repertoire of common and commonly understood rhetorical styles. We may identify a few of the more obvious among these as examples. The "military" style naturally used strong rhythms, sometimes in aggressive dotted patterns and usually in duple meters, simple diatonic harmony, and melodies that outlined triads in the style of trumpets and drums, even when those instruments did not actually appear. By contrast, the "singing" style employed flexible rhythm and a cantabile line set in a melody-and-accompaniment texture. The various dance types, each with its characteristic rhythmic patterns and phrasings, included most prominently the elegant, upper-class minuet (moderate triple meter), the lower-class waltz (fast triple meter), the gavotte (moderate duple time, with the phrases beginning and ending on the half measure), the bourrée (like a gavotte, but at a fast tempo), and the lively, bourgeois contredanse (in a fast duple or compound meter). The "brilliant" style featured rapid, virtuosic passagework. An especially impassioned style was the manner of the empfindsamer Stil (sometimes associated with the *Sturm und Drang* literary movement), which exploited such devices as the minor mode, chromatic harmony and melody, and recitativelike phrasing.

The use of the minor is rare enough to be noteworthy when it appears in the symphonies of Haydn and Mozart in the 1770s. Haydn wrote a handful of symphonies in minor keys during that period, and they have sometimes been regarded as evidence of a *Sturm und Drang* style in his output. He may have been responding to the influence of the works of C.P.E. Bach. Some of these symphonies have significant nicknames: No. 30 in D minor, (*Lamentatione*); No. 44 in E minor (*Trauersinfonie* or Mourning symphony); No. 49 in F minor (*La passione*). Mozart wrote only two symphonies in the minor mode (both in G minor). The earlier one (the "Little" G minor, K. 125) is astonishingly dark and intense, showing that the young composer commanded a depth of emotion far greater than is suggested by most of his works of these years, which tend to be in the galant manner.

The conventional manners had many kinds of usefulness. In the context of vocal music, particularly in opera, they could denote character or effect as they had in the Baroque period. The military style suggested the heroic or aggressive; the aria style, the amorous or tender; the empfindsamer Stil, emotional distress. The different dance types could indicate general spirit or specific social situations. In songs the dance styles maintained their affective values throughout the Classic period. The conventional styles can even be found in sacred music, where they are adapted, for instance, to the moods of the different movements of a Mass.

The standard expressive types also lent themselves to interpreting the structure of the sonata plan and sonata form. Contrasting material was needed to set off movements from one another or to indicate the contrasting functions of the different passages within a form. Military style offered a fine opportunity to establish tonality and make a strong initial impression. The aria type was appropriate for secondary themes and appears often as the predominant style in andante second movements; Mozart preferred this type for slow movements of sonata plan works. The empfindsamer Stil typically turns up in slow introductions and in slow movements with adagio or lento tempo indications, both of which are more characteristic of Haydn's works than of Mozart's. The brilliant style frequently serves as transitional and cadencing material, where rapid modulation or the limited harmonic vocabulary of alternating dominant and tonic chords make longer-phrased melody inappropriate.

It must be stressed that this flexibility to apply various affective styles freely within a single movement was one of the new elements of the Classic style. In practice, therefore, the construction of the sonata form may be viewed as necessarily predicated on the aesthetic premise of flexible expression. Similarly the freedom of the music to flow from one expressive state to another had to be grounded in a governing sense of form that related and shaped the listener's experience of the musical content. We cannot overlook the fact that in the Classic style, as in all music, aesthetic and technique, form and content are inseparably intertwined.

Questions for Reflection

❖ How are the ideals of the Enlightenment and of neoclassicism in artistic thought reflected in the musical style of the third quarter of the eighteenth century?

❖ Some music historians have argued for consideration of the eighteenth century as a unit, not divided in the middle between Baroque and Classic periods. What are the pros and cons of such a view?

❖ How did Haydn's and Mozart's careers differ, and what were the true causes of these differences?

❖ To what social causes can the successive operatic battles in eighteenth-century France (Rameau versus Lully, the Guerre des bouffons, and the Guerre des Gluckistes et des Piccinnistes) be linked?

❖ What elements of the Classic symphony can be traced to roots in Baroque instrumental or vocal music?

❖ Given the importance of convention in Classic musical design, what value should be placed on originality in music of the period, and how did the composer make each work individual?

Suggestions for Further Reading

The subject of the Classic style as a concept and a survey of the music are found in Friedrich Blume, *Classic and Romantic Music,* trans. M.D. Herter Norton (New York: Norton, 1970). Leonard Ratner, *Classic Music: Expression, Form, and Style* (New York: Schirmer, 1980) is based on contemporary sources.

On the sonata and sonata forms, see William S. Newman, *The Sonata in the Classic Era* (Chapel Hill: University of North Carolina Press, 1983), and Charles Rosen, *Sonata Forms* (New York: Norton, 1980).

On Gluck, see Martin Cooper, *Gluck* (London: Oxford University Press, 1935); Alfred Einstein, *Gluck* (New York: Dutton, 1954); Ernest Newman, *Gluck and the Opera* (London: Gollancz, 1967). The dedicatory preface to *Alceste* is included in Oliver Strunk, *Source Readings in Music History* (New York: Norton, 1950).

Among the biographies of Haydn, Karl Geiringer, *Haydn: A Creative Life in Music,* 3d ed. (Berkeley: University of California Press, 1982), and the monumental five-volume compilation by H.C. Robbins Landon, *Haydn: Chronicle and Works* (London: Thames and Hudson, 1976–1980), are especially recommended.

Alfred Einstein, *Mozart, His Character, His Work,* trans. Arthur Mendel and Nathan Broder (New York: Norton, 1962) is somewhat outdated; for more recent research, see Stanley Sadie, *The New Grove Mozart* (New York: Norton, 1983). Contemporary sources are compiled in Otto Erich Deutsch, *Mozart: A Documentary Biography,* 2d ed., trans. Eric Blom et al. (Stanford: Stanford University Press, 1965).

Notes

1. Alexander Pope, *Poetical Works,* ed. Herbert Davis (London: Oxford University Press, 1966), 66–67.

2. Karl Geiringer, *Haydn: A Creative Life in Music.* 3d ed. (Berkeley: University of California Press, 1983), 58–59.

3. Ibid.

18 THE HIGH CLASSIC PERIOD

The Position of Haydn and Mozart

After 1780 the potential of the Classic style was realized in the music of Haydn and Mozart. This is not to say that there were not many other fine composers. Indeed the general standard of musical craftsmanship reached a remarkably high level as a result of the inherent strength of the conventions of the period, the support of a still-powerful aristocracy, and the rise of commercial enterprise in music. What Haydn and Mozart accomplished, however, was the application of imaginative genius to sonata-plan works and the opera in ways that produced not only the most finely polished pieces of the age but also consistently masterful structural integration and depth of expression.

Haydn had achieved an international reputation by the end of the 1770s despite the fact that Prince Nicholas kept him on a short leash. Until Nicholas died in 1790, he did not offer his Kapellmeister occasions to go farther from Esterhaza than Vienna.

After 1781 Mozart settled in Vienna, where he supported himself by teaching, giving academies (subscription concerts), and writing compositions under commission or for publication. He was married in 1782 and began to raise a family, but the general insecurity of his income and his own poor management of money sometimes produced a hand-to-mouth existence. When Gluck died in 1787, Mozart received his appointment as chamber composer to the Emperor Joseph II, but at a much lower salary. In 1789 he took a tour northward into Germany, visiting Leipzig, Dresden, and Berlin, again contemplating possibilities for a good court position, but nothing came of the trip. Two years later,

257

when he was not yet thirty-seven years old, his health failed, and he died and was given a pauper's burial in a churchyard near Vienna.

Prince Anton Esterhazy, who succeeded his father Prince Nicholas in 1790, dismissed most of the court ensemble in order to save money. Haydn retained his title and salary as Kapellmeister, but he was free to move to Vienna and on the whole to pursue his career as he pleased. The most important events of the 1790s were two visits to London, arranged for him by the impresario Johann Peter Salomon (1745–1815) in 1791–1792 and 1794–1795. Haydn's last two sets of symphonies, six in each group, were written expressly for the concerts of his music in London. The English public was as taken with Haydn as it had been with Handel earlier in the century, and he was awarded an honorary Doctor of Music degree at Oxford. Haydn spent his last years in Vienna, composing a number of string quartets, several Masses, and his two great oratorios, *Die Schöpfung* (The creation, 1796–1798) and *Die Jahreszeiten* (The seasons, 1799–1801). As he passed seventy years of age, his health deteriorated, and though he was greatly honored by the musical world, he necessarily retired more and more from the public. He died in 1809.

Haydn's late oratorios were composed partly under the influence of an important patron of music in Vienna, Baron Gottfried van Swieten (1733–1803), who helped with the preparation of their librettos. Baron van Swieten had visited England and served as Austrian ambassador to Berlin, so he was more familiar with the music of Handel and J.S. Bach than most Austrians of the day. In the 1780s he held musical gatherings in his rooms and sponsored oratorio performances. Through him Mozart came to know the music of Bach, which affected Mozart's own mature style.

That Mozart and Haydn themselves recognized their unique position is clear from statements each made. Naturally each was thoroughly familiar with the other's works. Though Haydn continued to work at Esterhaza through the decade of the 1780s, he and Mozart met in Vienna, and they became good friends. Leopold Mozart proudly reported that on one occasion Haydn said to him, "Your son is the greatest composer known to me either in person or by reputation. He has taste and, what is more, the most profound knowledge of composition." Haydn also wrote in a letter of 1787,

> . . . if I could impress in the mind of every friend of music, but especially great persons, the inimitable works of Mozart *as deeply* and with *such musical understanding,* with *as great feeling* as I grasp them and feel them— then the nations would compete to possess such a treasure within their city walls. . . . It makes me angry that this *unique* Mozart is not yet engaged at some imperial or royal court! Forgive me if I get out of control, but I admire the man too much.

For his part, Mozart expressed his homage to Haydn in the dedication of a set of string quartets, in which he described the pieces as his children, and Haydn, whom he called his dearest friend, as their godfather.

In the present chapter we shall examine the accomplishments of the two great high Classic composers according to the various genres in which each special challenge was discovered and met.

Chamber Music

Haydn took an immensely important step in a set of string quartets published in 1781 as op. 33, sometimes called *Scherzi* quartets because Haydn headed their minuet movements "Scherzo" (joke), and sometimes known as *Russian* because they were dedicated to a Russian nobleman. In his dedicatory remarks, Haydn stressed that he had written the quartets in "an entirely new and special style." The new feature of the quartets is the unprecedented extent to which the four parts interact in handling the musical material. In contradistinction to the melody-oriented or fugal textures that had prevailed in the past, there was a new approach in which any part might come to the fore at any moment and then smoothly recede into an accompanimental role as it gave way to another member of the quartet. This does not exactly constitute counterpoint; it is more like a free-wheeling dialogue among the players. The great German poet Johann Wolfgang von Goethe (1749–1832) is supposed to have said on hearing Haydn's quartets that they resembled a conversation among four equally intelligent speakers.

This conversational texture depended on the creation of thematic material made up of clearly recognizable but brief motives rather than long, lyrical melodies. The motives must be able to maintain some aspect of their character despite adjustment to varying harmonic contexts; thus, they tend to have a sharp rhythmic identity and simple melodic profile. The motivic elements may fill extended thematic passages by reiteration of a single motive or by linking of various motives into melody. Their use is more striking, however, in the usually nonthematic parts of the sonata form, such as transitions, cadential segments, and "fantasy" sections. The constant or frequent appearance of motives that are identified with the stable presentation of tonal areas and therefore are thematic lends a high degree of integration to each movement. It is appropriate to refer to the conversational treatment of material as *development*. The use of that term for the third section of the sonata form when motivic working-out takes place there is therefore justified. However, it must not be forgotten that such motivic work can occur in any part of a form, so we must understand development also as a process or technique. Development may not apply to the third section of every sonata-form movement, and it may not be limited to that section.

Haydn's many string quartets after op. 33 continued to explore the possibilities of the motivic-conversational style. Likewise Mozart's six "Haydn" quartets reflect his recognition of Haydn's achievement. Mozart exploited the freedom of the different instrumental lines by stressing the lowest part in the three late string quartets dedicated to the cellist King Frederick William II of Prussia. Two late string quintets and the quintet for clarinet and strings faced Mozart with further challenges—stemming from their denser scoring and, in the case of the clarinet quintet, from timbral contrast—which he met brilliantly.

Symphony

As we would expect, conversational texture and motivic treatment greatly affected the symphony in the 1780s. As the use of the winds increased, the possibilities for exchange of motives among the instruments multiplied. In the hands of Haydn and Mozart the orchestra became less like a string body with wind reinforcement or concertato wind solos and more like a single large and subtle instrument. The integration of the symphonic score was worked out in the seven symphonies of Mozart's Vienna years and in the twenty-three that Haydn composed between 1786 and 1795, including five composed for Paris (nos. 82–87) and twelve for his London visits (nos. 93–104). Mozart's last three symphonies (all composed in the summer of 1788) and Haydn's London symphonies set a standard of classic perfection. Without abandoning the limits of the period's conventions, each establishes and solves its own compositional problems and is a unique masterpiece.

These symphonies addressed an audience different from that for which earlier symphonies had been intended. They suited performance for a large body of listeners in a concert hall rather than a private aristocratic audience. The music appealed to the concert-going audience by its animated rhythm, memorable thematic ideas, and interesting dynamic and orchestral effects. The orchestras in Paris and London were much larger than the ensemble for which Haydn had composed at Esterhaza. The London string group included sixteen violins; four each of violas, cellos, and basses; a full complement of woodwinds in pairs; two horns, two trumpets, and timpani; as well as keyboard. Paris offered twenty-two violins; six violas; nine cellos; six basses; and two each of flutes, oboes, clarinets, bassoons, horns, trumpets, and timpani. It must be noted that among the works of Haydn and Mozart few demand the entire wind complement. Except for a few symphonies, the scoring is likely to use only one flute; oboes or clarinets, but not both; and not necessarily trumpets and timpani.

Concerto

In the genre of the concerto, Mozart clearly takes precedence over Haydn. Haydn was not a virtuoso performer himself as Mozart was. In the Vienna years Mozart wrote a number of concertos to present himself to the public. In these works he achieved complete integration of thematic material and virtuoso work within the form, as well as classic balance between soloist and orchestra.

In one set of these Viennese concertos, written at the beginning of his period of independence, Mozart attempted not primarily to feature his own technique but to meet the needs of the popular market. He described how he hoped that they would suit different types of listeners and players, both connoisseurs and amateurs:

> The concertos are just in the middle between too easy and too difficult. They are very brilliant, pleasing to the ears, but naturally without falling into inanity. Here and there, too, only connoisseurs can get satisfaction [from them]; however, [they are composed] so that the nonconnoisseurs must be pleased with them, without knowing why.

He also contrived the wind parts so that, while they added to the total effect, they could be omitted, permitting performances not only when a full orchestra was available but also in chamber-music style with only a string quartet.

The later concertos, primarily written for performance by the composer himself at his academies, are more sophisticated. They take advantage of the full symphonic potential of the orchestra, working with the concertato opposition of instrumental colors so that there is considerable timbre contrast within the orchestra and a great deal of interaction between solo and tutti in the large structural solo sections. These works are not merely like keyboard sonatas with inserted ritornellos and gratuitous accompaniment. The integration that results yields a scoring in which there is perfect equilibrium between the need for virtuoso display of the solo part and a sense of ensemble in which every line has its important role to play.

In terms of structure, Mozart also achieves integration of the material of the ritornello sections with the sonata form outline pursued in the structural solo parts. The following diagram suggests how this might be accomplished in an abstract case:

Part 1				Part 2		
Section 1		Section 2		Section 3	Section 4	
Rit.	Solo		Rit.	Solo		Rit.
P1 P2 K	P1 (t)	P2 (as S1) S2	K	"fantasy"	P1 (t) P2 S2	K
I———I	I	V	V—V	modulatory	I	I—I

The opening ritornello may present several of the thematic ideas to be used in the solo, particularly P and K. Thus the opening ritornello proper begins, rather than precedes, part 1, section 1 of the form. When the solo enters with P1, it produces a sort of recommencement and reinterpretation of section 1. As the diagram indicates, a second theme (P2), associated in the opening ritornello with the tonic key, may signal the arrival of the contrasting key (P2 serving as S1). Another new theme in the contrasting key area (S2) may also be introduced in the solo part. A common closing theme may be shared by all three ritornellos, so that it appears not only at the end of the first ritornello but also at the ends of the two main structural parts of the sonata form. In large-scale first movements a brief orchestral tutti, resembling the first measures of the opening ritornello, may start the fourth section, so that the movement may be described as having a four-ritornello rather than a three-ritornello structure.

A later description of this form (unfortunately often repeated) refers to the opening ritornello in the Classic concerto sonata form as an "exposition," that is a part 1. This is misleading, because the ritornello does not establish the two contrasting key areas, the crucial determinant of any genuine Classic exposition. The misconception arises from the erroneous analysis of the form as fundamentally based in thematic, rather than tonal organization.

Mozart's Mature Operas

The most important popular genre in the eighteenth century was the opera. To succeed in the opera theater offered a composer the best chance to establish a major reputation. Court Kapellmeisters such as Haydn, of course, did not necessarily have to compose for the public opera theaters. Haydn's works for the Esterhaza palace opera (Fig. 18.1) were quite competent though not among his masterpieces, but he had exceptional success in gaining fame through other works. Of the two Classic masters, Mozart holds the crown in the operatic realm. As we have noted, Mozart's experience in opera composition was already substantial by 1780; before his fifteenth birthday he had composed in all the practicable theatrical genres—opera seria, opera buffa, and Singspiel—and he worked in these three types in the course of the 1770s. By his midtwenties, he had completely mastered the opera, and in the following years he produced one great work after another.

Opera Seria

Just before his summary dismissal from Archbishop Colloredo's service, Mozart had composed his finest work of the serious Italian type for production in Munich. This opera, *Idomeneo,* stands with those of Gluck as a masterpiece of the Classic opera seria. Its vocal writing is fully Classic, but it seems less self-consciously Apollonian than that of Gluck. In ensemble work Mozart surpassed Gluck, as he did all of his contemporaries, by setting contrasting characters and sentiments simultaneously in a fully integrated counterpoint. In *Idomeneo* Mozart also explored the possibilities of sonata form for structuring the music of opera.

Figure 18.1
Haydn is shown in this picture (by an unknown artist) conducting one of his own operas at the opera theater at Esterhaza. As was common for conductors of the time, he played the continuo part and directed the orchestra and singers from the keyboard. (*The Bettmann Archive*)

During his Vienna years Mozart did not have occasion to return to the opera seria except for *La clemenza di Tito*, composed quickly in 1791 for a coronation ceremony for the new emperor, Leopold II. This opera is based on a cut-down version of an old-fashioned libretto Metastasio had written in 1734. Its music is elegant and polished but noticeably restrained in style.

Singspiel

The history of Mozart's Viennese-period stage works partly reflects the musical inclinations of Emperor Joseph II. For a time Joseph was especially interested in cultivating a national German genre that would rival the Italian opera buffa. Mozart responded to this with the Singspiel *Die Entführung aus dem Serail* (The abduction from the harem) in 1782. The action unfolds in a Turkish pasha's palace, a popular setting with the Viennese, near as they were to the Middle East. This gave the opportunity for some "Turkish" music effects with the so-called Janissary music that was also a fad at the time. (The Janissaries were Turkish military units whose marches featured jangling percussion.)

In connection with *Die Entführung aus dem Serail* Mozart wrote to his father about the requirements of an opera libretto and said, "In an opera the poetry must be altogether the obedient daughter of the music." This absolutely contradicts Gluck's theories of fifteen years earlier, with which Mozart must have been familiar. It reflects his belief that the element of drama in opera derives from the music more than from the words. This thesis finds support in the opera through the controlled use of tonal relationships, musical styles, and dramatically opposed voice types. The pasha's fierce but comical servant, a bass, has violent rage music in remote keys; the music for the leading characters is taken from the opera seria, and the vocal styles expected from them include the passionately florid and the lyrically sentimental.

Collaboration with Da Ponte

In Vienna Mozart found a particularly effective librettist in the Italian court poet Lorenzo Da Ponte (1749–1838). The two men collaborated on three great comic works. The first of these, *Le nozze di Figaro* (The marriage of Figaro) dates from 1786. It is the greatest of all opere buffe. The story, originally by the French playwright Beaumarchais (1732–1799), involves a Spanish count who intends to take advantage of an ancient right by which the master may enjoy the first night with any new bride among his servants. He attempts to assert his authority with Susanna, fiancée of his valet Figaro, but in the opera buffa tradition, he is ultimately outwitted by Figaro, Susanna, and the countess. At its root, however, the story is not the slapstick stuff of common opera buffa but social criticism of aristocratic injustice with revolutionary overtones; Beaumarchais's original play was banned by the French government's censors under Louis XVI. The action is considerably complicated by several farcical subplots, including legal roadblocks to Figaro's marriage by an old lady who wants him for herself but who turns out to be his mother, unjust accusations by the philandering count against his faithful wife, disguises, and mistaken identities. The opera is extremely long, so that the two standard acts must each be subdivided into two.

Using all the expressive language of the Classic style, in *Le nozze di Figaro* Mozart created subtle and convincing delineations of individual characters and eloquent musical realizations of mood and thought. But Mozart's dramaturgical genius extended beyond these things. For one thing, in this opera he achieved precision of dramatic timing. Actors and directors find (or should find) that much of their work is simplified and clarified if they listen alertly to the score and let the music guide their actions and reactions. The music paces the movement, leads the character's thought process, and supplies the subtext behind the actual speeches in the libretto.

Especially effective in Mozart's operas from *Le nozze di Figaro* on is the composer's use of the principles of sonata form. By laying out substantial segments of the action according to the tonal structure of a sonata movement, Mozart articulated subordinate units within the plot. Each dramatic unit then possesses its own point of departure (tonic), destabilization (transition) and area of tension (dominant), crisis (modulatory), and resolution (tonic). Tonal planning is also evident over the opera as a whole; for example, the second act of *Figaro* concludes in the key of E flat and the third ends in C, while the key of the opera as a whole is D major.

The crowning glory of *Le nozze di Figaro* is Mozart's ensemble writing. The ensemble numbers define and develop the contrasting states of mind of the characters, the degree of conflict between their opposing ideas, and the working out of their relationships. Mozart's ability to lay out progress in the action during the continuous music of an ensemble number is best demonstrated by the immense ensemble finale to the second act (the first half) of *Le nozze di Figaro*. Da Ponte wrote in his memoirs,

> This finale, which must be intimately connected with the rest of the opera, is a sort of short comedy or little drama in its own right and requires a new plot and special interest. It is mainly in this part that the genius of the conductor, the strength of the singers, the grandest effect of the drama should shine forth. Recitative is excluded from it; everything is sung. And there must be found there every type of singing: adagio, allegro, andante, *amabile, armonioso, strepitoso* [noisy, boisterous], *arcistrepitoso, strepitosissimo*. With the last of these, the aforementioned finale almost always ends; in musical jargon it is called the *chiusa* [close], or rather the *strenta* [or *stretta*, meaning "strained"]—I don't know whether this is because here the force of the drama is most intense, or because it generally gives not one strain but a hundred to the poor brain of the poet who must write the text. In this finale, according to theatrical dogma, all the singers must appear together in the scene, even if there are three hundred of them— one, two, three or six, ten, sixty at a time—to sing solos, duets, trios, sextets, sessantets. And if the plot of the drama does not permit it, the poet must find a way to make it permit it, despite good judgment, reason, and all the Aristotles in the world—and if he then finds it going badly, so much the worse for him!

Although Da Ponte was writing in a humorous vein, the description would apply well to *Le nozze di Figaro*, except that the drama does not go badly at all. Obviously Mozart expected the libretto to be the servant of the music; whatever method he and Da Ponte used in working together, the result turns out to be musically and dramatically compelling.

The second collaboration of Mozart and Da Ponte was *Don Giovanni*, first staged in Prague in 1787. Far from the usual buffa type of opera, this work could only be termed "dramma giocoso." It deals with the legendary character Don Juan, the women whom he seduces, and his ultimate downfall. Although much of the action is lively, and comic moments occur, the story is neither farce nor social satire. It deals with the significant problem of a morally bankrupt roué who fascinates us by the apparent fact that he lives life at a higher pitch than average people. The effect is one of very dark humor, emphasized by the music's minor key; the overall tonality is D minor.

The more intense and serious parts of the action evoke long spans of continuous music, while the clear articulation of alternating set musical numbers and recitative carries the comic events. The climax arrives when the memorial statue of the man whom Don Giovanni killed at the opening of the opera returns at the end to take him to hell in the key of D minor. Trombones and an offstage demonic chorus add to the infernal effect. Moral order and musical stability are barely restored by the appearance of the surviving characters to sing the epilogue in D major. With its departures from convention in both subject and style, *Don Giovanni* seems fundamentally unaccountable within the Classic spirit.

The last of the Mozart and Da Ponte operas, *Così fan tutte* (Thus do all women), came in 1790. It also has a rather unusual plot, dealing with a cynical old fellow who sets out to demonstrate that women are always unfaithful lovers and succeeds by creating an entirely artificial environment in which the characters are completely at his mercy. Mozart had the skill to portray the artificially limited personalities with perfect clarity. His practice in laying out conflicts in ensembles and tracing complex courses of action also served him well. The general effect of the opera, in both story and music, is to recall the figures of Swift and Voltaire, exposing our sentimental delusions about ourselves with cool ruthlessness.

Die Zauberflöte

Mozart's last dramatic work to reach the stage was a Singspiel, *Die Zauberflöte* (The magic flute), written just a few months before his death. It is a fairy-tale story, set in the Near East and incorporating much of the lore of the Freemasons, an order to which Mozart and Haydn, like many free thinkers of the period, belonged. It treats the themes of brotherly unity and self-knowledge. Much of the plot incorporates Masonic symbols: day versus night, man versus woman, the number 3, and so on.

The music of *Die Zauberflöte* bids a convincing farewell to the ornamental and bravura style of eighteenth-century opera. The florid coloratura style is given only to the evil Queen of the Night, who is defeated in the end. The musical realization of the forces of good depends more on the Lied and the hymn than on traditional operatic music. Masonic symbolism also seems to have inspired some particular details in the music, including the keys and the threefold reiteration of the tonic chord that launches the overture.

A New Model for Expression

As we have observed, music after the arrival of the Renaissance took its models for expression from literature. In the Renaissance the model was poetry; in the Baroque period it was rhetoric. For music after the middle of the eighteenth century it is necessary to identify a new model.

The literary archetype for music beginning in the Classic period is drama (perhaps including the novel, which resembles drama in the sense that is relevant here). It might be reasoned that drama requires dialogue, and the achievement of the motivic, conversational texture in the High Classic period certainly corresponds to this. Further, the introduction of various themes and styles in a single movement might be regarded as parallel to the introduction of different characters or settings in the drama.

The essential feature of drama, however, is that it achieves its meaning only as a result of the entire action. To illustrate this point, while a poet might attempt to describe sorrow, and an orator might seek by rhetorical means to make his listeners feel sorrow, it remains the prerogative of the dramatist to unfold the causes of the emotion, to pursue the shape of the emotional experience, and to carry the experience through to closure. This is also essential to the music of the Classic style.

We have already observed that Mozart could use the tonal structure of sonata form to create dramatic units in his operas. From the opposite point of view, all music that employs tonally based structure resembles drama. It includes an exposition that sets up conflicting forces, a crisis in which the situation becomes volatile, a climax and resolution, and the bringing of everything into a unified perspective in a dénouement. Every musical movement in the period of tonal design necessarily finds its own interpretation of this dramatic shape. The way in which that shape is worked out is as much a part of the music's meaning as the character of its themes, key, and scoring.

Another dramatic aspect of the music of this period comes from the sense in which we interpret as dramatic those moments when events come together in a meaningful way. This is, of course, an inherent aspect of the Classic musical form, in which tonal arrivals are given significance by the simultaneous arrivals of themes, while tonal instability is often highlighted by motivic fragmentation or brilliant passagework. Other elements of musical style are also brought to bear on the significant moment, such as changes in dynamics, texture, and scoring.

To understand later developments of the dramatic model in music, it is important to recognize that the Classic sense of dramatic pacing requires a considerable degree of stability. The contrast must be established by a firm delineation of the opposing poles in the first part of the dramatic form. Only after that is accomplished can the crisis take place. Once the resolution occurs, it is again important, in the Classic way of thinking, to assert the recovery of stability by a somewhat extended continuation in which every important idea is tied up.

The Classic Beethoven

To the names of Haydn and Mozart we must add that of Ludwig van Beethoven (1770–1827) before we leave our discussion of the High Classic period. Beethoven's career began just as Mozart's came to an end, and he, with Haydn, carried the Classic period through to the opening of the nineteenth century. Beethoven took on great significance for the future of music thereafter, but the music he composed during the 1790s still belongs to the Classic era.

Beethoven's Early Years in Bonn

Beethoven was the son of a musician in the electoral court of Bonn. His father recognized his talent and hoped to make him another Mozart, but as a parent he did not have the wherewithal of Leopold Mozart to educate his son and promote his career. Indeed Beethoven's father was an irresponsible drunkard, and he succeeded only in pressuring young Ludwig, not encouraging him. He also left the boy with a very poor general education.

As a youth, Beethoven studied with the court organist Christian Gottlob Neefe (1748–1798) in Bonn. Beethoven was a gifted keyboard player and substituted for Neefe in the court ensemble. Later he played for the Bonn court orchestra as a violist, gaining valuable orchestral experience. In 1787 he traveled to Vienna, where he played for Mozart and may have had a few lessons from him. Mozart apparently gave him a great deal of encouragement. By the time he was twenty, Beethoven had also begun to compose, producing a number of promising works.

Beethoven's First Decade in Vienna

In 1792 Beethoven decided that he must leave Bonn to pursue his career in Vienna. He had met Haydn when the older master passed through Bonn on his way to London in 1790 (or possibly on his return in 1792), and it was arranged that he would study with him in Vienna. This project was sponsored by the patronage of one Count Ferdinand von Waldstein, who had come to Bonn from Vienna and who expressed the hope that Beethoven would "receive Mozart's spirit from Haydn's hands."

In his first decade in Vienna, Beethoven had three objectives: to polish his musical skills, to cultivate patronage that would support his career, and to present himself to the public. The first of these turned out to be a bit more complicated than he might have anticipated. His studies with Haydn did not proceed particularly well. Haydn was by this time a mature composer, interested in taking advantage of his freedom and his fame to fulfill his own career goals, and he had never cultivated the role of teacher. Beethoven discovered that Haydn was less than assiduous in correcting the errors in his exercises and secretly sought out another mentor. (Would that students were always so demanding of their instructors!) Johann Schenk (1753–1836) agreed to give Beethoven lessons on the sly. When Haydn left Vienna to make his second visit to London, Beethoven began to study with Johann Georg Albrechtsberger (1736–1809), one of the most important theorists and teachers of counterpoint in the period. Later Beethoven also had some instruction from the imperial Kapellmeister Antonio Salieri (1750–1825) in composing for the voice in the style of Italian opera.

Beethoven's relationship with the noble and wealthy patrons of music in Vienna was quite different from the traditional one. Rather than hire himself out to a single patron, he cultivated the support of a number of aristocratic families. In the earliest years he used his connections with the nobility in Bonn, particularly Count Waldstein, to gain introductions in Vienna. He was taken into the homes of various nobles, where he played private concerts, establishing a reputation as a virtuoso and as an improviser. Later he found opportunities to perform in public. Ultimately he succeeded in living on his own, making a living from his concerts and the publication of his music and enhancing his income by undertaking individual commissions from his patrons or dedicating works to them in the expectation of financial expressions of gratitude. In fact he was able to manage the sort of life at which Mozart had failed. This was possible partly because of Beethoven's personal strength of will—he could be very stubborn and even downright rude, even to the nobility—and partly because by the 1790s the Viennese aristocracy had to find new ways to support music without the substantial investment in household personnel of an earlier time.

The Music of Beethoven's First Vienna Period

Beethoven wisely did not present himself to Vienna in competition with Haydn; instead he sought ways in which he could excel while Haydn was engaged in his own activities. Beethoven led from strength, using his performance ability to spread his name. As a result, his works of the 1790s were composed mostly for the piano. From this period come half of his thirty-two piano sonatas and several pieces of chamber music with piano, including piano trios, sonatas for piano and violin and for piano and cello, and a quintet for winds and piano. He also composed three of his five piano concertos during these years. A few pieces of chamber music for strings without piano date from this time, but Beethoven did not produce quartets until the fine set of six composed in 1798–1800 and published as op. 18 in 1801. Only when it seemed certain that Haydn would not compose any more symphonies did Beethoven enter that arena; the First Symphony, op. 21, comes from 1800, and the Second Symphony, op. 36, from 1801–1802.

Beethoven's music up to 1802 reflects a period of absorption of the High Classic style and the production of works within that style. The years from 1792 to 1802 have been dubbed a stage of "imitation" by one of Beethoven's biographers, the French composer Vincent d'Indy. The music from this decade is clearly modeled on the styles of Haydn and Mozart, as well as other eighteenth-century composers. The forms and the handling of motives in the texture show that in his twenties Beethoven fully mastered the principles of Classic construction.

Beethoven's passionate and somewhat unpolished personality already comes through distinctly, however. The pieces seem strong but rough, generally weightier in texture and more rugged in dynamic contrasts than those of his predecessors. His ambition to make powerful statements is betrayed by the symphonic pretensions in his piano sonatas. The early sonatas reveal this most clearly. They include minuet movements, unusual in sonatas but characteristic of symphonies. There are effects reminiscent of specifically orchestral styles, including a "Mannheim rocket" theme in the very first sonata (op. 2, no. 1). The Sonata in C minor, op. 13, nicknamed *Pathétique,* starts with a symphonic slow introduction that draws from the idiom of the empfindsamer Stil. The slow movements are sometimes in the arialike, andante manner of Mozart's and sometimes in the more expressive, largo style of Haydn's. In the minuets—some labeled "scherzo," a type Beethoven would use consistently later—and the rondo finales, Classic forms shape not the elegant, light content of Classic convention but material of rumbustious humor. Altogether these works indicate an artist with a secure grasp of contemporary style and technique but with a personality and ideas that were bound to burst free with revolutionary significance.

Colonial and Revolutionary America

American music up to the nineteenth century was peripheral to the Western musical mainstream, in the sense that influence was directed only from Europe to America, never the reverse. Consequently American music will only be touched on in the present context to indicate its general position and to note a few special American developments and composers.

The Europeans who settled in the Americas brought the music of their homelands with them. The Spanish and French missionaries of the Roman Catholic Church sang both chant and polyphonic liturgical music in the New World in the sixteenth century. As we noted earlier, French Huguenot settlers and the pilgrims brought the Calvinist psalters with them to North America in the seventeenth century, and the first book printed in the British American territory was the Bay Psalm Book.

Music formed a smaller part of secular activity for the early colonists because there was little time or energy for leisure pursuits while the basic requirements of life had to be won from the land. As cities became established in the eighteenth century, however, musical activities increased. The wealthy and educated imported instruments and scores from Europe for domestic use. The larger cities—Boston, New York, and Philadelphia—began to have performances of concerts and ballad opera by the 1730s.

In New England the standard homorhythmic type of psalm setting was elaborated by the addition of brief passages of imitative polyphony, to form the *fuging tune*. These simple compositions did not pretend to the sophistication of the fugues of the late Baroque period. The term *fuging* simply refers to the use of *fuga* in the sense of contrapuntal imitation in general.

The finest composer of fuging tunes, and one of the most original musicians of the period, was the tanner William Billings (1746–1800) of Boston. He gave up his craft to become a professional musician—the first American to do so. He not only composed both sacred and secular works but also had a great deal to say about his art. He continuously insisted on his independence from established conventions; thus he takes a place in history not only for the considerable interest of his music but also for representing an important attribute of the American spirit.

A more-sophisticated music, employing concerted instruments and more elaborate forms, was cultivated by the Moravian Brethren, who came from central Europe seeking religious freedom in the mid–seventeenth century and settled mostly in Pennsylvania and North Carolina. Their musical life included not only sacred music but also instrumental works played in collegia musica, works both imported from the Old World and newly composed.

The leaders of the American Revolution included several notable figures interested in music. Benjamin Franklin, whose interests ranged over all sorts of areas, played the guitar and harp and invented a design for musical glasses. Thomas Jefferson hosted music parties at his home. Another signer of the Declaration of Independence, Francis Hopkinson (1737–1791), was actually a composer. Hopkinson's simple but charming song "My Days Have Been So Wondrous Free," of 1759, may be the first composition by an American-born composer. It was a favorite of George Washington's.

The Revolution itself inspired composers to write patriotic songs and marches aplenty. Another genre, already popular in Europe, was the pictorial *battle piece* for keyboard. These naive and amusing works included trumpet signals, marching music, loud and confused battle noises, laments for the fallen, and often quotations from well-known patriotic songs. James Hewitt's (1770–1827) "Battle of Trenton," a classic of the battle genre, was dedicated to George Washington.

Questions for Reflection

❖   In what ways does a High Classic instrumental movement seem to be operatic, and in what ways does the musical structure of the sonata help dramatize the structure of the action in an opera?

❖   How did the practical aspects of musical life shape the compositional activities of Haydn, Mozart, and the young Beethoven? In what circumstances did purely artistic motivations affect their output?

❖   How does the changing social context for musical performance in the last quarter of the eighteenth century help explain why Haydn's output of symphonies slowed considerably toward the end of his career, why Mozart composed far fewer and these also appeared more rarely as time went on, and why Beethoven composed comparatively few symphonies?

Suggestions for Further Reading

An outstanding study of the music of the High Classic composers is Charles Rosen, *The Classical Style: Haydn, Mozart, Beethoven* (New York: Norton, 1971).

On chamber music of Haydn and Mozart, see Rosemary Hughes, *Haydn String Quartets*, 5th ed. (Seattle: University of Washington Press, 1975); A. Hyatt King, *Mozart Chamber Music* (Seattle: University of Washington Press, 1969).

On the symphony, see H.C. Robbins Landon, *The Symphonies of Joseph Haydn* (London: Barrie & Rockliff, 1961); Georges de Saint-Foix, *The Symphonies of Mozart*, trans. Leslie Orrey (London: Dobson, 1947).

Cuthbert M. Girdlestone, *Mozart's Piano Concertos*, 3d ed. (London: Cassell, 1978) is a useful overview.

Two excellent studies of Mozart's operas are Edward J. Dent, *Mozart's Operas*, 2d ed. (London: Oxford University Press, 1960), and William Mann, *The Operas of Mozart* (London: Oxford University Press, 1960).

For many years the standard biography of Beethoven has been that of Alexander Wheelock Thayer, updated as *Thayer's Life of Beethoven*, rev. ed.

Elliot Forbes (Princeton: Princeton University Press, 1969). An important, insightful study is Maynard Solomon, *Beethoven* (New York: Schirmer, 1977).

A good, compact survey of American music is H. Wiley Hitchcock, *Music in the United States: A Historical Introduction,* 3d ed. (Englewood Cliffs, N.J.: Prentice-Hall, 1988). See also Gilbert Chase, *America's Music,* rev. ed. (New York: McGraw-Hill, 1966). On the colonial and revolutionary periods, see Irving Lowens, *Music and Musicians in Early America* (New York: Norton, 1964).

19

THE RISE OF THE ROMANTIC MOVEMENT

Philosophical Roots of Romantic Thought

The impetus toward a new way of thinking was embodied in the Enlightenment. Fundamental to this trend was a change in human values that arose in the second half of the eighteenth century. At this time society faced the deterioration of the old feudal class system in which people were categorized and treated as units in an artificial social hierarchy. Thinkers began to place greater emphasis on the innate worth of a person as a unique individual. Rousseau wrote in his *Confessions* (1765ff), "I am not made like anyone I have ever met; I even venture to believe that I am not made like anyone now alive."

This idea that human beings are essentially individuals and therefore cannot be lumped together into social castes and treated as so many sociological clones had revolutionary political implications, and it quickly began to affect the political scene. Rousseau's *The Social Contract* (1762) addressed the question of the function of government, which Thomas Hobbes had dealt with in the seventeenth century. Whereas Hobbes had viewed a monarchical, hierarchical system as essential to protect people from their own baser instincts, Rousseau proclaimed that any government was not ordained for the people but was an agreement among the people to organize under authority granted by them for the common good. The American Revolution (1776) soon took the theory to heart. The Declaration of Independence stated explicitly that government must be subject to the will of the people, not vice versa, and further that when a government no longer responds to the people's needs, they should form a better one. The motto of the French revolution of 1789–1792, "Liberty, equality, fraternity," reflects the assumptions that people should be fundamentally free from artificial constraints and that individuals must not be pigeonholed by class.

The possibility that individuals might rise by their own effort from a low position to one of prominence and power found its embodiment in the person of Napoleon Bonaparte (1769–1821). He began as a low-ranking military officer, but his leadership was so forceful that he was able to save France from the disastrous Reign of Terror that followed the revolution. Napoleon climbed the ladder of power rapidly until in 1804 he became emperor of France and for the following ten years dominated almost all of Europe. The thinkers and artists of his day regarded Napoleon's heroism and his tyranny with mixed emotions, but as a symbol for the victory of the human individual in the struggle against the powers of the system he could not be matched. As Lord Byron put it in a poem entitled "Napoleon's Farewell,"

Farewell to the Land where the gloom of my Glory
Arose and o'ershadow'd the earth with her name—
She abandons me now—but the page of her story,
The brightest or blackest, is fill'd with my fame.[1]

Politics and Social Revolution

Once the revolutionary spirit had been released, aggressive political reform movements became common. A second revolution in France in 1830 effected the replacement of the aristocracy by the bourgeoisie as the focus of political power. In 1848 political uprisings occurred in France, Germany, Austria, Italy, and Hungary. In the *Communist Manifesto* (1848) and *Das Kapital* (1867) Karl Marx (1818–1883) suggested that the proletariat should displace the bourgeoisie from power as the bourgeoisie had displaced the nobility. The new regard for the worth of the individual led to the abolition of serfdom in Russia by Czar Alexander II in 1861 and the American Emancipation Proclamation in 1863.

The expectations of individuals that their life could be comfortable and fulfilling did not depend exclusively on political liberty. The Industrial Revolution made much of the manual labor that had occupied the entire lives of the lower class obsolete and extended a comfortable life to more people than ever before. The mass production of relatively inexpensive goods meant that even those of comparatively modest means could attain some luxuries and the benefits of the arts and literature. Steam and electricity rendered travel and communication rapid, efficient, and reasonable in cost. Robert Fulton's steamship demonstrated the usefulness of steam for transportation in 1807, locomotives were in regular use in England by 1829, and by the middle of the century steamships and railroads were common. The telegraph was invented in 1832; the transatlantic cable was laid in 1866; and Alexander Graham Bell created the telephone in 1876. The effect of technological advances on the arts is no less significant. The photographic process, invented in 1839, made it possible to reproduce visual works, and Thomas Edison achieved phonographic recording in 1876.

The Concept of Organic Unity

A philosophical idea as characteristic of and important to the nineteenth century as the new view of the human individual was the concept of the organic unity of all being. The German philosopher Georg Wilhelm Friedrich Hegel (1770–1831) argued that natural and human history constitute the story of the self-fulfillment of a universal spirit through a process of dialectical opposition and synthesis. According to this plan, life supersedes inorganic matter, humanity is the culmination of life, and art and religion constitute the highest manifestations of human experience.

The willingness to pursue in science the idea that at a deep level all life is connected by organic processes made possible theories of biological evolution. In 1859 Charles Darwin (1809–1882) articulated the theory in a satisfactory form in *The Origin of Species*.

This organic manner of thinking inevitably affected the arts. We shall observe its effect in specific instances later.

Romantic Art

The term *Romantic*, which came to denote the new artistic approach that emerged at the end of the eighteenth century in literature and around 1800 in music, derives from the literary "romance." It therefore suggests a style that is "romancelike" or novelistic, concentrating on emotional conflict and climax.

Since the Romantic movement was inclined to stress the uniqueness of the individual, it seems only natural that artists chose to treat the part of experience in which individuals are most individual, the emotional life. In our rational, objective experience, we are all pretty much alike. We all find the stormy sky gray, the rain cold and wet, the lightning bright, the thunder loud. Whether we find such weather depressing, invigorating, or frightening is an individual, subjective matter. The German writer Friedrich Schlegel (1772–1829) put it this way: "Reason is but one and the same in all; however, just as each human being has his own nature and his own peculiar love, so each person also carries his own poetry in himself." The Romantic artist seeks not merely to depict the storm but also to treat its emotional possibilities and, in so doing, may take the audience through an entire range of emotional reactions. The work succeeds not by the accuracy of its depiction of content or its perfection of design, but by the effectiveness of its expression of emotion. The artistic movement of the nineteenth century that we call Romantic therefore belongs among the several swings of the aesthetic pendulum away from the Apollonian toward the Dionysian, a recurring phenomenon in music history.

In the late eighteenth century writers on aesthetics made an important distinction between the two qualities they called the beautiful and the sublime. The appeal of the beautiful is objective, controlled, and ultimately satisfying to the Apollonian, classical taste. The sublime depends on the power of the effect and the absence of control and has a subjective appeal. The philosopher Edmund Burke (1729–1797) wrote,

> The passion caused by the great and sublime in *nature,* when those causes operate most powerfully, is Astonishment; and astonishment is that state of the soul in which all its motions are suspended, with some degree of horror.
>
> . . . sublime objects are vast in their dimensions, beautiful ones comparatively small: beauty should be smooth, and polished; the great, rugged and negligent; beauty should shun the right line, yet deviate from it insensibly; the great in many cases loves the right line, and when it deviates, it often makes a strong deviation; beauty should not be obscure; the great ought to be dark and gloomy; beauty should be light and delicate; the great ought to be solid, and even massive. They are indeed ideas of a very different nature, one being founded on pain, the other on pleasure; . . .[2]

Romantic art generally inclines to the sublime rather than the beautiful; the aim is not aesthetic satisfaction but stimulation.

One characteristic of Romantic art is a preoccupation with longing or yearning. Sometimes this is directed toward a future object, but characteristically the object is inherently unattainable. Often the longing is manifested in nostalgia for the past, which is, of course, ultimately out of reach. This Romantic longing is actually experienced as an end in itself, not as a mere transitory state leading to fulfillment. The writer and composer E. T. A. Hoffmann (1776–1822) claimed that Beethoven's music aroused "just that infinite longing which is the essence of romanticism."

Themes in Romantic Art

The artistic emphasis on emotional experience led artists frequently to a few central themes, each of which possesses great power to evoke emotion. Naturally one of these themes is love, and the situation for the Romantic artist is usually one in which the love is unrequited, hopeless, or even fatal. The prototype for this sort of love was the protagonist in Johann Wolfgang von Goethe's *Die Leiden des jungen Werthers* (The sorrows of the young Werther, 1774), in which Werther finally commits suicide out of frustrated love.

A second subject to which we inevitably have an emotional response is death, and the mystery of death—inspiring fear, awe, or even triumph—was another common topic in nineteenth-century art, literature, and music. Death became an obsession for nineteenth-century artists in all fields. The longing for death offered the marvelous paradox of a fulfillment that was fatal to the person who attained it.

Closely related to death are religion and the supernatural, two more common themes for the Romantic artist. (A number of nineteenth-century artists turned to mystical religion out of the same desire for emotional experience that attracted them to art; they generally became Roman Catholics, finding Catholicism the most mystical of the Christian denominations.) The ideal figure for the exploration of the supernatural was Goethe's Faust.

Another emotion-inspiring area of life is politics, and the political movements of their day provided materials for the artists in all fields. They painted pictures of, wrote about, and composed music about the political events of their own time, particularly wars and battles. Alfred Lord Tennyson's *The Charge of the Light Brigade* (1855) offers an example of the glorification of sacrifice on the battlefield. The Romantics also pursued their national identities in recovering their history and ethnic mythology. The brothers Grimm, in their compilation of folk tales, were important contributors to this movement.

Yet another subject to which the Romantics, like people in all times, had a strong emotional response was nature. They were particularly interested in nature as it presented a conflict with or threat to human life, and as a reflection of human emotion. Storms, for example, turn up frequently in Romantic literature and art, partly because of the danger and the threat—or promise—of death that the forces of nature present and partly because the storm outside symbolizes the inner storm of emotion in the Romantic soul. By the same token, the peacefulness of a bucolic scene symbolized a moment of inner peace.

Techniques of Romantic Art

Unlike the art of the Enlightenment, which tended to strive for satisfaction in terms of refinement and intellectual design, that of the Romantic era concentrated on the strength of expression and shaping derived from emotional experience. Some aspects of Romantic technique can be identified in all the arts. These may be best understood if they are defined in terms of the opposition between the Classic and Romantic approaches.

One of these general techniques is the use of roughness rather than polish in the application of material in the artwork. This is perhaps most easily observed in the visual arts, where painters apply paint thickly to canvas in such a way that the brushwork remains clearly seen, as in the portrait of Chopin (Fig. 19.1) by Eugène Delacroix (1798–1863), or in sculpture where the strokes of the chisel are left and not polished away. In music the desire for a kind of ruggedness led composers to employ dissonance more frequently and freely and to explore brighter and more aggressive timbres.

Figure 19.1
Eugène Delacroix (1798–1863), *Frédéric Chopin* (1838). The portrait of the twenty-eight-year-old pianist and composer gives the impression of a visionary Romantic contemplating a distant world reserved for the genius alone. The roughness of the brushwork helps to create the impression that the painter must have captured this image in a rapid flash of Romantic artistic insight. (*Giraudon/Art Resource*)

In the same way, abruptness of change and sharp contrast are more likely to occur in Romantic art than in the more gracefully shaped works of the preceding era. In Romantic literature one finds shocking juxtapositions that would have seemed impossible self-contradictions in the eighteenth century; thus Byron in *Childe Harold's Pilgrimage* is able to speak of a scene as "Charming the eye with dread" and "Horribly beautiful." The juxtaposition of extremes of brightness and clashing colors in painting naturally became more common. In music contrasts and extremes in dynamics, for example, also arise more often, and we hear harmonic progressions that move abruptly between unrelated chords.

In structure, the Romantic artist placed the emphasis on unpredictability rather than pattern. This is, of course, in keeping with the ideal of unfulfilled longing. We must note, however, that the disruption of the audience's expectations of a pattern depends on the assumption that a pattern will appear, and thus the Romantic style depends on the Classic style though it thwarts Classic expectations. In poetry there is more freedom of meter and less end-stopping of lines in the Romantic work than in a Classic one, though the expectation of regular poetic meter and clearly end-stopped lines persists. The poetry of Walt Whitman (1819–1892) makes a good example, for its rhythm tends to be free of regular meter, and the lines are of extremely varied lengths. In works of visual art asymmetry and a sense of motion supersede symmetry and stability; the canvas is likely to be divided on a diagonal and into portions of unequal area. (Plate 7) Musical works present structural surprises, and forms tend to offer too little stability to balance large periods of instability, at least by Classical standards.

It was also possible to heighten expressiveness by creating a seeming mismatch between content and structure, which produces a sense of overloading that suggests that emotional expression had overwhelmed rational control. The poet William Blake (1757–1827) took advantage of this possibility by crafting verses that seem to embody much depth and seriousness in miniature, almost singsong rhymes. Composers could achieve the same effect by overloading a simple, four-measure phrase with chromatic harmonies that certainly are not required to clarify the structure, or by creating dynamic effects that seem excessive, rather than employing dynamics, as in the Classic style, simply as a means of articulating the design.

Finally, all the arts reflect the organic thinking of the Romantic philosophers by stressing organic continuity rather than architectural sectionalization. In the eighteenth century poems tend to have end-stopped lines that sit one on top of the other like building blocks; nineteenth-century poets used enjambment to create poems that grow on and on as if they were alive. Nineteenth-century painters increasingly blurred the outlines of shapes in their works, and this combines with asymmetry to create a more organic kind of form. In music we find that cadences blur, and movements quote one another and run together so that the divisions disappear.

Also part of the increasing Romantic sense of connectedness of things is the interpenetration of works of various art forms. There appear paintings based on poems, poems based on paintings, and musical works based on either. This is part of the explanation for the expansion of music related to extramusical topics in the Romantic period. Moreover, the relatedness of things provides links between art and the real world; novels, dramas, paintings, and musical works were based on the lives of artists, and in some cases the lives of the artists seems to have been lived in imitation of characters in novels. (Byron, from whom we have heard earlier, would be a case in point).

The Romantic Movement in the History of Musical Style

It can be argued, as it has been most notably by the great German music historian Friedrich Blume, that the Romantic movement in the history of music does not constitute a separate style but is inseparable from the Classicism of the late eighteenth century. From this point of view, Classicism and Romanticism form two phases in the life span of a single style. The Classic phase achieved the perfection of the technical aspects of the style, whereas the Romantic stage completed the exploration of the style's expressive possibilities. It must be emphasized, though, that this should not be understood to imply that expression was not important in the music of the Classic composers, or that no achievements in technique came from the Romantics.

What binds together the entire Classic-Romantic style period complex is the reliance on dramatic means of expression based on tonally grounded structure. The essential processes of drama—instability and stability, conflict and resolution, development and climax—provide the fundamental structural and expressive foundation of music from the second quarter of the eighteenth century until the end of the nineteenth. Moreover, in all this music the basis of the drama is tonal harmony. In the Classic phase, as we have seen, the drama tended to be structural and intellectual; in the Romantic phase, it naturally tended to be expressive and emotional. As mentioned above, however, Romantic expressiveness relies on distortion, frustration, blurring, and overloading of Classic form; that is to say, Romantic expression depends on the assumptions of Classic form and style. This must be kept in mind throughout this and the following two chapters.

Beethoven from 1802

Beethoven occupies a crucial position in the rise of the Romantic period. Having mastered the Classic style by the end of his first decade in Vienna and established himself as the successor of Haydn and Mozart, and having achieved a degree of economic success through dedications and commissions of works, his own concerts, and his publications, Beethoven proceeded to explore the potential of dramatic musical expression for emotional expression. The years from 1802 to about 1815 in his compositional career are often characterized by d'Indy's term *externalization;* a more recent biographer, Maynard Solomon, refers to this stage of Beethoven's career as his "heroic" period.

Beethoven and the Artist as Hero

The composer's compulsion to extend the existing style for greater expressive force was a natural part of his personality; he was undoubtedly constitutionally unable to rest on his mastery of an earlier generation's style. There was another factor, however, that impelled him to press forward. By 1802 he had been forced to recognize that he was losing his hearing, a terrible fate for a young composer just arriving at artistic maturity. It made him deeply embarrassed and uncomfortable around others, indeed genuinely antisocial, and drove him to the brink of suicide. He retreated from the city of Vienna to the spa town of Heiligenstadt, where he confronted within himself the disaster of his affliction. He wrote there the famous "Heiligenstadt Testament," in the form of a letter to his brothers Carl and Johann, which said in part,

> O, you men who think or pronounce me to be hostile, stubborn, or misanthropic, how greatly you wrong me—you do not know the concealed cause for that which appears thus to you. . . . But just consider that since six years ago an incurable condition has afflicted me, made worse by foolish doctors, who deceived me from year to year by the hope of getting better, finally forced me to face the prospect of a *long-term illness* (for which the cure may last for years or even be impossible). Born with a passionate, lively temperament, responsive to the amusements of society, I soon had to isolate myself, to spend my life alone. And if from time to time I wished to conquer all this, oh, how roughly I was thrown back by the doubly wretched experience of my bad hearing. And yet it was impossible for me to say to people, "Speak louder, shout, because I am deaf." Ah, how should it be possible for me to admit that I had a weakness in *a sense* that I should have had to a more complete degree than others had, a sense that I once possessed in the greatest perfection, as few in my profession, certainly, have or ever have had it. . . . But what humiliation when someone stood beside me and heard a flute from far away and I heard *nothing,* or someone *heard the shepherd sing* and also I heard nothing. Such incidents brought me near to despair; it would have taken only a little and I would have ended my life myself.

Yet Beethoven did find a reason to live, his art and his vocation to express his emotions and musical thoughts:

Only . . . Art . . . held me back. Ah, it appeared impossible to me to leave the world before I had brought out all that I felt I intended, and so I endured this miserable life, truly miserable, with a body so sensitive that a somewhat fast change can alter me from the best condition into the worst. Patience—that is what it is that I must now choose for my guide. I hope my decision to persevere until it pleases the pitiless Fates to break the thread will last. Perhaps it will get better, perhaps not—I am prepared. . . . O, men, when once you read these words, think that you did me wrong; and may the unhappy man console himself with finding one of his own kind, who, despite all the handicaps of nature, has nevertheless done everything in his ability to be accepted into the ranks of worthy artists and men. . . .

Virtue—that alone can create happiness, not money; I speak from experience. It was that, that lifted me up even in misery; that, next to my art, that I have to thank that I did not end my life by suicide.

So it is over. With joy I hasten toward my death. If it comes before I have had the chance to develop all my artistic abilities, then it will come too soon in spite of my stern fate, and I would wish it to be later. Yet even then I shall be content—does it not free me from an endlessly painful condition? Come when thou wilt—I am going bravely to meet thee. . . .

Heiligenstadt, October 6th, 1802

A few days later he added a postscript:

Heiligenstadt, October 10th

So I must take my leave of thee—and that sadly. Even the dear hope that I brought here, of at least being healed to a certain point—it must now forsake me completely. As the leaves of autumn fall, are withered, so it has dried up for me. Almost as I came here, I leave again. Even the high courage that often inspired me in the lovely days of summer has faded. O Providence, may one pure day of *joy* appear to me. So long already the sincere echo of true joy has been unknown to me. O when—O when, O Godhead—can I feel it again in the temple of Nature and of humanity? Never?—no—that would be too hard.

Returning to Vienna and his work, Beethoven thus asserted a heroic attitude toward life—the heroism of one who feels a mission and though he cannot conquer knows that he must never give up the struggle.

Another heroic inspiration was very strong in Beethoven's view of life— that of the ideals of the French revolution and of the personality of Napoleon. He believed in the liberty and equality that would give everyone the opportunity to rise to the pinnacle of personal achievement, and Napoleon represented the model for a man's capacity to raise himself in the world by his own talent and effort. Between 1802 and 1804, when Beethoven was writing his

Symphony No. 3 in E flat, he planned to entitle the work *Bonaparte*. When he heard that Napoleon had made himself emperor and was, after all, no less a tyrant than the king the revolution had deposed, Beethoven scratched out the name from the title page. The symphony was published with the title *Sinfonia eroica* (Heroic symphony) and the bitter inscription "to celebrate the memory of a great man."

Beethoven did not give up his own heroic ideals, however. There are numerous evidences of his disregard for the nobility of the aristocratic class and his belief in the nobility of achievement. He is reported to have said to one of his wealthy aristocratic supporters, "Prince, what you are, you are by accident of birth; what I am, I am through my own efforts. There have been thousands of princes and will be thousands more; there is only one Beethoven." To the writer Goethe, he said about the nobility: "You must make it very obvious how valuable you are to them, else they'll never know it: . . ."

Beethoven's Heroic Style

The assertive, heroic nature of Beethoven's personal character is evident in his music as well. In his works after 1802 the Romantic approach is unmistakable. An increase in degrees of contrast affects the scoring and dynamics, giving a rugged strength to the music. In many cases the rhythm has a relentless drive and energy, particularly in the scherzo movements that replace the minuets of the Classic four-movement sonata plan. Fragmentation of melody into mere motives together with unprecedented harmonic dissonance and surprise add to the sense of roughness.

In structure Beethoven's music during this period features much more instability than his predecessors', or even his own in earlier years; this can be expressed in harmonic and tonal fashion or in strong, syncopated rhythm. Climax and resolution tend to be delayed, so that the moment of the triumphal arrival of the tonic key, rather than the balance of tonal motion by tonal stability, becomes the goal. The third sections of sonata-form movements grow to prodigious size, distorting the Classic proportions of the form, while the process of development extends throughout the form. Ultimately the integrity of the separate movements is sacrificed, as in the Symphony No. 5 in C minor, op. 67, where the first movement ends in a peculiarly abrupt fashion, the leading motive of the first movement continues to appear in the later ones, the movements eventually run together, and the finale becomes the climax of an integrated four-movement whole. In all, symmetry is sacrificed in favor of continuous forward struggle, and the Classic designs are overloaded.

Such asymmetry and overloading leaves the listener with the sense that there is a new degree of emphasis on emotional content in Beethoven's music after 1802, for the Classical, Apollonian ideas of design cannot explain them.

In the *Eroica* Symphony, the title specifies the nature of this change, and many of the works of the period share its heroic character.

Most of Beethoven's greatest works are instrumental rather than vocal. Despite his study of vocal composition with the Italian opera composer Salieri, Beethoven's style of writing for the voice is not characteristically grateful to sing. He wrote Lieder and arranged a large number of folksongs, including many Irish, Scottish, and Welsh ones. He produced only a single opera (more strictly speaking, in view of its use of spoken dialogue, a Singspiel), *Fidelio*, op. 72 (composed 1805–1806 and revised in 1814). *Fidelio* is an example of the *rescue opera,* a type that became popular in postrevolutionary France. It has much to do with tyranny and freedom, personal strength, and heroism, and this content made the libretto appeal to the idealistic, revolutionary Beethoven.

Beethoven did not often find it necessary to explain the content of his instrumental music by adding titles, but there are some cases in which he did so, and this desire to make the nature of the expressive content explicit became an important element for later Romantic composers. Another of Beethoven's works with a programmatic title is the Symphony No. 6 in F, op. 68, the *Pastoral* Symphony (subtitled "Recollections of Country Life"), which might be regarded as an explicit counterpart to the *Eroica* or to the heroic-style Fifth Symphony, which premiered on the same concert. The title *Pastoral* draws attention to another aspect of Beethoven's Romantic character, his preoccupation with nature. He responded sensitively to nature, and many of his compositional ideas came to him in the outdoors; he carried small books of staff paper with him on his walks so that he could jot down ideas as they came to him. He once answered someone who asked where he got his ideas,

> That I cannot tell you with certainty; they come unsummoned, directly, indirectly—I could seize them with my hands out in the open air; in the woods, while walking; in the silence of the night; early in the morning, incited by moods which are translated by the poet into words, by me into tones—which sound and roar and storm about me until I have set them down in notes.

In these years Beethoven was interested not only in new approaches to musical content but also in technical problems. He became increasingly interested in the variation form, writing several sets of variations for solo piano and also using the form for movements of larger sonata-plan works. The last movement of the *Eroica* Symphony, for example, is a set of variations on a theme that Beethoven also used in several other works. Of particular importance is the manner in which Beethoven's variations do not merely decorate the theme but seem to take on different expressive content or personalities. This approach may be identified by the term *character variation.* Another interest of Beethoven's was the fugue, which appears not as a type of separate piece or movement but as a means of development within other, larger musical forms.

Beethoven's Sketchbooks

Throughout his life, and especially after 1800, Beethoven was more self-conscious about his compositional process than any other composer. He produced and carefully kept a large number of sketchbooks, which reveal something of his work on most of his major compositions. These books hold a special fascination because they give some insight into how Beethoven formulated his ideas and worked out the plans of movements, and they have been much studied by scholars in recent decades. One significant implication of these books is that for the artist himself the aspect of his biography most worth preserving was his work. What we can know about his day-to-day activities, his friends, his financial accounts, his style of life—the sort of things we can find out for other composers—is complemented to a unique extent for Beethoven by this enormous quantity of evidence of his inner biography, the part of his life that mattered most. To judge from the Heiligenstadt Testament, this is perhaps the way Beethoven wished posterity to know his biography.

Beethoven's Personal Life in His Middle Period

Beethoven did, of course, also deeply long for and treasure friendships with other people, despite his inevitable isolation because of his deafness, as the Heiligenstadt Testament proves. Unfortunately his personality and temperament were rough and stormy, and while he developed passionate affection for his friends, he could also fight bitterly with them and easily feel jealous and betrayed. He never married, but in 1812 he did have an important relationship with a woman, which has become famous as the affair of the "Immortal Beloved." He wrote her a long and impassioned letter, never sent but preserved among his papers, that was the source of great controversy, for it never actually gives her name. Its true addressee was identified only recently as Antonie Brentano (1780–1869), wife of an important figure in the history of German literary Romanticism. She was the dedicatee of Beethoven's *Diabelli* Variations, op. 120, and the presumed inspiration for his song cycle *An die ferne Geliebte* (To the distant beloved), op. 98, in 1815–1816.

Beethoven's Last Period

An die ferne Geliebte may mark the turning point between the end of Beethoven's middle period and the beginning of the final stage in his creative career. After 1815 Beethoven was almost totally deaf and experienced poor health, and he became more isolated than before. He was not entirely a hermit, however, and carried on conversations by having friends write their questions and statements in books, while he answered orally. These conversation books, preserving half of Beethoven's conversations, are an important source for scholars studying the composer.

In this period Beethoven fought a legal battle with his sister-in-law for custody of his brother's son Karl. Having no child of his own, he sought to establish a close relationship with the boy, but again his affection was frustrated.

Finally, after the end of the Napoleonic, heroic era, and with the rise of the reactionary Prince Metternich, Vienna was no longer the city it had been. Beethoven's revolutionary liberalism must have seemed out of step with the gay Viennese spirit of the time.

In the face of this isolation and personal frustration, Beethoven achieved fulfillment in his compositions. This period was dubbed one of "reflection" by d'Indy. Listeners have sensed in these pieces a meditative and profound concentration, and the works seem somewhat private, more a communication between the artist and the art itself than between the composer and the public audience. General style characteristics include an intense involvement with mastery of technical problems of composition, particularly counterpoint and motivic working out, and highly experimental treatments of the standard musical forms. The conventional key plans of Classic form give way to experiments with relationships between more distant keys, such as those a third apart. The developmental techniques of variation and fugue, already important in Beethoven's earlier, heroic style, are highly developed in his late works. At the same time there seems to be a certain disregard for such values as lyrical melody and the sensual beauty of sound. Often these works are extremely challenging to performers.

The final period works can be divided into two categories. In the first are the last five piano sonatas and string quartets. In these solo and chamber works Beethoven experimented with texture and form. The outward sonata plan and sonata form give way under the pressure of musical concentration, sometimes producing works in which the movement forms are difficult to classify and sometimes leading to works made up of a large number of short sections not fully articulated as independent movements. In the second category are two monumental masterpieces for voices and orchestra, the *Missa Solemnis* and the Symphony No. 9 in D minor, op. 125 (1822–1824). In the Ninth Symphony heroic idealism returns, but it undergoes a change into a vision of worldly struggle leading to utopian peace and harmony. The four movements are convincingly integrated, and the last is a vast and complicated realization of the Classic concerto sonata form for voices and orchestra. The key of D minor is supplanted by D major, the symphonic style gives way to a songlike theme, and absolute music is replaced by the explicit expression of ideas in the text of the "Ode to Joy" by the German poet Friedrich Schiller (1759–1805).

Beethoven's Influence on Nineteenth-Century Music

Beethoven cast a long shadow over the remainder of the nineteenth century, and one broader than the substantial influences his music had on the styles of later composers. In his life he represented a sort of myth of the Romantic artist, enduring physical affliction and social isolation and living for art alone. The model he provided of the artist expressing his own personality and the great ideals of the time in his music inspired later composers to view their calling as one of enlightening the world and challenging their listeners to meet them on their own terms, rather than of providing entertainment or diversion to suit a patron's or the public's taste. The strength and freedom with which Beethoven handled the Classical conventions of musical composition established the Romantic idea that the true artist must strive against conventionalism for originality.

The Romantic Lied

The early nineteenth century saw the song increase considerably in significance as an artistic genre. The leading composers of Lieder around the turn of the century were based in Berlin, forming a *Second Berlin School* (so named to distinguish it from the First Berlin School of the middle of the eighteenth century). Their style was predicated on musical simplicity and the intention to let the poetry speak clearly for itself. They espoused the ideal of *Volkstümlichkeit,* a term that does not translate into English easily but suggests both folklike simplicity and reflection of the national folk character. Among the leaders of this school was the Berlin composer and music director Karl Friedrich Zelter (1758–1832), a good friend of Goethe's. Though Romantic in much of his poetry, Goethe held, with Zelter, conservative ideas about the role of music in the song; he felt that the setting should essentially provide a medium for the delivery of the text, not an attempt to interpret it. Goethe's and Zelter's concern was to avoid a musical style that seemed operatic, for that would thwart the intimate, personal expression of the lyric poem.

On the basis of this ideal, a strophic text called for a strophic setting of neutral character, designed to suit the meter and verse structure of the poem. Both the intention of the Second Berlin School composers to achieve a folklike style and the Goethe-Zelter song aesthetic led to songs that employed strophic form with symmetrical melodic phrasing, light textures, and simple harmonies. The style was well suited to performance in the drawing rooms of the middle-class German bourgeoisie, and the music naturally had a lively market.

An alternative to the strophic Lied was the *ballad*. Unlike the lyric poetry of Lieder, ballad texts were narrative and dramatic in their content, and generally their poetic rhythm was quite irregular. As a consequence, musical settings of such ballads, best represented by those of the leading exponent of the genre, Johann Rudolf Zumsteeg (1760–1802), were through-composed. They could be very long and rambling, passing through numerous vocal styles and accompaniment textures, musical meters, and keys, so that only the story being unfolded in words and music held the work together. In some ballads recurring motives helped increase the coherence of the music.

Franz Schubert

The course of the development of the Lied was totally altered by the work of the Viennese composer Franz Schubert (1797–1828). Schubert, the son of a middle-class schoolmaster, played chamber music at home and was trained as a choirboy at the imperial choir school, where he studied under Salieri. At the age of sixteen Schubert abandoned his future as a schoolteacher for a career as a composer. He idolized Beethoven and hoped to follow in his footsteps, but he made little headway in the musical world. His many fine instrumental works—including piano music, chamber music, and symphonies—reveal that he knew Beethoven's music well but was an entirely different personality, more lyrical and less intense in his treatment of tonality and thematic development. Hardly any of Schubert's instrumental music was published during his lifetime. His theatrical works, of which he wrote quite a number, were unsuccessful. In the field of the song, however, he was perfectly original, and his works in the genre are truly epoch-making. (Fig. 19.2)

Schubert's contribution to the history of the Lied consists in his obvious insistence that the role of the composer should be equal to that of the poet in determining the emotional experience of the song. He combined the talent for melody that Austrian composers seem to have absorbed from their nearness to Italy, the dramatic possibilities of the ballad, and a Romantic insight into lyric poetry. Schubert composed both strictly strophic Lieder in the tradition of *Volkstümlichkeit* and ballads, the latter especially in his early years. In his mature style, however, beginning in about 1814, he made the music not merely a vehicle for the text or simply programmatically illustrative of the meanings of the words, but both of these and also an interpretation of the poem's content.

Essential to Schubert's way of interpreting poetry was his use of the piano. He invented myriad variants of simple broken-chord patterns, often comprising a kind of transfigured sound effect that not only suggested a background setting for the thoughts of the poet but also captured the emotional state of the speaker. The first masterpiece to accomplish this was Schubert's setting of

Figure 19.2
Moritz von Schwind (1804–1871), *A Schubertiad*. The artist von Schwind was a member of Schubert's circle of friends. The composer is depicted playing a song while another friend, Michael Vogl, on his left, sings. Clearly the milieu for which Schubert's Lieder were intended was not the recital stage of most of today's performances. (*The Bettmann Archive*)

Goethe's song from *Faust*, "Gretchen am Spinnrade" (1814); the constantly circling right-hand figuration in the piano part evokes not only the motion of a spinning wheel but also the disturbed feelings of Gretchen. Another fine example is the water music of various songs in the first of his two cycles, *Die schöne Müllerin* (1823), in which the piano part illustrates the flowing of the water but also changes from song to song as the stream reflects the different moods of the journeyman miller—now cheerfully sparkling, now peacefully flowing, now agitated.

Likewise, the great setting of Goethe's ballad "Erlkönig" (1815) employs an accompaniment rhythm that suggests the galloping of a horse and at the same time the frantic agitation of the riders. "Erlkönig" illustrates how Schubert could take advantage of every aspect of musical style: The melodic range is designed to distinguish the different speakers who appear in the story, the pacing of their lines depends on their mood, major and minor modes are freely used for their affective value, and sequentially rising harmony creates a sense of rising tension. Here, too, the form departs from the strophic convention to take a rondo- or ritornellolike form, which is derived from the content rather than the form of the text.

Schubert's most characteristic song form was the *modified strophic* design, comparable to the variation form in instrumental music. The strophic principle operated as far as the poetic content would allow, and then variation was applied. This gave the impression of the *volkstümlich* aesthetic without tying the composer's hands when it came to interpreting the ideas.

Schubert expressed the Romantic inclination to organically growing, multipartite works in his great song cycles. For *Die schöne Müllerin* and its successor *Winterreise* (Winter journey, 1827), Schubert took cycles of poems by the German poet Wilhelm Müller (1794–1827), both dealing with love and with the romantic protagonist's sensitivity to nature. These cycles, of twenty and twenty-four songs respectively, are unified largely by the narrative progress of the texts and by recurring poetic and musical images, rather than by explicit thematic quotation, a thoroughgoing tonal plan, or continuous music as in Beethoven's *An die ferne Geliebte*.

Early Nineteenth-Century Italian Opera

Of all parts of Europe in the early nineteenth century, Italy remained the most conservative in its music. Opera dominated the scene, and with the spread of public opera theaters it became the most popular social pastime. Everyone who could afford the price of a ticket attended the opera regularly, and the opera became for that time roughly equivalent to rock concerts or major sporting events in today's American society (with the exception that it could not be seen at home on television and therefore had to be experienced live in a public situation). Fans gave vocal support to their favorite stars and showed their disapproval in equally lively fashion. Vendors of refreshments sold their wares during performances, and the arias of minor characters gained the nickname *aria di sorbetto* (sherbet aria), because during them the boxholders often closed the curtains of their boxes to snack or converse, opening them again when the prima donna or primo uomo returned to the stage. Intermissions were filled by a ballet or other "half-time" entertainment.

Audiences frequently went to hear the same opera a number of times, but novelties were always in demand, and composers were kept busy producing new works at considerable speed. In many cases a major composer had help from assistants who wrote the recitatives and arias for lesser characters while he created the major arias and ensembles. It was not uncommon for a composer to borrow music from his own earlier works by parody, continuing the practice that had produced many works since the parody Masses of the Renaissance.

Certain factors made the composition of an opera as much a matter of craft as of high art: The genre incorporated a variety of conventions inherited from the eighteenth century, so that the work could be approached somewhat as a problem in filling out a predetermined scheme; and composers continued to have to meet, as had their late Baroque and Classic predecessors, the demands of the star performers. To be sure, the performers experienced their own pressures in learning new roles to keep up with the public demand for new operas, and sometimes having to do so at the last minute when a procrastinating composer submitted the score with the ink still wet on the page.

It will be understood from all of this that the Italian opera in the early nineteenth century remained comparatively closely tied to the Classic tradition and style. Indeed, the Romantic movement took hold more slowly in Italy than it did in northern Europe. The operatic styles current in the first quarter of the nineteenth century descended directly from the opera seria and opera buffa of the eighteenth century in a continuous tradition.

Rossini

The greatest Italian composer of the period was Gioacchino Rossini (1792–1868). He established a very successful career with his works in the major opera houses of Italy, beginning in 1810. By 1816 he had achieved notable success, and in that year he composed his most famous opera, *Il barbiere di Siviglia* (The barber of Seville). That the work belongs to the Classic tradition will be evident from the observation that the subject is taken from the first play in the trilogy by Beaumarchais from which Mozart's *Le nozze di Figaro* had come. It had already been composed by the Classic opera composer Giovanni Paisiello (1740–1816). Indeed, *Il barbiere di Siviglia* is even more clearly in the manner of the prototypical opera buffa, more low comedy and less concerned with social criticism than *Le nozze di Figaro*. Mozart's operatic composition had placed musical drama ahead of every other concern, and, while his vocal writing certainly showed off the voice, the Italian style that followed him seems to make vocalism its highest priority. When we compare Rossini's style to Mozart's, we find that Rossini's is more immediately grateful for the singers. Rossini's music tends toward greater lyricism and offers more opportunities for vocal improvisation than Mozart's, even though Rossini tried harder than his lesser contemporaries to maintain authority over the vocal lines, writing out more specifically the ornamentation he wanted sung.

Rossini's serious operas are classified as *dramma,* rather than opera seria. One example is his *Otello* (1816), which was composed immediately after *Il barbiere di Siviglia*. It is significant that the subject matter comes from Shakespeare. The great English Tudor dramatist began to gain appreciation throughout Europe in the nineteenth century because he was regarded as a model of the serious dramatist whose works succeeded despite their disregard for the academic "classical" unities of time, place, and action. In *Otello* Rossini first attempted to let the drama control the musical conventions, and he broke away somewhat from the older style.

Opera in France

The French opera maintained some of its characteristic features after the revolution but also added some new tendencies. The well-established use of large choruses and stage spectacle remained, as did the preference for a relatively undecorated vocal style in arias. All of these naturally suited the bourgeois public, which was impressed by effect and not by artificial vocalism. A popular subject for operatic treatment in this period was heroic rescue; we have already noted that Beethoven's *Fidelio* was modeled on French revolutionary rescue opera. New Romantic tendencies led to the inclusion of vivid settings in wilder natural surroundings and elements of the supernatural, both of which were not only Romantic in themselves but also gave the opportunity for striking stagings. The orchestra of the French opera was large and colorful, making special effects of instrumentation a characteristic feature. The Italian-born composer Luigi Cherubini (1760–1842), who settled in Paris in 1826, led the French movement toward Romanticism by his use of unusual, imaginative scorings and his willingness to break melodic and rhythmic regularity to achieve forceful expression of emotion.

By the early years of the decade of the 1820s it became evident to Rossini that to move with the times he must break away from the old-fashioned comfort of the Italian opera theaters and go north, where the new Romantic movement had already taken hold. He went to Paris to try his hand at the French style. He first adapted Italian works into French but eventually attempted original opera in that language. In 1829 he tackled the subject of William Tell, using Friedrich Schiller's drama as the basis for the libretto. *Guillaume Tell* offered much to the Romantic taste: the issue of political freedom from tyranny, a picturesque natural setting, and a love interest added for the opera. It evoked Rossini's most advanced music, including more harmonic and orchestrational originality than his earlier works, a good deal of choral material, and a less florid vocal style. After *Guillaume Tell* Rossini retired from composing opera. A variety of reasons for this may be adduced, but probably most convincing was simply that he found the Romantic style uncongenial to his talent and that it required more effort than it was worth to him to compete in the new age. He remained a prominent figure in musical society for nearly forty more years.

German Romantic Opera

The German nations produced a genuinely national and truly Romantic opera composer in the person of Carl Maria von Weber (1786–1826). Weber combined musical training under fine Austrian Classical composers and a background in the theater, and he became director (at the age of thirty) of a series of prominent opera houses, including the great opera at Dresden. With Weber's Singspiel *Der Freischütz* (The free marksman, 1821) German opera clearly achieved Romanticism. Weber took a colorful plot involving a wild forest locale, magically charmed bullets, and a love story, and combined it with equally colorful music. The overture immediately alerts the listener that something special is at hand, as it features unexpected and structurally inexplicable dynamic effects, a solo passage for a quartet of hunting horns, and ominous tremolos on mysterious, fully diminished seventh chords. The casting of the magic bullets in the "Wolf's Glen" scene, which includes the weirdest of music and calls for stunning supernatural stage effects, ranks as one of the most strikingly Romantic moments in the operatic literature. (Fig. 19.3)

In *Der Freischütz* Weber wove thematic threads through the musical fabric to give a deliberate organicism to the work; each musical idea in the sonata-form overture anticipates some theme from the drama. The use of *reminiscence themes* was even more thoroughgoing and explicit in *Euryanthe* (1823), which also moved in the direction of continuous opera by breaking down the closure of musical numbers. This Romantic tendency toward organic continuity became a central issue to Richard Wagner, who owed much to Weber's pioneering works.

The Social Context for Music in the Nineteenth Century

As we have seen, the social position of the composer changed radically with the decline of the patronage system at the close of the eighteenth century. The new arrangement, under which the composer worked more as a private entrepreneur, brought at once greater economic risks and possibilities for greater artistic independence. The artist became freer to express his own thoughts in new ways, untrammeled by the demands of a patron, but at the same time he could not live without appealing to the marketplace. As a result, in the nineteenth century there were generally three types of composers: those who had great artistic imaginations but found themselves subject to financial insecurity; those who succeeded by making a brilliant impression on the public and therefore achieved financial success; and many, little-known to posterity, who

Figure 19.3
Carl Wilhelm Holdermann, drawing of the Wolf's Glen scene from an early performance of Weber's *Der Freischütz*. Romantic interests in the supernatural and nature are evoked as the ghostly riders race through the air at the climactic casting of the magic bullets in the forest. (*Staatliche Kunstsammlungen, Schloßmuseum, Weimar*)

appealed to the mass market, writing competent and popular works but rarely masterpieces. Schubert belongs to the first category. He never achieved wide public recognition and was unable to take advantage of the free enterprise system to make a living as a composer; instead he relied heavily on the generosity of a circle of friends who believed in his talent and supported him through difficult financial times. The second type would include virtuoso performers and opera composers. Rossini became very wealthy through the success of his works on the stage, and of course Weber had financial security through his employment as a director.

The need to appeal to the public was tremendously important. A number of new popular styles arose. Throughout Europe, but especially in Italy, the opera house became the major social and entertainment center in most cities. After the devastating period of French occupation, and under the regime of Prince Metternich, Vienna's glittering social life produced the waltzes of the Strauss family (Johann, Sr., 1804–1849; Johann, Jr., 1825–1899; Josef, 1827–1870), which were exported and became popular all over Europe. Also attractive to the masses were virtuoso solo players, who toured the continent and even crossed the Atlantic giving concerts that often featured their own compositions. Their repertoire often included flashy arrangements of and variations on well-known popular and operatic melodies. By contrast, there was also a need for large quantities of parlor music to be performed by amateurs in the homes of the middle class. This was met by the production of songs, piano pieces, and short easy pieces for all sorts of solo instruments. The best of this literature had genuine artistic merit and survives as recital repertoire; most of it has faded into obscurity.

During this period there arose an important new type of musical institution, the modern music conservatory. The first such establishment was the result of the French revolution. The downfall of the aristocracy and the rise of a democratic system threatened to create a musical crisis. The Paris Conservatory was founded partly to provide music for the new audiences and new occasions under the postrevolutionary regime and partly to offer a means for educating new musicians now that the opportunity for private, apprenticeship-style training in the households of the nobility no longer existed. One of the greatest public prizes for composition, the *Prix de Rome,* was established in France in 1803 to provide the most gifted young composers both recognition and financial support in the new social situation. It allowed the promising artist a chance to enrich his background by a period of study in Rome, which was considered the center of classical culture. The Paris system was so successful that similar conservatories were soon founded in Italy, Austria, Germany, England, Russia, and the United States.

Questions for Reflection

✛   How convincing is the theory that the Classic and Romantic periods in music history are actually phases of the same style? What unifying name could be employed to identify that larger style period?

✛   In general, was the spread of democratic government and egalitarian thinking a positive or negative influence on quality in European music?

✛   Why was the writing of the biographies of composers largely a new interest beginning in the nineteenth century? The theory of the "biographical fallacy" suggests that works of art should be understandable in their own terms and not require knowledge of the artist's life. Is there a limit to this theory for nineteenth-century composers?

✤   How did developments in the field of literature affect music in the early nineteenth century?

Suggestions for Further Reading

The Romantic phase in music history in general is discussed in Friedrich Blume, *Classic and Romantic Music* (New York: Norton, 1970); Alfred Einstein, *Music in the Romantic Era* (New York: Norton, 1947); Gerald Abraham, *A Hundred Years of Music,* 4th ed. (London: Duckworth, 1974); Leon Plantinga, *Romantic Music* (New York: Norton, 1984). Aesthetic writings on early Romanticism can be found in Peter le Huray and James Day, eds., *Music and Aesthetics in the Eighteenth and Early Nineteenth Centuries* (Cambridge: Cambridge University Press, 1981).

For books on Beethoven, see the Suggestions for Further Reading for Chapter 18.

On Schubert, see Maurice J. E. Brown, *Schubert: A Critical Biography* (London: Macmillan, 1958); Otto Erich Deutsch, *Schubert: A Documentary Biography,* trans. Eric Blom (London: Dent, 1946); for more recent research, Maurice J. E. Brown and Eric Sams, *The New Grove Schubert* (New York: Norton, 1983). A survey of Schubert's Lieder is Richard Capell, *Schubert's Songs,* 3d ed. (London: Duckworth, 1973).

On nineteenth-century opera, see Edward J. Dent, *The Rise of Romantic Opera,* ed. Winton Dean (Cambridge: Cambridge University Press, 1976).

An excellent biography of Rossini is Herbert Weinstock, *Rossini: A Biography* (New York: Knopf, 1968).

On Weber, see John H. Warrack, *Carl Maria von Weber,* 2d ed. (Cambridge: Cambridge University Press, 1976).

Notes

1. Lord Byron, *The Poetical Works of Byron,* Cambridge ed. (Boston: Houghton Mifflin, 1975), 186.

2. Edmund Burke, *A Philosophical Enquiry into the Origins of Our Ideas of the Sublime and Beautiful,* ed. James T. Boulton (Oxford: Basil Blackwell, rev. ed. 1987), 57, 124.

20 THE MATURE ROMANTIC PERIOD

The Context for Mature Romanticism

By the late 1820s, with the deaths of Beethoven, Weber, and Schubert, the first phase of the Romantic period had come to an end. The essential tenets and procedures of Romantic expression based on the dramatic tonal language established in the eighteenth century were well established. It remained for the next generation, a group of composers who came to maturity between 1825 and 1850, to explore its possibilities.

The artistic bases for the Romantic musical style were at last clear and secure. Although the elements of musical style in the mid-nineteenth century had been inherited from the Classic period, by this time the courtly world of Haydn and Mozart seemed remote and old-fashioned; Beethoven was the model for much of the music of the Romantic movement. The new composers also had a substantial body of Romantic literary material on which to base their works; Goethe's vast oeuvre was substantially complete, for example.

The bourgeois revolution had settled down, so there was also a considerable degree of stability in the social and economic position of musical activity by this time. Such institutions as public concert series and opera houses had achieved a secure existence, and the commercial music-publishing industry was now thriving.

Composers' Life-Styles

The Romantic composers naturally had to adopt quite a different life-style from their Classic predecessors. Some managed to earn a living from composing, particularly the more prolific and popular opera com-

299

posers. More often, however, they found it necessary to obtain income from another source. Frequently they were players or conductors. Felix Mendelssohn Bartholdy (1809–1847) held the directorship of the Leipzig Gewandhaus orchestra, which he made into one of the premier ensembles in Europe. Virtuoso solo performers such as pianists Franz Liszt (1811–1886) and Frédéric Chopin (1810–1849) made money by playing. Each of these men was also involved in music teaching: Liszt began giving piano lessons while still a teenager and returned to teaching after abandoning his concert career; Chopin earned much of his living as a teacher; and Mendelssohn founded the Leipzig Conservatory. By contrast, the French composer Hector Berlioz (1803–1869), who had no significant performance skills, spent much of his life in the government-supported position of librarian for the Paris Conservatory.

In the Romantic period the biographies of composers take on an unusual degree of importance for their work. Not only does the subjective intention of the music make it helpful to know the details of the composers' personal experience, but also many of these works are implicitly or explicitly autobiographical. The operas of Giuseppe Verdi (1813–1901) must be understood in the light of his family life and his political views; Chopin's national heritage affected many of his works; Berlioz drew on his love life for inspiration; and Berlioz, Liszt, and Mendelssohn wrote works that reflected their travels. There is a degree of circularity here, too, for like Byron some of these composers enjoyed a romancelike life-style, deliberately cultivating their personae. As we shall see, the composers Liszt and Chopin in turn provided subjects for contemporary authors.

Composers' Literary and Artistic Activities

Writing about music was a very important activity for several of the major Romantic composers. Berlioz wrote music criticism for several Paris periodicals, the extremely important orchestration manual *Traité d'instrumentation* (1843), and his sometimes rather imaginative *Memoirs*. The German composer Robert Schumann (1810–1856) had contemplated becoming a poet before he decided on music. When his pianistic aspirations collapsed after he injured his hand, he turned not only to composing but also to journalism, founding in 1834 the *Neue Zeitschrift für Musik* (New music journal), which is still published after more than a century and a half.

The literary activities of Romantic musicians are significant for several reasons (besides their contribution to the income of the writers). It was a characteristic urge of Romantic artists to propagandize on behalf of their progressive movement. Schumann and Berlioz felt a mission to criticize the artificialities of old-fashioned, conventional Classicism and the banalities of trite and unimaginative popular compositions. Just as revolutionaries sought to change political and social institutions, and Victor Hugo had sought to change literature in his famous preface to his 1827 play *Cromwell,* these composer-critics wished to lead contemporary musicians and audiences into the new musical era. Embedded, not always particularly deeply, in their criticism is the ever-present Romantic manifesto that art and music should espouse values such as individualism, subjectivity, and progressivism.

The remarkable literary ability of these musicians also focuses attention on the Romantics' desire to draw the different arts together. Berlioz and Schumann wrote in a very lively style. Schumann, in particular, attempted a kind of poetic criticism that allowed him to write a literary work. Following the style of the early Romantic writer and composer E. T. A. Hoffmann, Schumann sometimes set a piece of music in a storylike context rather than describing it directly. Because people with poor artistic taste are commonly known as Philistines, after the enemies of Old Testament Israel, Schumann invented a mythical *Davidsbund* (League of David) that would combat them. Two of the fictional league's members, Eusebius and Florestan, represented respectively the sentimental and the aggressive aspects of Schumann's own Romantic personality; a Master Raro mediated between the two of them. Some of Schumann's characters were real, contemporary musicians, such as F. Meritis, a hardly disguised Felix Mendelssohn. Celia or Chiarina stood for Clara Wieck (1819–1896), daughter of Schumann's piano teacher and later Schumann's wife. Clara Wieck Schumann was a distinguished pianist and composer in her own right, who also managed the special difficulties in that time of combining a professional performing career with the obligations of a wife (widowed young) and mother. The fictional conversations of these *Davidsbündler* allowed Schumann to discuss music and to try to re-create in a literary form the spirit of the work under consideration. It is not, of course, a critical technique that can find favor in the twentieth century, but it clearly manifests the Romantic style and belief in the unity of the arts.

Mendelssohn's literary ability can be seen in the eloquence and wit of his immense correspondence, particularly with his very intellectual and artistic family. In addition he was a talented landscape artist with pencil, pen and ink, and watercolors, and he drew and painted many of the scenes of his extensive travels. Some pages of his compositional sketches are decorated by humorous caricatures.

Even when they did not create literary and artistic works, all the Romantic composers were avid and sensitive connoisseurs of the products of their contemporaries in other fields. They maintained intimate contact with artists and literary figures; they read voraciously; and they were constantly inspired by poetry, novels, and works of visual art. One cannot grasp the music of this period without a sense of the importance of these meetings of artistic minds.

Romantic Lyricism in Italian Opera

Romanticism slowly began to take hold in Italy after the first quarter of the nineteenth century. It manifested itself in literary terms by the appearance of new kinds of subject matter for librettos and in musical style by an increase in lyricism.

We can best understand the nature of the new type of Italian opera libretto if we think of it as novelistic. In earlier times the serious opera libretto had generally relied on ancient mythological or historical plots, but it now took up quite different subjects. Most often it adopted material from European history, commonly by borrowing from contemporary Romantic historical novels and dramas. The libretto of Gaetano Donizetti's (1797–1848) *Lucrezia Borgia* (1833), for example, came from a Victor Hugo play about the colorful Italian Renaissance duchess of Ferrara. The libretto of *Lucia di Lammermoor* (1835) came from Sir Walter Scott's 1819 novel of ill-fated love and violence in Scotland.

Lighter operas continued to take their characters and situations directly from contemporary life. Donizetti's opera buffa *Don Pasquale* (1843) is in the same vein as all the repertoire in its genre since the middle of the eighteenth century, including Rossini's *Il barbiere di Siviglia*, and his *L'elisir d'amore* (The elixir of love, 1832) takes place in a nineteenth-century country village. The semiserious love story set by Donizetti's contemporary Vincenzo Bellini (1801–1835) in his *La sonnambula* (1831) also unfolds in a modern Italian town. Of the two composers, Donizetti belongs more clearly to the traditional Italian type; he produced operas at a tremendous rate, on a variety of types of libretti, and with greatly varying quality. Bellini took a more characteristically Romantic approach; in his short career of ten years he composed just ten operas, all serious and all in an unusually polished style.

Style

Following the direction already anticipated by Rossini, Donizetti and especially Bellini wrote in a recognizably Romantic melodic and harmonic style but without making an abrupt break from their Classic past. The melodic writing can appropriately be described as more lyrical and vocal than Classic melody, which tended to adopt an instrumental style. Analysis of the vocal lines in Bellini's operas shows a pervasive tendency for the melody to proceed in a stepwise motion unlike the triadically based structures of the eighteenth century. There is considerable ornamentation of the linear contour, often producing a wide variety of beat divisions, so that the small-scale rhythm becomes quite flexible and naturally calls for considerable rubato in performance. From the point of view of expressiveness, this melodic style lends these operas an increased quality of intimate personal expression, even in passages of vocal virtuosic display.

On the phrase level, Bellini's and Donizetti's music mostly tends to be quite square and predictable. Symmetrically arranged two- and four-measure phrase lengths, expressing clearly directed tonal patterns of a few chords in slow harmonic rhythm, predominate. To give variety, however, Bellini in particular added altered and borrowed chords that catch the listener's ear easily in the generally simple diatonic context. Such harmonic shadings add to the general sense of Romantic subjectivity of expression.

The Italian Romantic opera composers developed a two-part structure for the large number or solo *scena ed aria*. After a free passage that mixes recitative and arioso-style singing, the first aria section is of a reflective nature and includes a slow, lyric movement sometimes known as a *cavatina*. This is often in two strophes and may be structurally closed or open-ended. A transitional passage leads to the fast and brilliant concluding movement known as *cabaletta*; it may be in binary form or have more than one strophe. The cabaletta expresses powerful emotion and becomes the climax to the scene. Such a forward-directed plan is obviously a much more dramatically conceived artistic shape than the now distant, rhetorical, eighteenth-century da capo aria, which the new scena structure supplanted.

The solo scena structure could incorporate interpolations for additional characters or chorus, and it could also be applied to a duet scene. In duets Donizetti took the lead in breaking away from an earlier tendency to make characters sing in parallel or to alternate stanzas; instead he had them express contrasting thoughts by contrasting melodic material, creating the "dissimilar duet."

Performance Practice

In the realm of performance practice, it is important to understand that the nineteenth-century opera singers enjoyed the opportunity in this repertoire to embellish the melodic lines and add improvisational cadenzas. The style is called *bel canto,* but of course it is quite the opposite of the seventeenth-century bel canto type. Rather than being simple and letting the fullness of the voice sound on each note, here the music aims to demonstrate vocal agility and technique. The composers assumed that this ornamentation would take place—the repetitions of sections in arias and the frequent cadential fermatas implicitly call for decoration—and for modern singers to sing none is inappropriate. Of course, these additions must be done in good taste, with the words and the dramatic context in mind, and within the limits of the performer's own skill. The best singers' voices of that time seem to have possessed more flexibility and less amplitude than came to be called for in later operas. Most opera houses were modest in size, pit orchestras were not very large, and the singers were able to perform from in front of the proscenium arch, so that sheer vocal power was not a major concern. (Fig. 20.1)

Giuseppe Verdi

The culmination of the Romantic Italian opera came in the works of Giuseppe Verdi. Verdi's career did not begin until 1836, after the retirement of Rossini and the death of Bellini. He built on the style of his predecessors and achieved still greater flexibility of harmony and phrase structure, which allowed him to express emotion more strongly. After Mozart, Verdi was the most effective opera composer in delineating character through musical means.

Verdi's selection and handling of librettos was the most careful of all the Italian opera composers. His librettos employed uniformly high quality literary sources, including works of the Romantic authors Victor Hugo, Byron, and Schiller, as well as the Romantics' beloved Shakespeare. Verdi also had an excellent sense of what succeeded on the stage, and he worked closely with his librettists, demanding all sorts of special adjustments. His operas are full of strong emotional situations, rapid action, and sharp contrasts. (He knew, too, that a liberal dose of violence and blood could be relied on to hold an audience's attention.) Even in his epic historical operas, there is a novelistic focus on the personal emotional lives of his characters.

The topics Verdi chose mirror some of the dominant events and forces in his life. He formed a close attachment to his patron, Antonio Barezzi, a wealthy merchant who became a father-figure to him. He married Barezzi's daughter, but within a few years his wife and both of their young children died, leaving deep emotional scars on the young composer. It is not surprising that, like Bellini, Verdi turned almost exclusively to tragic plots. Many of his operas explore in great depth the relationships between fathers and children.

Another topic of central importance among Verdi's operas is political liberty. Italy had long been not a unified nation-state but only a group of independent territories that were too weak to resist foreign control. Verdi came from the northern part of the peninsula, which was under Austrian domination. During the nineteenth century there grew up a nationalist movement known as the *Risorgimento* (resurgence), which hoped to cast off the oppressive foreign rule and establish Italy as a united country. Verdi supported this movement and expressed its ideals in several operas, especially *Nabucco* (1842), which was set in the biblical days of the Jewish exile in Babylon but which the audience recognized as resembling their own situation.

Nabucco was Verdi's first great success, and he followed it with other operas on political topics, heroism, and the overthrow of tyranny. Verdi naturally had continuously to deal with the Austrian censors, who feared the power

Figure 20.1
The interior of the Teatro alla Scala in Milan. This opera house was one of the most important of the nineteenth century. Many of the great Italian operas of Rossini, Donizetti, Bellini, and Verdi were introduced here. *(Alinari/Art Resource)*

of music and particularly of opera to arouse the public to revolt. Verdi even became a political symbol himself. Because the nationalists hoped to establish the King of Sardinia, Victor Emmanuel II, as King of Italy, they used Verdi's name as an acronym for "Vittorio Emmanuele, rè d'Italia" (Victor Emmanuel, king of Italy) and loved to flout the authorities by shouting "Viva Verdi!" at every performance of his operas. After unsuccessful uprisings in 1831 and 1848 the kingdom was finally established in 1861, and Verdi became a senator in the new government.

La Traviata (1853), the last opera of the first period of Verdi's career, is a striking example of the interaction between life and art in the Romantic experience. In 1847 Verdi encountered in Paris the singer Giuseppina Strepponi, who had been in the original cast of *Nabucco* but had abused her voice, accumulated several illegitimate children, and retired from singing to support herself by giving voice lessons. He lived with her in Paris, later took her away to his home in Italy, and finally married her. Only a few years earlier, the young French author Alexandre Dumas *fils* (1824–1895), son of the author of *The Three Musketeers,* had written the novel *La dame aux caméllias* (The lady with the camelias). Its plot was based on Dumas's experience with a well-known Parisian demimondaine, Marie Duplessis, who had left him for a wealthier life but died of tuberculosis soon thereafter at the age of twenty-three. The fictionalized story includes the theme of the young artist "rescuing" a fallen woman and the opposition of the young man's devoted father. Verdi, who must have seen Dumas's stage adaptation, selected this plot for *La Traviata.* The parallels with his own life, including his first wife's death and his relationships with Strepponi and with his father-in-law, Barezzi, are obvious. The musical work is related not only to the literary source in this case but also to two different real-life stories. It is not a question of direct autobiography here, of course, but Dumas's story offered Verdi an opportunity to explore a difficult love relationship, the complexities of family affection, and the tragic death of a young woman, matters with which his background made him especially sympathetic.

In his musical treatment of his material, Verdi used the devices of his predecessors but did not in any sense adopt them as molds into which to pour music. He carried the principle of the dissimilar duet beyond Donizetti's experiments, and he freely extended, abbreviated, or varied the standard scena structure. While his style is rooted in the "number" opera tradition, there are many cases where the divisions between numbers give way to the impulse toward dramatic continuity. Further organic connections sometimes arise in the music because of Verdi's employment of recurring melodic ideas in connection with certain dramatic elements or characters.

French Grand Opera

Opera in France developed somewhat differently from opera in Italy, though there was a degree of cross-influence between the two. Italian composers seem to have felt a greater urge to succeed in Paris than French composers did in Italy. As we have noted, Rossini went to Paris after his career was established in his native land, and Donizetti, Bellini, and later Verdi also composed works for Paris. The situation there called for some stylistic adjustments from each of them.

Parisian audiences tended to belong to the more vigorous elements of the Romantic movement. For them their composers developed the genre of *grand opera.* The term was originally intended as a way of distinguishing between the opéra comique, with its spoken dialogue, and opera that was sung throughout.

It also reflects the content and style of these works, however. Rather than concentrating on subtle expressions of personal feelings, grand opera presented striking experiences—the exotic, violent passions, and supernatural events. As a result, the librettos call for impressive and elaborate sets, costumes, and special stage effects. The librettist Eugène Scribe (1791–1861) developed the type. His librettos are long, occupying four or five acts, and they treat historical subjects of heroic or epic character with tragic outcomes.

The music of the grand opera matched the action. The Paris Opéra boasted the largest and most colorful opera orchestra in Europe. French opera also continued, as it had done historically, to exploit the use of the chorus on stage. The solo parts demanded both brilliance and power. Giacomo Meyerbeer (1791–1864), a German who had learned opera in Italy, brought the genre to its culmination with libretti provided by Scribe. Meyerbeer's *Robert le Diable* (1831) offered an operatic counterpart to the popular Gothic novel, while in *Les Huguenots* (1836) he handled a tragic love story set in the same turbulent period in French history that his contemporary Alexandre Dumas *père* (1802–1870) later dealt with in *The Three Musketeers*. *Robert le Diable* relied on maximum effect and minimum subtlety. *Les Huguenots* is much more sophisticated; in it Meyerbeer used dotted rhythms in minuet tempo to recall French Baroque music, and he wove in a cantus firmus treatment of the Lutheran chorale "Ein' feste Burg ist unser Gott" as a symbol for the Protestant faction.

The Cult of Virtuosity

We have already alluded to the importance of nineteenth-century virtuoso performers on the opera stage and in the concert hall. Among the most outstanding of the virtuoso soloists during the mature Romantic period was the violinist Nicolò Paganini (1782–1840), whose technical virtuosity and striking appearance combined with a sense of demonic possession in his playing to make him immensely effective on the stage. He must have seemed to his audience more a fictional character than a working musician.

Greatly influenced by Paganini's virtuosity when the violinist appeared in Paris in 1831, the young Hungarian pianist Franz Liszt determined to attain the same level of skill at the keyboard. After a period of intensive technical study Liszt reappeared as a recitalist and achieved his purpose. He toured throughout Europe in the 1830s and 1840s and won a fabulous reputation. His notoriety was not at all hindered by the fact that women found his tall, slender figure and gaunt good looks very attractive. A Romantic in his life as well as in his music, Liszt pursued liaisons with several women, including the

French countess Marie d'Agoult (who produced a novel about Liszt and three children by him) and the Russian princess Carolyne Sayn-Wittgenstein, both of whom left their husbands for the musician. (Fig. 20.2)

Liszt was the first musician regularly to perform recitals in which he appeared as the sole performer; until this time concerts had generally consisted of potpourri programs of various players in various genres. Liszt's repertoire included not only his own compositions but also transcriptions of other composers' works, including Beethoven's orchestral works, Schubert songs, and opera arias. He was famous for the "orchestral" sound he produced from the piano. His formidable piano technique allowed for large numbers of notes in chords played by the right hand. His speed and assurance in hand movement allowed coverage of the entire range of the keyboard, so that his music is sometimes written on three rather than the usual two staves. In addition, special effects arising from such devices as tremolos or rapidly repeated chords give the impression of increasing the available timbres of the instrument.

The musicologist Friedrich Blume has pointed out that virtuosity, in and of itself, is "antiromantic." In a sense, this is certainly true, for when virtuoso technique predominates over content in music, sincerity of emotional expression is sacrificed, and emotion is the essence of Romanticism. On the other hand, the position of the virtuoso performer in the nineteenth century constitutes another matter entirely. Such musicians as Paganini and Liszt became veritable cult figures. Because music is so effective and mysterious an art form, and because the virtuosos seemed to be able to accomplish superhuman feats in that medium, they found themselves regarded as mythical heroes or even priests of an artistic cult that could offer a transcendental experience to their audiences. Thus, while empty virtuosity contradicts Romanticism, the cult of the virtuoso actually represents a manifestation of Romanticism in nineteenth-century life.

There were plenty of empty and antiromantic virtuosos about, to be sure. In describing the musical situation as he observed it in the early 1830s, the composer-critic Robert Schumann wrote:

> . . . It cannot be said that the musical conditions in Germany at that time were particularly gratifying. On the stage Rossini still reigned; on the piano, almost exclusively Herz and Hünten. And yet only a few years had passed since Beethoven, C. M. v. Weber, and Franz Schubert lived among us.

The pianists Schumann singles out for scorn here, Franz Hünten (1793–1878) and Henri Herz (1803–1888), were representative of a type. They wrote and played mostly light rondos and arrangements and sets of variations on arias and popular songs. Their variations characteristically consist of mere series of decorative and mostly unoriginal formulas applied to a tune. The pieces they played showed off their technique rather than feeling or imagination; those they published and sold were simple versions for the self-entertainment of amateurs. At their best, they are still technically impressive today; more often

Figure 20.2

J. Danhauser, *Liszt and His Friends*. This Romantic painting shows a salon gathering in which Liszt plays for a group of notable artists, writers, and musicians. Standing, left to right, are Victor Hugo, Paganini, and Rossini; seated are Alexander Dumas, George Sand; and on the floor by the piano is the Countess Marie d'Agoult. Beethoven's pioneering Romantic spirit is represented by his bust on the piano. (*Staatliche Museen Preußischer Kulturbesitz, Nationalgalerie, Berlin (West)©Bildarchiv Preußischer Kulturbesitz, 1989. Photo: Jörg P. Anders, Berlin*)

they strike the modern listener as merely funny. Nevertheless, these composer-performers were immensely admired and financially successful. Herz's concert touring even brought him to the Western Hemisphere.

Lyricism and Virtuosity—Chopin

Schumann did discover a true musician among his pianistic contemporaries, however, in the person of Frédéric Chopin. Of French and Polish descent, Chopin began his career in Warsaw as a prodigy at the piano. In his late teens he traveled through Europe as a touring performer, arriving in Paris in 1831.

He settled in France and never returned to Poland. As a Romantic he naturally maintained patriotic feelings for his homeland, and he transfigured its native dances, the *mazurka* and *polonaise,* in stylized piano settings. His final public performance was a benefit for Polish refugees after the country had been taken over by Russia.

Chopin earned his living primarily by teaching and by the sale of his compositions, which he managed with considerable skill. Unlike many other virtuosos, Chopin preferred not to play in public. Instead he performed in the private Parisian salons where intellectuals and connoisseurs gathered to share ideas and artistic experiences. In this context one could meet the finest minds and talents of the time; among Chopin's acquaintances were such musicians as Liszt, Bellini, and Meyerbeer; the painter Delacroix, who created Chopin's famous portrait; the poet Heinrich Heine; and the novelist Honoré de Balzac. He pursued a stormy, novelistic love affair with the authoress George Sand (Aurore Dudevant), which she later described in a thinly fictionalized novel.

Chopin was a specialist, and the great majority of his works are for solo piano. (His other works include chamber music with piano, two concertos, a few other concert pieces with orchestra, and some songs.) He developed a lyrical style paralleling the operatic writing of Bellini, with similarly rather square phrasing made flexible by its ornamentation and rhythmic rubato. Chopin exercised much more harmonic freedom than Bellini, however, which allowed him remarkable liberty within the harmonic phrase directions of the tonal system. Compared to the pianism of Liszt, Chopin's is on the whole more fluid and less fiery, his lines more curvaceous, and his tone colors, aided by subtle pedalling technique, more shaded. At times, of course, it reaches its own moments of high drama.

What Schumann perceived on his first encounter with Chopin's music, the Variations for Piano and Orchestra on "La cì darem la mano" (the duet from Mozart's *Don Giovanni*), was the application of virtuoso technique to genuinely Romantic purpose. In these variations Schumann felt that Chopin had not merely decorated a tune but had interpreted the characters and emotional situations of the opera. Beethoven had brought the variation form into the Romantic spirit with his character-type variations, and Chopin, though he was somewhat sceptical of Beethoven's revolutionary musical tendencies, accomplished his own equivalent treatment of this still often vacuous form. This Romantic necessity for purely instrumental music to be imbued with emotional content characterizes all of Chopin's works.

Salons and Drawing Rooms

Much music was composed for domestic use throughout the Romantic period. In the case of Chopin, the composer intended his works primarily for his own performance in the elegant Parisian salons, where they would be heard by a well-educated and sophisticated audience. Such gatherings included conversation ranging over a variety of topics of current interest—the arts, philosophy, politics. The Parisian salons were imitated in many of the cities of Europe.

The middle class often experienced music at home in the parlor or drawing room, including chamber music, piano pieces, and songs. A great deal of the music written for this setting was flimsy in structure and superficial in content; it soon fulfilled its purpose—to entertain—and was set aside to yellow, turn brittle, and fall to dust. Some of the best composers, however, did not neglect this repertoire. Most of Mendelssohn's Lieder, for example, were accessible to the amateur performer and listener, but many of them have sufficient musical interest to have a legitimate place in song recitals today. Schumann's Lieder, which often employed outstanding poetry set to music of greater rhythmic and harmonic complexity, belong to the same genre as Mendelssohn's but are more challenging and interpret their texts with more sophistication. In America Stephen Collins Foster (1826–1864) wrote sentimental songs that have far less intrinsic musical interest; but their authentic simplicity has made them part of the folk literature of the United States.

It should be noted that in an era when women's lives were still generally expected to center in the home, the domestic environment provided the main musical outlet for women musicians. Certainly many talented women who could not find a professional outlet provided fine performances in middle-class drawing rooms. One noteworthy woman composer was Fanny Mendelssohn Hensel (1805–1847), Felix Mendelssohn's older sister. She matured as a musician in her mother's salon in Berlin, performed and directed music there, and composed piano pieces and fine songs, as well as larger instrumental and choral works. Felix respected Fanny as much as he did any musician, and he sought her musical criticism and advice throughout his life. Because of the family's perception of the social pressures that would fall on a woman composer, some of her songs were published under her brother's name. She was later able to release other works independently, but much of her music remains unpublished.

Instrumental Genres in Romantic Music

Piano Music

Such abstract genres as the sonata and symphony soon became obviously inadequate for instrumental music that evoked a high degree of subjective meaning. While these genres inherited from the Classic period continued, new ones grew up beside them that demonstrate the Romantic urge to stress emotional content over abstract form.

In the realm of piano music, the short, one-movement piece became very important. Because these pieces generally seem to express a particular character, the term *character piece* is often used to refer to them generically. The actual pieces may have any of a wide variety of titles, however. Beethoven and Schubert composed independent piano pieces, the expressive content of which they did not clearly specify; Beethoven employed the title "Bagatelle," while Schubert called his pieces "Impromptu" or "Moment musical." Chopin's character pieces include some whose names come from existing, abstract genres, such as preludes and etudes; these works are not merely explorations of keyboard figurations or exercises, however; each takes on a particular expressive style that seems to give it quite evident emotional content. Like many other composers, Chopin also wrote character pieces derived from dances, such as the mazurkas and polonaises already mentioned, and waltzes.

Another type of character piece was derived by imitation of vocal music. The Irish composer John Field (1782–1837), who worked in Russia, anticipated Chopin in creating a piano style that resembled the cavatina of Italian opera. He tried out the names "Pastoral" and "Romance" for his pieces but finally settled on "Nocturne," a title Chopin also adopted. Mendelssohn composed a number of piano pieces under the title "Lied" or, as they were published, "Lied ohne Worte" (Song without words). (These pieces often appear in print with specific titles that attempt to make their character more obvious, but Mendelssohn strongly objected to such verbal cues as merely confusing.) Chopin contributed to the repertoire of solo piano pieces with implied literary content in his ballades. Schumann often gave very specific titles to individual pieces, such as the famous "Träumerei" (Reverie, 1838), or even people's names, such as "Chopin" and "Paganini," which appear in the set *Carnaval* (i.e., a Mardi Gras masked ball, 1833–1835).

Orchestral Music

In the field of orchestral music, Mendelssohn was most responsible for the creation of a genre in which content was indicated by a title. In 1826 he established the genre of the *concert overture* with his Overture to *A Midsummer Night's Dream*, op. 21. Although he did not at the time intend the work as an instrumental introduction to a specific performance of Shakespeare's play, the operatic overture provided the best model for a one-movement orchestral composition with definite literary content. (Later he added a complete score of incidental music for an actual performance of the play.) The character portrayals are quite clear in the unusual thematic materials: The denizens of the fairy kingdom are evoked by the soft but rhythmically energetic "elfin-scherzo" style that was one of Mendelssohn's most original creations, while the buffoon Bottom in his ass's head inspired a melody with hee-hawing downward leaps. Mendelssohn followed the *Midsummer Night's Dream* Overture with other concert overtures based on literary works and on the inspiration of his travels. Other composers soon followed his lead. The concert overture normally takes the form of a sonata movement, often with a slow introduction. It thus does not attempt to outline a narrative sequence of events. Instead, its themes and styles capture the characters or qualities of its extramusical subject matter. The concert overture is therefore more appropriately thought of as "characteristic" than "programmatic" in intention.

A similar manner of thinking led to the *program symphony*. Beethoven's *Pastoral* Symphony had laid the groundwork for a multimovement orchestral work with explicit indications of emotional content. Beethoven referred to the symphony as a "sinfonia caracteristica," however, because, except for the arrival and passing of the thunderstorm in the fourth movement, the movements represent isolated "recollections of feelings rather than tone painting." Berlioz produced the greatest of all program symphonies in the *Symphonie fantastique: épisode de la vie d'un artiste* (1830), representing the love and death of a Romantic artist and partially inspired by autobiographical circumstances. This work is genuinely programmatic, in the sense that the movements are organized according to a narrative sequence of events and are connected by the recurrence in different guises of the musical motive of the woman who is the object of the protagonist's *idée fixe* (obsession). Few program symphonies have the overarching programmatic narrative of the *Symphonie fantastique*. Even Berlioz's own *Harold en Italie* (1834), a symphony for solo viola and orchestra originally written for Paganini, is actually episodic or characteristic, following the nature of Byron's *Childe Harold's Pilgrimage,* on which it is based. (See Plate 8)

The inspiration of Beethoven's Ninth Symphony engendered a number of large Romantic works for chorus and orchestra, though his successors naturally attempted such projects with a certain trepidation and attempted to deflect comparisons by somewhat different approaches and genre designations. Mendelssohn contributed two major works that he called "symphony-cantatas": the *Lobgesang* (Hymn of praise, also called Symphony No. 2, op. 52, 1840), consisting of three symphony movements and nine vocal numbers based on biblical texts; and *Die erste Walpurgisnacht,* op. 60 (1832–1833, rev. 1843), an orchestral overture and nine vocal movements on a dramatic ballad by Goethe, which Berlioz called "a masterpiece of Romanticism." Inspired by Shakespeare, Berlioz composed a "dramatic symphony," *Roméo et Juliette,* in 1839, which mixed choral and solo movements with orchestral ones.

Romantic Musical Style

As has already been indicated, the period of musical history from around the middle of the eighteenth century through the nineteenth century can be regarded as a single stylistic era with Classic and Romantic phases rather than as two entirely different periods. From a technical standpoint, both phases rely on the structuring of music at all levels by the principles of tonal harmony.

With regard to aesthetic premises, both share a concept of expression based on the shaping of events according to the literary model of drama. As has also been suggested several times in the foregoing discussion, the listener's perception of a musical statement as Romantic depends on an implicit set of expectations that the music will proceed according to Classic stylistic assumptions. With this in mind, we can identify some of the most important aspects of the Romantic treatment of the Classic-Romantic style.

Expansion of Sound Vocabulary

One of the obvious tendencies of nineteenth-century music was to expand the sound vocabulary inherited from the Classic composers. This includes exploitation of dynamic extremes and instrumental timbres. Beethoven's symphonies had already added wind instruments, bass drum, and cymbals to the orchestra. Naturally the most fruitful field for experiment was the opera pit, where dramatic necessity was often the mother of musical invention. Berlioz, who learned much from attending the opera in Paris, became the leading pioneer in this area. He called not only for extremes of loudness but also for remarkable new instrumental effects. Among his most famous passages are the last movement of the *Symphonie fantastique,* which features *col legno* playing by the strings, and the "Queen Mab" scherzo of *Roméo et Juliette,* which employs string and harp harmonics and antique cymbals. In such instances listeners who knew only the usual symphonic sound vocabulary would certainly find these unusual timbres striking and naturally sense them as indications of significant extramusical content. Berlioz himself recognized this effect in his extensive review of Rossini's *Guillaume Tell,* where he singled out for special praise the use of the triangle for "dramatic meaning" and pianissimo rolls on the timpani, in which he heard "one of those natural sounds whose cause remains unknown, one of those strange noises which attract our attention on a clear day in the deep forest and which redouble in us the feeling of silence and isolation."

The urge to find new sounds led to the invention of new instruments. One of the great inventors of wind instruments was Adolphe Sax (1814–1894) who patented the saxophone in 1846. Other new instruments—such as the ophicleide, a bass version of the keyed bugle, which had the folded-tube design of a bassoon and was called for in Mendelssohn's *Midsummer Night's Dream* Overture and other works—soon disappeared. Percussion instruments gradually increased in number and variety, a trend that has continued quite steadily through the twentieth century.

Romantic Harmony

The expressive effect to be attained by thwarting Classic harmonic expectations was well understood and marvelously exploited by the Romantics. Particularly effective in a musical style generally based on tonal directedness was the momentary use of nonfunctional harmonic progressions. At the opening of Mendelssohn's *Midsummer Night's Dream* Overture come the four chords I-V-iv-I, reversing the normal cadential progression and establishing the unreal atmosphere of the action of the play. A characteristic of Berlioz's writing is the construction of phrases that appear to follow the simple outline of motion between tonic and dominant but whose goals turn out to be quite distant harmonies.

Another way of exploiting the limits of tonal harmonic direction was that of Chopin, whose externally simple harmonic phrasing can pass through a rich mixture of chromatic harmonies along the way. To the ear tuned to straightforward tonal procedures this gives the effect of overloading the syntax, as if a poet were enriching a simple sentence with qualifying adjectives. The expressive result is one of supercharging the basic two- or four-measure phrase with emotion.

Form in Romantic Music

The Romantic composers also experimented with the possibilities of new interpretations of the dramatic form. Beethoven's *Eroica* had already indicated the direction. In the ideal sonata form of the Classic phase there is a substantial period of stability and resolution following the climactic return to the tonic. In Romantic dramatic shaping the climax is likely to be delayed as long as possible, and the time allotted to dénouement is minimal. Unusual and surprising things occur even in apparently traditional, absolute works, especially at the end. Mendelssohn's Symphony No. 3 in A minor, op. 56 (*Scottish*, 1842) ends with a coda that introduces a change of mode, tempo, and material, thus becoming almost a separate movement. Schumann, at the moment of the return to the tonic in the finale of his Symphony No. 2 in C (1845–1846), instead of recapitulating introduces a new theme. Not surprisingly, interpreters of such works were inclined to suggest programs for them, finding in them some kind of *plot archetype* (a term proposed by the musicologist Anthony Newcomb) that would be better understood as a Romantic literary shape than as a Classic symphonic design. Berlioz's programmatic and dramatic symphonies make their emotional contours explicit by this very technique.

A contribution of great importance in the Romantic musical style was the multimovement cycle. Cyclic unification of the disparate segments of a musical work stands as an abstract symbol of the Romantic thinkers' search for the unity in all things. It reflects the organic indivisibility of existence proposed by the early nineteenth-century German philosophers and soon to be realized in natural science by Darwin. Composers found that they could create this universal wholeness in a tangible microcosm, and they did so again and again.

In the opera there was always the overriding unifying presence of a plot.

This was increasingly reinforced by breaking down the distinction between set numbers and recitative so that the music would be continuous, and by using themes associated with recurring elements in the action. The leading opera composers moved in this direction in all the national opera styles. Notable examples can be found in Weber's *Der Freischütz* and Verdi's *La Traviata.* Other dramatic vocal works (even those that are not intended to be staged, such as Mendelssohn's *Die erste Walpurgisnacht),* follow similar procedures.

Song composers also seized on the idea of the cycle, as we have observed in the cases of Beethoven and Schubert. Schumann was Schubert's leading successor in the field of the Lied, and he also wrote several noteworthy song cycles. His exemplary *Dichterliebe* (Poet's love, 1840), based on texts by Heinrich Heine (1797–1856), is unified not only by the emotional progression of its texts but also by a tonal plan that proceeds in a well-directed circular fashion.

Schumann also used the cyclical principle in sets of character pieces for the piano. It was not unusual in the early nineteenth century for keyboard composers to create variation sets or sets of dances. Schumann adapted this procedure to incorporate sets of brief character pieces; one example is *Carnaval,* which is unified by a set of motives derived from the musical letters A, S (Es), C, H (in English A, E flat, C, B).

In large orchestral works cyclicity is established both by running the movements together (following the example of the third and fourth movements of Beethoven's Fifth Symphony) or by thematic references (following the example of the finale of Beethoven's Ninth Symphony). Berlioz's *Symphonie fantastique* is unified by the musical theme of the beloved, which he calls *idée fixe* because it represents the young artist's psychological fixation. He later used the term *idée fixe* again for the theme that represents the person of Harold in *Harold in Italy;* in that symphony Berlioz also imitates Beethoven's thematic recollections separated by orchestral recitative, from the Ninth Symphony. Mendelssohn's A-minor Symphony employs a slightly more subtle unifying thematic gesture, and in his well-known Violin Concerto in E minor, op. 64 (1844), the three movements proceed continuously. Schumann's Symphony No. 4 in D minor, op. 120 (1841, rev. 1851) has no pauses between movements; the material of the slow introduction recurs in the slow movement; the middle section of the slow movement (headed "Romance") returns in the trio of the Scherzo; and the finale is a virtual recapitulation of the first movement. All of this suggests that the work may be heard not as four movements but as a single large one.

Recognition of the Musical Heritage

It may be difficult for modern musicians to understand how little composers up to the nineteenth century concerned themselves with the music of their predecessors. Until around 1830 there seems to have been remarkably little interest in even the recent musical past. Schubert's music had hardly made an impression in his own lifetime, and to some musicians Beethoven seems to have appeared merely a radical of the uncomfortable revolutionary era. Haydn and Mozart belonged to the still-earlier, rejected age of frills and powdered wigs. Bach was mostly known only as a difficult composer of keyboard preludes and fugues that might be used for finger exercise, and Handel's oratorios were popular primarily in England. Baron van Swieten's attempt to spread the music of the Baroque masters to the Viennese had been generally restricted to a limited number of invited connoisseurs.

In Berlin, however, a group of musicians—the *Singakademie*, led by Karl Friedrich Zelter—knew Bach's music and sang it enthusiastically. In 1829 Zelter's most precocious pupil, Felix Mendelssohn, convinced his mentor to permit him to give a public performance of Bach's *St. Matthew Passion*. The event was a tremendous success. Bach's music came across as deeply impassioned, and a new interest in his works and in older music in general began to spread. Mendelssohn carried his propagandizing efforts on behalf of the music of earlier times to Leipzig, where his programs with the Gewandhaus Orchestra included "historical concerts," which reintroduced the world to Bach, Handel, Haydn, Mozart, Beethoven, and Schubert.

One result of this was that musicians began to unearth all the early musical works that were mouldering in libraries and private collections throughout Europe and to discover new musical experiences and new musical ideas. The publication of responsibly edited, complete collections of composers' works started in 1850 when, on the hundredth anniversary of his death, the works of Bach began to appear under the aegis of the *Bach-Gesellschaft* (Bach Society). Similar editions were set in motion for many other composers and for collections of assorted early music.

Another immensely important effect of this movement was the establishment of the idea of musical classics in the general sense. After the 1830s the realization that modern listeners might find delight or enlightenment in listening to works of a time (or, by extension, a culture) other than their own was generally accepted. This change in perspective altered and still controls our musical experience as listeners and performers.

The Midpoint of the Nineteenth Century

Students of music history have sometimes assumed that the nineteenth century comprises a unified whole that can be subsumed under the heading "Romantic." However, in the same way that it would be misleading to divide sharply Classic and Romantic phases in the history of music, it would be erroneous to think of the nineteenth century as one continuous development. In fact there is a significant break in musical thinking around the middle of the century.

The careers of most of the major Romantic composers came to an end or to a major point of articulation at about the same time. Mendelssohn died in 1847, Donizetti in 1848, and Chopin in 1849. Schumann was incarcerated in an asylum after an attempted suicide in 1853 and died in 1856. Verdi's opera style reached a culmination point in his three masterpieces *Rigoletto* (1851), *Il Trovatore* (1853), and *La Traviata* (1853), after which he took a new direction. We shall see that Liszt did the same even more deliberately and aggressively.

An extramusical signal for the end of the mature phase of Romanticism was the revolutionary year of 1848. Violent revolt swept across Europe. The continent was forced to realize that no satisfactory resolution had yet been reached to the problems that had brought about the French revolution sixty years earlier.

Questions for Reflection

✣   How did it happen that Romantic composers frequently seemed to have multiple talents and careers more often than composers of other periods?

✣   Why did Romanticism affect music in Italy more slowly than other countries?

✣   In what sense is the music usually thought of as "program music" genuinely programmatic rather than "characteristic"? How should the two types be defined to distinguish between them?

Suggestions for Further Reading

Collections of the writings of individual Romantic composers include Hector Berlioz, *The Memoirs of Hector Berlioz*, trans. and ed. David Cairns (New York: Norton, 1975), and Robert Schumann, *On Music and Musicians*, trans. Paul Rosenfeld, ed. Konrad Wolff (New York: Norton, 1969). For a study of Schumann's writings, see Leon Plantinga, *Schumann as Critic* (New Haven: Yale University Press, 1967). See also Oliver Strunk, *Source Readings in Music History* (New York: Norton, 1950).

The following biographies of Italian Romantic composers are recommended: Leslie Orrey, *Bellini* (London: Dent, 1969); Herbert Weinstock, *Vincenzo Bellini: His Life and Operas* (New York: Knopf, 1971) and *Donizetti and the World of Opera in Italy, Paris and Vienna in the First Half of the Nineteenth Century* (New York: Pantheon, 1964); Frank Walker, *The Man Verdi* (New

York: Knopf, 1962); and George Martin, *Verdi: His Music, Life, and Times* (New York: Dodd, Mead, 1963). Closer studies of Verdi are Julian Budden, *The Operas of Verdi*, 3 vols. (New York: Praeger, 1973–1982), and David Kimbell, *Verdi in the Age of Italian Romanticism* (Cambridge: Cambridge University Press, 1981).

On French grand opera, see William L. Crosten, *French Grand Opera: An Art and a Business* (New York: Da Capo, 1972); Karin Pendle, *Eugène Scribe and French Opera of the Nineteenth Century* (Ann Arbor, Mich.: UMI Research Press, 1979); and Jane F. Fulcher, *The Nation's Image: French Grand Opera as Politics and Politicized Art* (Cambridge: Cambridge University Press, 1987).

Some of the significant biographical studies of individual Romantic composers are Jacques Barzun, *Berlioz and the Romantic Century*, 3d ed. (New York: Columbia University Press, 1969) and Barzun's briefer *Berlioz and His Century* (Boston: Little Brown, 1969); Hugh MacDonald, *Berlioz* (London: Dent, 1982); D. Kern Holoman, *Berlioz* (Cambridge: Harvard University Press, 1989); Gerald Abraham, *Chopin's Musical Style*, 4th ed. (London: Oxford University Press, 1960); Arthur Hedley, *Chopin*, rev. M.J.E. Brown (London: Dent, 1974); Alan Walker, *Franz Liszt: The Virtuoso Years, 1811–1847* (New York: Knopf, 1983); Philip Radcliffe, *Mendelssohn*, rev. ed. (London: Dent, 1976); Joan Chissell, *Schumann*, rev. ed. (London: Dent, 1977); and Peter Ostwald, *Schumann: Music and Madness* (London: Gollancz, 1985).

William S. Newman, *The Sonata since Beethoven*, 2d ed. (New York: Norton, 1972) concludes Newman's monumental history of the sonata genre.

21 THE TWILIGHT OF ROMANTICISM

The New German School

The principles and the stylistic tendencies of mature Romantic music were carried even further by composers who took as their models the revolutionary directions indicated by Beethoven. These progressive composers constitute the so-called *New German School,* and they adopted as their slogan "the music of the future." The founders of the New German School were Liszt and Richard Wagner (1813–1883). Like the other nineteenth-century Romantics, they felt it necessary to write at length about their philosophical, artistic, and musical views.

In 1855 in the *Neue Zeitschrift für Musik* there appeared under Liszt's name a major essay in defense of program music as it was represented in Berlioz's *Harold en Italie.* In this essay the ideals of the progressive movement found their expression. Liszt sums up his guiding principle near the beginning of the article: "The artist can pursue beauty outside the academic rules without having to fear that he will fail as a result." This statement amounts to an assertion that reliance on convention is no longer essential in music. Indeed, in a passage that echoes Hegel's metaphysics, he argues that the old must necessarily yield to the new:

. . . Art, which arises from mankind as mankind evidently arises from Nature—which, as mankind is nature's masterpiece, will, as mankind's masterpiece, be endowed with ideas and feeling—art cannot escape the necessary evolution that inheres in all that Time begets. Its life principle, conforming to that of mankind, like the life principle of Nature, only continues to occupy a certain period in the same forms, and it goes from one to another in eternal process of change and drives mankind to create new ones at the same rate that they give up those that have decayed and become obsolete.

321

Liszt went on to say that the direction of musical development is toward more explicit emotional content and that the artist

> must demand emotional content from the formal container. Only when filled with the former does the latter have significance for him.

Therein lies the defense of programmatic music, for

> if music is not on the way to deterioration, . . . then it seems apparent to us that the programmatic symphony is destined to gain a firm foothold in the current period of art.

Moreover Berlioz is vindicated against the conservatives who would reject his music:

> . . . unusual handling of form is not the most unforgivable failure for which they reproach Berlioz; indeed, they will perhaps grant that he has done art a service in discovering new turns of phrase. But this they will never forgive: that *for him form has an importance that is secondary to idea,* that he does not, as they do, preserve form for the sake of form; they will never forgive him for being a thinker and a poet.

Naturally, Liszt himself put these principles into practice in his later works. In 1848 he retired from concert touring and settled in Weimar, where he turned his attention to large orchestral works. These included two programmatic symphonies in the genre established by Berlioz: the *Faust* Symphony (1854–1857), three movements portraying the leading characters in Goethe's work and concluding with the addition of voices to the orchestra; and the *Dante* Symphony (1855–1856), based on the *Divine Comedy.* Equally important are the *symphonic poems,* a designation invented by Liszt for single-movement orchestral works with specified programmatic content. Unlike those of concert overtures, the forms of Liszt's symphonic poems tend to depart from the convention of the sonata form. Though roots in the sonata form can be discovered in some of his works, in others the form is merely vestigial, making analysis of the works' forms as sonata forms more frustrating than helpful. The structure in the freest pieces can best be explained by reference to the events and shape indicated by the program; this is to say, they are works whose material is symphonic and whose structure is not that of an abstract musical form but of the program. While a program symphony remains a musical structure with literary content, the adjective *symphonic* and the noun *poem* suit this new genre precisely; the works amount to poems expressed in tones rather than words.

It should be emphasized here that the literary program did not necessarily precede the musical composition. In fact, in Liszt's best-known symphonic poem, *Les Préludes,* the music definitely came first. The program, a reflection on the fact that life, with its joys and its strife, is only a prelude to the great mystery of death, was adapted from one of the poetic meditations of the French Romantic author Alphonse Lamartine (1790–1869), which Liszt thought suitably expressed the poetic form and content of the piece.

The musical style that results from the insistence in the New German School that emotional content supersedes abstract form extends the principles that governed Romantic style. Naturally the palette of orchestral color should grow without apparent restraint. More significantly, harmonic style can become freer and more chromatic. In some of his latest works Liszt indulged in such extreme harmonic experiments that he practically abandoned tonality altogether. In regard to form every work strives for a unique structure. These forms tend to be based on continuous juxtaposition and interplay of motives, which Liszt called "thematic transformation," in predominantly unstable tonal contexts. In other words, the style of symphonic development found in the sonata-form movements of the preceding generations now becomes the process that rules the entire design. In the true Romantic fashion that was established in Beethoven's *Eroica,* the music moves from each climax to a higher one, with the final climax delayed as long as possible.

The Artwork of the Future

Liszt's friend and later son-in-law Richard Wagner carried the banner of the New German School into the theater. Wagner had a strong literary background, but he decided on a musical career, becoming an opera chorus master and later conductor. Despite his concentration on theatrical music, his musical idol was Beethoven. He began to compose operas in the 1830s, experimenting with Weber's Romanticism, Italian lyricism, and the French grand opera style. In the 1840s, while working in Dresden as the theater music director, Wagner found a mature German Romantic opera style in three works, *Der fliegende Holländer* (The flying Dutchman, 1843), *Tannhäuser* (1842–1844), and *Lohengrin* (1846–1848). In 1848 Wagner, like many artists of the time, became involved in the political uprisings that swept through Europe, and his revolutionary activities made him *persona non grata* in Germany. He went into exile in Switzerland.

For a few years Wagner did not compose but immersed himself in literary efforts. He produced several important treatises. *Das Kunstwerk der Zukunft* (The artwork of the future, 1850) took up the philosophical ideas of the New German School. He began by insisting that art arises from nature and that artifice and convention have no place in it:

> . . . art will not be what it can be and should be, until it is or can be the accurate, clearly conscious embodiment of actual humankind and of the

true, naturally necessary life of humankind—until, therefore, it must no longer borrow the conditions of its existence from the errors, perversities, and unnatural distortions of our modern life.

Then he argued that the art of the future ought to express the essence of the people or *Volk* (folk) from which it comes:

> The individual spirit, striving artistically after its salvation in Nature, cannot create the artwork of the future; only the collective spirit, fulfilled by Life, may do so. . . .
>
> The work of art is religion represented in living form; but religions are arrived at not by the artist—they arise only from the *folk*.

The artwork of the future, he adds, must be collective not only in embodying the character and aspirations of a folk but also in uniting different means of expression: gesture, speech, and music. For Wagner the history of music reached an important climax in the symphonies of Beethoven, particularly the Ninth, where music and speech combine. Beethoven, like a musical Columbus, discovered an entirely new world:

> . . . he plunged once more into that endless sea. . . . he *knew* the goal of the journey, and he was resolved to reach it. . . .
>
> The master thus passed through the most unheard-of possibilities of absolute tonal language—not that he quickly slipped by them, but rather that he expressed them completely, in the most forceful terms, out of the deepest fullness of his heart—until that point where the sailor begins to measure the sea's depth with his lead; . . . . Resolutely he threw the anchor out, and this anchor was the *Word*. . . .

Beyond Beethoven's Ninth Symphony comes the artwork of the future:

> Beethoven's *last symphony* is the salvation of music out of its own element to become *unified art*. It is the *human* gospel of the art of the future. Beyond it no *progress* is possible, for only the completed artwork of the future can follow immediately upon it, *the unified drama*, the artistic key to which Beethoven has forged for us.

The summation of Wagner's theories is already suggested here. The new artwork must be a *Gesamtkunstwerk* (universal artwork or collective artwork) that represents the collective experience of the culture from which it proceeds and also synthesizes into one entity gestural, verbal, and musical types of expression.

> The artistic person can only be completely satisfied in the unification of all types of art into the *collective* artwork. . . .
>
> Art's *true* striving is therefore the *all-embracing*: Everyone who is inspired by the true *artistic impulse* wishes to achieve, by means of the fullest

development of his special talent, not the exaltation of *this special talent,* but the exaltation *of humankind in general in art.*

The highest collective artwork is the *drama;* it can only be present in its *greatest possible completeness* when *each type of art in its greatest completeness,* is present in it.

Wagner's universal drama would have nothing to do with opera, however. As he proceeded to explain in *Oper und Drama* (Opera and drama, 1851), existing operatic styles amounted only to an aberration. Wagner associated himself with Gluck, agreeing that music's proper function was to serve drama. Mozart he regarded as a fine composer whose libretti had simply been too trivial to produce really great results. To Wagner the opera of the first half of the nineteenth century failed because of its inherently commercial nature. It aimed at pleasing the public—ironically the exact opposite of expressing the character of the noble *Volk.* The Italian opera, with its virtuosic arias, consisted of mere artificiality, which prevented any honest expression; and the drama served merely as an excuse for singing. French grand opera relied on effect rather than sincerity.

What was called for, Wagner proclaimed, was a reversal of the roles of music and drama. He proposed to effect this reversal in the artwork of the future, the Gesamtkunstwerk, which he would call not opera but *music drama.* The term is significant, and its parallelism to the term *symphonic poem* must be noted. As in that case, the noun derives from the literary model, the adjective denotes the use of tones as material. The structure of the music drama, therefore, is that of the drama, dictated by the artistic content. Music serves as a means to carry out the dramatic purpose.

Wagner's Music Dramas

At the same time that he was formulating his theories, Wagner began on a text that he would compose according to his new principles. Between 1848 and 1852, and with several false starts, he created a massive libretto entitled *Der Ring des Nibelungen* (The ring of the Nibelung) for an imposing cycle of four music dramas. The characters and action he borrowed from Norse mythology, but the libretto is also political; its ideological content concerns the destructive force of the lust for wealth and power. It took him over two decades to compose the four works in the *Ring* cycle: *Das Rheingold, Die Walküre, Siegfried,* and *Die Götterdämmerung.* The first complete performance did not take place until 1876. In the meantime, Wagner had returned to Germany under the protection of King Ludwig II of Bavaria, who had a special theater, the *Festspielhaus* (festival playhouse), constructed in the town of Bayreuth just for Wagner's music dramas.

Also during these years Wagner took a break from the composition of the *Ring* to create a pair of works, one tragedy and one comedy. The tragic love story *Tristan und Isolde* (1856–1859) deals with the problem of the conflict between Will and Idea explored by the philosopher Arthur Schopenhauer (1788–1860). The comedy, *Die Meistersinger von Nürnberg* (The Meistersingers of Nürnberg, 1862–1867), has to do with the struggle of the radical progressive artist against the closed-mindedness of the conservative artistic establishment. Wagner clearly found the subject directly applicable to his own career.

At the end of his life Wagner produced a last music drama in which he attempted to show the solution to the pessimistic dénouements of his earlier works. In *Parsifal* (1877–1882) he demonstrated that escape from the tragic human situation comes through the redemptive power of love, an idea suggested but not brought to fulfillment in a number of his earlier works.

Wagner's Librettos

Wagner's librettos are worth considering from the point of view of literary analysis. As we have noticed, their underlying content deals with substantial philosophical issues, whether psychological, political, or artistic. These are couched in subject matter derived from the Germanic tradition, including mythology, as in the case of the *Ring;* folk epics, as in the stories of Tristan and Isolde or Parsifal and the Grail; or history, as in the case of *Die Meistersinger*.

The poetic style of Wagner's texts also derives from old German poetic technique. Instead of using meter and rhyme, the familiar devices of English poetry, he employed the technique of *Stabreim* (stem-rhyme). The basis of Stabreim is the use of alliteration between the strong word roots or syllables. Thus we find passages such as the following, from the closing scene of *Die Götterdämmerung* (Fig. 21.1):

BRÜNNHILDE:

Verfluchter Reif!   Accursed richness!
furchtbarer Ring!   fearful ring!
dein Gold fass' ich,   I grasp your gold
und geb' es nun fort.   and now give it up.
Das Wassertiefe   Wise sisters
weise Schwestern,   of the watery depth,
des Rheines schwimmende Töchter   swimming daughters of the Rhine,
euch dank' ich redlichen Rat!   I thank you for your just counsel!
Was ihr begehrt   What you desire
ich geb' es euch: I give it to you:
aus meiner Asche   out of my ashes
nehmt es zu eigen.   take it for your own.

Figure 21.1
The final scene from Wagner's *Die Götterdämmerung*. Brünnhilde rides her horse onto the flaming funeral pyre of her beloved Siegfried, before the conflagration spreads to consume the evil world. *(The Bettmann Archive)*

Das Feuer, das mich verbrennt,	Let the fire that burns me
rein'ge vom Fluche den Ring;	purify the ring of the curse;
ihr in der Flut	you in the flood,
löset ihn auf,	dissolve it away
und lauter bewahrt	and always defend
das lichte Gold,	the gleaming gold
das euch zum Unheil geraubt.	so fatefully stolen from you.

The lines vary considerably in length, but each contains either two or three strong syllables, with a flexible number and placement of weaker ones. This produces a poetic diction that diverges sharply from the four-square structure we are more accustomed to, and it naturally finds an equivalent freedom and flexibility in the phrase structure of the music.

Wagner's Musical Style

In his music Wagner adopted a style that he developed not by altering the conventions of opera but by appropriating the instrumental procedures of the symphonic poem. The dramatic content is worked out in the orchestra, and the words and action on the stage function very like the program in a symphonic poem to elucidate the workings of the symphonic score. The importance of the orchestra led Wagner to create new scorings and even new instruments. In particular, he wished to achieve a full orchestral sound in any instrumental timbre, and thus had to multiply the winds. In the case of the brass family, he even devised a fuller horn scoring by designing an additional lower-pitched instrument commonly known as the "Wagner tuba."

Wagner's vocal style is far from the style of the opera of his contemporaries. It is almost exclusively syllabic, for one thing, declaiming the words with careful regard for the value of the syllables and inflection of the phrase. There is no place for vocal display; given the weight and richness of Wagner's orchestra, the singers must spend their effort on balance in the overall sound, in any case.

The harmonic syntax of Wagner's advanced works presses the tonal system to its limit. Often the harmonies are not governed by functional root movement but are the by-product of linear motion, which leads to free chromatic successions of harmonies. This results in a degree of tonal tension that, from the perspective of the listener whose general harmonic expectations remain those of the Classic-Romantic tonal framework, makes the music expressively supercharged. Wagner took special advantage of this in *Tristan und Isolde;* the free chromaticism and the refusal of the music to cadence evokes intense feelings of musical desire and frustration that parallel the sexual element of the action. Wagner did not abandon the central Classic-Romantic concept of long-range tonal planning to shape and unify a work, however. Despite the immediate harmonic instability of much of the music, clear tonal centers are established, departed from, and reestablished over the course of a music drama. The contrasts between the large key areas create differing levels of intensity by the same principle, though not following the same conventional details of structure, as in Classic form. Between the stage action and the keys certain consistent relationships are also set up whereby, for example, in the *Ring* dramas the key of E flat is associated with the river Rhine and D flat with Valhalla, the home of the gods. Thus the plot and the musical construction simultaneously trace a single dramatic contour.

As in the Lisztian symphonic poem, the processes of musical form in the music dramas are symphonic in the sense that they are derived from the manner of a symphonic development. The ideas form a highly integrated, weblike network rather than the sharply articulated sections of the Classic sonata form or the traditional opera. The musical material thus avoids much that defined form in the preceding period, such as four-square phrasing, clear cadential formulas, and "filler" passages for transitions and closings. Wagner described the resulting continuous flow of the entire musical line as *unendliche Melodie* (endless melody).

Unity and contrast come from the statement, juxtaposition, and developmental use of important motives. Such a musical element is commonly known as a *Leitmotiv* (leading motive). Wagner himself did not use the word *Leitmotiv*; instead he used the term *Grundthemen* (basic themes) for these musical units. In *Oper und Drama*, he described their use as resembling that in a symphonic development, where they would be intertwined, juxtaposed, developed, and combined. Rather than appearing as vocal melodies the Leitmotivs occur mostly in the orchestra. In many cases they are associated with characters, objects, or ideas in the text or on the stage; consequently they are not simply musical motives but also part of the dramatic material of the work. The idea of such associative themes was not original with Wagner—Weber provided the most direct model—but the root of Wagner's style in symphonic genres may have had as much to do with this aspect of his style as any operatic forerunner. His use of these motives was certainly far more thorough and vastly more complex than that of any of his predecessors. They cannot be explained simply as mechanical musical reflections of what is being sung or acted at the moment. Their occurrence in the absence of explicit references to the usual objects of their association permits the interpretation of the orchestral score as a deeper subtext for the direct statements in the libretto. Their interplay and transformation produces a network of relationships perceived in the hearing but too complex to be translated easily into language.

In Wagner's musical thought and composition, the principles of relation between theme and tonality in Classic-Romantic musical structure were stretched to the limit. The dramatic process in form had reached a climax of complexity. Composers following Wagner were faced with a variety of difficult alternatives: to find new things to say within the more stable language of Romantic form and expression; to try to press on further within the New German style; or to seek out new styles or models for musical art.

Late Romanticism

Austria

Many musicians in the second half of the nineteenth century disagreed with the New German School's challenge to the Classic-Romantic musical syntax. Indeed, some saw Wagner as abandoning essential musical truths. There were more conservative composers in many places, but composers who continued to explore the possibilities opened up by the Romantics clustered in Vienna, the center of the Classic tradition and home of Beethoven and Schubert; France, where a classicistic turn of mind had always had importance; and Italy, where the appeal to public taste in the opera house exercised some restraining force.

A leader among the anti-Wagnerians was the Viennese jurist and music critic Eduard Hanslick (1825–1904). In his aesthetic treatise *Vom musikalisch Schönen* (On the musically beautiful, 1854) he defined musical content as *tönend bewegte Formen* (tonally animated forms), and he attacked the idea that music could have any other content than that embodied in its own sound and structure.

The conservatives soon set up Johannes Brahms (1833–1897) as a model. Brahms was a north German who was trained in the compositional tradition of Mendelssohn and Schumann, but in the 1860s he made his permanent residence in Vienna, the city of Beethoven and Schubert. In his four symphonies, his concertos, and his chamber music, Brahms seemed to take up the course of musical development from Beethoven. He employed the Classic four-movement sonata plan, with interconnections among movements that do not approach the frequency and explicitness of those in Schumann's D-minor Symphony. His forms, including frequent use of the sonata form, can clearly be traced to the standard patterns of the Classic era. His music does not call for unusual instruments or performance techniques, though he had a highly personal style of scoring that was especially dense and rich. His harmonic language exploits the possibilities of the tonal system without offering any threat to it.

Brahms was a consummate craftsman in handling problems of musical structure. This is especially evident in his masterful use of counterpoint. He applied himself to rigorous study of contrapuntal technique, assisted by the editions of the works of Baroque composers that began to appear during his lifetime. He was a subscriber, for example, to the complete edition of Bach's works published by the *Bach-Gesellschaft*. He kept a collection of examples of parallel fifths and octaves in music. His own works contain many fugal and canonic passages, and he wrote a number of independent canons. In the finale of his Symphony No. 4 in E minor (1884–1885) Brahms wrote one of the greatest chaconnes in the history of music.

Brahms's pursuit of traditional genres of absolute music and his mastery of the intellectual problems of compositional technique should not be allowed to obscure his Romanticism, however. In piano character pieces and Lieder he continued in his own personal direction from the end of Schumann's and Mendelssohn's path. His large choral works, especially the deeply felt and moving treatment of death in *Ein deutsches Requiem* (A German Requiem, 1868), show him to have been as sensitive to Romantic concerns and extramusical content as any composer. In short, Brahms must be regarded as a late Romantic, whose music demonstrates that the Classic-Romantic style was not entirely exhausted after the middle of the century.

Brahms's treatment of rhythm possesses special interest. Taking up hints from Schumann, he frequently used hemiola, in which triple rhythmic beat groupings shift from one metrical level to another. With Brahms such shifts came to be more than momentary effects; they became structurally significant, making the rhythm in his works of greater importance as a determinant of structure than in any music since the fifteenth century.

Another late Romantic working in Austria was Anton Bruckner (1824–1896). Bruckner was a Catholic composer of sacred music who combined the great Roman Catholic tradition of choral writing with a rich and Romantic harmonic vocabulary. His symphonies are also important. They are expansive works with a grandeur that leads to stately sectionalism and a slow pace. They follow the direction of Schubert's late symphonies as Brahms's followed Beethoven's. Bruckner's themes are more lyrically than motivically conceived and consequently produce a rather slow-moving rate of development. By contrast to the works of the composers of the New German School, the emotionalism of Bruckner's symphonies seems perhaps deeper and certainly less demonstrative.

France

In France the late Romantic movement was manifested partly in the operatic genre known as *lyric opera,* of which the best example is the interpretation of Goethe's *Faust* (1859) by Charles Gounod (1818–1893). Lyric opera backed away from the spectacular hugeness of the grand opera and concentrated on the expression of personal feeling, mainly through an emphasis on the voice and the melody. The plots naturally focus on the characters and their subjective experience rather than treating serious philosophical or political matters. Consequently, Gounod's *Faust* is a love story rather than an exploration of the larger topics in Goethe's drama such as the demonic nature of genius or the crisis and resolution of the human condition. (Fig. 21.2)

In other vocal genres the French had something significant to offer as well. They produced some fine Romantic religious choral music, which, though it generally seems a bit oversweet in the twentieth century, was meant sincerely. Equally important, the French began in the second half of the century to understand the potential that the German composers had found in the song. They called their works in this genre *mélodies,* to distinguish them from the popular *chanson.* The composers at the end of the century were fortunate in having a significant burst of original activity in lyric poetry in their native language. Unlike the German Lied, the mélodie does not stem from a folk music tradition but from a native French Romantic gift for elegant, lyric melody.

The realm of absolute instrumental music also produced some late Romantic manifestations in France. The chamber music and the Symphony in D (1888) of César Franck (1822–1890) show that there might still be new things

Figure 21.2
The Opéra in Paris (1861–1874) designed by Charles Garnier (1825–1898). This lavish monument of the Second Empire in France was the site of many of the great operas of the late Romantic style. (*Giraudon/Art Resource*)

for a nineteenth-century Frenchman to say in a musical language that disregarded Berlioz and did not depend on unusual effects of orchestration and harmony or depart from conventional structures into original, programmatic ones.

Italy

In Italy we still have to deal mainly with opera. In the 1850s Verdi came more under the influence of the Parisian grand opera style, beginning with *Les Vêpres siciliennes* (The Sicilian Vespers, 1855), on a libretto by Eugène Scribe, and culminating with *Aida* (1871), written for performance in Cairo at the celebration of the opening of the Suez Canal and uniting political conflict, romance, and grand opera pageantry.

After *Aida* Verdi retired from composing operas for fifteen years. In 1874 he completed his massive *Requiem,* which used music originally intended for a collaborative work of several composers to commemorate Rossini but was eventually composed throughout by Verdi and dedicated to the memory of his friend, the Romantic novelist and political activist Alessandro Manzoni

(1785–1873). Full of operatic dramatic effects, the *Requiem* is more a Romantic expression of the fascination and awesomeness of death than a true sacred work. It seems more at home in the concert hall than in the church; indeed, its first two performances took place three days apart in the church of San Marco and the opera theater of La Scala in Milan.

In 1886 Verdi bowed to considerable pressure and reentered the field of opera with the first of two late works, both on subjects taken from Shakespeare. The librettos were by the younger composer Arrigo Boito (1842–1918), and the collaboration of Verdi and Boito constitutes one of the great composer-librettist relationships in the history of opera. Their first product was *Otello,* a Romantic interpretation of Shakespeare's tragedy *Othello* and a masterful character study of the protagonist. In *Otello* there is more symphonic scoring for the orchestra and greater musical continuity than in Verdi's earlier works, which may reflect the influence of Wagner, but it never overwhelms Verdi's Italianate emphasis on singing. Boito and Verdi worked together again on *Falstaff* (1893), adapted from *The Merry Wives of Windsor. Falstaff* must be considered one of the greatest Romantic operatic comedies. In this final work, his second and only successful comedy, Verdi brought back to the opera stage a complexity of ensemble writing and a sense of comic timing not heard since Mozart.

The Second Generation of the New German Style

Liszt and Wagner had plenty of followers, composers who took up the stylistic trend toward harmonic and structural freedom and faith in the guidance of extramusical content. Since we have called Brahms, Bruckner, and Franck late Romantic composers, we may distinguish these composers as post-Romantic.

Wolf and Mahler

Among the post-Romantic group two outstanding examples, exact contemporaries, matured in Austria under the shadow of Brahms and Bruckner. Hugo Wolf (1860–1903) made his mark primarily in the field of the song. In the German nineteenth-century tradition of highly literary musicians, Wolf worked as a critic. He approached poetry with intense concentration, and his songs are the artistic product of his study. He devoted himself to single poets, one at a time, producing collections of settings on texts by Eduard Mörike (1804–1875), Joseph von Eichendorff (1788–1857), and Goethe, as well as translations of Spanish and Italian texts. He presented his pieces not as songs by Hugo Wolf, but as poems by the writer, set to music by Hugo Wolf. Wolf's songs do not belong to the folk-based strophic Lied tradition, but seem more like Wagnerian music concentrated into miniature form. Wolf's harmony is often highly chromatic, his forms are free, and the piano parts are more expressive of the content than the declamatory vocal lines.

Gustav Mahler (1860–1911) represents another progressive approach. Mahler wrote songs, but unlike Wolf's they genuinely and even determinedly belong to the folk song genre. He was deeply interested in German folk poetry as well as folk musical style. Mahler worked as a conductor, including very prominent positions at the Vienna Hofoper (Court opera, 1891–1897) and the Metropolitan Opera in New York (1907–1911).

Unlike Wolf, Mahler composed important large-scale works. There are several song cycles that effectively combine the Lied tradition with symphonic scoring. The *Kindertotenlieder* (Songs on the death of children, 1901–1904) are a tender reflection on the ubiquitous Romantic topic of death, while *Das Lied von der Erde* (The song of the earth, 1907–1908) reflects the Romantic inclination to propose a philosophical world view. Mahler also composed nine symphonies (leaving a tenth unfinished) on a very large scale and with cyclical unity. The symphonies call for enormous orchestras, but often the instruments are used sparingly in chamberlike ensembles with clear and sometimes unusual timbre combinations. The Second, Third, Fourth, and Eighth symphonies include solo singers, and the Second, Third, and Eighth also require choruses. As this implies, Mahler's symphonies are largely directed by extramusical content, and this is true even when there is no actual text sung.

The extramusical content in some of Mahler's symphonies is specified by the use of melodic material borrowed from Mahler's own songs, including the orchestral song cycles *Lieder eines fahrenden Gesellen* (Songs of a wayfarer; 1883–1885, rev. 1891–1896) for the Symphony No. 1 in D (1888, rev. 1893–1896), and *Des Knaben Wunderhorn* (The boy's magic horn, 1892–1898) for the Second, Third, and Fourth symphonies. Another way Mahler achieves the sense of extramusical content is by using styles that have particular associations, rather in the manner of the eighteenth-century use of specific musical types for their expressive value; the symphonies contain passages in the styles of the Austrian popular dance called the Ländler, the march, the chorale, and, of course, the folk song.

Richard Strauss

The genre of the symphonic poem founded by Liszt was not taken up by Wolf and Mahler, but it led to the *tone poems* of the German composer Richard Strauss (1864–1949) in the 1880s and 1890s. In Strauss's tone poems the orchestra is very large and colorful, and the musical style is harmonically and structurally free and dominated by content. There are two different types of programs among Strauss's tone poems. One type is narrative, as in the popular

Till Eulenspiegels lustige Streiche (Till Eulenspiegel's merry pranks, 1895), which quite naturally adopts a flexible rondolike structure to follow a series of scenes centered around a single character, or in *Don Quixote* (1897), which was designed for somewhat the same purpose as a set of variations. The other type is more abstract and is best represented by *Tod und Verklärung* (Death and transfiguration, 1889), which employs a free treatment of sonata form.

Alexander Scriabin

A highly independent and progressive musical thinker who should be considered a member of the post-Romantic movement was the Russian pianist Alexander Scriabin (1872–1915). As a pianist, Scriabin naturally came under the influence of Chopin and Liszt. A mystical visionary and something of an eccentric, Scriabin developed original aesthetic and harmonic theories. He believed in synaesthetic experience and proposed multimedia artworks that would appeal simultaneously to the various senses; for his symphonic poem *Prometheus* (1910) he wanted to have a colored light show coordinated with the music. In the field of harmony he experimented with nontriadic chords, particularly his "mystic chord," built of a series of perfect, diminished, and augmented fourths.

Realism in Late Nineteenth-Century Opera

In the first half of the nineteenth century the Romantic movement in literature had already begun to give way to a more pessimistic view of the world. The Romantics had seen the collapse of their grand hopes that the inequities and injustices of society could be righted. A new group of authors began to explore the seamier side of life and to portray the destructive and violent aspects of the human condition. They took their topics from the life of the oppressed classes and depicted their characters as conditioned by situations that led them to unhappy ends they were powerless to escape. This movement is known as *realism*.

Realism also began to appear in opera in the late part of the century. In France it was represented by Georges Bizet's (1838–1875) *Carmen* (1873–1874). The opera is based on a story by Prosper Mérimée (1803–1870) about lower class characters in Seville. The action is dominated by raw, uncontrolled passion that ends in the violent murder of the licentious Carmen by the soldier Don José. Since *Carmen* employed spoken dialogue, it was classified as opéra comique and first staged at the Paris Opéra-Comique in 1875. Its reception was negative; the story was regarded as too immoral for the stage—murder had never been portrayed at the Opéra-Comique—and the acting, especially of Célestine Galli-Marié, who played Carmen, was considered too realistic and actually immoral. Both the conservative French audience and the high-minded Wagnerians rejected it. Later that year, but not until after Bizet's death, *Carmen* was presented successfully in Vienna, transformed into a grand opera by the substitution of recitative for the dialogue.

In Italy the realist movement produced an operatic style known by the Italian synonym *verismo*. The verismo composers chose plots that were unrestrainedly emotional and melodramatic, were set among the lower classes, and culminated in violence. Pietro Mascagni's (1863–1945) one-act opera *Cavalleria rusticana* (1890) deals with Sicilian peasants and moves rapidly toward its climax, a duel between a husband and his wife's lover. *I pagliacci* (1892) by Ruggero Leoncavallo (1858–1919), often performed as a companion piece to *Cavalleria rusticana,* tells of a traveling commedia dell'arte company, whose leader, Canio, finds that his actress wife is unfaithful. In the course of playing a cuckolded husband on stage Canio loses control and kills his wife and her lover.

The musical style of verismo opera features violent contrast. The vocal parts are more declamatory than in other Italian operatic styles and tend to have sweeping, wide ranges and high tessituras. Often they are heavily reinforced by orchestral doubling, which in turn demands considerable vocal power from the singers. The orchestras are large and colorful. The harmony is chromatic, which adds to the emotional intensity.

Giacomo Puccini

Giacomo Puccini (1858–1924), the most important composer of Italian opera at the turn of the century, belonged only partly to the verismo movement. His *La Bohème* (1896) is an example of Romantic realism; its characters are lower-class Parisian artists who are unable to escape their fate, but they are Romantically sympathetic figures, and the ending, while tragic, is not violent. On the other hand, *Tosca* (1900), which has a violent ending, takes place in an aristocratic setting. Puccini's music profits from the style of verismo, with powerful vocal lines that provide one climax after another and with colorful and attractive orchestration.

Exoticism

As the nineteenth century began to draw to a close, the old aesthetics and styles began to seem effete and worn-out. The Classic-Romantic musical language appeared trite; the New German style, a dead end. Composers began to look around for new ideas in an attempt to revitalize the western European musical tradition. One solution to this was *exoticism*, the application of new tonal patterns derived from musical styles from outside the leading musical nations of Europe.

There had been some awareness of these peripheral musical styles for a long time. The Austrian Classic composers, who were near Turkey, had imitated the jangling Janissary bands of Turkish guards. Chopin had adapted Polish dance rhythms in his mazurkas and polonaises, and Liszt and Brahms had written piano music that claimed inspiration from Hungarian gypsy violin playing. In the course of the century there had begun to be an awareness of Middle Eastern music as well; the French composer Félicien David (1810–1876) wrote piano pieces, choral-orchestral music, and operas on oriental topics, with mildly Middle Eastern turns of phrase in the melodies but Western harmonies. The New Orleans piano virtuoso Louis Moreau Gottschalk (1829–1869) brought to Europe piano pieces with styles derived from Creole, Caribbean, and South American visits.

Spain was a favorite region for mainstream composers who sought exotic material. Bizet's music, including *Carmen*, provides the best-known examples, though he never visited Spain himself and found his models in published collections of Spanish music. *Carmen's* famous "Habañera" is based on a melody by the Spanish composer Sebastian Iradier (1809–1865), whose style was formed in Cuba, while her "Seguidilla" shows the influence of flamenco style.

The exoticist movement reflects the growing awareness in western Europe of other musical cultures. A significant step was the publication of folk songs of various nations—including Spain, Russia, and Asian countries—though they were often regularized to make them more intelligible to ears accustomed to the mainstream musical tradition. A major event was the Universal Exhibition of 1889 in Paris, at which many Europeans first heard music of the Far East performed live by native musicians. Many composers set oriental subjects and attempted to imitate oriental music, not the least of whom was Puccini in his Japanese *Madama Butterfly* (1904) and Chinese *Turandot* (1926). As we shall see, oriental musical language took on great significance for the impressionist movement in France.

Late Nineteenth-Century Nationalism

Nationalism has already been discussed in the context of Romanticism. Chopin and Liszt, for example, who were both displaced natives of eastern Europe, felt strong ties to their homelands. In the later part of the century nationalism in music grew considerably stronger. There were two reasons for this. The first is essentially extra-musical: There was an increasing determination to achieve independence and national integrity in the regions that had long been dominated by Western empires, particularly the Austro-Hungarian empire. From a purely musical viewpoint there was a desire for an alternative musical language to either the Romantic or the post-Romantic styles. These motivations came together in the composers of these regions to produce important results.

Bohemia

One of the first regions to experience the nationalist movement in music was the area known as Bohemia, now western Czechoslovakia. The composer Bedřich Smetana (1824–1884), a patriot and political expatriate, expressed feeling for his native land in a traveloguelike cycle of symphonic poems entitled *Ma Vlast* (My homeland, 1872–1879), the best-known of which is "Vltava" (The Moldau). Most of his operas, including *Prodana nevesta* (The bartered bride, 1863–1870), have their settings among the Bohemian peasantry. Smetana's music does not depart radically from the German symphonic style, but he included quotations of folk tunes and melodic gestures derived from Bohemian folk music.

The next generation in Czech nationalism is represented by Antonin Dvořák (1841–1904). Like Smetana, Dvořák was trained in the German style. His career was abetted by the support of Brahms, whose music also influenced Dvořák's style, and of Hanslick. He spent a few years in the United States, where he held the directorship of the National Conservatory in New York and was much interested in African-American spirituals and Native American music. The presence of such an important European composer and his confidence in the future of music in America gave important support to American musicians. Nevertheless Dvořák soon succumbed to homesickness and returned to Prague. Dvořák's music shows the influence of folk songs—pentatonic and modal melodies are characteristic—and folk dance rhythms from both Czech and American sources; he rarely quoted borrowed material directly, however.

Russia

In Russia the deliberate westernization by which Peter the Great and Catherine the Great had attempted to strengthen their country's place among the nations of Europe continued to repress nationalist musical inclinations into the nineteenth century. After Napoleon's abortive invasion in 1812 (the inspiration for Tchaikovsky's familiar concert overture), however, there was a new spirit of Russian cultural self-esteem and an impulse toward indigenous styles of art. The Russian intelligentsia debated the direction their artistic rise should take; one party, the westernizers, believed in a high art modeled on that of Western Europe, while the other, the slavophiles, insisted that Russian art should come from the common folk.

Literature preceded music in the Russian nationalist movement. Alexander Pushkin (1799–1837) pioneered in writing literature in vernacular Russian rather than the literary, church-dominated language that had been used in the past. Nicolai Gogol (1809–1852) wrote novels of social satire. Feodor Dostoevsky (1821–1881) expanded the range of the novel in the direction of realism. The accomplishments of these literary figures provided musicians both inspiration and material for their work.

The emancipation from the Western tradition took place gradually. At the start of the century Russian music was dominated by Italian and German imported composers and styles. The first important Russian Romantic was Mikhail Glinka (1804–1857), whose operas took up Russian topics, though their music was still quite Italianate. Alexander Dargomyzhsky (1813–1869) brought a bit more idiomatic Russian style to his music; his opera *The Stone Guest* is based on Pushkin's treatment of the Don Giovanni story.

In the later part of the nineteenth century we find a clear distinction between Russian composers' approaches to music. Pyotr Il'yich Tchaikovsky (1840–1893) presents a relatively conservative, westernizing aspect. Although he did take up some patriotic subject matter, much of his music is absolute or draws its content from the broader Western European cultural heritage, as in the fantasy-overture *Romeo and Juliet*. Tchaikovsky's style does not diverge much from the Germanic tradition of tonal harmony and form. He did use folk song quotations and folk-style melody, however. His music seems particularly Russian in its deeply serious and intensely introverted, self-examining character.

The more strongly independent nationalistic movement in Russian music was the work of the group of five composers known as *moguchay kuchka* (mighty handful or mighty five). These composers, who mostly bypassed traditional conservatory training, relied heavily on folk music for their material and style. They were Alexander Borodin (1833–1887), a chemist; Cesar Cui (1835–1918), a military engineer; Mily Balakirev (1837–1910), the only professional musician; Modest Mussorgsky (1839–1881), a civil servant; and Nicolai Rimsky-Korsakov (1844–1908), a naval officer. They concentrated largely on vocal and program music with explicitly national content. The topics they chose included Russian history, as in Mussorgky's opera *Boris Godunov* (1872), which was based on a Pushkin play; landscape painting, as in Borodin's *In Central Asia* (1882); and their national music itself, as in Rimsky-Korsakov's *Russian Easter* Overture (1888), which was based on liturgical melodies of the Russian Orthodox church.

In attempting to create their national music the mighty handful quoted and imitated the style of folk tunes, which produced, in fact, quite a variety of music, since the large area they represented incorporated a number of different ethnic musics. For example, the melodies may be simple and diatonic with an emphasis on skips of fourths and fifths, or sinuous and chromatically ornamented in a more oriental style, depending on what regional culture served as the composer's inspiration. The rhythms sometimes depart from regular meters. The music of Russian folk culture was not the only thing that affected melody and rhythm; Mussorgsky created a special vocal style that deliberately resisted forcing Russian texts into patterns created for and suited to Italian or German. Instead he worked out a nationalist melodic style guided by natural linguistic declamation in his own language. The harmonies of much nationalistic Russian music are not particularly advanced in chromaticism or dissonance, but the harmonic progressions may be nonfunctional, reflecting modal qualities in the folk-song-based melodic content.

A special character accrued to the scoring of a great deal of the orchestral music of the mighty handful because of the work of Rimsky-Korsakov. He was an outstanding orchestrator, with a gift for brilliant sonorities of exoticist coloration. He occasionally assisted his compatriots in their orchestrations. When Borodin left his *Prince Igor* incomplete at his death, Rimsky-Korsakov finished the work. He also revised and reorchestrated Mussorgsky's opera *Boris Godunov* to help the music appeal to audiences who were not prepared for Mussorgsky's own rather stark and unsensual scoring. Rimsky-Korsakov himself recognized, however, that there might come a time when the musical public would be ready to hear Mussorgsky's own, less-polished sound, and suggested that then his arrangement could be discarded in favor of his compatriot's orchestration. Recent performances have indeed restored Mussorgsky's scoring, and some critics and audiences have found that its unconventional and sometimes even ugly sound contributes to its effectiveness.

Nationalism in Other Countries

The nationalist movement affected other regions as well as Bohemia and Russia. For the most part composers applied certain touches derived from their folk music to the general style of Romantic harmony. The music of the Norwegian composer Edvard Grieg (1843–1907), for example, is rooted in his training at the Leipzig Conservatory and the piano works of Chopin, but his melody employs inflections and figures of Norwegian folk music. The nationalistic output of the Spanish composer Isaac Albéniz (1860–1909) derives its character from the use of striking Spanish dance rhythms and melodies that capture the declamation patterns of Spanish speech and song.

The best composers of the English-speaking countries were slower to discover a national musical idiom. This may be partly the result of a certain degree of musical insecurity. Serious composers may have felt that it was necessary for them to show that they could master the mainstream European style before they could explore new directions. Certainly audiences, especially in America, believed (and in many instances still seem to believe) that high culture was better expressed in European rather than home-grown art. The

English composer Edward Elgar (1857–1934) wrote in a primarily German Romantic style, but his music sometimes manages to sound "English" for reasons that analysts have difficulty in explaining.

A number of American composers traveled to Europe to study in the late nineteenth century. Edward MacDowell (1860–1908) was trained in both France and Germany and proved that an American could become a fine composer in the European post-Romantic style, but he was nationalistic only in some of the titles of his characteristic and programmatic works and in his Suite No. 2 for orchestra (the *Indian* Suite), op. 48 (1891–1895), which employs Native American melodic material. A group of other American composers who also followed the pattern of study in Germany have become known as the Second New England School (by contrast to the First New England School, of whom William Billings was the most prominent). John Knowles Paine (1839–1906) composed with considerable craftsmanship in a style that did not go beyond that of the German Romantic symphonists Mendelssohn and Schumann. George Whitefield Chadwick (1854–1931) took the late Romantic style as his point of departure; passages in his symphonies recall the works of Brahms. However, there are some hints of nationalism in some of Chadwick's works: American folk melodic idioms appear, including those of Negro songs. Horatio Parker (1863–1919) also extended the German late Romantic style, notably in choral music, such as his impressive cantata *Hora novissima* (1892).

In addition to their music, these American composers hold special significance for the history of music in the United States because they estalished a high level of musical education for the following generations. Paine was professor of music at Harvard, Chadwick taught at the New England Conservatory in Boston, and Parker taught at Yale. To the men of the Second New England School must be added the first important American woman composer, Amy Beach (1867–1944). Beach was a piano prodigy, and many of her works feature that instrument, including not only solo pieces but also songs and chamber music. Although trained in America, Beach composed, like the rest of her New England compatriots, in essentially the mainstream European style with occasional use of American folk melodies.

The Situation at the End of the Nineteenth Century

As we consider the state of music at the close of the nineteenth century, two important things become evident. First, the Classic-Romantic style seemed to have passed its climax. Composers working within the style, the Viennese and French late Romantics in particular, left themselves vulnerable to the critical judgment that they were out of step with the march of progress and living in the past. The New German School, on the other hand, could be challenged by the accusation that in carrying the musical language to its expressive limit—that is, by stressing content, breaking down the stable tonal system, and rejecting tonally and thematically structured form—they left music incoherent.

The other major characteristic of the late nineteenth century in Western music is the division of musical styles. In the Classic phase of the late eighteenth century, there had been a considerable degree of conventionalism in musical style. In the Romanticism of the first half of the nineteenth century composers had produced clearly individual types of expression without threatening the assumption of a common musical language. By the end of the century, however, the Classic-Romantic *lingua franca* was threatened by the simultaneous existence of several contrasting aesthetics and styles: the relatively conservative late Romantic, including several regional variants; the progressive post-Romantic; and the diverse nationalist approaches. In effect, the Western musical world had become both larger and more complex.

As we shall see, the handwriting was on the wall for the twentieth century. Radical changes were due, and the world would not soon again, if ever, be as clear and simple as it had once seemed.

Questions for Reflection

❖   Why did the theories and musical works of Wagner have a wide-ranging influence outside of musical circles as well as among musicians?

❖   In what ways did musical developments in France and Italy after 1850 reflect the special situations and characteristic interests of those countries?

❖   How did the rise of national styles in music in the late nineteenth century differ from the appearance of nationally distinct musical styles in the sixteenth and eighteenth centuries?

❖   Would it be appropriate to refer to the developments in musical style in the second half of the nineteenth century as manneristic? Why or why not?

Suggestions for Further Reading

The music of the late nineteenth century is most commonly dealt with in general studies of the Romantic movement (for which see the Suggestions for Further Reading in Chapter 19) or by individual composers and works. The following may also be suggested: Bojan Bujic, *Music in European Thought, 1851–1912* (Cambridge: Cambridge University Press, 1988), a collection of aesthetic essays; Martin Cooper, *French Music from the Death of Berlioz to the*

Death of Fauré (London: Oxford University Press, 1951); Gerald Abraham, *On Russian Music* (London: Reeves, 1939); Gerald R. Seaman, *History of Russian Music* (New York: Praeger, 1967); Carl Dahlhaus, *Realism in Nineteenth-Century Music*, trans. Mary Whittall (Cambridge: Cambridge University Press, 1985).

Wagner's writings can be found in *Richard Wagner's Prose Works*, trans. William Ashton Ellis (London: Kegan Paul, Trench, Trübner, 1892–1912; several reprint editions are available). For Wagner's biography, see Ernest Newman, *The Life of Richard Wagner*, 4 vols. (London: Cassell, 1933–1947), or his one-volume *Wagner as Man and Artist* (New York: Vintage, 1960); Curt von Westernhagen, *Wagner: A Biography*, trans. Mary Whittall (Cambridge: Cambridge University Press, 1978). One of the best studies of the music dramas is Carl Dahlhaus, *Richard Wagner's Musical Dramas*, trans. Mary Whittall (Cambridge: Cambridge University Press, 1979).

A selection of books on other major late nineteenth-century composers follows:

Bizet: Winton Dean, *Georges Bizet: His Life and Work*, 3d ed. (London: Dent, 1975).

Brahms: Karl Geiringer, *Brahms: His Life and Work*, rev. ed. (London: Oxford University Press, 1961).

Bruckner: Robert Simpson, *The Essence of Bruckner* (London: Gollancz, 1967).

Dvořák: John Clapham, *Antonin Dvořák*, rev. ed. (New York: Norton, 1979).

Franck: Laurence Davies, *Franck* (London: Dent, 1973).

Mahler: Donald Mitchell, *Gustav Mahler*, a multiple-volume study including *The Early Years*, rev. P. Banks and D. Matthews (Berkeley: University of California Press, 1980); *The Wunderhorn Years* (Berkeley: University of California Press, 1976); and *Songs and Symphonies of Life and Death* (Berkeley: University of California Press, 1986).

Mussorgsky: M. D. Calvocoressi, *Mussorsgky*, rev. ed. Gerald Abraham (London: Dent, 1974).

Puccini: Mosco Carner, *Puccini: A Critical Biography*, 2d ed. (London: Duckworth, 1974).

Rimsky-Korsakov: Gerald Abraham, *Rimsky-Korsakov: A Short Biography* (London: Duckworth, 1945).

Scriabin: Hugh Macdonald, *Skryabin* (London: Oxford University Press, 1978).

Strauss: Norman Del Mar, *Richard Strauss: A Critical Commentary on His Life and Work* (Philadelphia: Chilton, 1962–1972).

Tchaikovsky: David Brown, *Tchaikovsky*, a multiple-volume biography, including *The Early Years, 1840–1874* (New York: Norton, 1978); *The Crisis Years, 1874–1878* (New York: Norton, 1982); and *The Years of Wandering, 1878–1885* (London: Gollancz, 1986).

Wolf: Frank Walker, *Hugo Wolf: A Biography*, 2d ed. (London: Dent, 1968).

22

THE ARRIVAL OF THE TWENTIETH CENTURY

A Crisis in Artistic Ideas and Styles

As we have seen, the New German School, and particularly Wagner, had a tremendous impact on the history of music at the end of the nineteenth century. In fact Wagner influenced thought not only in music but also in literature and painting. Many artistic thinkers regarded the triumph of content over structural convention and the application of artistic means for the expression of political and philosophical ideas as the wave of the future. "Wagnerism" became a general aesthetic movement.

Others, however, viewed the Wagnerian movement as completely misguided. To them the expression of philosophy and sociopolitical theory seemed a betrayal of the proper role of art, which they believed ought to be the creation of beauty and the expression of personal feelings. They also believed that the abandonment of governing principles of design threatened to make the work incoherent. To these critics the Wagnerian aesthetic and stylistic approach were justified (if at all) only in the personal expression of Wagner himself or, at its best, in Germanic post-Romanticism. These critics faced the task of discovering new principles and styles that would challenge post-Romanticism without reverting to the conservatism of the late Romantics.

Impressionism

As might be expected, the French, whose national predilection had long run in the vein of elegance and grace, found the New German style unsympathetic. As the century came to its close, they developed characteristically French approaches to painting, literature, and eventually music that offered alternatives to Wagnerism, expressed a French viewpoint with integrity, and were genuinely new. This movement is known as *impressionism* or *symbolism*.

The term *impressionism* was derived from a critical review of an 1874 exhibition of painting that included a work by Claude Monet (1840–1926) entitled *Impression: Sunrise, 1872*. The epithet was not meant in a complimentary sense; the critic who coined it intended to convey his objection to the style's lack of clarity. "Impressionist" thus joins the group of style designations, such as Gothic and Baroque, that were originally intended as derogatory but that we now use objectively.

The impressionist artist's intention was indeed to be vague. Impressionist paintings were supposed to capture the immediate, sensual impression of a moment's glance at a scene rather than to reproduce the scene's details. The painter Camille Pissarro (1830–1903) stated that "the Impressionists . . . stand for a robust art based on sensation." As a consequence, the favorite subjects for these painters were scenes with masses of small objects, objects in motion, water scenes, special tricks of light, and the sort of sensory perception one has in dreams rather than full consciousness. Monet studied light, painting a famous series of pictures of the facade of the cathedral of Rouen under the changing types of light during the day. (Plate 9)

Impressionists did not draw forms and fill in color but used dabs of paint; the more closely the observer looks, the less clear the picture seems. To get the effect of light emanating from the canvas the impressionists sometimes began by painting the surface a brilliant white, so that any place that is not covered by color is unusually bright. The colors tend to be pastels and primary colors rather than carefully blended shades. All of this technique makes analytical examination or the attempt to discover depth of feeling in impressionist works fruitless. Nothing is to be found there but purely sensual experience. In effect, both neoclassic intellectualism and Romantic emotionalism have been rejected and replaced with a new artistic criterion, sensual pleasure.

In literature a parallel movement to impressionism was symbolism. The symbolist poets created a style in which verbal images could be combined for their own sake, without significance beyond delight in the imagery itself, and words could be used for their abstract, musical sounds, with no regard for their meanings. The symbolist poet Paul Verlaine (1844–1896) summarized the aesthetic in the poem "Art poétique," much of which might equally serve as a description of impressionist painting:

> You must have music first of all,
> and for that a rhythm uneven is best,
> vague in the air and soluble,
> with nothing heavy and nothing at rest.

You must not scorn to do some wrong
in choosing the words to fill your lines:
nothing more dear than the tipsy song
where the Undefined and Exact combine.

. . .

Never the Color, always the Shade,
always the nuance is supreme!
Only by shade is the trothal made
between flute and horn, of dream with dream!

. . .

Let there be music, again and forever!
Let your verse be a quick-winged thing and light—
such as one feels when a new love's fervor
to other skies wings the soul in flight.

Happy-go-lucky, let your lines
disheveled run where the dawn winds lure,
smelling of wild mint, smelling of thyme . . .
and all the rest is literature.[1]

Verlaine was, of course, using the word *literature* as a term of derision, since it suggests complex structure and profound emotional expression. Like Pissarro, he espouses a robust style, stressing the sonorous value of words and delight in the suggestion of sensory images with no underlying deeper meaning.

Claude Debussy

The sensualism of the impressionists and symbolists inevitably reached music as well. The leading figure in musical impressionism was Claude Debussy (1862–1918). Debussy was an original genius; in his years at the Paris Conservatory he was notorious for his lack of discipline, but he managed nevertheless to win the prestigious Prix de Rome in 1883. He frequented gatherings of symbolist poets and impressionist painters, and he became strongly anti-Wagnerian, rejecting the Germanic emphasis on emotional expression and philosophical propaganda in music. At the same time, he did not espouse a return to the dominance of intellectual, structural values. Debussy once tried to disassociate himself from impressionism and symbolism, but this seems to have been because he understood the terms as derogatory labels by which critics dismissed the new styles out of hand. Like the ideals of his contemporaries in the other arts, however, Debussy's ideal for music was based on sensual appeal:

Music should humbly seek to *give pleasure* . . . . It is essential that beauty be *sensual*, that it give us immediate enjoyment, that it impose itself or insinuate itself into us without our making any effort to grasp it.

Impressionist music applies a new set of priorities based on this intention to the elements of musical style. The elements that can be comprehended most immediately—timbres and harmonic colors— receive the greatest emphasis. Less important are the elements that we understand only when tones unfold over time and when we compare sounds with each other, such as rhythm, melody, and harmonic function. Of least importance is musical form, for it requires attentive listening and mental synthesis over the length of an entire structure.

The importance of timbre for musical impressionism led to advances in instrumentation. New effects and new combinations were explored. The use of muted orchestral strings divided in many parts, as in the movement entitled "Nuages" (Clouds) from Debussy's three orchestral *Nocturnes* (1897–1899), gives a characteristically impressionistic sound, for example. The influence of exoticism is evident in the oriental-sounding unison flute and harp passage from the middle of the same movement. The third of the *Nocturnes,* "Sirènes" (Sirens), employs wordless voices as members of the orchestra.

The treatment of rhythm and melody in impressionism involves particular problems. The aim is to avoid involving the listener's analytical faculties. One result is melodic fragments that do not resolve themselves into singable lines; another is the creation of long and meandering lines that do not manifest any clear sense of direction. Rhythms often seem vague and unmetered, as in the improvisationlike flute solo that opens the *Prélude à l'après-midi d'un faune* (Prelude to the afternoon of a faun, 1894). This partly reflects the antianalytical tendency of impressionism, but it also stems from a new consciousness of the fluid rhythmic character of French poetry, which does not use syllable stress or meter in the manner of English or German verse. There are also, however, examples of rhythms that are physically driving like those of the middle movement, "Fêtes" (Fiestas), of the orchestral *Nocturnes.*

One of the impressionists' particular concerns was to avoid the creation of emotional tension by harmony (which had, of course, been the main source of both expressiveness and structure by the Classic-Romantic style). This was accomplished by avoiding traditional harmonic function. Particularly effective were those harmonies whose function was ambiguous, such as diminished seventh chords and augmented triads. A typical procedure is the "streaming" of chords in parallel motion, particularly seventh and ninth chords. The effect is more like that of parallel organum—a kind of enriched monophonic line— rather than true counterpoint or harmonic motion. Also helpful in reducing the sense of harmonic tension and directedness were scales without half steps (i. e., without the effect of leading tones), such as the whole-tone scale or the pentatonic scale; the latter also reflects the strong effect of exoticism on impressionism.

Impressionist music inherited from the Romantic movement a considerable reliance on literary texts or extramusical subject matter. Debussy was as interested in nature as the Romantic composers on the one hand or the impressionist painters on the other. The cloud impressions in "Nuages" from the orchestral *Nocturnes* and the impressions of the sea in the programmatic symphony *La Mer* (1903–1905) provide two excellent examples. Debussy's character pieces for the piano often rely on visual images—among the most familiar are the preludes "Voiles" (Veils, or Sails), "Des pas sur la neige" (Some steps in the snow), and "La cathédrale engloutie" (The sunken cathedral) from 1909 and 1910—but he did not hesitate to use other sensory suggestions in "Les sons et les parfums tournent dans l'air du soir" (Sounds and scents revolve in the evening air). He also employed the poetry of the symbolist poets. The *Prélude à l'après-midi d'un faune* is based on a poem by Stéphane Mallarmé (1842–1898), whose Tuesday evening salon soirées Debussy attended. The great opera *Pelléas et Mélisande* (1902) takes its plot from a story by Maurice Maeterlinck (1862–1949). Debussy also composed fine songs using texts by several of the leading symbolist poets, particularly Verlaine.

Diffusion and Limits of Impression

The impressionist movement was short-lived. Besides Debussy, it is mostly identified with the early works of his fellow French composer Maurice Ravel (1875–1937). The Germans were not naturally inclined toward such sensualism, but examples appear in other nations, as in some works of the English composer Frederick Delius (1862–1934), the American Charles Tomlinson Griffes (1884–1920), and the Italian Ottorino Respighi (1879–1936). Passages of impressionist style also appear in many other twentieth-century pieces that cannot be classified as belonging to the impressionist movement itself. Even Debussy progressed in his own style beyond sensualism and toward a new degree of abstraction, most notably in his ballet *Jeux* (1912) and in his late songs and chamber music.

The Aesthetics of Ugliness

By the close of the nineteenth century a sense of frustration and pessimism had arisen. The brave dreams of the Enlightenment, the physical comforts that became widely accessible after the Industrial Revolution, and the political revolutions of Romanticism had come and gone without providing the utopia they had seemed to promise. The opening of eyes that came with Enlightenment empiricism had revealed unpleasant truths about the human condition without giving any solutions. The Industrial Revolution had offered more creature comforts than ever before, but industrialization had also proved to be a dehumanizing force. Social, political, or economic changes in the external circumstances of life were clearly unable to create universal happiness and fulfillment.

Indeed, the realist aesthetic appeared to depend on the recognition that consciousness itself was grounded in tension and frustration. As early as 1864 Dostoevsky, in *Notes from Underground,* had his protagonist say,

> I know, for instance, that suffering is inadmissible in light stage plays. In the utopian crystal palace, it'd be inconceivable, for suffering means doubt and denial, and what kind of crystal palace would that be, if people had doubts about it? Nevertheless, I'm certain that man will never give up true suffering, that is, chaos and destruction. Why, suffering is the only cause of consciousness. And, although I declared at the beginning that consciousness is man's greatest plague, I know that he likes it and won't exchange it for any advantage. . . . With consciousness . . . we can at least lacerate ourselves from time to time, which does liven us up a bit. It may go against progress, but it's better than nothing.[2]

At the turn of the century Sigmund Freud (1856–1939) revealed the extent of the deeply rooted but repressed psychological baggage we carry, which no external change in circumstance can obliterate. Freud saw the roots of frustration and unhappiness as inherent in the human mind.

In view of such ideas, it is not surprising that artists began to question the assumption that art should purvey beauty and pleasure. From the Freudian point of view classic order and control, romantic feeling and joy in emotional expression, and the sensual appeal of impressionism all decline into mere repression of fundamental human conflicts and tensions. A new aesthetic stance, in which the venting of conflict and tension would be the central aim of art, naturally became appropriate; it offered perhaps a kind of artistic psychotherapeutic catharsis or at least a representation of the bitter truth. Dostoevsky's underground man writes,

> . . . I derived pleasure precisely from the blinding realization of my degradation; because I felt I was already up against the wall; that it was horrible but couldn't be otherwise; that there was no way out and it was no longer possible to make myself into a different person; that even if there were still enough time and faith left to become different, I wouldn't want to change myself; and that, even if I wanted to, I still wouldn't have done anything about it, because, actually, there wasn't anything to change into. Finally, the most important point is that there's a set of fundamental laws to which heightened consciousness is subject so that there's no

changing oneself or, for that matter, doing anything about it. Thus, as a result of heightened consciousness, a man feels that it's all right if he's bad as long as he knows it . . . .[3]

Clearly there were artists who found neither the richness of late Romanticism, as manifested, for example, in the music of Brahms or Verdi, nor the indulgence of the senses represented by the impressionists a satisfactory aesthetic approach for the new century. They sought new principles and styles suited to expressing the newly recognized, deeply rooted ugliness in the human psyche and in human behavior.

This new approach is exemplified in the operatic work of Richard Strauss in the first years of the twentieth century. Strauss explored the darker side of the human psyche in his opera *Salome* (1905), based on Oscar Wilde's play of the same name. It tells the riveting but revolting story of the stepdaughter of King Herod. Salome is consumed by sexual passion for the imprisoned John the Baptist, and when she is unable to seduce him she demands his head on a platter. She triumphantly kisses the gory head and is in turn killed at the order of the horrified king. Strauss's music extends the style of the Wagnerian music drama, expressing psychosis with extreme dissonance and wide-leaping melodic lines.

Primitivism

One important source of inspiration for artists who wished to explore the deep-rooted and unrefined aspects of the mind was the artistic styles and techniques of less-developed, non-Western cultures. To westerners who felt their own culture had developed to the point of decadence and had sublimated the deepest and truest elements of the psyche, such cultures seemed to offer access to the raw truth. Thus there arose a movement known as *primitivism,* which adopted stylistic idioms that imitated presumably primitive art in an attempt to approach the expression of less refined and therefore more genuine feelings.

In the visual arts the primitivist tendency is represented by the works of the French painter Paul Gauguin (1848–1903), who eventually abandoned his homeland for the uninhibited island environment of Tahiti. He developed a style that abandoned perspective and realism, and employed blocklike forms in simple colors. The religious icons of South Pacific culture appear in a number of his works, as unrealistic, sculpturelike figures with a powerful, brooding presence. (Plate 10)

As we have seen in the music of the exoticist or nationalist movements, styles based on those of non-Western musics could offer escape from the overripe luxuriance of the late Romantic and post-Romantic styles. In certain forms, as musical primitivists realized at the opening of the twentieth century, such musics could also provide ways to express the underlying powerful impulses in the human character.

In 1911 the Hungarian pianist and composer Béla Bartók (1881–1945) made an important experiment in primitivism with his "Allegro barbaro" for piano solo. In this work the piano was frankly treated as a percussion instrument. The irregular rhythms, narrow-range melodic gestures, and dissonant harmonies were derived from Hungarian peasant music.

The most notorious work of the short-lived primitivist movement was Igor Stravinsky's (1882–1971) score for the ballet *Le sacre du printemps* (The rite of spring), which appeared in 1913. Stravinsky had studied composition with Rimsky-Korsakov and was discovered by the great ballet impresario Serge Diaghilev (1872–1929), who commissioned the young composer to write music for his great dance company, the Ballets Russes in Paris. The first of Stravinsky's Russian ballets was *L'oiseau de feu* (The firebird, 1910), which was exoticist in the manner of Rimsky-Korsakov; the second was *Petrushka* (1911), which was more oriented toward the use of folk material and rather advanced harmonically. With *Le sacre du printemps* Stravinsky achieved a decisively new style that immediately brought him world fame, or at least notoriety. The ballet concerns imagined rites with which prehistoric Russian tribes greeted the arrival of spring, culminating in a human sacrifice. This brutal action was choreographed by the progressive Russian dancer Vaclav Nijinsky (1888–1950). The Parisian ballet audience, accustomed to late Romantic and brilliant exotic styles, was shocked by the presentation of such sheer ugliness on the stage, and a riot broke out at the first performance. There was so much noise in the hall that the dancers could not hear the orchestra. The occasion became one of the best-known performance events in the history of music. (In fairness it must be noted that at successive performances the audiences behaved more decorously.)

Stravinky's music calls for a very large and colorful orchestra. The complex rhythms he devised vary from the free, unmetered style of the opening to the heavily marked syncopation of the movement entitled "Dance of the Adolescents." The melodic material often gives the impression of wandering improvisation, and at other times it presents obsessive fragments of folklike tunes. The harmony is extremely dissonant, often with chords that superimpose the pitches of more than one triad at a time to create *polychords*. There is a certain centripetal tonal force produced by the use of pedal points and ostinatos; nevertheless, to some analysts the music seems to part decisively from tonality. It is hardly surprising that to some listeners *Le sacre du printemps* seemed to be an attempt to destroy music entirely. Yet it also became a landmark masterpiece of twentieth-century music, signaling the emancipation of modern music from both traditional stylistic techniques and from the aesthetic presupposition that music must be "beautiful."

Expressionism

The aesthetics of ugliness produced the artistic movement that came to be known as *expressionism*. The term is, of course, derived by opposition to impressionism, since it relies not on sensual appeal but on a deliberate attack on the senses. In the history of art it was only a step from the extreme emotional intensity of the late nineteeth century to the region where emotion gives way to psychosis. Thus expressionism is a logical outgrowth of Romantic emotionalism.

In terms of artistic technique, expressionism demanded rejection of the devices that had brought rational sense to artworks. In *Notes from Underground*, Dostoevsky described the technique for literature:

> I don't want to let considerations of literary composition get in my way. I won't bother with planning and arranging; I'll note down whatever comes to my mind.[4]

This creation of the sense that in a literary work the mind is allowed to leap randomly from one thought to another without rational coherence is termed *stream of consciousness*. It produces a distortion of reality, in which chronological time and logical progression of ideas are warped or twisted. This technique is familiar from the works of James Joyce (1882–1941) and William Faulkner (1897–1962).

Painters made use not only of distortions of form but also of clashing colors that attacked the viewer's visual sense. Such paintings were produced by the French group called "les fauves" (the wild animals), led by Henri Matisse (1869–1954). In Germany the Munich-based group called "Der blaue Reiter" (the blue rider), headed by Vassily Kandinsky (1866–1944), departed from the representation of physical reality altogether. Kandinsky's nonrepresentational canvases were often given titles derived from music, suggesting both their abstractness and their extreme emotional power. (Plate 11)

Arnold Schoenberg

Musical expressionism proceeded naturally from the intense emotionalism of the New German School and of verismo opera. It centered in Vienna, which was home to a group of expressionist composers who have become known as the Second Vienna School, in contrast to the Viennese triumvirate of Haydn, Mozart, and Beethoven during the Classic era. The leader of the group was Arnold Schoenberg (1874–1951). Schoenberg had begun his career in the post-Romantic style, exploiting extreme chromaticism for strong emotional effect, but this did not hinder his great admiration for the craftsmanly motivic development technique of Brahms. Schoenberg also became associated with Kandinsky and was a painter himself in the expressionist style. (Plate 12) He once described how an art work should function, in a manner that clearly suggests the extreme intensity of emotion in expressionism:

> . . . a work of art can produce no greater effect than when it transmits the emotions which raged in the creator to the listener, in such a way they also rage and storm in him.[5]

After about 1908 Schoenberg found a musical style that allowed the expression of the same sort of disruptive emotional excess as stream-of-consciousness literature and nonrepresentational painting. The essential feature of the style was the final abandonment of tonality. The presumption of a tonal center in music had never before been questioned in the history of Western music. The eventual arrival at the tonic had always provided a sense of coherence and satisfying closure in music, and, as we have emphasized, tonality was the fundamental principle of Classic-Romantic and even post-Romantic musical structure. The absence of tonality, or *atonality*, could naturally be expected to mark music with a feeling of both structural and emotional instability. Schoenberg also took both harmonic dissonance and melodic disjunction to new extremes.

Schoenberg's music was closely organized by intensive development of motives, based on the style of Brahms but in even more concentrated fashion. This helped to maintain some amount of coherence in compensation for the loss of tonality as a unifying force. Even so, the works of Schoenberg's period of free atonal expressionism tend to be divided into short movements, for he realized he did not have the tools to make longer expanses of music hold together. Most of these works are accompanied by poetic texts that provide a degree of coherence. Characteristic of this style is *Pierrot lunaire* (1912), a set of twenty-one settings of poems by the Belgian postsymbolist poet Albert Giraud for voice and a chamber ensemble consisting of various combinations of piano, flute or piccolo, clarinet or bass clarinet, violin or viola, and cello. The texts interpret the antics of commedia dell'arte clowns in a sometimes horrifyingly nightmarish way. In addition to a dissonant, atonal style and a scoring for instruments whose tone colors generally clash rather than blend, Schoenberg employed a special type of vocal declamation, *Sprechstimme* (speech-voice), in which the performer uses the timbre of regular speech but follows a contour of high and low, notated in detail on the staff. The entire effect is eerie and unreal. A phrase from No. 15, "Heimweh" (Homesickness), "krystallnes Seufzen" (crystalline sigh), captures the idea of perfectly concentrated emotional expression that is the essence of expressionism.

Alban Berg

Following Schoenberg's lead, his student Alban Berg (1885–1935) took up the expressionist cause. Berg was a rather unstable personality and had contemplated suicide shortly before he found a degree of fulfillment in his studies and friendship with Schoenberg. One of Berg's best-known works is the opera *Wozzeck* (1922), written shortly after the end of World War I and reflecting on the horrible effects of man's inhumanity to man. Berg wrote the libretto based on an early nineteenth-century play by Georg Büchner (1813–1837) about a soldier who is victimized by his captain, experimented on by his company doctor, and betrayed by his wife. He finally cuts his wife's throat and drowns himself. Berg employs atonal style and Sprechstimme, but not continuously. These devices for extreme expressive effect are set into relief by appearing in juxtaposition with chromatic tonal music in advanced post-Romantic style and with regular singing and speaking. *Wozzeck* in a sense continues the Wagnerian and Straussian music drama one step further; it even uses Leitmotiv technique.

As was the case for Schoenberg in his atonal pieces, Berg's problem was to maintain some coherence over the span of a long work. His solution in *Wozzeck* was to design each act as a set of movements within a larger form. Thus the first act, "situation," incorporates a suite; the second, "complication," is structured as a five-movement symphony; and the third, "dénouement," comprises a series of inventions on different types of musical ideas.

Advantages and Problems in Atonal Expressionism

The atonal, expressionist aesthetic and style suited a certain aspect of the early twentieth-century cultural context very well. Because expressionism captured some truths about the human experience and because the later twentieth century has not reached a consensus that the psychological and social foundations on which the style was based were erroneous or have gone out of date, it has continued to find sympathy with modern listeners. Nevertheless expressionism gave composers technical problems, since it was not an easy matter to write atonal music by empirical methods or to give atonal material coherent form in the absence of a harmonic center. Solutions to these problems were developed only after intensive effort over a period of several years. We shall return to this matter shortly.

An American Original: Charles Ives

One of the most independent thinkers in music history, the American composer Charles Ives (1874–1954), worked in relative obscurity in the first two decades of the twentieth century. Ives was a native of Connecticut; his father, George Ives (1845–1894), had been a bandmaster in the Civil War. George Ives studied acoustics and undertook a number of experiments with musical phenomena, including the use of polymeters and simultaneous multiple tonal-ities, microtones, and spatial arrangements of musicians in antiphonal group-ings. Charles Ives was often recruited to assist with these projects, and they clearly made a lasting impression on him.

Ives worked as a church organist and studied music under Horatio Parker at Yale University. After he graduated, he took a position with the Mutual Insurance Company in New York and later cofounded an independent com-pany, making a very good living in business while he composed in the eve-nings and on weekends. For many years Ives's music was little known. Al-though most of his compositions date from before 1920, it was not until the 1940s that his work gained much attention. His first important success came with the performance in 1939 of his Second Piano Sonata (*Concord, Mass., 1840–60*), composed between 1909 and 1915. He won the Pulitzer Prize in 1947, ironically for a work composed in 1904, his Third Symphony.

In addition to composing, Ives also did a good deal of writing. He set out his ideas about music in the "Essays before a Sonata," written to accompany the *Concord* Sonata, and the "Postface" to his song collection *114 Songs*. He also dictated an autobiography, *Memos*. A powerful force in Ives's thinking was the tradition of the American pioneering spirit, and he maintained a strong belief in the ideals of the New England transcendentalist philosophers Ralph Waldo Emerson (1803–1882) and Henry David Thoreau (1817–1862), such as faith in the spark of truth in each individual's intuition, self-reliance, and rejection of conventional behavior. Ives consequently went out of his way to avoid stylistic convention or traditional assumptions in his music. Nothing seems to have struck him as too outrageous to be considered, and rugged individualism and originality for its own sake justified any sort of experimentation. He wrote in the epilogue to "Essays Before a Sonata" that

> . . . beauty in music is too often confused with something that lets the ears lie back in an easy chair. Many sounds that we are used to do not bother us, and for that reason we are inclined to call them beautiful. Frequently, when a new or unfamiliar work is accepted as beautiful on its first hearing, its fundamental quality is one that tends to put the mind to sleep.[6]

For Ives, the ultimate vice was to be lazy or to rest in the past.

Ives's musical oeuvre includes pieces in a wide variety of genres. Besides four symphonies, his orchestral works include other multimovement sets and a number of shorter works. There are important examples of chamber music and keyboard pieces, together with choral music and about a hundred and fifty songs.

Ives put his ideas and his unusual experiences into practice in his music and became one of the first avant-garde composers of the twentieth century. His father's experiments that he had known in his youth led him to compose using quarter tones, antiphonal ensembles, and mutually contradictory metrical combinations (*polymeter*). He sometimes called for unusual techniques, including the use (in the *Concord* Sonata) of cluster chords on the piano, played by laying a length of board on the keys. He also pioneered in the use of a collagelike technique for constructing works, often quoting well-known spiritual songs and national patriotic tunes in the context of free material of his own composition. The *Concord* Sonata is notable for this, as are some of his familiar orchestral works, such as the First Orchestral Set (*A New England Symphony* or *Three Places in New England*), and chamber music, such as the Fourth Violin Sonata (*Children's Day at the Camp Meeting*). Ives also took a flexible attitude toward manners of performance for his music that anticipated the later ideas about indeterminacy in composition. He frequently rearranged material from one medium to another, offering options for the players; in the last movement of the *Concord* Sonata there is an optional part for flute, should the instrument be available. He anticipated and even valued the possibility of mistakes in performance, and in some scores actually wrote in deliberate "mistakes."

The use of melodic quotations in collage reflects not only Ives's interest in experimentation and concern for specifying content in his music but also his dedicated patriotism. The majority of his instrumental works carry programmatic or characteristic titles, and often their individual movements do the same. In the *Concord* Sonata, for example, the four individual movements are named for leading nineteenth-century literary figures: "Emerson," "Hawthorne," "The Alcotts," and "Thoreau." The four separate symphonic poems "Washington's Birthday," "Decoration Day," "The Fourth of July," and "Thanksgiving" were later assembled into a symphonic cycle called *Holidays*.

Ives ranks as the most distinctively American composer up to his time. His posthumous influence far outweighed the neglect he experienced during his life. Once his music began to be heard in the 1940s and to be studied seriously after his death, he became a model or ideal for many later composers. His works and his attitudes encouraged composers to test the limits of music itself. That the United States developed into the leading center for avant-garde experimentation in the middle of the century may be due to many factors; certainly one of them is the music and musical thought of Charles Ives.

Questions for Reflection

✛ Is the music of the so-called impressionist style more appropriately associated with the aesthetic problems and positions of impressionist painters or with those of symbolist poets? How valid is a literary model for musical expression in regard to this music, compared to the music of the preceding centuries?

❖ Why did ballet become a particularly important genre for composers in the twentieth century?

❖ Should "beauty" have an essential place in defining art? How is *beauty* defined? Is expressionist music really not "beautiful"? not "music"? not "art"?

Suggestions for Further Reading

A good survey of music through the first half of the twentieth century is William W. Austin, *Music in the Twentieth Century* (New York: Norton, 1966). An interesting discussion, written by a composer and with considerable emphasis on aesthetic issues, is Eric Salzman, *Twentieth-Century Music: An Introduction,* 2d ed. (Englewood Cliffs, N. J.: Prentice-Hall, 1974).

Debussy's musical essays are collected in *Debussy on Music,* ed. F. Lesure and R. L. Smith (New York: Knopf, 1977). For Schoenberg's writings, see Arnold Schoenberg, *Style and Idea,* ed. Leonard Stein, trans. Leo Black (New York: St. Martin's Press, 1975). Some of Ives's most important essays are in *Essays Before a Sonata and Other Writings,* ed. Howard Boatwright (New York: Norton, 1961), and *Memos,* ed. John Kirkpatrick (New York: Nortion, 1971).

The following list is a selection of biographies of composers discussed in this chapter:

Bartók: Paul Griffiths, *Bartók* (London: Dent, 1984).

Berg: Mosco Carner, *Alban Berg: the Man and the Work,* 2d ed. (New York: Holmes & Meier, 1983).

Debussy: Edward Lockspeiser, *Debussy: His Life and Mind* (London: Cassell, 1965–66).

Ives: H. Wiley Hitchcock, *Ives* (London: Oxford University Press, 1977).

Ravel: Arby Orenstein, *Ravel, Man and Musician* (New York: Columbia University Press, 1975).

Schoenberg: Willi Reich, *Schoenberg: A Critical Biography,* trans. Leo Black (New York: Praeger, 1971).

Stravinsky: Eric Walter White, *Stravinsky: The Composer and His Works,* 2d ed. (Berkeley: University of California Press, 1979).

Notes

1. Paul Verlaine, *Paul Verlaine: Selected Poems,* trans. and ed. C. F. MacIntyre (Berkeley: University of California Press, 1948), 181, 183.

2. Fyodor Dostoyevksy, *Notes from Underground,* trans. Andrew MacAndrew (New York: New American Library, 1961), 118.

3. Ibid., 94–95.

4. Ibid., 122.

5. Arnold Schoenberg, *Style and Idea,* ed. Leonard Stein, with translations by Leo Black (New York: St. Martin's Press, 1975), 450.

6. Charles Ives, *Essays before a Sonata and Other Writings,* ed. Howard Boatwright (New York: Norton, 1962), 97.

23

BETWEEN THE
WORLD WARS

A Period of Readjustment

The two decades between the end of World War I and the beginning of World War II form a period of reorganization in the cultural life of the West, particularly in music. After the horror of World War I, which was by far the most terrifying manifestation until that time of the violence that mankind could wreak on itself, it seemed necessary to regain control both of political conditions and the arts. In the sphere of politics, the United States emerged from the war as the world's leading power. It had determined the outcome of the war but had been geographically removed from the fighting and destruction. This placed the United States in a position for the first time to assume a role of cultural leadership.

The midpoint of this period, however, was occupied by an economic crisis as severe as that of the war, the Great Depression of 1929. The Western nations had settled down politically for the moment, only to discover that they did not have control of their economy. No balance was established between supply and demand, between the economy of the producers of goods and that of the holders of capital. The result was disaster in the monetary and banking system. Eventually government had to intervene to readjust the economic system.

It is not surprising to find in the arts of this period an attempt to gain or reestablish some of the sense of control that had been foregone in the sensualism of the impressionists and the emotional excesses of the expressionists. This took place both among artists who continued the directions of development we have already observed and among others who turned their backs on those directions and attempted to discover other, more objective ways of proceeding. In music the expressionist camp established systematic procedures for atonal composition, while other composers rejected atonality and sought new (or returned to older) tonal techniques.

One important part of the attempt to reestablish political stability was the formation of the rigidly governed fascist police states of the Axis powers. Under Hitler, in particular, political control was achieved, but at a terrible cost. Artistic freedom was heavily repressed in favor of a government-ordered conservatism. One practical result of this was the emigration of important writers, artists, and composers, as well as scientists and scholars, especially to the United States. This emigration was accelerated by the outbreak of World War II. By the early 1940s a number of the best European artistic minds were living and working in United States, which reinforced its importance in the development of Western culture.

The Twelve-Tone Method of Composition

As we have noted, the expressionist composers faced two important technical challenges in atonal composition: finding a systematic process for producing atonal music; and finding a satisfactory way to provide structural coherence in a musical style that had abandoned the traditional means of unifying musical compositions, tonality itself. During World War I, and for a few years thereafter, Schoenberg and some other composers devoted themselves to solving these problems. By the early 1920s Schoenberg had achieved his goal, creating a simple, flexible, and intellectually elegant system, the *twelve-tone method* of composition. His work deserves a place beside that of the other great codifiers of musical systems, such as Guido of Arezzo, Franco of Cologne, Philippe de Vitry, Gioseffe Zarlino, and Jean-Philippe Rameau.

The twelve-tone system grows logically from the governing axiom that in order to avoid tonality no pitch class among the twelve of the equal-tempered chromatic system should receive greater exposure than any other. To assure this, the twelve pitch classes are simply arrayed in an order—called the *prime* or *original row, set,* or *series*—such that none is repeated. The series must be stated in its entirety before the first of its pitch classes can return. There are, mathematically speaking, 12 factorial ($12 \times 11 \times 10 \times 9 \times 8 \times 7 \times 6 \times 5 \times 4 \times 3 \times 2 \times 1$), or 479,001,600 possible series, and although not all of these make good musical material for composers—twenty-four, for example, are chromatic scales—the possibilities are certainly many and varied.

In addition to providing equal play of the pitch classes, and therefore atonality, the twelve-tone system obviously creates very strict structural unity. The difficulty then becomes finding ways to provide variety. This is accomplished by using various permutations of the original series. Because a simple transposition still gives the twelve pitch classes of the series equal exposure, while the musical patterns of intervals are recognized as representing the series, transposition is permitted, as long as it applies to the entire series. Other manipulations of the series are also possible. One of these is interval-for-interval (melodic) *inversion,* which again gives equal articulation to the twelve pitch classes and, as composers in polyphonic textures have known for centuries, can be perceived audibly as derived from the original. Another possibility is to use the series in *retrograde,* or reverse order—the old contrapuntal device of cancrizans. It is also possible to combine these two permutations into the *retrograde inversion.* (Fig. 23.1) The four principal forms of the series—original, retrograde, inversion, and retrograde inversion—plus the possibility of the transposition of each to begin on any of the twelve pitch classes, gives the composer plenty of room to manoeuvre, so much so, in fact, that in practice composers generally found it necessary to restrict their vocabulary of series forms and transpositions for any given piece. In summary, the twelve-tone method yielded rational control of atonality, the means by which expressionist composers had originally sought to voice our least rational impulses.

If at first the twelve-tone method seems artificial, mathematical, and mechanical, it is not necessarily so in practice. Schoenberg insisted that in composing according to this method his students should first devise the series and then compose exactly as they would in any other system. That is, a composer whose style was dense and rich, heavily laden with dynamic nuance, and complex in rhythm would continue to compose in that manner with twelve tones, while another who preferred light, transparent textures, few but sharp dynamic contrasts, and clearly defined rhythm would compose in that style. All that their pieces would necessarily have in common would be atonality, just as two composers working within the tonal system might share only that aspect of style.

There is, as might be expected, a tendency for the procedures by which twelve-tone music is composed to show some bias in favor of contrapuntal textures, since the material is determined in linear fashion to a degree. It is perfectly possible, however, to construct chords by using pitch classes of the series simultanously (as long as the pitch classes are taken from the series together in their place) or from simultaneous appearances of forms of the series. There is also a bias in favor of variation form, since the permutations of the series amount to variations on it. Nevertheless, all sorts of musical forms can be designed in twelve-tone composition, even including some sonata-form plans.

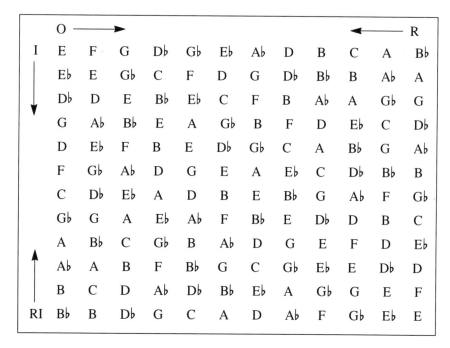

Figure 23.1
Schoenberg's pitch material for his Suite for Piano, op. 25 is shown in this matrix. The original row (prime set) is shown across the top row of the square and its inversion down the left-hand column. Each row and column then contains the original or inversion transposed to a different pitch. The retrograde and retrograde inversion are found by reading rows from left to right and columns from bottom to top, respectively.

Schoenberg after 1920

When Schoenberg began using the twelve-tone system in the 1920s, he still retained his inclination to work with short musical units. His Suite for Piano, op. 25, completed in 1923, provides a good example; the Baroque suite structure offered a model for a unified work in several brief movements. Gradually he turned to larger works as well. The Variations for Orchestra, op. 31 (1928), form an intermediate stage between the group of separate movements and the long, continuous work. By 1930 he was able to sustain the twelve-tone method through the length of an opera in *Moses und Aron.*

The antisemitism and artistic conservatism of the Hitler era in Germany forced Schoenberg to leave for the United States in 1933. He eventually settled in southern California, where he became a professor at the University of California at Los Angeles. He was a fine teacher of theory and composition who demanded of his students that they master composition within the tonal system and that they discover fundamental principles of artistic expression rather than simply following rules. The flexibility of Schoenberg's teaching may be estimated by the fact that among his many successful students was the jazz pianist and composer Dave Brubeck (b. 1920).

Adaptations of the Twelve-Tone Method

The use of the twelve-tone method in expressionist music was not always strict. In his Variations for Orchestra, for example, Schoenberg introduced some materials that are not derived from his series, notably the pitch sequence B A C H (i. e., B flat, A, C, B natural). Berg, as might be expected from our earlier observations about the mixing of materials in *Wozzeck,* was inclined to combine twelve-tone and tonal ideas. His last completed work, the Violin Concerto (1935), is based on a series that allows for the presentation of tonal patterns such as triads and seventh chords, and it quotes both a folk song melody and a chorale harmonized by Bach. The Violin Concerto was composed as a memorial to Manon Gropius, the eighteen-year-old daughter of Gustav Mahler's former wife Alma, and it has clear programmatic content in the Romantic tradition. Also indicative of Berg's romantic inclinations are the emotionally suggestive headings of the movements in his Lyric Suite for string quartet (1925–1926): 1. Allegro gioviale, 2. Andante amoroso, 3. Allegro misterioso and trio estatico, 4. Adagio appassionato, 5. Presto delirando, 6. Largo desolato. It has also been discovered that the Lyric Suite had a hidden autobiographical program. Berg thus appears as the most romantic of the Second Vienna School composers.

Serialism

A very different approach to the twelve-tone method was explored by Schoenberg's other most important student in Vienna, Anton Webern (1883–1945). Webern began to study with Schoenberg in 1904 while he was still completing his Ph.D. degree in historical musicology with a dissertation on the Renaissance composer Heinrich Isaac. He was an important conductor and teacher. His early atonal works show considerable focus and concentration, which may be heard as evidence of either great emotional intensity—especially in his vocal works, where content is explicit and considerable effort is required of the singer—or cool objectivity. All of Webern's works are very brief; the longest of his thirty-one opus numbers lasts only ten minutes. They have been compared to the Japanese haiku form in poetry because of their power to evoke a great deal with the most limited means.

Webern's greatest importance comes from his approach to the process of twelve-tone composition. His use of material and procedures is characteristically rigorous and extremely economical, with a great deal of organization already attained within the construction of the series. He also extended the idea of serialization to musical style elements other than pitch, creating series of rhythms, dynamics and articulations, and timbres. This type of composition is sometimes given the name *serialism*. The serialization of timbres produces a type of instrumentation in which each player may have only a note or two or three before passing the line on to the next player. This technique has been likened to the impressionist painters' pointillism, which created a picture out of detached points or dots of color. Schoenberg had envisioned such a style and called it *Klangfarbenmelodie* (tone-color melody). Intricate contrapuntal constructions are also part of Webern's personal style; the Symphony, op. 21 (1928), for example, begins with a double canon that controls pitch, duration, and timbre.

The extremely thorough organization in Webern's music is not particularly easy to perceive. Melodic flow is obscured by the tendency of adjacent pitch classes to come from distant registers and to sound with differing timbres. Serialized duration values do not characteristically produce a metric grid against which they can be measured and ordered, so they often seem entirely irregular. Nevertheless, the music does have a high degree of coherence, derived from the treatment of the series and the economy of material, and it repays study and repeated, concentrated listening.

Webern's economy and attention to detail made him even more a model for later composers than Schoenberg; Stravinsky later called Webern his "standard for music." The ideals of economy of means and intellectual control, of course, are those of the Apollonian or generally classic aesthetic in art, as is the ability to serve as a model for other artists. Some of Webern's pieces also adopt the external structure of Classic genres. The Symphony, op. 21, consists of a first movement in sonata form and a finale in the form of a theme and variations. The Concerto for Nine Instruments, op. 24 (1934), adopts the traditional three-movement concerto plan.

Webern's extended serialism thus produced a classic aesthetic out of technical devices originating in the Romantic/post-Romantic/expressionist stream of historical development in music. While the intensity of expression cannot be denied in Webern's works, they clearly suggest a cooler and more objective direction at the same time.

Artistic Objectivity

The first half of the twentieth century was generally a period of new assertion of the objective side of the human mind. To many artists it seemed time for a new exploration of intellectual, analytical, and practical matters. The move-

Figure 23.2
The shop block of the Bauhaus in Dessau, Germany. The movement for objectivity in the period between the world wars affected architecture as it did music. The Bauhaus school produced simple, geometrical designs, in which the pure service of function superseded decoration. Composers responded to the same motivations with a simplified style and functional *Gebrauchsmusik*. (*Marburg/Art Resource*)

ment in painting known as cubism, led by Pablo Picasso (1881–1973) and Marcel Duchamp (1887–1968), focused on analytical vision; objects were reduced to geometrical shapes, and various planes or stages in an action could be depicted simultaneously. (Plate 13) In the field of architecture and design the Bauhaus school in Munich produced simple, unornamented, purely functional works—flat, boxlike buildings of steel, concrete, and glass, and furniture in molded geometrical shapes. (Fig. 23.2)

Not all composers after World War I followed the path of the Second Vienna School, of course. Many believed that the principle of tonal unity and organization in music continued to offer opportunities for original thought and work in the twentieth century. Moreover, a revitalization of tonality, it might be reasoned, could restore a sense of reason and control in music.

The tonal music of the period after World War I is often classified as *neoclassic*, both specifically because much of it draws on the tonal basis, clear textures, and forms of the Classic-Romantic styles and more generally because of its aesthetic objectivity. In practice, however, a variety of widely divergent tonal styles emerged in these years. It might therefore be possible to identify subcategories to describe different types of works, including those based on late eighteenth-century classicism, which we might call neo-Classic, as well as those that harken back to other stages of musical style, such as neo-Romantic, neo-Baroque, and even neo-Renaissance and neo-Medieval. These stylistic roots may also intertwine in individual works, complicating the picture further. And, of course, there appeared new types of tonal composition not based on older techniques at all.

Neoclassicism

France

At the turn of the century a trend toward objectivity and simplification had already arisen, particularly in France, where intellectuality had traditionally been highly regarded. A leader in this was Erik Satie (1866–1925), a rather eccentric composer whose musical style derived from his strongly anti-German inclinations, his sense of the limitations of his own compositional skill, and his wry wit. Satie employed clear, sparse textures, simple melodic and rhythmic design, and a diatonic harmony that suggested the eighteenth century. He also referred in his subject matter to the classicism of antiquity, as in the piano solo pieces *Gymnopédies* (1888) and his cantata *Socrate* (1918). His sardonic sense of humor paralleled that of Ives. According to a characteristic, if fictitious, story, when Satie was accused of writing formless music, he responded with *Trois morceaux en forme de poire* (Three pieces in the form of a pear). His *Vexations* (1893) comprises a passage that is to be repeated 840 times. Together with his seemingly perverse titles for his works, like *Embryons desséchés* (Dessicated embryos, 1913), he parodied exaggerated expressive markings in scores, with such indications as "Like a nightingale with a toothache." Satie also paralleled Ives in being something of an experimentalist; his ballet *Parade* (1917) uses the sounds of a roulette wheel, a typewriter, and gunshots.

The trend toward neoclassicism begun by Satie grew quite strong in France. Debussy's style in his later years began to become less impressionist and more intellectual. Even more of a neoclassicist, Ravel always maintained a more detached and objective style than Debussy's; Stravinsky once referred to him as a "Swiss clockmaker." The suite *Tombeau de Couperin* (1917) for solo piano (later orchestrated) is a direct homage to the French galant style. In the Piano Concerto in G (1931) Ravel combined brilliant exoticist and impressionist orchestration with traditional eighteenth-century structural design, including sonata form, in a clear, brilliant texture. This work also shows the influence of jazz.

Under the influence of Satie and of the writer and artist Jean Cocteau

(1889–1963), a group of younger French composers took up the resuscitation of objectivity in music. This group—Louis Durey (1888–1979), Arthur Honegger (1892–1955), Darius Milhaud (1892–1974), Germaine Tailleferre (b. 1892), Francis Poulenc (1899–1963), and Georges Auric (1899–1983)— was dubbed "les six" by a critic in 1920, on the model of the Russian "mighty five." Although they differed in personality and style, they shared a rejection of impressionism and expressionism and a belief in the strength of tonality. Durey and Tailleferre did not achieve longlasting success. Honegger, who came from a German-Swiss background, was somewhat inclined toward German seriousness and weightiness in his style. Poulenc's music reflects the influence of early nineteenth-century Romantic lyricism as well as of the popular *chanson*. Milhaud, the most progressive of the group, was affected by Latin American music and by jazz, as exemplified in his *La création du monde* (The creation of the world, 1923). He also explored the extension of tonality to polyharmony and bitonality. Auric is mostly important as a composer of film scores, an important and rapidly growing new field for composers in this period.

Stravinsky's Neoclassic Music and Thought

Stravinsky, it will be remembered, had moved to Paris at the time of the early Diaghilev ballets. After World War I he worked in France and Switzerland, absorbing the neoclassic spirit of French musical aesthetics, though his music invariably bears such fingerprints of his own style as bright and percussive scoring, biting dissonances, irregular rhythms, and ostinatos. His works in the years from World War I to the middle of the century all share a high degree of objectivity and a predilection for structural and textural clarity, but they draw on a variety of musical traditions.

Ballet continued to be an important genre in Stravinsky's career, including works in a wide variety of styles. The ballet score *L'histoire du soldat* (The soldier's tale, 1918), for chamber ensemble, is influenced by popular dance styles and jazz; that of *Pulcinella* (1919) parodies its material from pieces by Pergolesi. *Les noces* (The wedding, 1923) is a ballet to be performed to a cantata; the dancers are accompanied by chorus, solo singers, four pianos, and percussion. *Le baiser de la fée* (The fairy's kiss, 1928) evokes the spirit of Tchaikovsky.

Stravinsky found inspiration and models for his other works of the 1920s, 1930s, and 1940s in many places. The opera-oratorio *Oedipus Rex* (1927) is derived from Sophocles. The *Symphony of Psalms*, commissioned by the Boston Symphony Orchestra for its fiftieth anniversary in 1930, uses the chorus in a fashion that suggests medieval chant. Baroque fugal and concerto styles can be heard in the Octet for Winds (1923) and the *Dumbarton Oaks* Concerto for chamber orchestra (1938). The Symphony in C (1940) is modeled on the

Classic symphony, and the opera *The Rake's Progress* (1951), which is based on a series of engravings by the eighteenth-century artist William Hogarth (1697–1764), uses the style of eighteenth-century number opera and recalls the setting of English ballad opera.

Stravinsky came to the United States in 1939 to present a series of lectures at Harvard University. These lectures, published as *Poetics of Music*, outline Stravinsky's aesthetic position, a strongly objective view of music with emphasis on form and craftsmanship. He wrote that the exalted standing given to musicians and other artists in recent times was unjustified, and he argued that the maker of artworks should be regarded as a skilled worker:

> The word *artist,* which, as it is most generally understood today, bestows on its bearer the highest intellectual prestige, the privilege of being accepted as a pure mind—this pretentious term is in my view entirely incompatible with the role of the *homo faber* [man who makes things]. . . .
>
> It was the Renaissance that invented the artist, distinguished him from the artisan and began to exalt the former at the expense of the latter.
>
> At the outset the name artist was given only to the Masters of Arts: philosophers, alchemists, magicians; but painters, sculptors, musicians, and poets had the right to be qualified only as artisans.[1]

He further described his own approach to composing, not as a process of allowing his fantasy to run unchecked, but as a rigidly controlled method:

> . . . The creator's function is to sift the elements he receives from his imagination, for human activity must impose limits on itself. The more art is controlled, worked over, the more it is free. . . .
>
> My freedom thus consists in my moving about within the narrow frame that I have assigned myself for each one of my undertakings.
>
> I shall go even farther: My freedom will be so much the greater and more meaningful the more narrowly I limit my field of action and the more I surround myself with obstacles. Whatever diminishes constraint, diminishes strength. The more constraints one imposes, the more one frees one's self of the chains that shackle the spirit.[2]

This passage clearly recalls the classical restraint advocated by Alexander Pope in his *Essay on Criticism,* " 'Tis more to guide, than spur the Muse's steed. . . ."

Because World War II had broken out, Stravinsky remained in the United States. He resided in California and became an American citizen in 1945. After *The Rake's Progress* he entered a new stylistic phase, making use of serial technique. In view of Stravinsky's aesthetics, it is natural that he was most strongly influenced in his serial works by Webern rather than by Schoenberg. Even within this technique, however, his music never fails to sound like Stravinsky.

Germany

In Germany Richard Strauss continued to work within the tradition in which he had already established himself. Even he, however, largely abandoned the expressionist material with which he had dealt in *Salomé*. In *Der Rosenkavalier* (1910) he took up a plot based on the eighteenth-century galant and adopted a lighter touch, though he adapted the post-Romantic harmonic and orchestral vocabulary to this purpose.

Hitler's government adopted Wagner as its artistic prophet. Strauss became its model composer and was appointed head of the state music ministry. Absorbed primarily in his music, Strauss did not immediately realize the meaning of his position. When he did understand the role in which he had been cast, he attempted to back away from the Nazis. He lived long enough to find himself cleared of complicity.

New Tonal Theory

Progressive composers in Germany in the 1930s found their music prohibited by the fascist government. Even those who did not reject tonality, however, might find their work suppressed as too dissonant. This was the case with Paul Hindemith (1895–1963). Hindemith, who was well established as a teacher in Germany, finally moved to the United States in 1937 and taught for several years at Yale University.

Hindemith was deeply committed to the necessity of tonality as a musical force, but his approach to tonal composition differed in an important sense from that of the other composers of tonal music just discussed. He developed his own theory of harmonic and melodic construction based on the harmonic constituents of musical tones. The theory is described in his book *The Craft of Musical Composition* (1937). Hindemith ordered melodic and harmonic intervals hierarchically, based on relationships found in the overtone series. He put his ideas into practice in some of his compositions, though he was not rigidly bound by his own abstractions. Later composers did not adopt Hindemith's methods, either; the importance of Hindemith's work is more generally in setting an example for creation of new tonal styles independent of the Classic-Romantic syntax.

Another of Hindemith's important contributions to the music of the middle twentieth century was his commitment to the type of compositions that he called *Gebrauchsmusik* (use-music). Gebrauchsmusik includes all compositions that arise from or are intended for particular, practical situations. This attitude is objective in the sense that it promotes usefulness rather than personal expression as the motivation for artistic endeavor. Hindemith, for example, wrote works for various unusual groupings of performers, for instruments that had been neglected as soloists, for amateurs, and for teaching. He also wrote such practical compositions as scores for radio plays and films.

Some of Hindemith's music seems to merit classification as neo-Romantic. Notwithstanding his analytical mind and his commitment to practicality, his music is often rich and intense, giving a sense of underlying depth of personality, especially in his vocal and programmatic compositions. Probably his most familiar work is the symphony *Mathis der Maler* (1934), three movements based on the masterpiece of the German Renaissance painter Matthias Grünewald (ca. 1475–1528), the Isenheim altarpiece (see Plate 4). In its connection of the musical work to another art form, the explicitness of its content, and its intensity of expression, Hindemith's symphony returns to the Romantic tradition. This romanticism is even greater in the opera on which the symphony is based (1935). In the plot Matthias Grünewald confronts the political crisis of the German Peasants' Revolt and must work out his role as artist in the world at large. This profound moral problem obviously reflects the experience and concerns of Hindemith himself. Such personal involvement of the composer in his music clearly marks the work as romantic. Hindemith also drew on the historical tradition of German music by incorporating chorale material in the opera and symphony, another romantic thing to do.

Hindemith and composers like him demonstrate how difficult, indeed inappropriate, it is to pigeonhole composers' ideas and styles. In his invention of new musical procedures Hindemith was progressive; in his objectivity he was a classicist; in his personal expressiveness he was a romanticist. A more distant historical perspective may make it easier to judge artists and art and establish simpler pictures of musical eras. There is constant danger of oversimplification, however, and such cases in more recent times should warn us that glib generalizations about older musical styles must be avoided.

The Influence of Regional Musics

As we have seen, an important influence on social, political, and cultural life in the late nineteenth and early twentieth century was the growth of a spirit of nationalism among smaller, less powerful, and often oppressed peoples. Indeed, World War I began as the result of this spirit when a radical member of a Serbian (slavic) nationalist movement assassinated the Austrian Archduke Ferdinand of the old and powerful Austro-Hungarian empire in 1914. Culturally, there was at the same time a rebirth of interest in folk art. Though nationalism and exoticism had already influenced music in the Romantic period, serious scientific study of ethnic art did not arise until later. When it did, it led to awareness of new materials and creative methods.

Two important Hungarian collectors of Eastern European ethnic music, Béla Bartók and Zoltán Kodály (1882–1967), were both pioneers in ethnomusicological research and composers. (Fig. 23.3) Kodály's music is the more conservative; it sets national elements in the context of relatively traditional chromatic tonal harmony. Kodály is probably best understood as representative of post-Romantic nationalism. He was also an important pioneer in music education, developing a new way of teaching music to young children and composing a large quantity of choral music for school use. His importance in the history of this field is at least as great as his compositional output.

Bartók was more progressive; his ethnomusicological research in Eastern Europe and the Middle East made it obvious to him that the Western tonal system was not the only possible means of organizing tonal materials. He wrote,

The outcome of these studies was of decisive influence upon my work, because it freed me from the tyrannical rule of the major and minor keys. The greater part of the collected treasure, and the more valuable part, was in old ecclesiastical or old Greek modes, or based on more primitive (pentatonic) scales, and the melodies were full of most free and varied rhythmic phrases and changes of tempi, played both *rubato* and *giusto*. It became clear to me that the old modes, which had been forgotten in our music, had lost nothing of their vigour. Their new employment made new rhythmic combinations possible. This new way of using the diatonic scale brought freedom from the rigid use of the major and minor keys, and eventually led to a new conception of the chromatic scale, every tone of which came to be considered of equal value and could be used freely and independently.[3]

Bartók did not actually quote folk tunes directly or try to compose new folk music; he thoroughly assimilated into his works elements of the folk music he had studied, and he looked to that music for new ideas for organizing musical materials. He experimented with scales other than the major and minor scales and with rhythms other than those in duple and triple meter, and thus he arrived at a rejection of the Classic-Romantic tradition parallel to that achieved by other composers of the time.

Bartók's contribution to Gebrauchsmusik includes the set of graded piano teaching pieces in the six volumes of the *Mikrokosmos* (1926, 1932–1939). Many of these short pieces employ the unusual scale patterns and irregular rhythms of Hungarian and Rumanian folk melodies.

The third movement of Bartók's well-known *Music for Strings, Percussion, and Celesta* (1936) illustrates his experimental techniques. This haunting movement employs very unusual sounds, extending the range of musical

Figure 23.3
Béla Bartók recording Hungarian folk songs for his ethnomusicological
research. His study of folk music led him to new tonal and rhythmic patterns
in his own compositions. (*Bartók Archivum*)

tones to include effects that until that time might have been rejected as mere
noise, including timpani glissandos and violent pizzicatos in which the strings
snap on the fingerboard. Bartók referred to this type of music as "night music."
The same movement illustrates one of the composer's favorite forms, the
symmetrical arch or bridge form, in which sections are arranged in the fashion
of a palindrome. The *Music for Strings, Percussion, and Celesta* was also an
important experiment in the spatial separation of antiphonal groups of instruments.

That Bartók also shared in the broader neoclassical movement is illustrated by his compositions in the genres of traditional absolute music, including most importantly the concerto (three for the piano and two for violin) and
chamber music. His six string quartets are among the most important works
in that genre of the twentieth century. The Concerto for Orchestra (1943)
brings the Baroque type of concerto into a twentieth-century idiom.

Like Schoenberg, Stravinsky, and Hindemith, Bartók emigrated to the United States when the political situation in Europe became insupportable. He was employed on an ad hoc basis by Columbia University and died of leukemia after five years in New York.

The Music of Socialist Realism in the Soviet Union

Nationalism in the nineteenth century had provided a source for progressive musical styles. In the twentieth century, however, nationalism generally represents a conservative trend, its aesthetic motivation being to create art that appeals to common people rather than more-advanced styles that seem to disregard the public in favor of experimentation. This was particularly true in the Soviet Union in the first decades after the revolution of October 1917.

The Soviet revolution probably had more direct impact on a nation's culture than any other political event in history. Under the philosophical premises of totalitarian socialism, all the arts, especially music, had to be reconciled with socialist theory. Lenin insisted that:

> Art belongs to the people. It must penetrate with its deepest roots into the very thick of the broad working masses. It must be understandable by these masses and loved by them. It must unite the feeling, thought, and will of these masses, inspire them. It must awaken in them artists and develop them.[4]

This argument has two significant implications for musical life. The first was relatively straightforward, that music should be made accessible to the people. This could be carried out simply enough under the state's authority. Music became part of schooling for everyone, and conservatory training was made to conform to very high standards. People were brought to concert halls and opera houses in programs organized by the government, while musical groups of all kinds, including symphony orchestras, chamber ensembles, popular bands, and choruses, were sent to industrial plants, army barracks, and so on.

The second implication of the socialist philosophy of the place of the arts in the state presented a more complicated and more important problem for music. This was the question of what musical style was appropriate under the new system. Two different musical organizations offered two strongly divergent answers. On one hand, the Russian Association of Proletarian Musicians took a conservative stance and denounced modern Western music as decadent and the music of the Classic-Romantic style as the product of effete bourgeois society. The RAPM stood for a new, accessible, "Soviet" art. On the other hand, the Association for Contemporary Music defended the independence of the artist and insisted that the Soviet Union should seize the leadership in the most progressive styles of the day.

By about 1930 the RAPM had gained ascendancy, and the Association for Contemporary Music had collapsed. The RAPM was characterized by intolerance and incompetence, however, and this led to a weakening of conservatory training, lower standards, and music of clearly poorer quality. In 1932 the level of serious musical life in the Soviet Union had declined to such an extent that the Central Committee of the Communist Party intervened. It created the Union of Soviet Composers and promulgated in music the aesthetic of *socialist realism,* adopted from the literary principles of the writer Maxim Gorky (1868–1936). The central principles of socialist realism are that art must be understandable by the masses, that it must be worthy of the great classical and Russian traditions, and that it must be optimistic and thereby help to build socialism.

In practice the effort to maintain socialist realism led to a repressive attitude toward ambitious new music. A crisis came in 1936 when *Pravda* viciously attacked the opera *Lady Macbeth of the District of Mzensk* by one of the country's leading composers, Dmitri Shostakovich (1906–1976). The work was accused of "leftist distortion" and decadent "formalism" and judged "primitive," "vulgar," and "petty-bourgeois." Shostakovich was forced to apologize, admit his error, and withdraw the score. To a later party resolution regarding correct Soviet musical style, he responded with marvelous obsequiousness:

> . . . every time that the Party corrects errors of a creative artist and points out deviations in his work, or else severely condemns a certain tendency in Soviet art, it invariably brings beneficial results for Soviet art and for individual artists. . . .
>
> . . . when the Party and our entire nation . . . condemn this tendency in my music, I know that the Party is right; I know that the Party shows solicitude for Soviet art and for me as a Soviet composer. . . .
>
> I am deeply grateful for it and for all the criticism contained in the Resolution.[5]

Shostakovich's immediate musical response to the controversy over *Lady Macbeth* was his Symphony No. 5 (1937), which he offered explicitly as the "creative reply of a Soviet artist to just criticism." This work follows in the tradition of Beethoven's Ninth Symphony, whose key it shares. It purports to be a programmatic depiction of the "stabilization of a personality" in its progression from the "tragically tense impulses of the earlier movements into optimism and the joy of living."

In a manner similar to that of Shostakovich's symphony, the Fifth Symphony (1944) of Sergey Prokofiev (1891–1953), who returned in 1936 to his native Russia after many years in the West, is programmatic in an autobiographical way. He described it as the culmination of a period in his own creative life and as "a symphony of the grandeur of the human spirit." Such programmatic content helped Soviet composers justify the exploitation of dissonance, for it can be argued that the resolution of dissonance to consonance establishes an optimistic overall picture. Tonality, therefore, was deemed absolutely essential in Soviet music.

The careers of Shostakovich and Prokofiev reveal that a great composer can produce great works even under the most trying conditions. They also indicate the effect of socialist realism on Soviet music: strong pressure in the direction of neo-Classicism and neo-Romanticism.

The United States

The impulse for the composer to reach to the audience rather than forge ahead in total disregard of the public's ability to comprehend the music brought conservatism not only to the Soviet Union, where it was legislated, but also to practical musicians in other nations. This is particularly evident in the career of the American composer Aaron Copland (b. 1900). Like a number of other American composers of his generation and later, Copland studied in France with Nadia Boulanger (1887–1979), one of the most important composition teachers of the first half of the century. Copland began as a neoclassicist, but by about 1930 his style had become rather complex and austere. He realized that he was beginning to leave the general listener behind and deliberately turned to a simpler, more popular style in an attempt to bridge the gap between composer and public. He developed a tonal style that was transparent in scoring, clear in rhythm, tuneful, and based on triadic harmony with sometimes modal and sometimes bichordal tendencies. A particular characteristic of Copland's style is the use of folk material, from both the United States and Latin America. Explicit content makes the music even more accessible. Like Stravinsky, Copland wrote several important scores for ballets. These are on American nationalistic subjects: *Billy the Kid* (1938), *Rodeo* (1942), and *Appalachian Spring* (1944), the last written for the great American choreographer Martha Graham (b. 1893). His participation in the Gebrauchsmusik movement produced several significant film scores. Only after the midpoint of the century did Copland turn to more progressive techniques, including serialism.

Several American composers in Copland's generation explored a variety of styles within the broad range of tonal idioms. These reach from Copland's relatively simple, folk-based style, through rich neo-Romanticism in the music of Howard Hanson (1896–1981), to the edge of expressionism in that of

Roger Sessions (1896–1985). The great output of these composers and numerous other Americans in the decades of the 1930s and 1940s demonstrates that the United States had reached the first rank of Western musical nations within a very short time.

Jazz

The multiplication of serious musical styles in the period after World War I included not only the fragmentation of the mainline tradition but also the rise of a musical tradition that had grown outside the "high" Western culture into the forefront of serious musical development. Jazz evolved out of the oral tradition of black American slavery, uniting the powerful syncopated rhythms of the African heritage, the formulaic improvisational melody of slave calls and black church singing, and the melody-and-accompaniment texture and harmonic progressions of Western art music.

In the 1920s jazz moved with the emigration of African-Americans out of the South into the cities of the North, where it quickly became popular. The reasons for its appeal to the wealthier, "cultured," white upper class are, of course, complex. Certainly part of the explanation of its success must be sought in the same curiosity for new and different experiences that led to exoticism in Europe in the nineteenth century. In addition, the fact that the music of "serious" composers had grown so difficult undoubtedly left a gap that the simpler, more accessible jazz could fill. The rhythms were lively, the harmony tonal, and the chamberlike scoring and clearly patterned twelve- and sixteen-bar blues forms easy to follow. Moreover, as in any period, the element of virtuosic performance and the excitement presented by the fundamental risk factor in improvisation were bound to captivate the audience. To musicians the rise of commercial recording and broadcasting meant that composing and playing in a popular style could provide a very handsome income.

In the 1930s and early 1940s commercialism produced the big band sound and the style of swing. This represents a distinct part of the growing process in the history of jazz. The leaner, simpler, "classic" sound of 1920s Dixieland jazz was enriched by larger ensembles and made more "romantic." As a result of the greater size of the ensembles, it became necessary to compose the music more thoroughly. Improvisation was generally limited to one featured performer at a time, and star virtuosos multiplied. The function of the music also changed, as it was increasingly used for dancing.

Incorporating Jazz into Traditional Genres

It did not take long for composers to incorporate the new concepts and sounds of jazz into the more traditional musical genres. We have already noted the influence of jazz in the neoclassic music of Stravinsky, Ravel, and Milhaud.

The American composer George Gershwin (1898–1937) trained as a classical pianist and composer but began his (popular songs and Broadway musical shows, also introduce and popular music into more-sophisticated works such as the Rha (1924) for piano and jazz band (later rescored for piano and orchestr , *American in Paris* (1928), and the opera *Porgy and Bess* (1935).

The Avant-Garde

During the period between the world wars a number of highly original individual composers began to produce remarkable new works that stretched the limits of music in unexpected directions. The foundations of the avant-garde movement were in part abstract and philosophical. Charles Ives's ideas about the independence of the individual had already produced remarkable experimental results in his music. In 1907 the post-Romantic German-Italian composer Ferruccio Busoni (1866–1924) had written a document entitled *Entwurf einer neuen Aesthetik der Tonkunst* (Draft for a new esthetic of music), in which he proposed that:

> The creator should adopt no traditional law on trust and faith, and treat his own creation as an exception to that law from the outset. For his individual case he must seek out, formulate a suitable individual law and destroy it again after the first complete application, in order not to fall into repetitions in a later work himself.
>
> The creator's problem consists in setting up laws, and not in following laws. Whoever follows given laws ceases to be a creator.

The exploration of new sounds for music was perhaps the most important area of work in the avant-garde. In 1913 the Italian painter, inventor, and composer Luigi Russolo (1885–1947) wrote a manifesto entitled *L'arte dei rumori* (The art of noises), in which he advocated the use of sounds more akin to everyday noises than to traditional musical tones. Russolo also experimented with compositions for noise machines of his own invention. The American composer George Antheil (1900–1959) produced his *Ballet mécanique* in 1927, with percussion, eight pianos, a pianola, and an airplane propellor; it was later revised to incorporate anvils, bells, buzz saws, and car horns. Honegger even participated, in a somewhat more conservative fashion, in the movement to absorb modern mechanical sounds into music with his *Pacific 231* (1924), a symphonic poem about a train.

Busoni's student Edgard Varèse (1883–1965), an early emigrant to the United States, was among the most important of the avant-garde composers of the 1920s and 1930s. Like others, his interests included the expansion of the repertoire of sounds that could be accepted as musical tones, particularly percussive sounds, as in his most famous work, *Ionisation* (1931), for thirteen percussionists. Varèse also moved away from organization of music according to melody and harmony and created large sound events instead. In 1936 he described his musical constructions in terms of visual and spatial metaphors:

> . . . you will find in my works the movement of masses, varying in radiance, and of different densities and volumes. When these masses come into collision, the phenomena of penetration or repulsion will result. Certain transmutations taking place on one plane, by projecting themselves on other planes which move at different speeds and are placed at different angles, should create the impression of prismatic aural (auditory) deformations.[6]

Other American composers tried not only new sounds but also new types of tonal organization. Henry Cowell (1897–1965) experimented with sound produced by playing the piano on the inside rather than via the keyboard and also led in the use of tone clusters. The sometime hobo Harry Partch (1901–1974) invented new instruments under such curious names as blue rainbow, Castor and Pollux (which is also the title of one of his compositions), crychord, cloud chamber bowls, quadrangularis reversum, and chromelodeon; he worked in a private tonal realm with forty-three pitches to the octave. A younger composer, John Cage (b. 1912), got new sounds out of the piano in the 1930s and 1940s by inserting small objects of various types between the strings; the instrument thus modified is known as the *prepared piano*.

Questions for Reflection

❖   How did the effects of the two world wars parallel or differ from the effects of earlier wars on music?

❖   Compare the exploration of the mathematical aspects of music in serialism to the application of mathematical thinking in earlier periods. What does this comparison suggest about the expressive models for music in the twentieth century?

❖   How does the increasing globalization of culture in the twentieth century relate to the growing identification of national styles in the period between the two world wars? Could it be argued that a "Western tradition" in music came to an end in the twentieth century?

❖   What are and are not valid roles of government in relation to the arts? How do capitalist and socialist political systems differ in their understanding and practice in this area?

❖ How does the avant-garde and the reaction to it in the twentieth century resemble or differ from other progressive movements in the early centuries of the Western musical tradition?

Suggestions for Further Reading

A general survey of the periods discussed in this and the following chapter is Arnold Whittall, *Music since the First World War* (London: St. Martin's, 1977). An interesting chronology, including a collection of documents, is Nicolas Slonimsky, *Music since 1900*, 4th ed. (New York: Scribner's, 1972).

Some writings of composers are collected in Elliott Schwartz and Barney Childs, eds., *Contemporary Composers on Contemporary Music* (New York: Holt, Rinehart & Winston, 1967).

On serialism, see George Perle, *Serialism and Atonality*, 5th ed. (Berkeley: University of California Press, 1981).

On Soviet music, see *Music and Musical Life in Soviet Russia, Enlarged Edition, 1917–1981* (Bloomington: Indiana University Press, 1983).

Two helpful surveys of jazz are Frank Tirro, *Jazz: A History* (New York: Norton, 1977), and Mark C. Gridley, *Jazz Styles: History and Analysis* (Englewood Cliffs, N. J.: Prentice-Hall, 1988).

Selected books by and about individual composers include:

Copland: Aaron Copland, *Music and Imagination* (Cambridge: Harvard University Press, 1985), and N. Butterworth, *The Music of Aaron Copland* (New York: Universe, 1986).

Gershwin: Edward Jablonsky, *Gershwin* (New York: Doubleday, 1987).

Hindemith: Paul Hindemith, *The Craft of Musical Composition* (New York: Associated, 1954) deals with the technical aspects of composing, whereas his *A Composer's World* (Cambridge: Harvard University Press, 1952) discusses more philosophical matters. For a biography, see Ian Kemp, *Hindemith* (London: Oxford University Press, 1967).

Honegger: Arthur Honegger, *I Am a Composer*, trans. Wilson O. Clough and Allan Arthur Willman (New York: St. Martin's, 1966).

Kodály: Laszlö Eösze, *Zoltan Kodály*, trans. István Farkas and Gyula Gulyás (London: Collett's 1962), and Erno Lendvai, *The Workshop of Bartók and Kodály* (Budapest: Editio Musica, 1983).

Milhaud: Darius Milhaud, *Notes without Music*, trans. D. Evans (New York: Knopf, 1970).

Partch: Harry Partch, *Genesis of a Music*, 2d ed. (New York: Da Capo, 1974).

Poulenc: Keith W. Daniel, *Francis Poulenc: The Man and His Songs* (Ann Arbor, Mich: UMI Research Press, 1982).

Prokofiev: Harlow Robinson, *Prokofiev: A Biography* (New York: Viking, 1987).

Satie: Rollo Myers, *Erik Satie* (New York: Dover, 1968).

Sessions: Roger Sessions, *The Musical Experience of Composer, Performer, Listener* (Princeton: Princeton University Press, 1950), and *Questions about Music* (Cambridge: Harvard University Press, 1970). Andrea Olmstead, *Roger Sessions and His Music* (Ann Arbor, Mich.: UMI Research Press, 1985).

Shostakovich: Christopher Norris, ed., *Shostakovich: The Man and His Music* (London: Marion Boyars, 1982).

Webern: Anton Webern, *The Path to New Music*, ed. Willi Reich, trans. Leo Black (Bryn Mawr: Presser, 1963), and Hans Moldenhauer, *Anton von Webern* (New York: Knopf, 1979).

Notes

1. Igor Stravinsky, *Poetics of Music in the Form of Six Lessons*, trans. Arthur Knodel and Ingolf Dahl (Cambridge: Harvard University Press, 1947), 51–52.

2. Ibid., 63, 65.

3. "The Life of Béla Bartók," *Tempo* 13 (Autumn 1949), 4–5. Reprinted by permission of Boosey & Hawkes, Inc.

4. Gerald Abraham, "Music in the Soviet Union," in *The New Oxford History of Music*, Vol. 10, *The Modern Age: 1890–1960,* ed. Martin Cooper (London: Oxford University Press, 1974), 640.

5. Nicolas Slonimsky, *Music since 1900*, 4th ed. (New York: Charles Scribner's Sons, 1971), 1370–1371.

6. "Edgar [sic] Varèse, 'Great Sound Builder' Is Here," *The Santa Fe New Mexican*, 15 June 1936, quoted in Fernand Ouellette, *Edgard Varèse*, trans. Derek Coltman (New York: Orion, 1968), 84.

24
IN THE SECOND HALF
OF THE TWENTIETH
CENTURY

History and Contemporary Music

It is extremely difficult to place the events and artifacts of one's contemporary culture into historical perspective. Much of the music of the past has faded into obscurity, leaving the historian a preselected body of evidence. Because the winnowing-out process of history has not yet separated the wheat from the chaff of the latest music, however, contemporary attempts to generalize about style may overlook what to later times will seem the greatest and most significant composers and works.

It will be wise to remember several truths about the history of music as we approach the music of our own time. First, all composers in any era compose contemporary music. Second, all composers have roots in their past and must choose the degree to which they will continue in traditional directions or attempt to launch new ones. Third, composers become great for a variety of reasons—some because of their mastery of existing styles and others because they envision new styles that later artists will bring to completion. Finally, circumstances external to music itself, and therefore outside the control of the musician, often have powerful and unforeseeable effects on the development of the art.

In the second half of the twentieth century, many composers continued to employ the musical styles of the first half of the century. These styles, some of which met hostile receptions at their first appearance, are heard by audiences with increasing acceptance as they become more familiar. Time will tell which works become lasting masterpieces and which fade from view. Only history determines what styles, genres, and composers ultimately attain historical prominence. The focus of the following discussion will be on some of the newer musical ideas and styles in the period since World War II.

Total Control

The development of musical structure following Webern led a number of composers to concentrate on achieving more and more control over each aspect of musical style. The extension of the serial technique was increased to cover every aspect of the music, and often the series governing different elements were interrelated according to complex mathematical formulas.

A pioneer in this area was the American composer Milton Babbitt (b. 1916), who taught first mathematics and then music at Princeton University. In 1947 and 1948 he worked systematically at the control not only of melodic and harmonic material but also of duration, dynamics, articulation, and scoring by mathematical-musical serial techniques.

The Frenchman Olivier Messiaen (b. 1908) was a European leader in the broadening of serial composition. Messiaen's interests range from the songs of birds, which he has transcribed avidly, to mystical Catholicism. Much of his music is characterized by subjectivity and programmatic content or orientation. He has absorbed a variety of musical materials, which he sometimes juxtaposes and sometimes synthesizes into an eclectic style, including new types of tonal patterns and scales, ancient Greek poetic meters, non-Western additive rhythms, impressionist sonorities, medieval chant, oriental music, and birdcalls. His experiments in rhythmic organization include the invention of complex sequences of durations in what he calls "nonretrogradable" rhythms, that is, symmetrical or palindromic patterns. In the piano piece "Mode de valeurs et d'intensités" (Mode of values and intensities, 1949), No. 2 from his *Etudes de rythme,* Messiaen serialized pitch, duration, loudness, and articulation in a systematic fashion in which each element is connected with the others. The use of such techniques need not lead to such abstract music, however; in Messiaen's *Quatuor pour le fin du temps* (Quartet for the end of time, 1940) they are combined with other elements of his style to evoke an apocalyptic, mystical vision.

A student of Messiaen at the Paris Conservatory, Pierre Boulez (b. 1925) followed this trend with his *Structures I* (1952). This work for two pianos establishes total control by interrelated series of twelve each of pitches, durations, dynamic levels, and articulations. In later works, such as the well-known *Le marteau sans maître* (The hammer without a master, 1953–1954), a set of songs and instrumental pieces for alto voice, flute, guitar, viola, and percussion on poems by the surrealist poet René Char, Boulez began to seek some flexibility to offset the purely mechanical tendencies of total serialization. After an active international career as a conductor, Boulez became director of the Institut de Recherche et de Coordination Acoustique/Musique (IRCAM) in Paris, one of the leading centers of new music.

Following World War II a center for avant-garde music was established in Darmstadt, Germany, where an annual International Summer Course for New Music was begun in 1946 to bring up to date German composers who had missed out on new developments during the repression of the Nazi period. A leading German figure in the total control movement was Karlheinz Stockhausen (b. 1928), whose *Kontra-Punkte* (1953) for chamber orchestra was totally serialized.

Some thorny new aesthetic questions arise in connection with totally serialized music. For example, once the initial planning is completed, does not the writing of the music become a purely mechanical matter? The composer's role is one of conception and predetermination of the course of the music; does the idea that specific moments during the playing out of the piece express anything disappear? If so, what place does expression have in the sound experience? If the composer's ideas belong primarily to the process of mathematical conception and planning, will the appeal of the music resemble that of an elegant equation, and will there be any special justification for actual realization of the music in performance?

Totally serialized music also presents enormous problems for performers. The execution of the score depends on clear distinction of often very rapid or subtle rhythms, dynamic levels, and articulations of individual notes, as well as technically awkward passages for traditional instruments. Moreover, the means by which performers have conventionally expressed themselves in their playing have been usurped by the composers, so that players might be frustrated by the sense that there is ultimately nothing for them to do except produce the designated musical tones with as much precision as possible.

There are thus both aesthetic and practical problems in total control music. It is not surprising that even the leading composers of this style later turned in other directions. The techniques of serialism are for many composers tools to be used as they wish, not rigid, inviolable laws.

The Exploration of New Timbres: Extended Techniques

As we have already observed, one major issue for avant-garde composers before World War II was the addition to the available repertoire of new timbres, either never yet heard or earlier dismissed as mere noise. After 1945 this concern remained an important one, resulting in what are called *extended techniques* for existing instruments and the voice.

Some of the composers interested in new timbres continued to achieve remarkable innovative effects by using traditional instruments in unusual ways. The Polish composer Krzysztof Penderecki's (b. 1933) "Threnody to the Victims of Hiroshima" (1960), for example, employs a string orchestra of fifty-two instruments in ways that produce surprising sounds. Rather than restricting the players to precise pitches, Penderecki calls for "bands of sound" that may be introduced by having the players spread from a unison in different degrees upward and downward; they may then return from the band of sound by reversing the process. The timbre thus departs from a single tone into a roaring sound and then refocuses on the unison again. In addition, Penderecki demands a variety of string techniques: arco and pizzicato, playing over the fingerboard, at the bridge, between the bridge and the tail piece, on the tail piece itself, col legno and col legno battuto, and even striking the body of the instrument. In such music, melody and harmony do not actually exist as style elements at all, and tonality is not an issue.

The American composer George Crumb (b. 1929) has also made important experiments with unusual sound production from voices and instruments, as well as the introduction of some uncommmon sound sources. *Ancient Voices of Children* (1970), on texts by the Spanish poet Federico Garcia Lorca (1898–1936), calls for a soprano soloist and offstage boy soprano. The onstage voice is modified by singing into a piano with the dampers released, and the vocalists must produce a variety of nontraditional sounds, including not only Sprechstimme and dramatic speaking but also percussive and nonverbal sounds, flutter-tongue rolls, and a "metallic" timbre. The same work calls for electrically amplified traditional instruments. *Black Angels: Thirteen Images from the Dark Land* (1970) requires an electrified string quartet, the players supplementing their regular instruments by maracas, tam-tam, and crystal glasses.

One result of this is that descriptions of new music cannot rely on traditional terminology. As we have already noted, Varèse found it more appropriate to speak of his works in spatial terms, referring to the collision and penetration of masses and volumes. There are no standard musical definitions for such usage, and new vocabularies are continually tried for new works. Much remains to be done in this area, if indeed any common terminology can be established. The creation of new timbres and the use of extended techniques thus carry with them entirely new possibilities for musical organization and style elements, going far beyond the mere addition of the sounds themselves to the available catalogue.

Such experiments in timbre as those of Penderecki and Crumb inevitably lead to new types of notation. In some cases these are directed to the reader of a score in an attempt to give some visual image of the sound, as in Penderecki's notation of dense bands along the staff. In other cases they address the performer, giving instructions for unusual performance techniques. In the latter case the notation may bear little symbolic relationship to the sounds actually heard. This is not a radical new idea, for it has been the case with some older notations, as well, such as those for string harmonics or tablature. Given the desire of composers to create ever-new timbres and effects, the composition and performance of such music often requires mastering a new notation for each new piece. Scores commonly have tables of notational symbols that look rather like the tables of *agréments* in French Baroque keyboard collections and serve exactly the same purpose.

Noteworthy is the use of texts or programs to explain the nontraditional sounds. This also has predecessors in the past. It will be recalled, for example, that Monteverdi justified his use of seconda prattica harmonic dissonance by textual considerations. Similarly, in the late nineteenth century textual programs accounted for unusual structural designs in symphonic poems. That new and strange musical techniques still seem to demand connection to extramusical content is evidenced by the common observation of nonmusicians who, on hearing a new style, remark that it sounds like music for a horror film.

Electronic Music

After 1937 Varèse gave up composing because he could not create the sounds in his aural imagination by traditional means. He resumed composition only in the 1950s, when adequate new, electronic sound sources became available. Important early centers for electronic music were located at the studios of the French Radio in Paris and at the Columbia-Princeton Electronic Music Center in New York, headed by Otto Luening (b. 1900) and Vladimir Ussachevsky (1911–1990). Electronic composition spread rapidly through the United States and Europe and was firmly rooted within a couple of decades.

In the early years of electronic composition the sources of sound available to composers were those of recorded tones and noises. By the 1940s composers equipped with tape recorders and microphones were already collecting all sorts of sounds to experiment with and combine into compositions. This sort of composition is known as *musique concrète*. The first tape music dates from 1948 and was created by Pierre Schaeffer (b. 1910) and Pierre Henry in France. A fine American example from a few years later is Ussachevsky's *Linear Contrasts* (1957), which uses the sounds of a gong, a harpsichord, and voices, though these sounds are so modified that their sources are not particularly evident.

The synthesizer, introduced in the 1950s, made it possible to generate tones directly on tape by electronic means, including sine, square, and sawtooth waves, and "white" noise. With the introduction of such purely electronic tones, composers had cleaner, more predictable raw material ready-to-hand in the studio.

The electronic studio offered the composer not only new sounds but also new means for modifying and manipulating sound. With fairly simple devices, tones could be played backward or at different speeds, altered in volume or pitch, and filtered or reverberated to change timbre. By means of overdubbing, that is, recording several sounds on a single segment of tape, complex new sounds could be created out of simpler ones.

The composition of music was also facilitated by electronic means. Even the tape recorder offered quite a few possibilities. For example, playing taped sounds backward produced retrograde motion. Several taped lines could be superimposed and recorded in counterpoint. Splicing small pieces of tape created rhythms that could then be measured out in centimeters rather than seconds. For the purposes of serial composition, a sequence of tones on tape could be spliced into a *tape loop* to be run through a machine in circular fashion while various means were applied to modify the series electronically. The synthesizer, which not only generated tones but could also put out tones in series, facilitated composition and gave the composer much more complete control over his or her material and compositional process. It was only natural that composers of the total control style, such as Stockhausen, would turn to electronic means to extend their control. Composition directly on tape meant that they did not have to rely on the approximations of notation or to find and trust live performers. Babbitt, for example, became associated with the Columbia-Princeton Electronic Music Center. His 1961 *Composition for Synthesizer* employs all synthetic sounds and serial procedures that can often be clearly heard.

Computers

The introduction of the computer in composing eliminated a great deal of manual labor and gave the composer even more control over the music. The mathematical calculations of total serialization are, of course, naturally suited to the computer. The use of a computer in tandem with a synthesizer facilitates both delicate adjustments in the sound material itself and the actual composition of pieces. Charles Dodge (b. 1945) explored the possibilities of computer-synthesized music in his *Changes* (1969–1970), which belongs to the total control tradition, and the humorous, madrigalistic *Speech Songs* (1973), in which the computer was used to synthesize words as well as pitches, rhythms, and timbres.

The Performer

Electronic composition calls into question the role of the performer in late-twentieth-century music. The composer's direct control of the sound on tape or in digital storage on the computer eliminates the need for players, while the ever-increasing capabilities of synthesis also began to put players out of work. Some composers, however, have found good reason to combine live performance with electronic composition. An example is the Argentine native Mario Davidovsky (b. 1934), whose various compositions entitled *Synchronisms* combine different live performers with taped sounds. One advantage of this is that it provides a human presence and a degree of flexibility in the music; such works make a more effective presentation in a public concert than music coming from immobile electronic speakers on the stage. In addition, the risk involved in the interplay between performer and tape, which requires a very precise rhythmic sense on the part of the player and sometimes the musicality to blend live and electronic timbres, lends a special interest to the performance.

Composers have recently found ways to use electronic sound sampling and synthesis in performance. This has produced a new relationship between player and electronic technology, in which the performer has considerable control in the creative musical process. In addition, an entirely new kind of live performing musician, the synthesizer operator, has now been added to many kinds of music.

Indeterminacy

Some composers, however, have questioned the seemingly fundamental assumption that in the course of the history of music it is inevitable that composers should take greater and greater control of musical sound and structure. They reason that most music has involved some degree of flexibility in actual execution and that this aspect of the art deserves more exploration. This philosophy has led to the idea of *indeterminacy* in musical composition. The music of indeterminacy is also sometimes called *chance music* or *aleatory music* (from the Latin *alea*, meaning dice).

We observed earlier that Charles Ives anticipated later composers' explorations of this idea. The concept of indeterminacy was pioneered most notably by the avant-garde composer John Cage. Cage, strongly influenced by Eastern mystical philosophy, argues against the historical Western compulsion for rigorous control and precision in art. Instead he values freedom, flexibility, and randomness.

In indeterminate music the composer generally exercises partial control.

He might establish the conditions for the performance (i. e., the form of the work) but relinquish control over the actual sound, as in Cage's *Imaginary Landscape No. 4,* which calls for twelve radios tuned to various frequencies and manipulated according to a specific set of instructions but playing whatever happens to be broadcast at the time. On the other hand, the composer may provide fixed sound materials but give up control of the organization, as in *HPSCHD* (1969) by Cage and Lejaren Hiller (b. 1924), in which scored and recorded sounds are provided, but the form is generated anew for each performance by random processes.

Cage's significance consists not only in his works but also in the aesthetic that underlies them. He has written and talked extensively about the art; his book *Silence* (1961) explores his thoughts. In what is perhaps Cage's most famous piece, *4′ 33″,* which consists of four minutes and thirty-three seconds in which the performer (or performers, since the scoring is indeterminate) does nothing, one is left to ponder whether the music truly consists of the performer's silence, of the incidental sounds in the performance space, or of what goes on in the minds of the players and audience.

Indeterminacy, Performers, and Computers

Indeterminacy is, for many more recent composers, one of many elements to be used in expressing ideas, not necessarily the main point of a piece. Crumb, for example, has employed structures in which performers take up musical fragments according to various instructions in maplike scores, passing with some freedom from one musical unit to another. Even Boulez, coming from the tradition of total control, has worked in such open forms, leaving decisions about the order of movements in his Third Piano Sonata (1957) up to the player.

The freedom thus given to performers has had several effects. Entirely new regions of creativity and virtuosity have opened up for performing musicians. They must not only handle technically difficult material but also be able to respond in the course of performance to unanticipated or unprecedented demands. In many cases they must learn to read notations made up of graphic symbols that do not correspond to fixed notes and rhythms. They must exert their own creative imaginations in ways not called for by the standard repertoire of the common practice periods.

There are also points of contact between indeterminacy and the mathematical ways of musical thinking associated with computer applications. Stockhausen's *Momente* (1964) employs serialism to determine different degrees of control and freedom in the music. The Rumanian-born French composer Yannis Xenakis (b. 1922), who came to music from a mathematical background, has employed computers to generate random numbers to be used in composing.

Minimalism

The important style known as *minimalism* or as *systematic* or *process* music is related to the ideas of Cage. In this style the composer establishes only a few brief musical motives. These are played in continuous repetition, perhaps with periodic additions of new ones or deletions of ones already used. (Fig. 24.1) A well-known example is *In C* by Terry Riley (b. 1935). It consists of fifty-three motives, to be used in ostinatolike fashion as long as the performers wish. This results in a musical form that evolves continuously in slow-moving, apparently suspended time. Steve Reich created similar effects by presenting a single musical motive in several simultaneous lines that are slightly out of phase. He used either electronic media, as in *Come Out* (1966), which is based on a recorded phrase spoken by a young African-American man describing his experience in a police station, or live performers, as in *Piano Phase* (1967) for two pianists, or *Violin Phase* (1967), which combines live performance and tape.

The expressive effect of minimalist music is often hypnotic, rather like the chanting of a mantra. Indeed much of the aesthetic basis for this type of music comes from Eastern mystical philosophies. Such music denies many of the traditional Western concepts that have governed music for at least two centuries, that is, dialectical resolution of dualistic opposites; development; and a sense of beginning, middle, and end.

Mixed-Media and Performance-Oriented Music

There has been a recent trend in the direction of exploiting the special advantages of the live performance experience for the combination of aural, visual, and gestural materials in music. Crumb's *Vox balanae* (The voice of the whale, 1971), for amplified flute, cello, and piano, is to be played by performers in masks under blue lighting. Other works require the players to move about on the stage during the course of the performance. In a way such music is the antithesis of purely electronic music, for it attains its interest and appeal in precisely the elements that do not suit simple electronic playback through speakers or headphones. In some cases the performance activity actually takes precedence over the sound in the impression the work makes.

Works such as the immense operatic creations of Philip Glass (b. 1937) combine such compositional devices as minimalism and collage, text, and action and stage design. Glass's groundbreaking *Einstein on the Beach* (1975) is his best-known work in this genre. Glass also pursues philosophical issues.

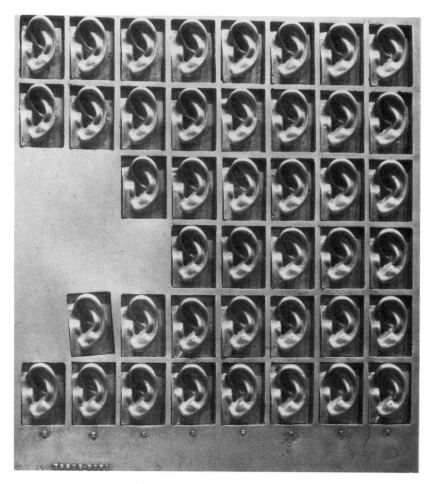

Figure 24.1
Tomio Miki (b. 1937), *Untitled (Ears)* (1964). Minimalism in visual art, as in music, often depends on simple repetition of a small design or motive, frequently presented in a phased manner. (*Collection, Museum of Modern Art, New York. Phillip Johnson Fund.*)

Einstein on the Beach deals with science and technology in relation to society, and *The Voyage*, commissioned for the five-hundredth anniversary of Columbus's discovery of the New World, deals with the innate human urge to discover. In their combination of media and use of music to make a philosophical statement, these works are a sort of reincarnation of the Gesamtkunstwerk.

As we have already noted, the use of multiple media and text, program, or staging helps audiences gain access to new and esoteric musical styles. It also belongs to the romantic aesthetic in the broad sense because it emphasizes the connection of music and extramusical experience. Also characteristic of this music is a return to diatonic, triadic harmonic sonority (not necessarily associated with functional harmonic progression, however), a deliberate attempt to appeal to the public and to reestablish connections with the music-historical tradition. In some cases, notably in works by George Rochberg (b. 1918), part of the material is taken from actual works of earlier composers, in a modern application of the parody technique that dates back to the Renaissance. These tendencies have led recent critics to characterize this sort of music as the New Romanticism. It falls into a completely separate line of development from the late Romantic or post-Romantic music of the turn of the century, as well as from the neo-Classic, neo-Romantic stream of the middle of the century, however. This close historical juxtaposition of Romantic styles is significant, for it indicates both the rapidity of musical change in the twentieth century and the considerable fragmentation of the Western musical tradition.

Jazz and Pop Music

The genres of popular music in the West from the time of World War II also demonstrate stylistic fragmentation. Jazz continued to develop, producing its own avant-garde in the style of bop in the late 1940s, represented by such musicians as Charlie Parker (1920–1955) and Dizzy Gillespie (b. 1917). Improvisation with extreme freedom from the underlying harmonic plan of a piece, as in the highly creative saxophone playing of John Coltrane (1926–1967) and Ornette Coleman (b. 1930), led to dissonant, atonal "free jazz" beginning in the late 1950s. At the same time there were "third stream" experiments in combining jazz with the mainstream tradition. The leader both in developing the theory and in actual composition of third-stream music was Gunther Schuller (b. 1925).

In the 1950s the African-American dance music style known as rhythm and blues, an offspring of jazz, combined with white country-western music to produce rock and roll. The affluent, youth-oriented society of the postwar era in the United States soon made rock music, and pop music in general, a dominant cultural force. The pop tradition forms its own history, making it possible to trace various phases. The British rock group the Beatles in the early 1960s may, for example, fairly be said to represent the high classic phase in rock music. One of the greatest minds in rock is Frank Zappa (b. 1940), who links advanced rock with the mainstream tradition of Stravinsky and the avant-garde of Varèse and Cage. Rock music quickly reached into the latest technology of the musical avant-garde and soon returned new ideas to non-popular composers. In addition, the trend toward multiple media found its own rock music realization in the visual effects added to rock concerts and the television music video.

Rock and pop music also quickly became widely diverse, including a variety of subcategories, often addressing separate ethnic and social groups within the large, heterogeneous American and European population. While American and British rock music became internationally popular, national rock idioms have also developed around the world, influenced by local folk music traditions.

Composers in Late Twentieth-Century Society

The twentieth century presented a new set of conditions under which composers must work. In Eastern Europe during the period of socialist state control, composers and other artists found themselves supported financially by the government but subject to aesthetic and stylistic restrictions. Their situation was in certain senses ironically similar to that of earlier composers working under the system of noble patronage. In the West the free-enterprise system tended to support popular musicians as well some nonpopular composers, such as a few of the minimalists, who became popular cult figures. Market economics thereby took over the function of the patron, with no less control over the composer's development.

Other composers obtained funding through government or private agencies created to support the arts. In these cases much of the artist's time and energy was taken up in application processes, and the monetary awards naturally depended on the judgment of committees. Commissions, though available, were never easily found, and the accumulation of a list of grants and prizes became important to the composer as a means of keeping his or her career alive.

Perhaps the most important alternative—one relied on by many outstanding composers—was an academic position at a college, university, or conservatory. In this situation, however, teaching absorbed a substantial part of the composer's energy, and the nature of the academic environment tended to favor a somewhat intellectual approach to music. However, the university must not be overlooked as a source of musical patronage in the late twentieth century, either for composers or for public performance of music other than popular music.

Women and Minority Composers

In the late twentieth century, women and minorities made significant progress in gaining access to composing and conducting careers, which had traditionally been the nearly exclusive domain of white men. Despite women's having won a political voice in the Western democracies in the first half of the century, genuine cultural and musical independence for women remained a goal approached only slowly and won by dint of considerable determination and strength. An important milestone for women was marked in 1983 when Ellen Taaffe Zwilich (b. 1939) became the first woman to win a Pulitzer Prize for composition, with her Symphony No. 1 (*Three Movements for Orchestra*).

African-American composers also had difficulty in making their careers. A ground-breaking composer in the years between the world wars was William Grant Still (1895–1978), the first African-American to have his works performed by major musical organizations and the first to conduct a major orchestra. Much of his music employs African-American folk material and is thus truly nationalistic in a sense that cannot quite be applied to such usage by white composers, whose use of those same materials might better be regarded as exoticist. The range of musical and extramusical influences the black composer can draw from his or her special heritage is illustrated by the works of T. J. Anderson (b. 1928), who employs jazz idioms and draws programmatic inspiration from both urban and rural black life. Anderson's works are by no means merely "ethnic," however, and some belong to the post-Webern part of the Western tradition.

The shrinking of the world also brought East and West together to blend and diversify musical cultures. A major contributor to this development was the Indian sitar virtuoso Ravi Shankar (b. 1920), whose tours to Europe and the United States beginning in the 1950s made a considerable impression on Western musicians, in both popular and "classical" spheres. Indian and African drumming styles influenced the compositions of some of the minimalist composers. A later interaction was that of the West with Japan. Toru Takemitsu (b. 1930) combined aesthetic and stylistic ideas from both hemispheres, notably in *November Steps* (1967), a large-scale concerted work for the Japanese *biwa* and *shakuhachi*, with an orchestra of Western instruments.

The Situation at the End of the Twentieth Century

Though it may still be too early to judge, it is possible that the twentieth century marks a major watershed in the history of musical ideas and styles in Western culture. For one thing, the aesthetics of recent music—from that of total control to that of indeterminacy—no longer seem to draw on the literary models that have dominated Western theories of musical expression since the Renaissance. Indeed, fundamental assumptions about musical expression that lasted from the sixteenth through the nineteenth centuries have been radically challenged by the new theories of objectivity, serialism, indeterminacy, and minimalism. Stravinsky clearly rejected the idea that music derives its models from literature, saying that it is

. . . far closer to mathematics than to literature—not perhaps to mathematics itself, but certainly to something like mathematical thinking and mathematical relationships. . . . I am not saying that composers think in equations or charts of numbers, nor are those things more able to symbolize music. But the way composers think—the way I think—is, it seems to me, not very different from mathematical thinking.[1]

There is, in addition, a certain broadening of culture that comes with wider and more rapid communication throughout the world. One manifestation of this is the permeation of Western composers' works by philosophies and musical material drawn from other cultures. Western music has at the same time been spread throughout the world, and its influence can be heard in some other indigenous repertoires.

To complicate the picture still further, Western musical culture has fragmented into a variety of subcultures and different musical styles. Even in the case of works that combine techniques of different schools, such fusions merely create more substyles; it seems impossible to find a basis for identifying stylistic or aesthetic conventions that would justify viewing the Western music or musical thought of this period as in some sense unified. This fragmentation began with the individualism and drive for originality in the early nineteenth century, and it is not surprising that there should be a shattering of the Western tradition in the twentieth. The Western musical tradition was synthesized out of disparate regional cultures in the Middle Ages. It seems to have come full circle in the course of ten or twelve centuries. It may no longer be possible to approach music history in as direct a fashion hereafter.

The study of music history has much to teach us and can enrich musical ideas and styles. It cannot, however, prophesy directions for the future. The best one can hope is that the future of our musical tradition will be as lively, diverse, and challenging as the past.

Questions for Reflection

✤   At what periods in the Western musical tradition have there been dramatic developments in the addition of new timbres to the compositional palette comparable to those in the twentieth century? Are there other significant parallels between those periods and this one?

✤   How has the development of purely recorded music and the general dominance of playback systems over live performance in the late twentieth century altered the position of the listener in music?

✤   Do developments in Western music in the late twentieth century demand rethinking of the traditional Western definitions of music?

✤   Can the development and position of popular music in the United States

and Europe in the post–World War II era be paralleled to any earlier developments in the Western musical tradition?

Suggestions for Further Reading

For a good general study of music since World War II, see Paul Griffiths,
Modern Music: The Avant-Garde since 1945 (London: Dent, 1981). American
contemporary music is discussed in John Rockwell, *All American Music: Composition in the Late Twentieth Century* (New York: Knopf, 1983).

On electronic music, see Herbert Russcol, *The Liberation of Sound* (Engle-
wood Cliffs, N. J.: Prentice-Hall, 1972); Jon Appleton and Ronald Perera, eds.,
The Development and Practice of Electronic Music (Englewood Cliffs, N. J.: Pren-
tice-Hall, 1975); Elliott Schwartz, *Electronic Music: A Listener's Guide,* rev. ed.
(New York: Praeger, 1975); David Ernst, *The Evolution of Electronic Music* (New
York: Schirmer, 1977); and Paul Griffiths, *A Guide to Electronic Music* (London:
Thames & Hudson, 1979).

On rock music, Carl Belz, *The Story of Rock,* 2d ed. (New York: Oxford
University Press, 1972), is now somewhat out of date. Jim Curtis, *Rock Eras:
Interpretations of Music and Society, 1954–1984* (Bowling Green, Ohio: Bowling
Green State University Popular Press, 1987), gives a somewhat personal read-
ing of the history of rock music.

On women in music history, see Carol Neuls-Bates, ed., *Women in Music*
(New York: Harper & Row, 1982).

Books by and about some of the individual composers discussed in this
chapter include the following:

Boulez: Pierre Boulez, *Notes of an Apprenticeship,* trans. Herbert Weinstock
(New York: Knopf, 1968), and Paul Griffiths, *Boulez* (London: Oxford University Press, 1979).

Cage: John Cage, *Silence* (Middletown, Conn.: Wesleyan University Press,
1961), and Paul Griffiths, *Cage* (London: Oxford University Press, 1981).

Messiaen: Olivier Messiaen, *The Technique of My Musical Language* (Paris:
Leduc, 1956), and Robert Sherlaw Johnson, *Messiaen* (Berkeley: University of
California Press, 1980).

Stockhausen: Karl H. Wörner, *Stockhausen: Life and Work,* trans. and ed.
Bill Hopkins (Berkeley: University of California Press, 1973).

Notes

1. Igor Stravinsky and Robert Craft, *Conversations with Igor Stravinsky* (Garden City, N. Y.:
Doubleday, 1959), 17.

RESEARCH AND WRITING
IN MUSIC HISTORY

General Principles for Writing about Music

One of the most important aspects of studying the history of music is to learn to form and to express your own ideas about the music you hear. Discovering and sharing musical experiences are no less genuinely musical activities than composing or playing music. Your reading about music should be only a step toward talking and writing intelligently and effectively about it.

To write effectively about music is inevitably difficult, since by its nature music expresses its ideas nonverbally. As Felix Mendelssohn once pointed out, the difficulty in all writing about music is that the music itself is always perfectly precise and definite, whereas words are imprecise and ambiguous. Nevertheless, we need to communicate about music and our experiences in hearing, playing, and studying it. When we succeed in sharing our thoughts about music, we enrich each other's musical lives.

It should be a pleasure to hear and study music and to exchange ideas about it. Whenever possible write about music that matters to you. You might select music for an instrument that you play, or settings of poems that you love. When you do not have the freedom of choice, however, enjoy the opportunity to make the acquaintance of unfamiliar music. Study to understand new pieces and composers; understanding is the first step toward liking a new work. Your interest in your subject will help to make your writing interesting. If your reader discovers that you are not interested in the music, he or she will soon lose interest also.

There are many types of writing about music, each with particular requirements of content and style. A simple essay might begin by establishing

the historical and biographical context in which a musical work was composed and then proceed to an analysis of the music. A more challenging
project would be to compare the histories and stylistic characteristics of two
or three pieces. Program notes require a special approach from the musically
knowledgeable writer, since the description of the music in program notes
must take into account that the audience may not have specialized or technical
vocabulary. A performance review or critical essay allows the expression of
personal judgments, but it also demands especially clear and well-argued
reasoning. Finally, a research paper calls for thorough documentation, careful
construction, and a highly precise style.

It generally works best to approach writing about music in an "inductive"
way, first establishing facts and then using them as the basis for conclusions
and judgments. In other words, start by asking and answering the "what,
when, where, and who" questions about the music, then go on to the "how and
why." Do not neglect these latter questions; they are harder ones, but they are
the ones that produce interesting and significant results.

Research Sources

When you begin to write about music, you will want to make yourself familiar
with some basic research sources and tools. The standard encyclopedic reference source on music in English is *The New Grove Dictionary of Music and
Musicians,* edited by Stanley Sadie (London: Macmillan, 1980). This monumental work has spawned a variety of smaller dictionaries and books on
particular topics that update the original twenty-volume set. Among the best
one-volume references are *Baker's Biographical Dictionary of Musicians,* edited
by Nicolas Slonimsky (7th ed., New York: Schirmer, 1984), for information
about performers and composers, and *The New Harvard Dictionary of Music,*
edited by Don Michael Randel (Cambridge, Mass.: The Belknap Press of Harvard University Press, 1986), for discussions of other topics.

It is important to go beyond such basic reference books, of course. The
articles in *The New Grove Dictionary of Music and Musicians* generally provide
substantial bibliographies that will give you a good start. General and specialized reference sources are listed in Vincent H. Duckles and Michael A. Keller,
Music Reference and Research Materials (New York: Schirmer, 1988). For further material, with brief summaries of the contents of each item, you should
consult the series *RILM Abstracts* (Répertoire internationale de la littérature
musicale). Periodical articles about music are also indexed in *The Music Index*
and *Music Article Guide.*

Several very extensive series of studies of music history by periods provide
more detailed coverage than can be incorporated in any single-volume history.

Largest of these is the *New Oxford History of Music* published by Oxford University Press. W.W. Norton and Company pioneered in producing a set of classic volumes, The Norton History of Music Series, devoted to the main periods of Western music history and has begun to release a second series, The Norton Introduction to Music History, in a more up-to-date format. A set of more concise volumes is published by Prentice-Hall as the Prentice-Hall History of Music Series.

You will also want to use the very best editions of musical scores you can find. The compositions of almost all the leading composers in the Western tradition have been published in complete editions that can be relied on for accuracy. A number of major composers' complete works are currently appearing in new scholarly editions based on the most authoritative original sources and sophisticated methods of research. Less prolific composers whose output may not warrant individual editions are often represented in collected editions. A useful index to all these editions is Anna Harriet Heyer, *Historical Sets, Collected Editions, and Monuments of Music: A Guide to Their Contents* (Chicago: American Library Association, 1980).

Finally, a word of warning: Avoid such materials as program notes and recording notes as sources for information or critical judgments. There are exceptions to this rule, for example, when a composer has provided comments on the music especially for a certain performance or recording. But program and recording notes are notoriously unreliable. They may be written by authors who do not have the time or background to base their writing on thorough research and musical analysis. Their purpose also makes it unlikely that they offer balanced and objective information and evaluation. If you do discover interesting facts or ideas in these materials, be sure to verify them in more reliable sources.

Writing about Music, Culture, and the Other Arts

As this book stresses, music cannot be understood separately from the context of history and the development of philosophical and aesthetic thought. In writing about music, you should try to keep in mind how music and the lives and thoughts of musicians reflect the times and places from which they come, and how they in turn affect their contemporaries and successors.

When you relate music to works in other fields, be careful to think about them in more substantial terms than superficial details. Consider the aesthetic foundations of the works—what ideas they seek to express and how they seek to express them. Pay attention not only to the use of similar subject matter of works in different art forms but also to similarities in the methods and forms of their construction.

Be sure when you compare music to the visual arts or literature that you draw reasonable relationships. Choose as examples works that have enough in common to make comparison sensible. Examples must come from the same time and place, share subject matter, have the same relative scope, serve similar functions, or in some other way justify comparison. Otherwise any connections between them will seem accidental, and their differences will be meaningless.

Writing about Composers' Lives

Music always arises out of the experiences of real live people. The biographies of composers can help us to understand much about how and why they produced their music. You should discover as much as you can about the events and ideas that provide the backgrounds for composers' works and the circumstances and purposes that surrounded the creation of the music.

Although practically anything in composers' lives might turn out to have affected their music, it is not true that *everything* affected *every* work. When writing about music, therefore, you need not include every detail of the composer's life. Concentrate on the facts that surrounded the composition of the specific work or works you wish to discuss. In addition, state explicitly what the connections between the composer's life and music are.

In writing about the works of artists, it is easy to succumb to the "biographical fallacy" and interpret the works as mirroring the lives of their creators. Artists, poets, and composers express their ideas and reflect their experiences in their works, but they do not present their biographies as directly as writers sometimes seem inclined to think they do. (Even when artists treat autobiographical subjects, they are most likely to do so in ways that reflect considerable imagination.) Be careful therefore not to interpret musical pieces as expressing the details of composers' lives.

On the other hand, our most important understanding of a composer as a person must come from his or her music. The nature of an artist's life is such that day-to-day or personal matters hold a relatively insignificant position in comparison to the art itself. Insipid musical ideas and undisciplined musical forms cannot be redeemed by the observation that the composer was kind, generous, or in any other way admirable as a person. By the same token profound musical insights and masterful handling of musical materials overshadow a composer's objectionable character traits or disagreeable personal behavior. To the extent that we care that a composer is a musician, that composer's music is the most important evidence of his or her biography.

Descriptive and Analytical Writing

Music itself should always be at the heart of your writing, but you will probably discover that to write successfully about music itself is difficult. One of the
most frustrating types of writing to read is the essay about music that merely
consists of a guided tour through the score or a blow-by-blow account of a
performance. We soon give up reading such descriptions in frustration. If we
want to know how the music goes, we would prefer to go directly to a performance, a recording, or a score. Of course, there is much to be said for effective
descriptions of particular things that take place in a piece of music. When you
write about music, be as simple, direct, and precise as possible. You must
master a certain vocabulary of musical terms and learn to use them properly.
However, avoid using technical jargon when ordinary language will do.

Be sure you choose analytical methods appropriate to the music you
discuss. According to a long tradition, curricula for music theory and analysis
concentrate on the study of triadic, functional harmony. This theoretical approach is not generally appropriate for music other than that of the eighteenth
and nineteenth centuries, however. Nevertheless, you should not shy away
from analyzing and writing about earlier and later music. For the earlier periods in the Western musical tradition a basic understanding of the church
modes and the principles of intervallic consonance and dissonance provide
the foundations for harmonic analysis. Discussing the most complicated analytical problems of early music, those of fourteenth-century rhythm, requires
in addition a bit of skill in arithmetic. The analysis of some twentieth-century
music, especially pieces in free atonal and serial styles, can be quite challenging and profits from some special techniques, also. Remember that in most
cases composers have developed their musical styles without waiting for theorists to design analytical techniques to explain it. Writers about music are still
working out the necessary methods to deal with recent styles.

A useful book on analysis is Jan LaRue, *Guidelines for Style Analysis* (New
York: Norton, 1970). It provides a systematic approach to the various components of musical style (sound, harmony, melody, rhythm, growth) and has
established some standard symbols for identifying elements of a piece of music
and methods for diagramming musical structures.

Writing musical analysis must then go beyond description and beyond
naming the various events in a work. Identifying harmonies, devices of counterpoint, and standard musical forms is only the beginning. Analysis should
undertake to answer the more challenging questions of how musical elements
interact to make an effective work, the functions of harmonic progressions for
which we have no conventional identifiers, why the form of a piece or movement departs from standard procedures. These questions and others like them
are difficult to answer, but they hold the reader's interest because they probe
the musical character of the individual work.

Analysis should eventually lead to broader and deeper insights about a work. Its direct purpose is to show how the different elements of style work together in the music. Its ultimate goal, like that of every aspect of writing about music, should be the understanding of the ideas a musical work expresses.

Writing Style

Because music is an art, writing about it presents special problems of literary style. The material about which we are writing has sensuous and subjective qualities that we cannot easily translate into language. We cannot do justice to the music if we try to avoid those qualities, but neither can we allow them to carry us away.

The sensuous nature of musical material requires vivid and specific descriptions. Try to write about the things that take place in a piece of music with the most explicit nouns and active verbs you can find. Do not avoid adjectives and adverbs either. We cannot increase the value of our discourse about music by adopting a tone of artificial objectivity and neutrality. To describe a melody as conjunct may be accurate, but the description is so empty that it does not distinguish between the fluid smoothness of a Renaissance vocal motet line and the energetic wiggling of a Baroque instrumental part. To say that a certain melody is directed upward hardly captures the nature of a particular musical experience, if what the listener hears is a brilliant trumpet arpeggio that rockets abruptly out of the orchestral texture.

On the other hand, we need to resist any urge to indulge in flamboyant imagery or fanciful metaphors in our writing. The romanticism of a few generations ago produced many amusing examples of this sort of "purple prose." A violin line may wiggle, but it is not like a worm; the tone of a trumpet is often brilliant, but it does not call the orchestra to arms.

Another principle to remember is to write about the music directly. Focus on the music's history, purposes, character, and construction. Let those factors support any opinions you may want to present. In the context of well-presented evidence a critical judgment should not be mistaken for a statement of fact. When you come to express your impressions and judgments, you can generally do so without prefacing each statement with the words "I think" (or something deadly, such as "In the present writer's opinion"). To begin with "I think" also has the disadvantage of turning the sentence into a statement about the writer rather than about the music. Your reader is likely to be more interested in reading about music than about you and will learn more about you from what you think about music than from what you say about yourself, anyway.

In expressing your judgments and particularly in writing conclusions make sure that general statements really follow from the facts that you have already presented about the music. An unfortunately frequent type of conclusion in student papers observes, for example, that Beethoven was one of the greatest composers who ever lived, that everyone should know his music, and that his works will continue to be played and appreciated as long as civilization lasts. All this may be true, but it is unlikely that any particular essay has demonstrated it. When in doubt about the ending of your essay, consider whether perhaps a simple summary conclusion will make a good ending or whether it might be best simply to stop.

Some Practical Considerations

When you begin any kind of writing, consider your subject and your reader. Be sure that the subject is appropriate to your interests and abilities, the medium in which you are writing, and your reader. Keep in mind the reader's reason for reading your work, his or her technical knowledge, and how much background information he or she will already have. Decide what the most important points are that you wish the reader to understand, and how to organize and present them in convincing fashion. Think about how much background and explanation you need to supply.

When you have collected your information, analyzed the music, and decided on a general approach, make an outline. The purpose of the outline is to allow you to organize your information and thoughts without having to concern yourself with the problems of creating elegant prose. Do not hesitate to try more than one outline, if you can envision more than one way to arrange your material, then choose the best of your options. In outlining, try to make sure that each outline entry has real content; a good way to do this is to make a sentence outline, in which each entry is a complete sentence with its own subject and verb. Check your outline to make sure that it allows for everything you want to say; if it does not, you may find that when you try later to include additional items, the flow of the writing becomes difficult to follow.

Perhaps the most difficult stage for most writers is the time when they sit facing a blank sheet of paper (or video display screen) and have to begin. The best solution is simply to begin, without concern for polish, and to get your thoughts on paper (or disk). You need not start at the beginning of the introduction and work through to the end of the conclusion. It often works better to begin with the straightforward statements of fact or some other stylistically simple portion of the essay. It is much easier to correct and polish rough writing than to create a literary masterpiece in your head before starting to write at all. Even if you discard entire paragraphs, you have wasted no more time than if you had spent the same amount of time just staring at a blank page.

Do not forget to give credit for any quoted words, facts, or ideas you have taken from others. Plagiarism includes not only failing to identify quotations but also neglecting to acknowledge and cite sources for information and ideas. In different types of writing credit is given in different ways. Less formal writing, such as program notes or reviews, generally allows for acknowledgment within the course of the prose—readers of performance notes or the daily newspaper do not expect footnotes. More formal papers such as research papers require detailed citations, either as footnotes or in the more recent style with parenthetical references in the text.

Once you have completed your draft, reread and critique it carefully and objectively. You might want to check the following, making several passes through the draft, if necessary:

- *Introduction.* Does the essay begin in such a way that it catches the reader's interest? Is your subject or main point clearly stated? Can the reader get a good sense of the approach that you have taken?
- *Statements of fact.* Are all the statements of fact true? Are they well supported by documentation or analysis? Are they clearly and objectively stated? Is each one necessary? Are they presented in the best order?
- *Paragraph organization.* Does each paragraph have a single topic? Is the topic clearly presented to the reader in a topic sentence (usually the first sentence of the paragraph)? Do the paragraphs lead logically from each to the next?
- *Opinions and conclusions.* Are your opinions logically and clearly based on the facts as you have presented them? Are your judgments and conclusions objective and fair?
- *General style.* Have you kept the music in the forefront of the reader's attention? Have you achieved the tone you intended? Have you used the best words to say what you mean? Are too many sentences short and choppy or long and complicated? Have you double-checked for grammatical errors arising from the revision process and for typographical errors? Have you read the essay aloud, listening to hear whether it sounds natural and pleasant?

A thorough writers' guide specifically directed toward musical writing is Demar Irvine, *Writing about Music,* 2d ed. (Seattle: University of Washington Press, 1968). This book offers helpful suggestions about the step-by-step mechanical procedures of writing a paper, general rules of grammar and principles of style, and comments on different types of writing. Its models for footnote references and bibliographic form are unfortunately now outdated and should not be used. A small handbook giving up-to-date formats as well as other technical recommendations is D. Kern Holoman, *Writing About Music* (Berkeley and Los Angeles: University of California Press, 1988).

For most of us writing is not primarily an art but a craft. Like any other craft it is not automatic; it requires attention to technical details, trial and criticism, and much practice. It is worth the time, effort, and thought needed to do it well. Also like any other craft it grows more satisfying as we work harder at it. Experiment with different approaches and styles in writing about music and develop your enjoyment of this aspect of musical experience.

Appendix B

PRONOUNCING CHURCH LATIN: A QUICK REFERENCE

Vowels

a is pronounced as in father: *sanctam* (sahngk-tahm).

e is pronounced as in *egg*: *ante* (ahn-teh).

i is pronounced as in machine: *filii* (fee-lee-ee)

y is pronounced the same as *i*: Kyrie (kee-ree-eh).

o is pronounced as in tone: *omnia* (ohm-nee-ah).

u is pronounced as in ruler: *unum* (oo-noom)

qu is pronounced as *kw*: *qui* (kwee).

Note: When two vowels appear together, each is pronounced: *mei* (meh-ee). (This rule does not apply in the cases of certain diphthongs—see below.) In singing, the first vowel is sustained and the second sounded on passing to the next syllable.

Diphthongs

ae and *oe* are pronounced like *e*: *saeculum* (seh-koo-loom).

au and *eu* are treated as single syllables, but each vowel is pronounced distinctly. In singing, the first vowel is sustained, as in other combinations of two vowels: *lauda* (lah-oo-dah).

Consonants

The consonants *b, d, f, k, l, m, n, p, q, s, t,* and *v* are pronounced as in English.

c before *e, i, y, ae, oe* is pronounced *ch:* coelo (cheh-loh); in all other cases, *c* is pronounced *k:* cantus (kahn-toos).

cc before *e, i, y, ae, oe* is pronounced *tch:* ecce (eht-cheh).

ch is pronounced *k:* cherubim (keh-roo-beem).

g before *e, i, y, ae, oe* is soft (as in gel): genitum (jeh-nee-toom); otherwise, *g* is hard (as in go): gaudeamus (gah-oo-deh-ah-moos).

gn is pronounced *ny:* agnus (ah-nyoos)

h is mute, except in mihi (mee-kee) and nihil (nee-keel).

j is pronounced as *y:* Jesu (yeh-soo).

r is lightly rolled with the tongue.

sc before *e, i, y, ae, oe* is pronounced *sh:* ascendit (ah-shehn-deet).

th is pronounced as if the *h* were absent, as in *Thomas.*

ti before a vowel and after any letter except *s, t,* or *x,* is pronounced *tsee:* gratia (grah-tsee-a).

x is pronounced *ks:* ex (ehks).

xc before *e, i, y, ae, oe* is pronounced *ksh:* excelsis (ehk-shehl-sees).

Page 41: Reprinted from William Tydeman, *The Theatre in the Middle Ages*. Copyright © 1978 by Cambridge University Press. **Page 54:** Reprinted from James McKinnon, "The Church Fathers and Musical Instruments," Ph.D. Dissertation, Columbia University, 1965. Copyright © 1967 by James William McKinnon. **Page 75:** From *The Paradiso* by Dante Alighieri, translated by John Ciardi. Copyright © 1961, 1965, 1967 and 1970 by John Ciardi. Reprinted by arrangement with New American Library, a Division of Penguin Books USA Inc., New York, New York. **Page 226:** Reprinted from Charles Burney, *An Eighteenth-Century Musical Tour in Central Europe and the Netherlands*, edited by Percy A. Scholes. Copyright © 1959 by Oxford University Press. **Page 236:** Reprinted from Alexander Pope, *Poetical Works*, edited by Herbert Davis. Copyright © 1966 by Oxford University Press. **Pages 240–41:** From *Haydn: A Creative Life in Music. 3rd revised and enlarged edition* by Karl Geiringer. Copyright © 1983 Karl Geiringer. Reprinted by permission of The University of California Press. **Page 278:** From Edmund Burke, *A Philosophical Enquiry into the Origins of Our Ideas of the Sublime and the Beautiful*, edited by J. T. Boulton. Oxford: Basil Blackwell, revised edn. 1987. Reprinted by permission of J. T. Boulton. **Page 347:** Reprinted from Paul Verlaine, *Selected Poems*, trans./ed. by C. F. MacIntyre. Copyright © The Regents of the University of California. **Page 350:** From *Notes from Underground* by Fyodor Dostoyevsky, translated by Andrew MacAndrew. Copyright © 1961 by Andrew MacAndrew. Reprinted by arrangement with New American Library, a Division of Penguin Books USA Inc., New York, New York. **Page 373:** Reprinted from "The Life of Béla Bartók," *Tempo* 13 (Autumn 1949), pages 4–5. Copyright © 1945 by Boosey and Hawkes Music Publishers, Ltd. Used by permission of the publishers. **Page 375:** Reprinted from Gerald Abraham, "Music in the Soviet Union," in *The New Oxford History of Music*, vol. 10, *The Modern Age: 1890–1960*, edited by Martin Cooper. Copyright © 1974 by Oxford University Press. **Page 376:** Reprinted with permission of Charles Scribner's Sons, an imprint of Macmillan Publishing Company from *Music Since 1900* by Nicolas Slonimsky. Copyright © 1971 Nicolas Slonimsky.

INDEX

WORLD EVENTS | MUSIC AND MUSICIANS | FIGURES IN THE ARTS AND HUMANITIES

MUSIC AND MUSICIANS

1728: Gay and Pepusch, *The Beggar's Opera*
1728–1800: Niccolo Piccini
1729: Bach, *St. Matthew Passion*
1732–1809: Franz Joseph Haydn
1735–1782: Johann Christian Bach
1737–1791: Francis Hopkinson
1742: Handel, *Messiah*
1746–1800: William Billings
1750–1825: Antonio Salieri
1752: Johann Joachim Quantz, *Versuch einer Anweisung die Flöte traversière zu spielen*
1753: C.P.E. Bach, *Versuch uber die wahre Art das Clavier zu spielen*
1756: Leopold Mozart, *Versuch einer gründlichen Violinschule*
1756–1791: Wolfgang Amadeus Mozart
1758–1832: Karl Friedrich Zelter
1760–1802: Johann Rudolf Zumsteeg
1760–1842: Luigi Cherubini
1770–1827: Ludwig van Beethoven
1770–1827: James Hewitt
1781: Haydn, String quartets, op. 33, published
1782–1837: John Field
1782–1840: Nicolo Paganini
1786: Mozart, *Le nozze di Figaro*
1786–1826: Carl Maria von Weber
1791–1864: Giacomo Meyerbeer
1792–1868: Gioacchino Rossini
1797–1828: Franz Schubert
1797–1848: Gaetano Donizetti
1801–1835: Vincenzo Bellini
1803: Beethoven, *Eroica* Symphony
1803–1869: Hector Berlioz
1804–1857: Mikhail Glinka
1805–1847: Fanny Mendelssohn Hensel
1809–1847: Felix Mendelssohn-Bartholdy
1810–1849: Frédéric Chopin
1810–1856: Robert Schumann
1811–1886: Franz Liszt
1813–1883: Richard Wagner
1813–1901: Giuseppe Verdi
1818–1893: Charles Gounod
1819–1896: Clara Wieck Schumann
1822–1890: César Franck
1824–1884: Bedřich Smetana
1824–1896: Anton Bruckner
1829: Berlioz, *Symphonie fantastique*
1829–1869: Louis Moreau Gottschalk
1833–1887: Alexander Borodin
1833–1897: Johannes Brahms
1838–1875: Georges Bizet
1839–1881: Modest Mussorgsky
1840–1893: Pyotr Il'yich Tchaikovsky
1841–1904: Antonin Dvořák
1843–1907: Edvard Grieg
1844–1908: Nicolai Rimsky-Korsakov
1848: Liszt, *Les Preludes*
1857–1934: Edward Elgar
1858–1919: Ruggero Leoncavallo
1858–1924: Giacomo Puccini
1858–1931: George Whitefield Chadwick
1859: Wagner, *Tristan und Isolde*
1860–1903: Hugo Wolf
1860–1908: Edward MacDowell
1860–1909: Isaac Albéniz
1860–1911: Gustav Mahler
1862–1918: Claude Debussy
1863–1919: Horatio Parker

WORLD EVENTS

1751: *Encyclopédie* begins to be published
1755: Samuel Johnson, *Dictionary*
1762: Rousseau, *The Social Contract*
1763: First excavations at Pompeii
1769: James Watt, steam engine
1776: Adam Smith, *The Wealth of Nations*
1776: Declaration of Independence
1789: French Revolution
1804: Napoleon Bonaparte becomes emperor of France
1815: Defeat of Napoleon at Waterloo
1830: Revolution in France
1837–1901: Reign of Queen Victoria in England
1839: Invention of photography
1848: Revolutions in Europe; Karl Marx, *The Communist Manifesto*
1859: Charles Darwin, *The Origin of Species*
1861–1865: U. S. Civil War
1861: Unification of Italy

FIGURES IN THE ARTS AND HUMANITIES

1729–1797: Edmund Burke
1748–1825: Jacques Louis David
1749–1832: Johann Wolfgang von Goethe
1749–1838: Lorenzo Da Ponte
1757–1827: William Blake
1759–1805: Friedrich Schiller
1770–1831: G.W.F. Hegel
1772–1829: Friedrich Schlegel
1775–1851: J.M.W. Turner
1776–1822: E.T.A. Hoffmann
1788–1824: Lord Byron
1791–1824: Théodore Géricault
1791–1861: Eugène Scribe
1798–1863: Eugène Delacroix
1799–1837: Alexander Pushkin
1803–1883: Ralph Waldo Emerson
1804–1871: Moritz von Schwind
1813–1837: Georg Büchner
1817–1862: Henry David Thoreau
1821–1881: Feodor Dostoevsky
1825–1904: Eduard Hanslick
1840–1926: Claude Monet
1842–1918: Arrigo Boito
1844–1896: Paul Verlaine
1848–1903: Paul Gauguin
1856–1939: Sigmund Freud